Francophone Jewish Writers
Imagining Israel

Contemporary French and Francophone Cultures, 40

Contemporary French and Francophone Cultures

This series aims to provide a forum for new research on modern and contemporary French and francophone cultures and writing. The books published in *Contemporary French and Francophone Cultures* reflect a wide variety of critical practices and theoretical approaches, in harmony with the intellectual, cultural and social developments which have taken place over the past few decades. All manifestations of contemporary French and francophone culture and expression are considered, including literature, cinema, popular culture, theory. The volumes in the series will participate in the wider debate on key aspects of contemporary culture.

Recent titles in the series:

LUCILLE CAIRNS

Francophone Jewish Writers

Imagining Israel

LIVERPOOL UNIVERSITY PRESS

First published 2015 by
Liverpool University Press
4 Cambridge Street
Liverpool
L69 7ZU

British Library Cataloguing-in-Publication data
A British Library CIP record is available

ISBN 978-1-78138-262-2 cased

Typeset by Carnegie Book Production, Lancaster
Printed and bound in Poland by BooksFactory.co.uk

This book is dedicated with deep love and gratitude to my family: my mother Dorothy Scott Cairns (née Samuel), my father John Cairns (1930–1981), my sister Angela Cairns and my brother Jonathan Cairns.

Contents

Acknowledgements

I am grateful to the British Academy for the Small Research Grant (2011) which enabled me to conduct structured interviews with a number of Francophone Jewish writers in whose work Israel occupies a significant position. I am also indebted to the writers interviewed or, in a small number of cases, questionnaired, for their time, good humour, and patience: Eliette Abécassis, Jean-Luc Allouche, Myriam Anissimov, Karin Bernfeld, Ami Bouganim, Yaël Hassan, Paula Jacques, Marco Koskas, Esther Orner, Chantal Osterreicher, Henri Raczymow, Michaël Sebban and Michel Warschawski. I would like to thank Bruno Chaouat, whose enormous erudition and generous intellectual exchanges have been a vital irrigator of this project; Anthony Cond, my superb editor at Liverpool University Press; Ben Kasstan, for his invaluable flow of suggestions for textual and human interlocutors; Keith Reader, for reading and commenting on a first draft of the book, and for his intelligent, extremely well-informed and stimulating contributions to debate on the Israeli-Palestinian question in particular; and Vered Weiss, an Israeli-born and Israeli-raised scholar now working in the UK who has provided information and insights of great value for this study.

Author's Note

All translations of French quotations into English, and thus any errors therein, are mine. I would like to highlight one particular difficulty: the problem of adequately translating the ideologically loaded terms 'colonie'/'colonialiste', which, depending on the speaker/writer, are sometimes used pejoratively, sometimes more neutrally. Accordingly, I have chosen to translate as 'colony'/'colonialist' what seem from context to be pejorative uses, and 'settlement'/'settler' what seem from context to be more neutral usages. I would also like to make clear an explicit choice about use of the English present tense: very often I have deployed this to render the French historic present used in many of the texts, in order to convey their sense of vivid immediacy.

Introduction

While its perspective is mainly literary, this book may be of interest to scholars and students in a wide variety of fields: colonial and postcolonial studies, conflict studies, French/Francophone studies, history, identity studies, Israeli studies, Jewish studies and political science. The subject of the book is rare within some of these disciplines: autobiographies, memoirs and novels by French-language Jewish writers[1] that, through their mediation of affect, emotion and politics, dynamically transform Francophone Jewish imaginings of Israel. Where appropriate, analysis of the primary texts is preceded by contextualizing material from a number of secondary texts, largely also by French-language Jewish writers, drawn from the domains of history, journalism, philosophy, politics, psychoanalysis, sociology – and, in one instance (Chapter 3), cognitive psychology, cognitive science and social psychology. Yet the primary texts remain primary in more senses than one. Apart from the precedence my analysis gives to the literary texts over the ancillary discursive texts, there are two other dimensions to that primacy. First, I hold that the deepest of psychic responses and subsequently the richest of contributions to these Jewish imaginings of Israel are stimulated by creative works. Second, the choice of *topoi* examined in the various chapters arose not from any pre-determined ideological schema, but from the salience of these *topoi* in the primary texts themselves.

This book foregrounds the differing emotional investments in Israel of, on the one hand, Francophone Jews physically domiciled in Israel and, on the other, diasporic Jews domiciled mainly in France for whom Israel nonetheless forms a central point of affect. Why Israel, why *French*-language Jewish writers, and why their coupling? Israel is at once a fraught geopolitical reality in the realm of international politics and a prominent site within Jewish cultural imaginaries that transcends national boundaries. However, it has often been claimed that the country enjoys a 'special' relationship with France, which until 1967 was its greatest ally. Even before the foundation of the state of Israel in 1948, France had shown solidarity with Jewish survivors of the Shoah desperate to emigrate to what was then Palestine. In so doing, it had openly defied its Second World War ally Britain, which since 1923 had held a Mandate over the historically disputed territory of Palestine. This solidarity emerged most strikingly in the world-famous Exodus affair. The Exodus 1947 transported 4,500 Jewish refugees from French docks to Palestine in July 1947; when it was intercepted and returned by the British to France, the French coalition government dominated by the socialists refused the British demand to enforce disembarkation of the survivors. In the twenty-first century, Israel has a large Francophone community (estimated at some 800,000), while France has the largest Jewish community in Europe (estimated at some 600,000). But Franco–Israeli relations have undergone radical, largely negative transformations under the Fifth Republic (1958–). This is due to factors ranging from the aftermath of French decolonization; the fallout of the Six-Day War in 1967 and de Gaulle's insulting of Israel in the same year[2] – resulting in a rupture that, in historian Élie Barnavi's words, 'mettait fin à une alliance extraordinairement forte, quasi sans précédent dans les annales des nations' (Barnavi and Rosenzweig, 30) ['put an end to an extraordinarily strong alliance, virtually without precedent in the history of nations']; the foreign policy priorities of French presidents after de Gaulle; and, in the new millennium, the seeping of politics and affect from the Israeli–Palestinian conflict into the French *banlieues*[3] (France is home to both the largest Jewish and the largest Arab populations in Europe). It is that last factor which gives this book its most obvious relevance to current global concerns. By the same token, the book provides insights (in Chapter 5) into tensions between two ethnic minorities, Arab and Jewish, in a contemporary French society lacking the social cohesion, indeed the ethnic in-difference, to which its Republican ethos aspires.

This book is original inter alia because it interrogates one of the most controversial nation states in the twenty-first century (Israel) from the perspective of a European country with a unique relationship to it (France), and more particularly from the perspective of those French citizens with the greatest stake in its continued existence – French Jews. It also, if only implicitly, advocates the inclusion of Israel within the conception of *francophonie* ('the French-speaking world'), which is blocked 'en raison du veto des participants arabes' (Ben-Rafael and Ben-Rafael, 26) ['because of the Arab members' veto']. The conception of *francophonie* is one of the means by which France seeks to promote its *rayonnement* ['influence'] within countries with which it usually has ties based on previous colonial rule of such countries. Although Israel has never been under French colonial role, as previously stated, Israel has a large Francophone community of some 800,000 citizens, and after Hebrew, English, Arabic and Russian (all languages one would expect to predominate), French is the most commonly spoken language in Israel (Ben-Rafael and Ben-Rafael, 59). To this we should add the facts that the five French cultural centres in Israel set up by the French government constitute the 'réseau d'institutions francophones le plus dense dans le monde pour un pays où le français n'est pas une langue officielle' (Ben-Rafael and Ben-Rafael, 75) ['the densest network of Francophone institutions in the world for a country where French is not an official language'], and that '77% des Juifs de France y [en Israël] ont de la famille' (Blanc 2012a, 53) ['77% of French Jews have family [in Israel]'].

Regarding the research context of this book, there have been a number of French-authored historical, philosophical, political and sociological studies which either bear directly upon or else reflect relations between France and Israel. Notable amongst these are Badiou and Finkielkraut's *L'Explication* (2010), Balibar, Brauman, Butler et al.'s *Antisémitisme, l'intolérable chantage: Israël, une affaire française* (2003), Barnavi and Rosenzweig's *La France et Israël: une affaire passionnelle* (2002), Benbassa's *Être juif après Gaza* (2009), Brauman and Finkielkraut's *La discorde: Israël-Palestine, les Juifs, la France* (2006), Charbit's *Les Intellectuels français et Israël* (2009), Debray's *À un ami israélien. Avec une réponse d'Élie Barnavi* (2010), Eytan's *Sarkozy, le monde juif et Israël: mariage d'amour ou de raison?* (2009), Hecker's *La défense des intérêts de l'État d'Israël en France* (2005), Marcus's *Soixante ans d'amour contrariées: les relations franco-israéliennes de 1948 à aujourd'hui* (2008), Primor's *Le Triangle des passions: Paris, Berlin, Jérusalem* (2000), Rosman's *La France et Israël 1947–1970. De la création de l'État d'Israël au départ des Vedettes de Cherbourg* (2009) and Sieffert's *Israël-Palestine, une passion française: la France dans le miroir du conflit israélo-palestinien* (2004). Relatively few of these studies challenge Israel's right to exist as a Jewish state, though this in no way means that they ignore or deny Palestinian concerns and rights. From them emerges a mapping of the vicissitudes of the 'special' relationship during the Fifth Republic particularly,[4] with extensive reference to its successive presidents, who either, as in the case of de Gaulle, openly offended Israel or, more commonly, as with Pompidou, Giscard d'Estaing, Mitterrand and Chirac, were more interested in courting the Arab world than in preserving friendship with Israel. Eytan focuses on the exception of Sarkozy (2007–2012), who established warmer relations with Israel than any of his predecessors (notwithstanding the overtures of Mitterrand, which were invariably double-edged).[5] Hecker moves beyond politics and diplomacy to emphasize the anti-Israel bias of the French press (see Chapter 5); Barnavi and Marcus extend this attribution of anti-Israeli bias to the French media more generally, particularly to television (also Chapter 5). Some of these studies, however, distinguish themselves through the adoption of a sharply critical stance towards Israel that some readers would regard as an anti-Zionist position (in the minimalist sense of appearing to contest the legitimacy of a state founded on Zionism, particularly the form which that state took after the Six-Day War of 1967):[6] Badiou within Badiou and Finkielkraut (2010), Balibar, Brauman, Butler et al. (2003), Benbassa (2009), Brauman within Brauman and Finkielkraut (2006), Debray (2010) and Sieffert (2004).

Notwithstanding the professional standards of neutrality and detachment commonly (if somewhat naively) expected of historical, philosophical, political and sociological studies, much of the material in the works referred to above is charged with its own affect, at the very least subliminally. This is clearly discernible to the reader able to disaggregate the purely factual from the rhetorical. Indeed, the very adoption of a Zionist or anti-Zionist position, and arguably even the adoption of a position which simply does not contest Israel's right to exist, which for anti-Zionists is in itself a partisan position, cannot but negate neutrality. But there is a large gap between simple adoption of such a position and head-on exploration of the affect with which the position is subconsciously or unconsciously shot through, or head-on exploration of the intense emotions felt by the human beings comprising the polities of the two countries forming this 'special' relationship.

In contrast, the mediation of the relationship in French *literature*, a more compelling vehicle for head-on treatment of emotions, has received minimal critical attention. Two exceptions are Anny Dayan-Rosenman's chapter 'The Israeli–Palestinian Conflict in France: A Conflict in Search of Novelistic Representations' (in Debrauwere-Miller, 2010) and my own article 'Righteous Realism Versus Postmodern Play: The Israeli–Palestinian Conflict in Female-Authored French Fiction' (Cairns, 2014). These aside, there are no publications entirely germane to the present monograph, which presents sustained analysis of Francophone *literary* representations of Israel (and not just of the Israeli–Palestinian conflict within such representations) along with that country's passionately charged rapport with France.

What is it about literary texts specifically that makes them such a compelling vehicle for exploring the unique relationship between France and Israel? First, for both Jews and non-Jews, Israel is an eminently emo*tive* subject. Literature explores and indeed often privileges the emotions. In simultaneously reflecting but also creating new forms of the emotions infusing that relationship, these literary texts offer a valuable aperture for understanding that is absent from most historical, philosophical, political and sociological studies. In so doing, these literary texts participate in the ongoing genesis of a Francophone Jewish imaginary about Israel. This imaginary is based on both emotion and affect. Recent work in the emergent field of cultural emotion studies has been concerned with the distinction between these two terms. While the word 'emotion' is common, 'affect' is a less familiar term, originally coined by Freud to denote 'psychic energy'. As Harding and Pribram (16) observe, '[s]ome theorists (Gibbs, Probyn) advocate the reintroduction of affect as a way to counter the dismissal of the biological'. For such theorists, the word 'emotion' tends to designate the more conscious and the more linguistically invested, and the word 'affect' that which has more of an obvious bodily dimension. Brian Massumi, for instance, insists on 'the irreducibly bodily and autonomic nature of affect' (28). In the case of Israel, where physical violence is an everyday reality and suicide bombings are always a very real risk, the body is particularly vulnerable, and what might be called a form of corporeal logic may impact intensely on the subject's psyche. But the distinction between the terms 'emotion' and 'affect' is by no means universally applied or watertight. As Margaret Wetherell points out, '[s]ometimes "affect" includes every aspect of emotion and sometimes it refers just to physical disturbance and bodily activity (blushes, sobs, snarls, guffaws, levels of arousal and associated patterns of neural activity), as opposed to "feelings" or more elaborated subjective experiences' (2). My book adopts a compromise, preferring the word affect where what in the vernacular would be called an emotion is experienced largely unconsciously and/ or is invested with a particular intensity that may well have a bodily dimension (such as anxiety, fear and anger, which induce trembling or accelerated heartbeat).

The prominence of emotion and affect in this book does not imply neglect of the cognitive and ethical. Indeed, I treat these four aspects of human ontology as interrelated. While political science has 'often viewed passion as the enemy of reason' (Groenendyk, 455), as Harding and Pribram note, '[p]roponents of cognitive psychology argue that not only are emotions largely cognitive processes but they are also integral to the functioning of reason' (7). This book bears in mind Nussbaum's view of emotions as 'intelligent responses to the perception of value' and, as such, 'part and parcel of the system of ethical reasoning' (1). This is not to deny the validity of Hogan's remark that, when successful, literature 'induces empathic emotions. It too involves distortions, through emotion-intensifying idealization and ideological biases' (184). Inspired by impetuses within cultural emotion studies, cultural geography, history, philosophy, political science and sociology, my enquiries form a cross-disciplinary nexus.

Subtending these enquiries are two basic research questions. How do French-language Jewish writers mediate Israel in their literary works? Within such mediations, what are the roles of emotion, affect, cognition and ethics? To answer these questions, the book appraises 44 primary texts, published between 1965 and 2012, by 27 authors, both male and female, covering the full cultural spectrum of Jews: Ashkenazim (of Central or Eastern European descent), Sephardim (of Spanish or Portuguese descent, tracing a lineage back to the Jews expelled from Spain and Portugal in 1492) and Mizrahim (of Middle Eastern or North African descent). This spectrum provides a purview of Francophone Jewish perspectives on Israel that is both nuanced and culturally comprehensive. Analysis of the primary texts will be complemented by selective references to structured interviews with (or, in a small number of cases, questionnairing of) French-language Jewish writers (six men and seven women, ranging in age from 35 to 75) which I conducted in 2011. More detailed consideration of the interviewees' responses is given in the final chapter (Chapter 7).

It is important that the 'special', indeed unique, relationship between France and Israel be investigated now, in the aftermath of such events as the Gaza war of 2008–2009, the flotilla episode of 2010 and the Gaza war of 2014. All three events resulted in sharply increased public hostility towards Israel in France, which in turn – due to a common but erroneous conflation of Israelis with Jews generally – led to an increase in antisemitic attacks both verbal and physical in France. In fact, it is often argued that even before those inflammatory events, antisemitism[7] had increased in France as a direct consequence of 9/11. Literary scholar

Bruno Chaouat, who is also an esteemed expert on Franco-Jewish–Israeli relations, makes just such a case:

> Il y a bien eu des attaques antisémites, et que la réaction fût ou non disproportionnée, on n'avait pas vu brûler de synagogues en France depuis longtemps, ni agresser des enfants identifiables par des signes extérieurs de judéité. (2007, 159)

> [there certainly were antisemitic attacks, and whether or not the reaction was disproportionate, for a long time France hadn't seen synagogues burning, or children visibly identifiable as Jewish being attacked]

Chaouat's argument is supported by reference to numerous empirical data.[8] One of the questions he poses chimes semantically with one of the salient foci of the present monograph, namely affect, and reinforces the intense affective rapport between France, Israel and Jews:

> Y a-t-il ce qu'on pourrait appeler un affect juif du 11 septembre? [...] Pour le dire autrement: pourquoi faire du 11 septembre une date césure dans l'expérience des Juifs de diaspora – césure qui s'est traduite par une augmentation notable de l'émigration juive française vers Israël, en dépit des déclarations d'amour jaloux adressées par la République à *ses* Juifs? Les Juifs de France, depuis le 11 septembre, ne sont-ils pas déchirés entre le touchant « Ne partez pas, nous vous aimons » de la République, et le non moins touchant, « Revenez chez vous » des autorités israéliennes? Abandonnés, les Juifs de France? Persécutés? Peut-être, mais pourquoi ne pas l'admettre, en même temps jalousement chouchoutés par leurs deux amours, Tel-Aviv et Paris. (2007, 157)

> [Is there such a thing as a 9/11 Jewish affect? [...] To put it another way: why make of 9/11 a transitional date in the experience of diasporic Jews – a transition manifested by a notable rise in French-Jewish emigration to Israel, despite the declarations of jealous love made by the Republic to *its* Jews? Are not French Jews, since 9/11, torn between the Republic's touching 'Don't go, we love you', and the Israeli authorities' no less touching 'Come back home'? Have French Jews been abandoned? Persecuted? Perhaps, but, why not admit it, at the same time they've been jealously overindulged by their two loves, Tel Aviv and Paris]

Notable in Chaouat's questions is a lexicon of emotion: *amour, jaloux, déchirés, touchant, jalousement*. Although now working in the US academy, Chaouat was born and raised in France, retains links with French Jews and so speaks from an informed position. His questions evince the emotional dilemma for French Jews posed by the global convulsion that 9/11 induced.

Chaouat's questions imply that both the events of 9/11 and their fallout in France worsened French Jews' fears of antisemitism, prompting them to make the *aliyah* – that is, to emigrate from the diaspora to Israel, the only country in the world where Jews will not become a persecuted minority. In late 2012, the French magazine *Respect* stated that:

> Chaque année, environ 2000 Juifs quittent l'Hexagone pour faire leur aliya [...] Proportionnellement, la France se classe fournisseur numéro un des candidats à l'aliya. (Serero, 43)

> [Every year, around 2,000 Jews leave France to make their *aliyah* [...] Proportionately, France is the number one supplier of applicants for the *aliyah*]

That French preponderance was confirmed more recently by figures from 2014:

> Près de vingt mille nouveaux immigrants, tous pays confondus, sont venus en Israël en 2013; un chiffre en hausse de 7% par rapport à 2012, tandis que l'Alya française a augmenté de 63% sur l'année. (Orès, 26)

> [Taking all countries of origin together, nearly 20,000 new immigrants came to Israel in 2013; 7% up from 2012, whereas French *aliyah* has increased by 63% over the year]

Respect's figure represents a significant increase on the pre-9/11 figures, but this is attributed more to the consequences of the Second Intifada (generally thought to have begun in 2000 and ended in 2005) than to those of 9/11:

> Avant les années 2000, on était à 800–1000 olim par an, explique Ariel Kandel. Durant la seconde Intifada, il y a eu un grand pic de 3000. Maintenant, la moyenne est autour de 2000 départs par an. (Serero, 44)

> ['Before the 2000s, we had 800–1,000 immigrants per year', explains Ariel Kandel. 'During the second Intifada, there was a peak of 3,000. Now, the average is around 2,000 departures per year']

Although in the new millennium, French Jews did not become a minority persecuted by the state, they certainly did become more subject to aggression by individual French citizens or small groupings of French citizens, often but not always of Arab origin. The most extreme such acts of aggression in recent years were the murder on 19 March 2012 of four Jews, including three children, at the Ozar Hatorah Jewish day school in Toulouse by the Islamist Mohammed Merah; and the murder of four Jews in a kosher supermarket in Paris on 9 January 2015, by militants claiming allegiance to al-Qaeda and the Islamic State extremist groups.

Eleven years after 9/11, the former president of the American Jewish Committee, Valérie Hoffenberg, made the following asseveration:

> lorsqu'en France on est toujours avec un sentiment de minorité avec des problèmes d'angoisses, le lien avec Israël est plus développé. Aux Etats-Unis, vivre en tant que juif est facile. En France, les choses se sont améliorées, mais je pense qu'on retrouve beaucoup plus de gens qui expriment une hostilité à l'égard d'Israël et que l'on fait face à une désinformation nettement plus forte qu'aux Etats-Unis. [...] L'autre grande force est l'attachement profond, inconditionnel des juifs de France avec Israël. (66)

> [while in France there is still a sense of being a minority with problems of fear, the link with Israel is stronger. In the United States, it's easy to live as a Jew. In France, things have improved, but I think that there are many more people who express hostility to Israel and that you face much greater disinformation than in the United States. [...] The other great force is the deep, unconditional attachment French Jews have for Israel]

Hoffenberg's formulation 'attachement profond' is partly echoed by a formulation in a later article by Chaouat: 'l'attachement *vital* à Israël' (2011, 190). In this article, Chaouat engages penetratingly with another French-Jewish thinker, indeed professional philosopher, Elisabeth de Fontenay, and more particularly with her *Actes de naissance. Entretiens avec Stéphane Bou* (2011). In her responses to Stéphane Bou's questions, she first recalls her adolescent indifference to Zionism. This indifference was to be transformed by an event that preceded 9/11 by 34 years and proved both cataclysmic and catalytic for world Jewry in a very different way from the American catastrophe:

> La Guerre des Six Jours a tout changé, car la panique que j'ai ressentie devant la possibilité d'un nouvel anéantissement a été un moment fondateur. [...] Avec la plupart des Juifs, y compris quelques antisionistes militants, je me suis découvert un attachement *viscéral* à l'existence d'Israël. (Fontenay, 13)

> [The Six-Day War changed everything, because the panic I felt at the prospect of a new annihilation was a foundational moment. [...] Like the majority of Jews, including a few militant anti-Zionists, I found within me a *visceral* attachment to Israel's existence]

Interestingly, de Fontenay cogently rebuts her interlocutor's implicature that a philosopher should eschew affect, particularly in the last sentence below, which avers that emotional attachment to Israel in fact constitutes a reasoned historical and political commitment (thus reflecting the views of Harding, Pribram and Nussbaum alluded to above):

> « *Viscéral, la philosophe assume ce mot?* »
>
> C'est ainsi que je ressens les choses, et je vous dirai que je n'y peux rien, quelles que soient les critiques que j'adresse, depuis la première guerre du Liban, à la politique des gouvernements israéliens et à leur manque de considération pour les attentes du peuple palestinien. Mais cet attachement émotionnel, profondément ancré, est en même temps un engagement réfléchi historique et politique. (13–14)
>
> ['Visceral, you the philosopher accept this word?'
>
> That's how I feel about things, and let me tell you that I can't help it, whatever criticisms I've made, since the first Lebanon war, of the policy of Israeli governments and of their lack of consideration for the Palestinian people's expectations. But this emotional, deeply rooted attachment is at the same time a reasoned commitment that is both political and historical]

Further congruence with Harding and Pribram's and Nussbaum's theories is evident in de Fontenay's support for the creative potential of pathos when it ushers in the conceptual: 'Il peut y avoir une fonction inventive du pathos et, quand il charrie des concepts, je trouve que ce n'est pas mal du tout' (102) ['Pathos can have an creative function and, when it brings to bear a conceptual dimension, I think it's no bad thing at all']. Affect and concept will not be equally present in this book's analyses of the primary texts, but their varying valencies will often be illustrated, together with their conscious responses to each other.

In all subsequent chapters, analysis of the primary texts will be structured in order of publication date. This approach is designed to allow readers to trace evolutions over time in the treatment of the various *topoi* examined, and to bring into their line of vision certain intertextual links in which writers respond, consciously or unconsciously, to the treatment of these *topoi* by previous writers. Such affective and/or cognitive responses may be divergent or even oppositional; conversely, they may be consensual, even refrain-like. Given the irreducibility of these multiple French-Jewish voices imagining Israel to single affective and/or cognitive idioms, it cannot be stressed too much that the goal of this monograph is to be helpfully introductory and expository, and not meretriciously synthesizing. My study is in some senses a phenomenology (in the restricted sense of that word, associated with the human sciences rather than with philosophy) that attempts carefully to describe numerous and diverse Francophone Jewish imaginings of Israel as mediated by literature. Mindful of the hyper-polemical nature of much of the material, I avoid totalizing analyses, and hope that from the materials provided readers will draw their own, informed conclusions.

Notes

1   The formulation 'French-language Jewish writers' rather than 'French-Jewish writers' is used because although all of them write and publish in French, not all of these writers are French – though the majority are, and even the exceptions have been deeply imbued by French culture.

2   At a press conference on 27 November 1967, de Gaulle referred ostensibly to the Jewish people generally but plainly targeted Israel specifically as 'un peuple d'élite, sûr de lui et dominateur' ['an elite people, sure of itself and domineering'].

3   The literal translation of *banlieue* is 'suburbs', but the French original has strong connotations of deprivation and urban decay.

4   One exception is Rosman, who, in only treating the period from 1947 to 1970, inevitably focuses more on pre-Fifth Republic relations between France and Israel. But it is significant that Rosman says of Franco–Israeli relations during her chosen period that 'S'y mêlent constamment du passionnel' (9) ['Passionate feelings were always part of the mix'].

5   The vicissitudes of this 'special' relationship are presented by Olivier Rafowicz as ongoing, shot through by a love-hate dynamic, but nonetheless enduring by virtue of that very emotivity: 'Je crois que les Français et les Israéliens ont […] une relation de « je t'aime moi non plus », mais il subsiste quand même une forte relation émotionnelle malgré les problèmes politiques parfois et les divergences d'analyses' (105) ['I think that the French and the Israelis have […] a "love-hate" relationship, but even so there persists a strong emotional relationship despite the political problems they sometimes have with each other and the differences in their analyses'].

6   The Jewish Virtual Library provides information on the differing movements within Zionism, but also a useful general definition: 'the national movement for the return of the Jewish people to their homeland and the resumption of Jewish sovereignty in the Land of Israel' (http://www.jewishvirtuallibrary.org/jsource/Zionism/zionism.html). Chapter 2 of this book throws into relief the complexities of the highly contested concept of 'Zionism'.

7   After some hesitation (since 'anti-Semitism' is the form recommended by the Oxford English Dictionary), I have chosen to use the noun 'antisemitism' as opposed to 'anti-Semitism', because the latter implies, dubiously, that there

is such a thing as 'Semitism' against which 'anti-Semitism' might react, and is currently the object of debate among scholars of antisemitism. I am grateful to Bruno Chaouat for bringing this point to my attention. Following the same logic, I use the adjective 'antisemitic' as opposed to 'anti-Semitic'.

8 Chaouat writes: 'Voir, parmi de multiples sources d'informations sur cette montée des actes antisémites après le 11 septembre 2001, la Commission Nationale Consultative des Droits de l'Homme (http://www.commission-droits-homme.fr). Voir aussi le *Chantier sur la lutte contre le racisme et l'antisémitisme*, Rapport présenté par Jean-Christophe Rufin, Ecrivain, médecin et responsable de nombreuses associations d'aide humanitaire, Remis à Monsieur le Ministre de l'Intérieur, de la Sécurité Intérieure et des Libertés Locales le 19 octobre 2004 suite à une lettre de mission en date du 29 juin 2004 (document consultable sur le site du Ministère de l'Intérieur). Voir bien sûr Pierre-André Taguieff, *La nouvelle judéophobie*, Fayard, 2002' (2007, 172) ['Among the multiple sources of information about this rise in antisemitic acts after 11 September 2011, see the National Consultative Commission on Human Rights (http://www.commission-droits-homme.fr). See also *Chantier sur la lutte contre le racisme et l'antisémitisme*, a report by Jean-Christophe Rufin, a writer, doctor and head of numerous humanitarian aid associations, presented to the Minister of the Interior, Domestic Security and Local Freedoms on 19 October 2004 following a briefing letter dated 29 June 2004 (the document can be consulted on the website of the Ministry of the Interior). See, of course, Pierre-André Taguieff, *La nouvelle judéophobie*, Fayard, 2002'].

CHAPTER ONE

Historical Foundations of Israeli Nationhood

This chapter considers literary representations of some key constituents in the historical foundations of Israeli nationhood. Due to its historical precedence, the first is Messianism, and its persistence in twenty-first-century Israel (1.1). Second is the status of the early Zionist pioneers who, in the heroizing national narrative, had fertilized the desert in Palestine, cleared the marshes, developed the economy, withstood the antisemitism of the British mandate and (after founding the nation via the declaration of the state of Israel made by David Ben Gurion on 14 May 1948), created a new, radically egalitarian social model in the institution of the kibbutzim (1.2). The third and most sustained focus is on the multifaceted relationship of Israeli citizens with (memories of) the Shoah (1.3). Some of the writers considered below reflect a belief that the Shoah was the chief factor enabling the foundation of Israel, and thus that it even had a redemptive value (1.3.1). Set against this in the writings of others is the desire of the ex-Yishuv (Jewish community in Palestine before 1948) and of sabras (Israeli Jews born in Israel) to occlude the Shoah as shame-inducing (1.3.2). Other writers still present the Shoah as a source of current anti-Israeli sentiments in France (1.3.3); as instrumentalized for Zionist (1.3.4) and/or wider Israeli political ends (1.3.5); and as terrifying template for the possible future destruction of Israel (1.3.6).

Some semantic clarifications are needed before addressing the above. Nationhood is a material reality, but it is also a form of myth. The word 'myth' is polysemic, and it is not used here to designate fiction or falsehood. Rather, I use it to signify a mental construct, both affective and cognitive, based on a sense of common history and narrative that has united and inspired a sense of transcendence in a given group of people. In our context, that group of people is a nation. Nationhood denotes a sense of belonging to a nation, which in turn can be construed as a sense of nationality. Benedict Anderson's approach to the word 'nationality' is apposite: 'nationality, or, as one might prefer to put it in view of that word's multiple significations, nation-ness, as well as nationalism, are cultural artefacts of a particular kind' (4). I conceive of nationhood precisely as cultural artefact, and of the nation as a nation in Anderson's terms: 'an imagined political community' (6). Before leaving Anderson, it is worth recalling his remarks on the nation and Israel in particular: 'The significance of the emergence of Zionism and the birth of Israel is that the former marks the re-imagining of an ancient religious community as a nation, down there among the other nations – while the latter charts an alchemic change from wandering devotee to local patriot' (149). Zionism is treated in Chapter 2 of the present study. Suffice it to say here that 'the birth of Israel' indeed involved a move from the religious to the patriotic. But that move was neither total nor definitive, as the first section of this chapter demonstrates.

1.1. Messianism

Like 'myth', 'Messianism' is a slippery term; in the context of the present study, it will be used to mean a personal or collective attitude which bestows on the geographical entity formerly known as Palestine and now known as Israel a divine and liberating role in the accomplishment of an exceptional mission. Messianism was one of the foundational reasons for the birth of Israel, as is reflected in the primary texts this chapter will go on to consider, and for a number – according to some accounts, a growing number – of Israelis it remains a crucial factor in their conception of Israeli nationhood. One example of such accounts is that of the historian Diana Pinto, which forms a fitting incipit to analysis of the primary texts:

> Aujourd'hui le Talmud et la Torah définissent le style de vie d'une proportion toujours croissante de la société israélienne, au grand dam du projet sioniste des pères fondateurs. Eux souhaitaient créer un État normal comme tous les autres dans l'esprit du nation building qui suivit la Première Guerre mondiale. Leurs descendants doivent maintenant batailler contre une vision nationale fondée sur le messianisme biblique et territorial. (2012, 23–24)

> [Nowadays the Talmud and the Torah define the lifestyle of an ever-growing section of Israeli society, to the detriment of the founding

fathers' Zionist project. They wanted to create a normal state like any other in the spirit of nation building that followed the First World War. Their descendants must now fight against a national vision founded on territorial and biblical Messianism]

Pinto further insists on the enduring importance of Messianism for understanding contemporary Israel's drive towards progress, be it spiritual or material:

Le grand passé biblique et talmudique n'est pas révolu – il ne cesse de renaître toujours plus fort sous nos yeux – mais désormais il conditionne le futur, et ce faisant il transforme le contenu du terme « progrès » et le tire dans deux directions opposées mais, et c'est là la force d'Israël, parfaitement complémentaires. D'un côté ce terme est désormais cantonné au domaine de la technologie, de la médecine et des avancées scientifiques aux connotations neutres. De l'autre, il est investi d'une signification nationale métahistorique et, pour certains, même messianique. (2012, 14)

[The great Talmudic and biblical past isn't over – it's constantly being reborn ever stronger before our eyes – but now it conditions the future, and in so doing transforms the content of the term 'progress', drawing it in two opposed but, and this is Israel's strength, perfectly complementary directions. On the one hand, this term is now confined to the field of technology, of medicine and of scientific, advances with neutral connotations; on the other, it is invested with a metahistorical national meaning that is, for some, even Messianic]

As we will see, Pinto's stress on the inveterate influence of Messianism in the contemporary period resonates particularly with Bouganim (2010), Warschawski (2002) and Raczymow (2010).

The earliest of the primary texts featuring Messianism is journalist and novelist Joseph Kessel's *Terre d'amour et de feu* (1965). In this emotive narrative of his various visits to Palestine/Israel, Messianism is historically framed as a form of madness ultimately vindicated as rational by, precisely, historical processes. The Zionists' refusal of the 1903 British offer of Uganda as a Jewish homeland and acceptance of nothing other than what was then an arid and materially uninviting Palestine turned out, asserts Kessel, to have been the right move: 'Les événements donnèrent raison aux fous' (9) ['Events proved the mad men right']. This Messianism-madness coupling, with ultimate negation of the madness component, also features in Ami Bouganim's *Le cri de l'arbre* (1983), a novel which focuses on reluctant immigration from Morocco to Israel in the early 1960s. Its epigraph from the Talmud refers to the eponymous tree's cry: 'Le cri de l'arbre qu'on abat s'étend aux quatre coins de l'univers' ['The cry of the tree that is felled reaches the four corners of the universe']. When towards the end of the novel Yéhiel descends into what from all normative perspectives is insanity but is actually prophetic truth, he identifies with this felled tree. Before the descent he makes an impassioned appeal to the secular Ashkenazi authorities who have no time for the central role of Messianism in these North African Jews' lives, nor for the religious motivation of their immigration to Israel:

> La Tora est notre charte de vie, et c'est pour insuffler un sens nouveau à l'alliance qui y est consignée que nous sommes là. [...] La présence des Juifs sur cette terre représente un enjeu qui concerne toutes les nations, or vous en corrompez la signification et la portée en reniant la dimension religieuse de notre retour. (199)

> [The Torah is our life charter, and it is in order to breathe new meaning into the alliance which is recorded in it that we are here. [...] The presence of Jews on this land is an issue that concerns all nations, but you corrupt its meaning and its import by denying the religious dimension of our return]

The response of the functionary is mockingly dismissive, and denies yet reveals the power differentials between the Ashkenazi elite and the North African underdog in early 1960s Israel, which will be explored in greater detail in Chapter 3:

> – Un Messie, un Messie-philosophe s'est annoncé pour les Marocains, s'exclame le fonctionnaire, à la bonne heure, mazal tov! Nous avons tous, les Orientaux comme les Occidentaux, connu les mêmes misères et traversé les mêmes difficultés. Le gouvernement fait par ailleurs tout ce qu'il peut pour venir en aide aux couches déshéritées de la société israélienne. (199)

> ['A Messiah, a philosopher-Messiah has announced himself for the Moroccans', exclaims the functionary. 'That's great, congratulations! All of us, Easterners and Westerners, have experienced the same poverty and gone through the same difficulties. In addition, the government is doing all it can to help the most deprived levels of Israeli society']

A previous rhetorical question posed by Yéhiel has already exposed the tension between the secular Zionism of the government elite and the Messianism of the North African immigrants:

> Quels sont ces discours et ces déclarations dont on nous abreuve, et que nous avons été rédimés par le sionisme qui, à notre messianisme, n'est

qu'insipides palabres, et que nous faisons la fine bouche quand nous est présentée la liberté – de quelle liberté parlent-ils donc? de celle dont nous jouissions au Maroc ou de celle que nous endurons en Israël? – sur un plateau d'argent, et que nos plaintes et nos revendications ne sont qu'ingrates jérémiades inspirées par je ne sais quelle mentalité viciée? (187)

[What are all these speeches and declarations they shower upon us? That we've been redeemed by Zionism which, for our Messianism, is nothing but vapid, never-ending talk; that we turn up our noses when presented with freedom – so what sort of freedom are they talking about? The sort we enjoyed in Morocco or the sort we endure in Israel? – on a silver platter; that our complaints and demands are nothing but ungrateful whining inspired by who knows what kind of tainted mentality?]

In *Entre vents et marées* (1998), which again focuses on Moroccan Jews whose immigration to Israel is highly conflicted, Bouganim draws out that same tension, beginning with the pre-immigration period just after an earthquake in Morocco:

Surtout ils sentaient, de toute leur sensibilité messianique, que l'heure du salut avait réellement sonné et qu'il serait pour le moins dommage de mourir dans un vulgaire tremblement de terre ou un ridicule raz de marée alors qu'ils pouvaient mourir, les armes à la main, au service de Dieu. Pourtant, personne ne parlait de partir en Israël, de crainte d'être accusé de menées sionistes; en revanche tous évoquaient la possibilité de s'installer au Canada, pour ne pas attirer le mauvais œil sur leur véritable destination, et la plupart de ceux qui disparaissaient sans avertir et sans laisser de traces se retrouvaient quand même en Israël. (86–87)

[Above all they felt, with all their Messianic sensibility, that the hour of salvation had really struck and that it would be a shame, to say the least, to die in a vulgar earthquake or a ridiculous tidal wave when they could die, bearing arms, in the service of God. However, nobody mentioned leaving for Israel, for fear of being accused of Zionist manoeuvres; on the other hand, everyone brought up the possibility of settling in Canada, in order to avoid the evil eye being cast on their actual destination, and the majority of those who vanished without warning and leaving no trace nonetheless ended up in Israel]

The fear of being accused of Zionist manoeuvres clearly indexes the anti-Zionism of many religious Jews who opposed the creation of a Jewish state before the coming of the Messiah. Clashing with that belief was aspiration to a better life in Israel, away from their inferior status of dhimmitude in postcolonial, Muslim-dominated North Africa. In a more recent novel, *L'arbre à vœux* (2010), Bouganim satirizes the whole ideological configuration of Messianism. The satire operates in the sanctification (86) and mediatization (91) of Ari, a humble man who makes the mistake of giving idiosyncratic public speeches about the Messiah (88–89). The tragicomic result of Ari's unwilling propulsion to fame is his assassination by a crazed religious fanatic. This seems to be an ironic allusion to the 1995 assassination of Israel's then Prime Minister Yitzhak Rabin, whose views, this time on peace for Israel via concessions to the Palestinians, had been rather too idiosyncratic for his assassin Yigal Amir – a real-life religious fanatic. Indeed, in my 2011 interview with him, Bouganim trenchantly condemned Messianism as a highly destructive feature of contemporary Israel. In that interview, Bouganim made the following comments: Israel represents a Messianic adventure that is going wrong; all the energy invested in the creation and protection of Israel, including among the secular, were and still are Messianic; those who set the tone in Israel are without fail Messianists; in these conditions, Israel is doomed to failure.

Relative to Bouganim's purview on Messianism, that of Michel Warschawski in *Sur la frontière* (2002) is a parallax. Warschawski views Messianism and Zionism as having been historically convergent, endorsing an argument in Seffi Rachlevsky's *Messiah's Donkey* (1998) that 'le sionisme a été l'« âne du messie », le bras séculier et inconscient par lequel se réalise la volonté divine et la rédemption du peuple juif' (249) ['Zionism was the "Messiah's donkey", the secular and unconscious arm through which divine will and the redemption of the Jewish people are realized']. Warschawski (249) endorses Rachlevsky's conclusion that:

> Le résultat des élections de 1996[1] a signifié pour le judaïsme religieux le signe de la victoire. Sa voie est la voie gagnante, et la certitude messianique s'est encore affermie. À l'avancée vers la rédemption par la conquête de territoires et la venue d'un certain messie,[2] s'ajoute une nouvelle avancée: celle du retour à la foi du peuple d'Israël. (Rachlevsky, 319)

> [For religious Judaism, the result of the 1996 elections was a sign of victory. Its path was the winning path, and Messianic certainty was further strengthened. A new advance was added to that towards redemption through the conquest of territories and the coming of a certain messiah: the return to faith of Israel's people]

But Warschawski later distinguishes Messianism from Zionism in the new millennium:

d'un côté, un Israël dont les références restent l'épopée sioniste des années 20 à 70 et le rêve d'une reconstitution de l'union sacrée autour des valeurs d'un colonialisme à visage humain et, de l'autre, la fuite en avant vers une Judée archaïque, messianique, nationaliste et intégriste. (263–64)

[on the one hand, an Israel whose references remain the Zionist epic of the 1920s to 1970s and the dream of reconstituting the sacred union around values of colonialism with a human face and, on the other, a headlong rush towards a fundamentalist, nationalist, Messianic and archaic Judaea]

For both Bouganim and Warschawski, however, Messianism is never a purely religious phenomenon, but always thoroughly saturated by the political – and indeed, since the late 1970s it has become a potent fillip to the right wing in Israeli politics.

The complex relationship between Messianism and Zionism is also hinted at in Line Meller-Saïd's *Cela ne sera pas un rêve* (2009). This novel's third-person narrative focalizes upon Léa, a Polish Jew born in 1898 who emigrates to Palestine in 1924. Her *aliyah* is inspired by news from a member of her community who has already reached Palestine, after which she thinks obsessively about leaving for the Promised Land. Even if the word *messianisme* is not used explicitly, its basis is certainly what drives her and, it is implied, has affected all other Jews through millennia:

Eretz Israël, la terre mythique, la Terre promise! *Et l'Éternel dit à Moïse: Monte sur cette montagne et regarde le pays que je donne aux enfants d'Israël.* Quel juif a échappé à cette image véhiculée par les prières au cours de milliers d'années? Et quand cette image se nourrit du désir profond de donner au peuple juif une terre où il ne sera plus pourchassé, massacré, une terre où il vivra en paix selon ses propres lois, quelle idéologie laïque pourrait récuser cette aspiration? (29)

[*Eretz Israël*, the mythical land, the Promised Land! *And the Eternal said to Moses: 'Climb this mountain and look at the country I give to the children of Israel'.* Is there any Jew who hasn't come across this image borne by prayers over thousands of years? And when this image is fed by the deep desire to give the Jewish people a land where it will no longer be hunted, slaughtered, a land where it will live in peace according to its own laws, what secular ideology could object to that aspiration?]

Similarly to Warschawski, Meller-Saïd here conjoins Messianism and Zionism via the rhetorical question of the free indirect speech focalized on Léa. The yoking of the two ideological configurations also subtends

her religious parents-in-law's decision to emigrate to Palestine (54).
Indeed, greater fuel is added to the fire of their beliefs by a particular,
ancient slant:

> Tout quitter n'est pas facile à cet âge mais une pensée profonde confortait
> leur projet: morts et enterrés en Terre Promise, ils feraient partie, selon
> une antique croyance, de ceux que le Messie ressusciterait avant les autres
> à la fin des temps (54)

> [Leaving everything behind isn't easy at that age but a profound thought
> backed up their plan: dead and buried in the Promised Land, they would,
> according to an age-old belief, be among those whom the Messiah would
> raise from the dead before others at the end of time]

Meller-Saïd's novel has an innocent, arguably naïve tone, but it sincerely
attempts to render a historical reality (and indeed is preceded by
a laudatory preface from the distinguished French Jewish historian
Benjamin Stora): that of pre-Shoah Polish Jews living in an increasingly
antisemitic country and holding a sincere belief in the transcendent,
sacred qualities of making *aliyah* to the biblical Promised Land.

Innocence and naivety are entirely absent from Henri Raczymow's
rendering of Messianism in *Eretz* (2010). This first-person account of the
author's visit to Israel in 2009 is shrewd, rueful, and elegiac in tone. The
elegiac tonality derives from the haunting memory of Raczymow's dead
brother, who had emigrated to Israel many years before. *Eretz* makes
only two explicit references to Messianism, but both are potent. The first
is connected to the euphoria first experienced after Israel's unpredictable
victory in the Six-Day War of 1967 and lasting until the far less victorious
war of 1973: 'En Israël, l'euphorie, messianique ou non, dura jusqu'à la
guerre du Kippour, en 1973' (34) ['In Israel, the euphoria, Messianic or
not, lasted until the Yom Kippur war, in 1973'].[3] Raczymow's second
reference to Messianism erects a critical barrier between himself and the
ideology when it is used to justify annexation of land:

> Ceux qui, « messianiques », occupaient les territoires comme les zélotes
> avaient occupé, jadis, la forteresse de Massada sur la mer Morte et
> avaient préféré se suicider, hommes, femmes, enfants et bétails, plutôt que
> de négocier avec les Romains. Ceux qui empêchaient la paix d'advenir;
> ceux qui empêchaient l'avènement de cet État résolument laïc que tu
> appelais de tes vœux. (100)

> [Those 'Messianic' types who occupied the territories as the Zealots
> had formerly occupied the Massada fortress on the Dead Sea and had
> preferred – men, women, children and cattle – to commit suicide rather

than negotiate with the Romans. Those who prevented peace from coming about; those who prevented the coming of that resolutely secular state you so fervently wished for]

Both Bouganim and Raczymow frame the confluence of Messianic beliefs (of which the Six-Day War's annexation of land was regarded as a partial biblical realization) and the Israeli right's adamant position on what have come to be known as the Occupied Territories as the most potent of obstacles to the peace process. Similarly, journalist and essayist Martine Gozlan identifies the cathexis of Messianism as the root cause of a cataclysmic event that, intentionally or not, ended what seemed like a breakthrough in the peace process in the 1990s – the assassination of Rabin in 1995 (allegorized, as we have seen above, in Bouganim's *L'arbre à vœux*):

> Trois semaines avant la guerre, le fils du Rav Kook, Zvi Yehuda Kook, clamait: « Où sont Jérusalem, Sichem, Hébron? » Et, vingt jours plus tard, l'étoile de David flottait sur ces villes! La victoire de 1967 a donc été interprétée comme un signe de Dieu. Soudain, on pouvait créer des colonies et être plus pionnier que les pionniers, plus religieux que les religieux. Les messianistes pouvaient à leur tour devenir des modèles, et faire des adeptes. En face, Itzhak Rabin n'offrait pas une identité, mais il ouvrait un chemin; c'était le guerrier, le pain et le vin des sabras, la jeunesse israélienne nourrie des idéaux des pionniers. Et c'est pour cette raison qu'on l'a tué. On l'a assassiné non parce qu'il faisait la paix mais parce qu'il était populaire. Son meutrier, Yigal Amir, a compris que Rabin était l'unique symbole capable de barrer la route au messianisme. (174–75)

> [Three weeks before the war, Rav Kook's son, Zvi Yehuda Kook, was shouting 'Where are Jerusalem, Sichem, Hebron?' And twenty days later, the Star of David was floating over those towns! The 1967 victory was therefore interpreted as a sign from God. Suddenly, you could create settlements and be more pioneering than the pioneers, more religious than the religious. The Messianists in their turn could become models, and gain followers. On the other side, Yitzhak Rabin wasn't offering an identity, but he was opening up a path: the warrior, the bread and wine of the *sabra*s, Israeli youth nourished by the pioneers' ideals. And it was for this reason that he was killed. He was assassinated not because he was making peace but because he was popular. His murderer, Yigal Amir, realized that Rabin was the only symbol standing in the way of Messianism]

Also of interest here is that Gozlan opposes the religious Messianists with the secular Zionist pioneers, whereas some of the primary texts discussed above have intermittently made parallels between the two. In Gozlan's vision, Rabin was the idealistic product of those pioneers. It is to the role of the latter in the historical foundations of Israeli nationhood that we will now turn.

1.2. Early Zionist pioneers

In the Zionist narrative, the heroic status of the early pioneers of the Yishuv derives from their formidable material, economic and politico-military feats. The material and economic feats consisted in their transformation, through back-breaking physical labour, of land legally purchased from Arabs, from a state of either arid desert or infertile marshes into highly productive agricultural units. The politico-military feats consisted in their combating either moderately (as with the Haganah, a paramilitary organization that restricted itself to Jewish self-defence) or more violently (as with the Irgun, which split from the Haganah in order to go on the offensive) the antisemitism of the British mandate that governed Palestine 1922–1948. Immediately after the Second World War, the British Mandate heavily impeded the establishment of a Jewish homeland in Palestine. This was in contradiction of Britain's own Balfour Declaration of 1917, which had stated, 'His Majesty's government view with favour the establishment in Palestine of a national home for the Jewish people, and will use their best endeavours to facilitate the achievement of this object'. British impediment contrasted sharply with French support (extending to the secret supply of weapons) for the more extreme self-defence branch of the Yishuv, the Irgun, whose tactics were condemned by many as terrorist. Gozlan refers to this support in the French press (47), in the French capital, which she inscribes as a metonym for educated and cultured France (50), and in both ex-French Resistance and French diplomatic circles (50). To support her claim she cites Shmuel Katz, the Irgun's emissary to Paris in 1948, who details with extreme precision this French provision of arms to the Irgun (50).

These are some of the main historical facts about the early Zionist pioneers, but how are they portrayed by French Jewish writers? Their heroic status emerges vividly in a number of the primary texts, although its mediation can be critical, wry and even ironic (in the case of Jacques, Peskine, Raczymow and Rosenthal). As Robert Wistrich and David Ohana remarked in 1995,

[h]istorical 'Revisionism' is in fashion in Israel as in most of the western world as established views of the past are criticized, reassessed or openly debunked. The heroic view of the Israeli War of Independence as a struggle of the few against the many or of a uniquely peace-loving Zionist movement facing intransigently hostile Arab enemies has been challenged by a new generation of Israeli historians [...] During the past decade it has become a commonplace of much Israeli historiography to question and undermine these and other 'myths' at the core of Israeli self-perception which had created structures of thinking and propaganda that long shaped Israeli policy. Along with the war of 1948 (and virtually all of Israel's subsequent wars), the heroes of Zionism and Israel have also come in for a battering. (vii)

Historical revisionism is relatively rare in our literary corpus, with an entirely critical, wry or ironic take on the heroic status of the early Zionist pioneers being restricted to four of 11 texts. These four will be considered at the end of this section, as exceptions to the rule, though they will be preceded by texts which start to question that status. In *Une année si ordinaire* (2004), Esther Orner directly condemns historical revisionism, which in her account equates to sheer mendacity about the pioneers:

> J'ai téléphoné à l'autre Maya, ma cousine à Bruxelles. Elle est allée écouter des conférences sur « Les nouveaux historiens ». Ilan Greilsamer a raconté que lors d'une conférence à Haïfa, quelqu'un s'est levé pour dire que l'assèchement des marais était un mythe sioniste. Un vieil homme qui avait vécu cette époque glorieuse, probablement enfant ou adolescent, a protesté. Rien n'y a fait. Une sorte de révisionnisme. Non pas une sorte. Du révisionnisme tout court. (83–84)

> [I phoned the other Maya, my cousin in Brussels. She's been to listen to lectures on 'The new historians'. Ilan Greilsamer said that at a lecture in Haifa, somebody got up to say that the draining of the marshes was a Zionist myth. An old man who had lived through that glorious period, probably as a child or adolescent, protested. It didn't make any difference. A sort of revisionism. Not a sort. Revisionism period]

Indeed, the dominant approach in our primary texts is one of valorization, at times tipping into mythification. The latter typifies much of Joseph Kessel's *Terre d'amour et de feu* (1965), the following serving as an apt illustration:

> Ceux qui, à travers tous les obstacles, au prix de cent épreuves, gagnèrent la Palestine, étaient véritablement le sel de la terre. Les mains presque nues, dans la fièvre, la pénurie, et un milieu hostile, ils ont défriché,

asséché, planté, fondé villes, villages et ces extraordinaires colonies collectives: les Kibboutz. Ils ont fécondé l'avenir. Ils ont rendu possible ce qui ne l'était pas.

J'ai eu la chance de connaître, sous les tentes, dans les baraquements misérables, parmi les champs stériles, sur les chantiers paludéens, les hommes et les femmes de ces années héroïques. (9–10)

[Those who, despite all obstacles, after a hundred ordeals, reached Palestine, truly were the salt of the earth. Practically bare-handed, suffering from fever and shortages, and in a hostile environment, they cleared, drained, planted land, founded towns, villages and those extraordinary collective communities – the *kibbutzim*. They made the future fertile. They made the impossible possible.

Under tents, in shabby huts, surrounded by sterile fields, on malaria-ridden building sites, I had the good fortune to meet the men and women of those heroic years]

The material and economic achievements of the early Zionist pioneers on the land are here evoked in exalted, almost epic terms. The register used to evoke the politico-military feats adds triumphalist terms:

A la veille de la deuxième guerre mondiale, ils étaient environ un demi-million. Il se trouva parmi eux assez de volontaires pour former, au sein de l'armée anglaise, une brigade juive. Elle se battit admirablement.

Mais elle fut aussi le noyau de la Haganah, de la Palmach, les bataillons clandestins qui allaient assurer la naissance et la vie d'une nouvelle nation. [...]

[...] Le colosse britannique fut harcelé, harassé par une poignée d'hommes. L'Angleterre déposa son mandat, le mit à la disposition des Nations Unies. Là, une majorité très nette vota l'indépendance d'Israël. (10–11)

[On the eve of the Second World War, they numbered about half a million. Among them were sufficient volunteers to form a Jewish brigade within the English army. It fought admirably.

But this brigade was also the core of the Haganah, of the Palmach, the secret battalions that were to ensure the birth and the life of a new nation [...]

[...] The British giant was harassed, exhausted by a handful of men. England set down its mandate, leaving it at the disposal of the United Nations. There, a very clear majority voted for Israel's independence]

Kessel's emphasis on the disparity between the Yishuv's tiny numbers pitted against the mammoth imperial power of Britain underscores their implied courage, valour and unfathomable strength, first in support of Britain during the Second World War, then against Britain when it sought to suppress the Jewish movement for independent statehood in the immediate post-war period. In evoking the War of Independence (also known as the First Arab–Israeli War) that followed Ben Gurion's declaration of the state of Israel, Kessel reprises the trope of disparity and ratchets up his rhetoric in a final sentence where litotes achieves lapidary impact:

> Le 14 mai 1948, cet État voyait le jour. [...]
> Le lendemain matin, six nations arabes attaquaient Israël. [...]
> Seul un miracle pouvait éviter l'anéantissement.
> Le miracle eut lieu. (11)
>
> [On 14 May 1948, this state was born. [...]
> The following morning, six Arab nations attacked Israel. [...]
> Only a miracle could prevent annihilation.
> The miracle happened]

Kessel's eulogy is not limited to the more dramatic peripeteia of the Yishuv/the Israelis pitted against the British/the Arabs. He also insists on the great benefits to the Arabs in pre-Second World War Palestine of the early pioneers' impressive infrastructural work:

> Les Arabes s'aperçurent que, contrairement à ce que les seigneurs avaient affirmé, l'immigration juive était profitable au peuple. Des terres qui semblaient sans avenir possible – sables, marécages – se couvraient de cultures et d'arbres. [...] Enfin, le développement des routes, l'installation de l'électricité, l'œuvre sanitaire – toutes choses auxquelles les Arabes ne contribuaient en rien, ils en bénéficiaient à l'égal de ceux qui les avaient créées. (26–27)
>
> [The Arabs realized that, contrary to what the lords had asserted, Jewish immigration was beneficial to the people. Land that had seemed to have no possible future – dunes, marshes – was being covered with crops and trees. [...] In short, the Arabs benefited from the development of roads, the installation of electricity, health facilities – all things to which they contributed nothing – just as much as those who had created them]

Kessel's tenor oscillates between the hard-headedly material and the quasi-mystical. An example is his presentation of a 'model' example of the Zionist pioneers' virtuoso successes:

> C'est l'Emek, vallée de Jezréel.
>   Voici trois ou quatre ans, cette terre appartenait encore à un riche Syrien de Beyrouth. Elle n'était alors qu'un inculte marécage. Mais les sionistes

savaient, d'après la Bible, que ce sol fut entre tous fécond, qu'il avait été le grenier et le jardin de la Palestine. Ils l'achetèrent. Et maintenant ceux qui passent dans cette région ne la reconnaissent plus. Ce ne sont que champs ensemencés, routes solides et plantées d'arbres, villages et colonies. Maintenant l'Emek est devenu la plus glorieuse réussite du sionisme, son espoir le plus vivace, sa fierté la plus légitime. (57)

[This is Emek, Jezreel Valley.

Three or four years ago, this land still belonged to a rich Syrian from Beirut. At that point it was just an uncultivated marsh. But the Zionists knew, from the Bible, that this soil among all was fertile, that it had been the granary and the garden of Palestine. They bought it. And now those who pass through this region don't recognize it. It is full of sown fields, solid roads planted with trees, villages and communities. Now Emek has become Zionism's most glorious success, its most enduring hope, its most legitimate source of pride]

Pre-empting resistance from non-religiously/non-mystically inclined readers, Kessel cannily observes a more secular but no less glorifying approach to explaining the unfathomable successes of the pioneers:

Pour ceux qui n'acceptaient pas la simple explication du miracle, il en fallait une autre.

Et c'était la condition intellectuelle, morale et spirituelle de chacun des adversaires en présence.

Les Juifs, s'ils se trouvaient dans un état d'infériorité écrasante par le rapport du nombre des soldats et des armes, l'emportaient de beaucoup par la technique.

Ils avaient plus de spécialistes militaires qu'il n'en fallait, vétérans de toutes les grandes armées alliées de la deuxième guerre mondiale. Ils avaient des pilotes, des tankeurs, des parachutistes, des commandos américains, canadiens, anglais, australiens, sud-africains, russes, finnois. Ils avaient des savants. Une industrie [...]. (173)

[For those who didn't accept the simple explanation by miracle, another was needed.

And it was the spiritual, moral and intellectual state of each of the enemies facing each other.

If the situation of the Jews was overwhelmingly inferior in terms of numbers of soldiers and weapons, they very much had the upper hand in terms of technique.

They had more military specialists than you could wish for, veterans from all the great allied armies of the Second World War. They had pilots, tank crew, parachutists, American, Canadian, English, Australian,

South African, Russian and Finnish commandos. They had scientists. An industry [...]]

His trump card, however, is a final explanation based neither on Messianism nor intellectual meritocracy:

> Les hommes de ce peuple ne luttaient pas pour des conquêtes ou des avantages économiques ou des convoitises politiques. Ils défendaient leur vie profonde et toute nue. Et ils disaient:

> Nous possédons la plus sûre des armes secrètes. Elle tient en deux mots:
> « Où aller? » (174)

> [The men of this people were not fighting for conquests or economic advantages or political greed. They were defending their very life at a deep, naked level. And they said:

> 'We possess the surest of secret weapons. It consists in five words:
> "Where else can we go?"']

The aporia of the last line is affectively potent, presenting the heroism of the pioneers on a poignantly human footing: that of beleaguered desperation. For in the light of 2,000 years of persecution, pogroms and, most recently, the Shoah, there seemed to be no place in the world for Jews *other* than a renascent Israel.

Kessel's dithyramb to the early Zionist pioneers is certainly rivalled by Line Meller-Saïd in *Cela ne sera pas un rêve* (2009). An early example of stress on their heroic courage and self-sacrifice comes in the narration of Léa's decision to go to Palestine to help create a Jewish nation. This is despite her father's dire warnings of its multiple dangers after his own reconnaissance trip (and despite, too, his threat to disinherit her):

> – Israël est un désert plein de brigands, de moustiques et de maladies. Ce n'est pas un endroit pour fonder une famille et encore moins pour élever des enfants. Je ne te laisserai pas aller là-bas. Et inutile d'insister, je ne reviendrai pas sur ma résolution.
> [...]
> Elle affronte la colère de son père:
> – Je ne peux plus reculer. J'ai dédé partir et je partirai. (33)

> ['Israel is a desert full of bandits, mosquitoes and illnesses. It's no place to start a family and still less to bring up children. I won't let you go there. And there's no point pushing the matter, I won't go back on my decision'.
> [...]
> She faces her father's anger.
> 'I can't turn back. I've decided to leave and I'll leave']

When staging Léa's final, hard-fought arrival in Palestine, the narrative emphasizes both the thrusting modernity and the strong cultural capital of Jewish pioneers in Tel Aviv:

> Tel-Aviv [...] la ville nouvelle, spacieuse, dominant les bords de mer, où s'élèvent quelques immeubles cossus, aux styles novateurs, bâtis par des architectes venus faire leurs preuves dans ce pays tout neuf: leur penchant pour la modernité cadrait avec l'esprit pionnier de l'époque. (41)

> [Tel Aviv [...] the new, spacious city overlooking the seashores, where opulent, innovative buildings rise, built by architects who had come to prove themselves in this entirely new country: their taste for modernity matched the pioneering spirit of the era]

The impression of relative luxury that flows from this, evident in Tel Aviv's architectural sophistication, is strategically balanced by accent on the hardship willingly endured by the vast majority of the pioneer settlers:

> La vie est difficile pour tous et le travail rare. Les budgets sont restreints, il n'y a pas assez d'argent pour payer les salaires. Il faut prendre ce qu'on vous attribue. Une embauche dans sa spécialité? Ce sera pour plus tard! [...]
>
> Abraham, malgré sa frêle constitution, casse des cailloux pour empierrer des chemins et les rendre carrossables. Deux, trois journées de travail par semaine, très peu, trop peu pour couvrir les besoins de la famille. (46)

> [Life is hard for everyone and work is hard to come by. Budgets are limited, there isn't enough money to pay salaries. You have to take what you are given. A job in your own field? That'll be for later on! [...]
>
> Despite his frail constitution, Abraham breaks pebbles to gravel the tracks and make them suitable for vehicles. Two or three days' work per week, not much, not enough to cover his family's needs]

As well as economic privation and hard manual labour, what is also foregrounded is the danger bravely faced by the pioneer settlers in the face of deadly Arab riots and attacks. All of these ordeals are willingly embraced by Léa, for whom simply being in Palestine is a source of enduring happiness:

> les conditions de sécurité restent précaires: en marge des émeutes meurtrières arabes qui endeuillent périodiquement diverses régions, sont toujours à craindre des attaques sporadiques de fanatiques encouragés par leurs dirigeants farouchement opposés à la renaissance nationale juive.

[...] Elle accepte volontiers toutes les contraintes actuelles en échange de ce sentiment de bonheur permanent qui perdure en elle malgré les conditions difficiles de son existence. (46–47)

[Moreover, security conditions remain precarious: alongside the murderous Arab riots that periodically plunge various regions into mourning, there is always the fear of sporadic attacks from fanatics egged on by their leaders, who are fiercely opposed to the national Jewish rebirth.

[...] She willingly accepts all the current constraints in exchange for this feeling of permanent happiness that persists in her despite the difficult conditions of her existence]

The characterization of Léa borders on a muted form of hagiography. In rhetorical terms, she functions as a metonym for the early Zionist pioneers in general, for whom the survival of their nascent nation is the supreme value.

Looping back in time to one of the earliest of our primary texts, that value, so prominent in both *Terre d'amour et de feu* and *Cela ne sera pas un rêve*, also features in Marc Hillel's *Tu vivras dans ton sang* (1971). However, Hillel's novel is less grandiloquent than Kessel's or Meller-Saïd's in its construction of pioneer heroism. The following extract depicts the strength and courage exacted from those fighting for their aspirational Jewish state and constantly risking death in the process. The first-person narrator in the extract is, in fact, already a survivor – of Vichy France, and of the death faced every day as a former member (along with his comrade Zéroubavel) of the French Resistance. Now he is a Jew resisting attacks on Israel by Arab countries following the declaration of the state of Israel in 1948 (after which Egypt, Syria, Transjordan, Lebanon and Iraq had immediately invaded Israel):

Durant plusieurs jours, avec quelques heures de repos seulement, nous fûmes soumis à un dur entraînement de commandos, dans une forêt de palmiers, située à l'orée d'une vaste étendue de sable: le Néguev. [...] La guerre, qui se développait sur tous les fronts à la fois, avait besoin de ceux à qui elle était familière; et nous étions, Zéroubavel et moi, de ceux-là, une minorité parmi les nouvelles recrues. (244–45)

[For several days, with only a few hours' rest, we were subjected to a tough training course for commandos, in a palm forest situated on the edge of a vast stretch of sand: the Negev. [...] The war, which was developing on all fronts simultaneously, needed those who had experience of it; and we, Zéroubavel and I, were amongst those, a minority among the new recruits]

Hillel's account of the War of Independence also diverges from the exalted bombast of Kessel or the patriotic positivism of Meller-Saïd in noting the more banal and thus more human, more affectively legible disposition of Avigdor, an army major. Avigdor expresses doubts about 'heroic' self-sacrifice, even if he ultimately privileges the survival of the larger collectivity and the ideal of a sovereign Jewish nation:

> Plus déroutant encore était le comportement du commandant. Avigdor traitait de stratégie militaire comme s'il se fût agi de l'élevage de ses poulets sur les bords du Jourdain. Avec lui, la guerre prenait un visage humain, presque sentimental:
>
> – Pour la première fois depuis deux mille ans, soupira-t-il, entre deux gorgées de café tiède, des Juifs vont donner à d'autres Juifs l'ordre d'aller se faire tuer. Je sais, et heureusement pour nous, que je ne suis pas le seul dans mon cas. Malgré tout, la conscience en prend un sérieux coup. Hélas, si nous voulons survivre, il n'y a pas d'autre moyen! Alors, tant pis pour nos vieux préceptes pacifistes! Tout de même, camarades, ce n'est pas de gaieté de cœur que nous allons faire ce que le pays attend de nous. (259)

[More disconcerting still was the behaviour of the major. Avigdor dealt with military strategy as if he were raising chickens on the banks of the Jordan. With him, war took on a human, almost sentimental face:

'For the first time in two thousand years', he sighed, between two gulps of lukewarm coffee, 'Jews are going to give orders to other Jews to go and be killed. I know, and it's fortunate for us, that I'm not the only one in this situation. Despite everything, it's a hard blow to the conscience. Alas, if we want to survive, there's no other way! So, too bad for our old pacifist principles! All the same, comrades, we're not exactly going to be happy doing what the country expects of us']

The heroism trope is presented still less vaingloriously in Bouganim's *Le cri de l'arbre* (1983). Here it is implicitly denigrated as a self-serving sacred cow of the Ashkenazi elite, who exploit it to denounce what they perceive as the indolence of recent North African immigrants to Israel in the early 1960s:

> Quels sacrifices avez-vous consentis, quels efforts avec-vous investis, quels dangers avez-vous affrontés? Où étiez-vous quand bravant la malaria et les pillards arabes, les premiers pionniers assainissaient le marais, déblayaient la pierraille, fertilisaient le désert? Nous vous avons sortis de vos taudis pour vous transplanter sur une terre conquise par le sang, les larmes et la sueur de plusieurs générations d'hommes et de femmes épris de liberté. Où étiez-vous alors? (198)

[What sacrifices did you consent to, what efforts did you put in, what dangers did you confront? Where were you when, braving malaria and Arab pillaging, the first pioneers were draining the marshes, clearing the loose stones, fertilizing the desert? We brought you out of your hovels to transplant you to a land conquered by the blood, sweat and tears of several generations of men and women in love with freedom. Where were you then?]

The critical edge of Bouganim's *Le cri de l'arbre* is also found in Jean-Luc Allouche's *Les jours innocents* (1984), but in less trenchant and more wistful form. The critique is preceded by lyrical, incantatory evocation of the wonder felt by the third-person narrator (based on Allouche himself) during the first part of his stay in Israel as a young French Sephardic Jew. Idealization is most apparent in the prose cameo of the country's founding pioneers, presented in the Promethean metaphor as superhuman beings of literally mythical power:

> Il ne pouvait ignorer, cependant, quelle grandeur, quel sursaut prométhéen avaient animé les fondateurs de la nation convalescente, érigée à bout de bras, contre le monde, contre l'Histoire; quelle folie salubre les avait saisis et poussés à briser la fatalité de l'asservissement, à revendiquer leur statut de sujets libres, à se vouloir maîtres d'eux-mêmes, à rendre à leur peuple rompu son antique fierté. (78)

> [However, he could not ignore the grandeur, the Promethean leap that had driven the founders of the convalescent nation, which they'd raised up high with their outstretched arms, against the world, against History; what healthy folly had gripped them and driven them to break the inevitability of enslavement, to demand their status as free subjects, to try to be their own masters, to restore to their broken people its ancient pride]

However, *Les jours innocents* also comes to express a melancholic disillusionment with the pioneers' ideals. Such ambivalence features more concisely in Valérie Zenatti's *Quand j'étais soldate* (2002). Set in 1988, this autobiographical novel about a young woman's military service in Israel stages a heated dialectic between fellow female soldiers, prompted by Daniéla's allusion to unjust treatment of Palestinians:

> – Arrête! Ça n'a rien à voir! Nous avons une histoire particulière, les Juifs ont été persécutés partout pendant des siècles, et les pionniers sionistes se sont sacrifiés pour que l'on puisse vivre ici en paix ...
> – Justement si, « ça a à voir », a coupé Daniéla. Tant que nous aurons cette image romantique et irréprochable de nous-mêmes, nous continuerons à opprimer un peuple sans même nous en apercevoir.

[...]

Je n'ai pas dit un mot. Je n'avais pas de mort proche à exhumer. Je pensais aussi que Daniéla n'avait pas tout à fait tort, mais qu'il fallait dire les choses autrement, expliquer, sans faire autant de mal, sans provoquer ces crises de larmes, sans tout remettre en question. (124–25)

['Stop! That's got nothing to do with it! We have a specific history, Jews were persecuted everywhere for centuries, and the Zionist pioneers sacrificed themselves so that we could live here in peace ...'

'Actually, it *does* have "something to do with it"', Daniéla interrupted. 'As long as we have this romantic and perfect image of ourselves, we'll carry on oppressing a people without even realizing it'.

[...]

I didn't say a word. I had nobody to dig up who'd been close to me and had died. I also thought that Daniéla wasn't entirely wrong, but that she should have said things differently, should have explained, without causing so much hurt, without provoking fits of tears, without calling everything into question]

Through dialogical exchange, the novel presents a thesis – the self-sacrificing heroism of the early Zionist pioneers – followed by an antithesis – that in late twentieth-century Israel such a purview is self-aggrandizing romanticism, and, moreover, politically blinding. The synthesis resides in the first-person narrator's acceptance of the critique, set against a call for greater sensitivity to the intense affective import for ordinary Israelis of conventional Israeli historiography and collective memory (however constructed, mediated and partly questionable that collective memory might be).

We have traced a development from texts that confine themselves to exalting the heroism of the early Zionist pioneers to those that question such exaltation, albeit with varying degrees of scepticism. The approach of the final four texts to be considered in this section recalls Wistrich and Ohana's allusion (1995, vii) to the debunking of myths. An early exemplar is Paula Jacques's *Un baiser froid comme la lune* (1983), a picaresque, satirical and humorous novel with pronounced autobiographical basis. The following extract shows pure persiflage:

Zoltan Gadol eut un sursaut. Il ramena ses jambes au sol. Il dévisagea sévèrement le solliciteur. Il entama le panégyrique d'une patrie, non plus élective, mais légitime. Et historique. Tobias approuva sans réserve. Il exprima son admiration pour les pionniers sionistes, et un regret, sincère ô Architecte de l'Impossible, de n'avoir pas participé à l'épopée; la conquête de la Terre sainte était le fait d'âmes d'élite. Lui, pauvre hère,

devait se contenter d'en louer la prouesse à distance. A un clin d'œil
en direction de sa fille, elle comprit qu'il estimait le prix de l'héroïsme:
exorbitant. Le borgne vanta longuement la beauté et la prospérité du
pays arraché aux marécages. Tobias le félicita d'avoir contribué à son
peuplement. (203–04)

[Zoltan Gadol jumped. He lowered his legs back to the ground. He stared
severely at the supplicant. He began the eulogy of a country that was no
longer elective, but legitimate. And historic. Tobias agreed unreservedly.
He expressed his admiration for the Zionist pioneers, and a regret, a
sincere regret, O Architect of the Impossible, for not having taken part in
the epic; the conquest of the Holy land was for elite souls. He, miserable
wretch, had to make do with praising it at a distance. From a wink in
his daughter's direction, she realized that he was assessing the price of
heroism: exorbitant. The one-eyed fellow vaunted at length the beauty
and prosperity of the country torn from the marshes. Tobias congrat-
ulated him on having contributed to its population]

The main protagonist Tobias is a comically hapless and impressionable
immigrant to Israel and the action is taking place in 1958. Initially, he
admires the monumental achievements of the pioneers, as is clear in
his humorously humble simile: 'Les pionniers d'Israël, ces architectes
du rêve avéré, l'intimidaient à l'égal d'un analphabète admis à un
cours d'université' (213) ['The pioneers of Israel, those architects of the
dream come true, intimidated him as if he were an illiterate admitted
to a university course']. Despite the humour, what follows closely is
not entirely mocking of a typical *kibbutz*, which sustains the ethos and
praxis of the earlier pioneers, and whose members combine intellectual,
artistic and manual prowess:

Aviv Midbar abritait une forte concentration d'intelligences et de vertus.
Certains possédaient des diplômes de médecin, d'ingénieur, de juriste.
Ils occupaient en ville des fonctions gouvernementales, tel le ministre
des Transports, siégeaient dans des chaires scientifiques ou initiaient les
enfants au kibboutz aux sciences humaines, à la musique, à la peinture
comme Yossele Yossipovitch, critique d'art dans un journal de Tel-Aviv.
Leurs tâches accomplies, ils prenaient leur part des travaux de la ferme où
leur savoir excellait. (213–14)

[Aviv Midbar was home to a strong concentration of intelligence and
virtues. Some were qualified doctors, engineers, lawyers. In town they
occupied governmental posts, such as Minister of Transport, held
academic chairs or introduced the *kibbutz* children to the human sciences,
to music, to painting, like Yossele Yossipovitch, an art critic for a Tel Aviv

newspaper. Once their tasks were done, they took part in the farm work, where their knowledge was excellent]

Gradually, however, an almost inhuman quality creeps into this perceived perfection. Narration focalized upon Tobias's contemplation of the Israelis' valiant husbandry of the land obliquely suggests a form of tampering with nature by comparison with the Arab's (in)action on the land:

> En regardant du côté opposé, là où la luxuriance marquait une frontière, l'œil était frappé d'une différence, de nature à expliquer l'antagonisme des habitants de la plaine. Du côté arabe, la terre reposait en son harmonie intacte et austère, les maisons faisaient souche avec la rocaille. Du côté juif, la moindre parcelle verdoyait, les arbres défiaient le ciel, le plus petit monticule se hérissait d'édifices criards, pressés, poussés à la hâte. Le domaine des pionniers, pris à la gorge, proliférait comme l'action suisse en bourse, la campagne palestinienne retenait ses offrandes indolentes. (242)

> [Looking at the other side, where luxuriance marked a frontier, the eye was struck by a difference that could explain the antagonism between the inhabitants of the plain. On the Arab side, the land lay in its austere intact harmony, the houses on a line with the rocky ground. On the Jewish side, even the smallest plot was green, the trees defied the sky, the smallest hillock bristled with garish, busy buildings that had grown in a rush. The domain of the pioneers, over which they had a stranglehold, proliferated like Swiss shares on the stock market, the Palestinian countryside kept back its lazy offerings]

In contrast to a non-interventionist harmony with nature respected by the Arabs, this passage mischievously implies in the Israeli approach a hungry appetite for dominance (here of nature) that reaches almost Nietzschean proportions. In *The Will to Power*, Nietzsche defines the eponymous will as 'an insatiable desire to manifest power' (110); for more, and more seriously, on the possible influences of Nietzsche on Zionism, see Chapter 2. Many other surreptitious digs are made at the ten-year-old Israeli nation and its still pioneering spirit, but the sharpest occurs in narration of the abrupt ending to Tobias's brief and unsuccessful dwelling in the Promised Land. He is rightly accused of petty crimes, but there is burlesque in the Israeli authorities' verdict that the greatest of his crimes were his desertion of the still-beleaguered Land and his perceived insult to the Herculean efforts of its pioneers and founders:

Grivèlerie à l'hôtel Zion, vol de papiers et usurpation du cercueil d'un citoyen français, dette envers l'Office d'immigration, fuite clandestine et, pis que tout: destruction de la Téoudat Zéhout. Aux crimes envers la Loi, il faut ajouter le délit d'opinion. Le ressortissant – le langage vous a de ces cruautés – a déserté la patrie en péril. Il s'est rendu coupable de couardise, de mépris pour la petite sueur des pionniers et la grande mission des fondateurs. (286)

[Non-payment of a restaurant bill at the Zion Hotel, theft of papers and usurpation of a French citizen's coffin, debt to the Immigration Office, secret escape and, worse than anything, destruction of the *teudat zehut*.[4] To crimes against the Law should be added expression of opinion contrary to that of the ruling body. The citizen   language can be so cruel – deserted the endangered country. He was guilty of cowardice, of contempt for the humble sweat of the pioneers and for the great mission of the founders]

Brigitte Peskine's *Buena Familia* (2000) is not as wittily coruscating as Jacques's *Un baiser froid comme la lune* in its assessment of the pioneers and of the new state of Israel, but it is far from the starry-eyed vision of Kessel, Hillel and Miller-Saïd. Of particular interest are its Turkish-Jewish narrator's imputation of gender imbalances and Zionist propaganda:

J'expliquai à Simone que l'État tout neuf que les Juifs venaient d'arracher à la culpabilité internationale n'avait pas besoin de vieilles femmes mais d'hommes jeunes et courageux. Simone était habituée à être servie, à bien manger, à dormir dans un lit confortable. Elle n'avait pas idée de la dureté de la vie, de la misère des camps où l'on parquait les nouveaux immigrants, de la rusticité des *Sabras*, dont les parents avaient labouré la terre de leurs mains presque nues … Il fallait être aveuglé par la propagande pour ignorer que les conditions de vie étaient tout à fait primitives, la nourriture immangeable, la chaleur torride, sans parler des moustiques, du manque d'hygiène et de l'écueil de la langue, surtout pour les femmes! Les garçons avaient appris l'hébreu à l'école, eux … (227–28)

[I explained to Simone that the brand new state the Jews had managed to pull from the teeth of international guilt needed not old women but brave young men. Simone was used to being served, to eating well, to sleeping in a comfortable bed. She had no notion of the hardness of life, the poverty of the camps where new immigrants were penned in, the rustic simplicity of the *sabra*s, whose parents had ploughed the earth almost bare-handed … You'd have to be blinded by propaganda not to know that the living conditions were entirely primitive, the food inedible, the heat scorching, not to mention the mosquitoes, the lack of hygiene and the language pitfall, particularly for women! The *boys* had learnt Hebrew at school ...]

Equally clear in Peskine's novel are the bitter divisions in early Israeli society, between the Yishuv pioneers and the Shoah survivors who arrived after the creation of the state of Israel, and between the Ashkenazim and the rest of the Israeli population:

> Nul n'ignorait l'antagonisme rampant entre les nouveaux arrivants et les pionniers qui avaient construit le pays. Les seconds reprochaient aux premiers de n'avoir pas émigré avant l'Holocauste. Les premiers se demandaient si les leaders juifs, en Palestine, avaient vraiment tout essayé pour les sauver.
> – L'État d'Israël a été créé par des Ashkenazes pour des Ashkenazes, conclus-je. (227)

> [Nobody was unaware of the creeping antagonism between the new arrivals and the pioneers who had built the country. The latter criticized the former for not having emigrated before the Holocaust. The former wondered if the Jewish leaders in Palestine had really tried everything to save them.
> 'The state of Israel was created by Ashkenazim for Ashkenazim', I concluded]

The arrogance ascribed to the Ashkenazim by Peskine is also a charge implicitly levelled by Olivia Rosenthal in her ludic but politically challenging novel *Les Fantaisies spéculatives de J. H. le sémite* (2005).[5] In this novel, the narrator's mother is forthright: 'La Palestine n'est pas un pays, dit-elle, c'est une terre déserte que les Juifs ont fertilisée et que pour cette raison ils ont le droit de posséder' (72) ['"Palestine isn't a country", she said. "It's a desert land that Jews fertilized and that they therefore have the right to possess"']. The view of this French Ashkenazi woman partially mirrors the final line cited above from Peskine's first-person narrator; both assert that it was Ashkenazi Jews who literally, materially created Israel in its modern avatar, and both – explicitly in Peskine's case, implicitly in Rosenthal's – assert that this heroic feat has been taken to signify their right to exclusive ownership of it.

The final text that participates in, if not a debunking, then a contestation of the pioneer heroism myth is *Eretz* (2010). Henri Raczymow's fleeting evocation of the early pioneers, filtered through address to his dead brother who had emigrated from France to Israel, at first appears fairly neutral, arguably even positive in its evocation of a ruggedness and free spirit:

Le pays lui-même a tant changé. Il n'est plus le pays pionnier, rude, un peu anarchique, que tu as connu, où il fallait se battre, souviens-t'en, pour accéder aux autocars Egged, ce pays que tu as passionnément aimé (46)

[The country itself has changed so much. It's no longer the tough, rather anarchic, pioneer country that you knew, where people had to fight, remember, to get on Egged coaches, that country you loved passionately].

However, one memory of his brother's tales is succeeded by a comparison that implies a Stalinesque brainwashing at work in the *kibbutzim* (see Chapter 2):

Tu nous racontais ces expéditions du shabbat à la plage, distante de quelques kilomètres. Vous grimpiez à trente sur une charrette tirée par un tracteur poussif, vous chantiez des chants de pionniers, vous traversiez d'autres kibboutzim, on eût dit un film soviétique à la louange de l'homme nouveau, du travail collectif, de la vie au grand air, que sais-je … (49)

[You told us about those Shabbat expeditions to the beach, a few kilometres away. Thirty of you would climb onto a cart drawn by a wheezing tractor, you'd sing pioneer songs, you'd go through other *kibbutzim*, it could have been a Soviet film in praise of the new man, of collective work, of life in the open air, I don't know …]

The last four clauses here dovetail with Jacques's more amusing but no less critical portrait of an indoctrinated community whose strength has faintly Nietzschean connotations (1983, 242; again, for more on the possible influences of Nietzsche on the early Zionists, see Chapter 2). While Raczymow's parallel is with Soviet totalitarianism, totalitarianism was of course also a defining feature of the Soviet regime's supposed opposite, the Nazi regime. It is to the most notorious product of the Nazi regime, the Shoah, and the role of the Shoah in the historical foundations of Israeli nationhood, that the rest of this chapter is devoted.

1.3. The Shoah

As historian Levana Frenk noted in 2011, whereas studies conducted from 1965 to 1975 showed that the majority of Israelis accorded more importance to the creation of the state of Israel and the War of Independence than to the Shoah,

[u]ne étude récente, menée par Yaïr Auron sur l'évolution des identités dans la société israélienne, montre qu'aujourd'hui la Shoah a pris la

première place. Elle est devenue l'événement fondateur et constitutif de l'identité juive, et le ciment unificateur de la société juive israélienne (30)

[a recent study conducted by Yaïr Auron on the evolution of identities in Israeli society, shows that now the Shoah has taken first place. It has become the foundational and constitutive event for Jewish identity, and the unifying cement of Israeli Jewish society][6]

While the Shoah is central to contemporary Israeli identity, French literary mediations of the relationship between the Shoah and Israelis are far from uniform: quite the contrary, they present a number of paradoxes. In this, they mirror divisions within Israel itself on that relationship. Focusing on the 1950s, Yechiam Weitz observes that 'The memory of the Holocaust and its victims was accompanied by unending political strife. These debates were always harsh, bitter, full of tension and emotional. Occasionally, they were violent and even deadly' (130). As we will see below, the primary texts suggest that such strife certainly persisted well beyond the 1950s.

1.3.1. The Shoah and redemptive value

Idith Zertal is one of the New Historians of Israel (other notable names include Benny Morris, Ilan Pappé and Avi Shlaïm) who engage in 'revisionist' historiography about Zionism, the state of Israel and particularly the 1948 War of Independence. In the following excerpt, Zertal describes (but clearly does not approve of, as the rest of her book makes plain) the ascription of redemptive value to the Shoah relative to the foundation of the state of Israel:

> le nouvel État né des ruines du peuple juif et dépeint comme l'antithèse de son histoire, tout en étant perçu comme le vengeur du sang de millions de Juifs assassinés (« Nous, le peuple juif souverain d'Israël, sommes les rédempteurs du sang de millions de Juifs », avait déclaré Ben Gourion), reconstruisait la Shoah dans le processus téléologique de rédemption d'Israël [...] (152)

[Moreover, the new state born from the ruins of the Jewish people and depicted as the antithesis of its history, while at the same time being perceived as avenging the blood of millions of murdered Jews – 'We, the sovereign Jewish people of Israel, are the redeemers of the blood of millions of Jews', Ben Gurion had declared – reconstructed the Shoah in the teleological process of Israel's redemption]

Towards the end of her study – a sustained indictment of what she perceives as the exploitation of Shoah memory to legitimate Israeli oppression of the Palestinians[7] – Zertal develops a swingeing analysis of the redemption thesis (which, interestingly, she allies to negative Messianism):

> C'est la proximité historique entre la Shoah et la constitution de l'État d'Israël, et le rôle décisif de celle-ci dans l'obtention et la formation de celui-là, qui avait engendré ce type de messianisme catastrophiste et, avec lui, un nouveau – ou bien antique et renouvelé – mythe de destruction et de rédemption, d'impuissance et de toute-puissance, détaché de l'historique et du politique. (233)

> [It is the historical closeness between the Shoah and the constitution of the state of Israel, and the decisive role of the former in obtaining and forming the latter, which had caused this type of utterly pessimistic Messianism and, with it, a new – or else ancient and renewed – myth of destruction and redemption, of impotence and of omnipotence, detached from the historical and the political]

The main grounds for Zertal's censure are that the thesis is ahistorical (234). A number of the primary texts also problematize the redemption thesis, but not necessarily for the same reasons as Zertal.

The first of the primary texts to allude to the redemption thesis is Allouche's *Les jours innocents* (1984), where it is presented ambiguously:

> Il ne pouvait méconnaître, non plus, l'ombre portée de la catastrophe qui avait emporté dans la tourmente d'Europe ces millions d'âmes dont l'absence diffuse endeuillait jusqu'à l'air respiré. Ce pays n'était-il pas leur rédemption? (80)

> [He could not be unaware, either, of the shadow of the catastrophe which had swept away in the European storm those millions of souls whose diffuse absence plunged everything into mourning, down to the very air people breathed. Was this country not their redemption?]

It is not at all clear that the rhetorical question here is posed by the homodiegetic narrator; indeed, it is more likely to reflect what he infers is the majority Israeli view. And it is equally unclear at this point in the narrative that Allouche's early enchantment with Israel is later subject to deep disillusion, the view of the Shoah expressed here being no obvious exception to that disillusion. Ambiguity on the question is also woven into Eliette Abécassis's *L'Or et la cendre* (1997), but by other means: two different characters taking clearly opposed stances. Espousal of the redemption thesis is represented by Mina, a deeply religious Jew. Though what she actually says is that 'Auschwitz est le purgatoire, est l'Etat d'Israël est la rédemption du peuple juif, un avant-goût des temps messianiques' (79) ['Auschwitz is the purgatory, and the state of Israel is the redemption of the Jewish people, a foretaste of Messianic times'], this has been preceded by an assertion that the two phenomena are inseparable (79). That inseparability reappears later on: 'Mina disait qu'Israël était la Rédemption après l'exil et la souffrance (218) ['Mina said that Israel was the Redemption after the exile and the suffering']. Yet it is important to note that Mina is a French, not an Israeli Jew, as well as a Shoah survivor, and that a counterpoint to her religious belief in the redemptive value of Israel as a product of the Shoah is provided in a secular Israeli character, Ron Bronstein (though he is also the son of a Shoah survivor who went on to commit suicide 46 years after the end of the Second World War). Bronstein opines, 'on ne peut pas dire qu'Israël soit la Rédemption après la souffrance, parce qu'il n'y a pas de sens à la souffrance, contrairement à ce que prétendent certains théologiens juifs' (81) ['you can't say that Israel is the Redemption after the suffering, because suffering has no meaning, contrary to what certain Jewish theologians claim'].

In view of this reference to Jewish theologians propounding the redemption thesis, it is interesting that in *Sur la frontière* Warschawski (2002) points to the converse: the objections of religious Israeli Jews who believe that the Zionist establishment exploited the memory of the Shoah in order to accelerate the creation of the state of Israel (218). Finally, in *Eretz* (2010) Raczymow also rejects the redemption thesis, for he cannot see the slightest meaning, be it political, theological or metaphysical, in the Shoah (and here he partially converges with Abécassis's character Bronstein, who rejects the idea that the Shoah has any theological meaning). However, Raczymow tempers this cognitive rejection with the affect of empathy:

> je pense toujours que la Shoah est un événement dépourvu du moindre sens, ni politique, ni théologique, ni métaphysique, et qui ne relève d'aucune rédemption possible. Reste que, si l'on se place du seul point de vue juif (ce à quoi, faut-il le dire, nul n'est tenu), chaque soldat israélien tué au combat pour la défense de son pays est tout aussi héroïque que Mordechai Anielewicz admiré pour être tombé face aux nazis les armes à la main et non asphyxié dans la chambre à gaz comme un animal d'abattoir. C'est ici, en Israël, et seulement ici que l'expression « Plus jamais ça » revêt un sens. (68)
>
> [I still think that the Shoah is an event lacking in the slightest meaning, be it metaphysical, theological, or political, and which has nothing to

do with any possible redemption. The fact remains that, if you look at things purely from a Jewish standpoint (which nobody is obliged to do, it should be said), every Israeli soldier killed while fighting in defence of his country is just as heroic as Mordechai Anielewicz, who was admired for falling weapon in hand faced with the Nazis and not being suffocated in a gas chamber like an animal in a slaughterhouse. It's here in Israel, and only here, that the expression 'Never again' takes on a meaning]

Immanent in the Israeli slogan 'Plus jamais ça' is oblique shame at the manner in which millions of Jews died and an adamant determination that Jews should never again become victims. As such, it provides a natural segue to our next section.

1.3.2. *The Shoah and shame*
Philosopher Elisabeth de Fontenay posits this shame as a worldwide Jewish phenomenon, but appears to put its *terminus ad quem* in the 1960s:

> Vous ne pouvez pas vous représenter à quel point, jusqu'aux années 1960, en Israël, en Europe, aux Etats-Unis, la plupart des Juifs ont eu honte de ce qui était arrivé à eux-mêmes et aux leurs (50)

> [You can't imagine how much, right up to the 1960s, in Israel, in Europe, in the United States, most Jews were ashamed of what had happened to themselves and to their families]

Historian Diana Pinto states that Shoah survivors had been 'peu écoutés dans l'Israël naissant car ils n'avaient pas fait le bon choix sioniste de partir « à temps »' (2012, 193) ['rarely listened to in the nascent Israel because they hadn't made the good Zionist choice to leave "in time"'], indicating the ex-Yishuv's scorn for Shoah survivors as a source of shame to be muffled. Broadly coalescing with Fontenay in targeting 1960s Israel, in *Sur la frontière* Michel Warschawski (who emigrated from France to Israel at the age of 16) focuses, like Pinto, on this scorn felt by non-diasporic Jews. A traumatic memory relays how an individual *sabra* displays a shame-inducing contempt felt widely in Israel for those Shoah victims who had not been 'strong' enough to survive the death camps:

> Celle qui deviendra plus tard ma compagne, une Sabra elle aussi, avait l'habitude de traiter de « savonnette » quiconque n'était pas assez fort à son goût. Cette expression israélienne est une allusion blasphématoire à l'utilisation faite par les nazis de la graisse des Juifs massacrés à Treblinka et à Auschwitz. « Blasphématoire » est le mot qui m'était venu à l'esprit en l'entendant la première fois. Je me souviens d'en avoir ressenti

un tremblement dans tout le corps, comme si on avait traité ma mère de
prostituée, ou comme si quelqu'un avait uriné devant le tabernacle à la
synagogue. C'était absolument incroyable et pourtant terriblement banal
dans cet Israël des années 60 où la faiblesse était considérée comme une
tare. (213)

[The woman who would later become my partner, also a *sabra*, had the
habit of calling whoever wasn't strong enough for her taste a 'soapbar'.[8]
This Israeli expression is a blasphemous allusion to the use the Nazis made
of the fat of Jews slaughtered at Treblinka and Auschwitz. 'Blasphemous'
is the word which came to mind when I heard it for the first time. I
remember having felt a trembling in my whole body, as if someone had
called my mother a prostitute, or as if someone had urinated in front of
the tabernacle in synagogue. It was absolutely incredible and yet terribly
common in that Israel of the 1960s where weakness was considered a
defect]

The intensely negative affect here is patent in the reference to bodily
trembling, which recalls Brian Massumi's reference to 'the irreducibly
bodily and autonomic nature of affect' (28) already noted in the
Introduction. Warschawski's body here reacts involuntarily to a literally
shocking admixture of outrage and humiliation. It is striking that the
first signifier that comes to Warschawski's mind to qualify the injurious
expression is 'blasphématoire', which even for a non-religious Jew would
suggest a devastating infringement of due respect, in this case for Jews
murdered in the death camps. Warschawski offers a possible explanation
of such infringement whereby, in a move of ethical checkmate, he shifts
the source of shame from the Shoah victims to the Yishuv that made
little attempt to prevent their extermination or even to mitigate its
devastating extent:

un sentiment de culpabilité et d'échec: l'existence d'une communauté
juive en Palestine, moderne, armée et partiellement souveraine, n'a pu
empêcher le judéocide et trop peu, bien trop peu, a été entrepris pour – si
ce n'est arrêter le massacre – du moins sauver le maximum de Juifs. Dans
l'inconscient d'Israël, surtout dans les années qui suivent la création de
l'État, le sentiment de culpabilité est bel et bien là. (216–17)

[a feeling of guilt and failure: the existence of a Jewish community in
Palestine, modern, armed and partially sovereign, had been unable to
prevent the Judaeocide and too little, far too little, was undertaken to – if
not stop the slaughter – at least save as many Jews as possible. There was
certainly a feeling of guilt in Israel's unconscious, especially in the years
following the creation of the state]

That usually unavowed sense of ex-Yishuv guilt in the first few years of the young state's existence is soberly acknowledged by Yaïr in Yaël Hassan's *Souviens-toi Leah!* (2004), a novel partly inspired by the non-fictional experience of the author's grandparents, who were themselves killed in the Shoah. Yaïr is an ex-Yishuv member, having emigrated to Palestine as a teenager in 1932 and immediately assimilated to a new mode of life:

> Ne m'as-tu pas demandé toi-même ce que nous faisions nous, ici, pendant que nos frères d'Europe se faisaient massacrer? Tu as raison. Nous n'avons rien fait ... Ou si peu. [...] Et sais-tu quelles furent alors les mesures prises par les dirigeants du Yishouv? Ils organisèrent des manifestations, des veillées mortuaires, des prières publiques dans les synagogues. Il y eut une journée de jeûne, des cours dans les écoles consacrés au massacre des Juifs, des drapeaux noirs au balcon. Voilà, pour répondre à ta question, Leah, ce que nous avons fait pour aider nos frères. (114)

> [Did you yourself not ask me what *we* were doing, here, while our European brothers were being slaughtered? You're right. We did nothing ... Or so little. [...] And do you know what measures the leaders of the Yishuv took? They organized demonstrations, wakes, public prayers in synagogues. There was a day of fasting, school classes devoted to the slaughter of the Jews, black flags on the balcony. That, to answer your question, Leah, is what we did to help our brothers]

However, Hassan's novel emphasizes less a sense of ex-Yishuv contempt for Shoah survivors than of deep insensitivity to them – or, to put it more charitably, of resistance to cognitive dissonance. The latter derives from the mismatch between awareness of the diasporic Jew's suffering and despair and the reasoned will to make a clean break from them, for the greater good of building a new, entirely positive and robust Israeli nation. The first-person narrator Leah, herself a Shoah survivor, conveys both sides of the binary (65). Her ruminations begin by registering the aversion of former Yishuv members to hearing about the traumas of the Shoah survivors. These Yishuv members had made very considerable material sacrifices to take in and offer a new life to the Jewish refugees; in return, they required a mnemonic moratorium on past sufferings and a willingness to contribute to the construction of a strong, future-oriented Jewish state informed by the new collectivist values of the *kibbutz*. Accordingly, Leah's need to put into language her traumatizing experiences, to speak and to be heard, is collectively censored. The psychic claustrophobia produced by this prohibition of memory, and of speech expressing that memory, is vividly expressed in the affectively charged metaphor of being walled in:

> Alors que j'avais tant espéré pouvoir parler, que j'avais besoin de pouvoir hurler mon histoire à qui voudrait bien l'entendre, on m'imposa le silence, on m'y emmura (65–66)

> [Whereas I'd so much hoped to be able to talk, needed to be able to yell my story at whoever would listen to it, silence was imposed on me, I was walled up in it]

The damage caused by imposed silence is also forcefully conveyed in Meller-Saïd's *Cela ne sera pas un rêve*. Reacting to her young daughter's abhorrence for the verbal outpourings of a Shoah survivor, Léa affirms the deontic duty of ex-Yishuv members such as herself and *sabra*s like her daughter not to occlude the survivor's suffering, and indeed their deontic duty actively to listen (81–82).

So far, this chapter has identified a number of patterns within the primary texts' inscription of the Shoah. But the merits of aggregated representation should not eclipse those of attention to singular phenomena, where the latter are significant. The last four sections of this chapter focus on such singular phenomena, found in one or, at most, two primary texts each. In three of the four cases, this is preceded by consideration of non-literary perspectives, from a literary scholar (Bruno Chaouat), two philosophers (Elisabeth de Fontenay and Jacques Derrida), a historian (Zertal), an essayist and journalist (Martine Gozlan) and a psychoanalyst (Daniel Sibony).

1.3.3. *The Shoah as source of current anti-Israeli sentiment in France*

Bruno Chaouat implies that the Shoah, or more precisely its perverted memory, is one source of current anti-Israeli sentiments in France:

> il est devenu de plus en plus incontestable que la délégitimation de l'État d'Israël, telle qu'elle se formule aujourd'hui à un degré de sophistication théorique sans précédent, se nourrit de trente ou quarante ans de perversion de la mémoire de la Shoah, perversion qu'Alvin Rosenfeld, dans un jugement d'un pessimisme radical, n'hésite pas à appeler « la fin de la Shoah ». (2011, 204)

> [it has become increasingly incontestable that the delegitimation of the state of Israel, as it is now formulated with an unprecedented degree of theoretical sophistication, has fed for thirty or forty years on corruption of the memory of the Shoah, a corruption that Alvin Rosenfeld, in a radically pessimistic judgement, doesn't hesitate to call 'the end of the Shoah']

While Chaouat's remark does not refer overtly to France, most of the cultural references of the powerful article in which it is located are French. The primary text within our corpus that similarly alleges perversion of the memory of the Shoah in France specifically is *Mon cœur de père* (2012). In this autobiographical narrative, Marco Koskas makes the following observation about twenty-first-century France:

> Sur Facebook, ce matin, je lis que les nouveaux manuels d'histoire décrivent Israël sous le jour le plus noir: colonialisme, occupation, etc. Après les médias, c'est au tour de l'école de fausser la réalité de ce pays magnifique. Pourquoi tous ces mensonges? Pourquoi ce déni? Sans doute pour se délester du poids de la Shoah, qui a rendu l'antisémitisme illégal et intellectuellement intolérable. Aujourd'hui c'est cette illégalité qui est en train de devenir intolérable à la société, et non la Shoah elle-même. Il me semble, du moins ... (198–99)

> [I read on Facebook this morning that the new history textbooks describe Israel in the most negative terms: colonialism, occupation, etc. After the media, it's the schools' turn to distort the reality of this magnificent country. Why all these lies? Why this denial? No doubt to offload the weight of the Shoah, which made antisemitism illegal and intellectually intolerable. Now it's this illegality that is becoming intolerable to society, and not the Shoah itself. That's how it seems to me, at least ...]

For Koskas, then, current anti-Israeli sentiments in France spring from France's wish to be rid of its historical guilt about connivance in the Shoah. If a formerly victimized people (Jews) can be cast as oppressors (Israelis), the people who formerly victimized them (the French under Vichy) can wipe the conscience-slate clean. While 'Il me semble, du moins' may suggest that this is a tentative hypothesis, it is one that Koskas also advances in an unpublished article entitled 'Peut-on encore être un écrivain juif en France?':[9]

> Du même coup, les interdits qu'a créés la Shoah s'avèrent trop contraignants, comme s'ils avaient empêché un certain antisémitisme cérébral de s'exprimer librement depuis la Libération; comme si enfin, il était urgent de se défausser de sa culpabilité coloniale sur l'état d'Israël, aux prises lui aussi avec d'acerbes nationalismes arabes. Peu à peu le sionisme est ainsi devenu, non pas la seule utopie du XIXeme qui ait produit de la démocratie et des richesses, mais un gros mot.

> [By the same token, the taboos created by the Shoah prove too restrictive, as if they had prevented a certain type of cerebral antisemitism from

expressing itself freely since the Liberation; as if, finally, it were vital to dump your colonial guilt on the state of Israel, also grappling with bitter Arab nationalisms. So, instead of the only utopia of the nineteenth century to have produced democracy and wealth, Zionism has gradually become a rude word]

Koskas's mention of Zionism leads us to the next singular but significant motif in Jewish-French literary representations of the Shoah and its relation to Israel.

1.3.4. *Instrumentalization of the Shoah for Zionist ends*
Elisabeth de Fontenay is forthright in claiming an Israeli instrumentalization of the Shoah that, while not specifically identified as Zionist, seems to cohere with contemporary Zionist-inspired policies:

> je dirai seulement qu'il y a une certaine instrumentalisation par Israël qui n'a pas voulu *se charger* de l'Extermination avant le procès Eichmann, et qui s'en sert maintenant trop souvent pour justifier les débordements des limites de son droit (89–90)

> [All I will say is that there is a certain instrumentalization by Israel which didn't want to *burden itself* with the Extermination before the Eichmann trial, and which now too often uses it to justify going beyond the limits of its right]

A similar critique by Jacques Derrida is cited by de Fontenay's interlocutor Stéphane Bou:

> Il est possible et nécessaire, sans le moindre antisémitisme, de dénoncer cette instrumentalisation, par exemple ce calcul proprement stratégique (politique ou autre) qui consisterait à *se servir* de l'holocauste, à l'utiliser à telle ou telle fin. On peut juger cette fin contestable, ou détestable la stratégie qu'elle commande, sans dénier le moins du monde la réalité de cette monstruosité passée, à savoir l'holocauste dont certains voudraient ainsi s'emparer et se servir. (Fontenay, 184)

> [It is possible and necessary, without being in the slightest bit antisemitic, to denounce this instrumentalization, for example that purely strategic calculation (political or otherwise) that would consist in *making use of* the Holocaust, in utilizing it for such-and-such an end. We can deem this end contestable, or the strategy it governs appalling, without in any way denying the reality of that past monstrosity, namely the Holocaust which some would like to appropriate and exploit][10]

De Fontenay's elaboration of her initial declaration brings into play the Palestinian question:

> Maintenant, force est de constater que l'instrumentalisation de la Shoah fonctionne en deux sens contraires. D'un côté, il y a ceux qui ont eu intérêt après 1961 à radicaliser la menace arabe pour légitimer une politique d'expansion. D'un autre côté, il y a ceux qui tiennent à accentuer la réalité d'un lien de cause à effet entre la Shoah et Israël pour mieux rappeler que les Palestiniens n'y sont pour rien. (193)

> [We now have to note that the instrumentalization of the Shoah works in two opposite ways. On the one hand, there are those in whose interests it was after 1961 to radicalize the Arab threat in order to legitimize an expansionist policy. On the other, there are those who insist on stressing the reality of a causal link between the Shoah and Israel, to strengthen their reminder that the Palestinians have nothing to do with it]

The Palestinian question is also raised by Zertal, who implies that Shoah victims are exploited by Israel in order to justify its bellicosity:

> Régulièrement, et en fonction des circonstances, les victimes de la Shoah sont rappelées à la vie et assument un rôle central dans le débat politique israélien, en particulier dans le contexte du conflit israélo-arabe, et plus spécifiquement lors des crises graves, voire des guerres. De fait, depuis 1948 et jusqu'à la crise actuelle, qui a commencé en octobre 2000, il n'y a pas eu de guerre ou de conflit qui n'aient été perçus, définis et conceptualisés par la société israélienne dans des termes liés au génocide. (9)

> [Regularly, as particular circumstances require, Shoah victims are called back to life and assume a central role in Israeli political debate, particularly in the context of the Israeli–Arab conflict, and more specifically at times of serious crises, or even of wars. Indeed, since 1948 and right up to the current crisis, which began in October 2000, there hasn't been a war or conflict that hasn't been perceived, defined and conceptualized by Israeli society in terms linked to the genocide]

It should be noted that Zertal's thesis on the instrumentalization of the Shoah has been subjected to ferocious critique by the philosopher Elhanan Yakira. Commenting on precisely the passage cited above, Yakira satirically ventriloquizes Zertal:

> Comme Israël est coupable de toutes ces guerres – auxquelles l'ont poussé, ainsi qu'à l'occupation des terres arabes, un mythe de la force et une angoisse existentielle irrationnelle – , la Shoah, ou son instrumentalisation, est à l'origine de tout ce mal (270)

[As Israel is guilty of all these wars – into which, along with the occupation of Arab lands, it has been driven by a myth of strength and by an irrational existential anguish – the Shoah, or its instrumentalization, is the root of all this evil]

Yakira finds many faults in Zertal's approach, including what he regards as a weak methodology that focuses selectively on discourse rather than on history (280) – although it is clear from the subtitle of Zertal's book, *La Nation et la mort: la Shoah dans le discours et la politique d'Israël*, that the Shoah in discourse (as well as in politics) is precisely her main object of enquiry. For our purposes, Yakira's key charge is that Zertal engages in a false dialectic which, ironically, involves the very malfeasance with which *she* charges Israel – viz. that of instrumentalization of the Shoah – for her *own* political ends:

> au nom de la Shoah, du scandale de son instrumentalisation, de l'ignominie que constitue la mobilisation au service de l'armée, du militarisme, de la « nation et de la mort », au nom de l'indignation morale devant le manque de respect dû la Shoah, sa commercialisation, etc. – la Shoah est en fait mobilisée au service d'une critique généralisée d'Israël; non pas contre telle ou telle politique du pays, mais contre l'israélianité en tant que telle ou contre les prétendus fondements (n'avons-nous pas parlé de « communauté victimaire »?) de son identité collective. (270)

> [in the name of the Shoah, of the scandal of its instrumentalization, of the ignominy constituted by mobilization in the service of army, militarism, 'nation and death', in the name of the moral indignation felt when faced with lack of due respect for the Shoah, its commercialization, etc. – the Shoah is in fact mobilized in the service of a generalized criticism of Israel; not against any particular policy of the country, but against Israeliness as such or against the so-called foundations of its collective identity – have we not talked about 'victim community'?]

I will not attempt to arbitrate here between Zertal and Yakira. However, I do agree with Yakira that Zertal engages in a generalized criticism of Israel rather than its particular governmental policies at any one time. Witness the following, which, while filtered through reference to an Israeli commentator, presents a damning portrait of Israel that Zertal endorses:

> Dans l'esprit d'Elkana, il y avait un lien direct entre les « leçons » de la Shoah, telles qu'elles étaient systématiquement instillées dans la conscience nationale et l'univers mental d'Israël à travers la commémoration, l'éducation et l'endoctrinement, et les actes de violences

« irréguliers » commis par les soldats et les colons israéliens contre les civils palestiniens. (131)

[To Elkana's mind, there was a direct link between the 'lessons' of the Shoah, as they have been systematically instilled in Israel's national consciousness and mental universe through commemoration, education and indoctrination, and the acts of 'illegal' violence committed by Israeli soldiers and settlers against Palestinians civilians]

Two primary texts intersect with Zertal's polemic. In fact, in the last sentence of the following, Warschawski's *Sur la frontière* relays a view that goes even further in condemning Zionist instrumentalization of the Shoah:

Le monde religieux, qui se sentait dépositaire de la mémoire du judaïsme européen massacré, accusait l'establishment sioniste d'avoir considéré le génocide comme un facteur d'accélération du processus de création de l'État d'Israël. Certains étaient même convaincus que, pour les sionistes, le judéocide était un phénomène positif qui contribuait à l'épuration du peuple juif, facilitant ainsi la régénération future des rescapés en Palestine. (218)

[The religious world, which felt itself to be the guardian of the memory of slaughtered European Judaism, accused the Zionist establishment of having considered the genocide an accelerating factor in the process of the creation of the state of Israel. Some were even convinced that, for the Zionists, the Judaeocide was a positive phenomenon which contributed to the purification of the Jewish people, thereby facilitating the future regeneration of the survivors in Palestine]

The shock of that last sentence is slightly mitigated by the suggestion in 'Certains étaient même convaincus' that this view is both minoritarian and perhaps implausible. However, Warschawski's conscious decision to include it may lead the reader legitimately to infer his will that this view be considered. Raczymow, for his part, recalls in *Eretz* (2010) his brother Alain's claim – with which he seems to concur – that Zionists have cynically recuperated the six million Jews slaughtered in the Final Solution in order to justify both the creation of Israel and its subsequent behaviour:

quand tu tins courageusement ces propos à ton commandant, tu n'étais déjà plus sioniste. Tu ne partageais déjà plus les valeurs de ce pays, fondées précisément sur la récupération des « six millions ». Toutes les expositions, tous les musées en Israël qui relataient la Shoah terminaient leur parcours didactique par le « renouveau », la « renaissance », une manière de rédemption de la Catastrophe par la création de l'État juif.

Tel était le sens du « plus jamais ça ». Le « plus jamais ça » n'était pas un souhait, pas davantage un mot d'ordre moral, c'était le fondement même de l'État, sa raison d'être, son programme ici et maintenant et à jamais. Israël se justifiait *ipso facto* par la Shoah. (113)

[when you bravely said these things to your army major, you had already stopped being a Zionist. You no longer shared the values of this country, values founded precisely on the recuperation of the 'six million'. All the exhibitions, all the museums in Israel that told the story of the Shoah ended their didactic path with 'renewal', 'rebirth', a sort of redemption of the Catastrophe through the creation of the Jewish state. Such was the meaning of the 'never again'. The 'never again' was not a wish, no more than it was an expression relating to morality, it was the very foundation of the state, its reason for being, its programme here and now and forever. Israel justified itself *ipso facto* through the Shoah]

It is significant that Raczymow's recollection of this claim is preceded by praise for Alain's challenge to an army major's rebuke ('tu tins courageusement ces propos à ton commandant') of his refusal to participate in unjustified violence against Palestinians. The raising of the Palestinian question adumbrates the widened political purview of our next section.

1.3.5. Instrumentalization of the Shoah for political ends
Within the secondary literature, Gozlan takes a nuanced stance, asserting not so much that the Shoah is instrumentalized for Israeli political ends generally, but rather that the Shoah's traumatic psychic legacy conditions all political choices in Israel:

Nous sommes l'un et l'autre: le déporté et le combattant, le squelette en haillons et le soldat vigoureux, l'extermination et la souveraineté. Cette dualité, qui ressurgit à chaque crise, conditionne tous les réflexes individuels et collectifs, tous les choix politiques. Pour ne pas être un déporté promis au brasier, il faut être un combattant. Pour ne pas être un squelette dans la fosse, il faut être un soldat resplendissant. Pour ne pas être exterminé, il faut être souverain. (208–09)

[We are both: the deportee and the combatant, the skeleton in rags and the sturdy soldier, extermination and sovereignty. This duality, which resurfaces with each crisis, conditions all individual and collective reflexes, all political choices. In order not to be a deportee doomed to the inferno, you have to be a combatant. In order not to be a skeleton in the pit, you have to be a radiant soldier. In order not to be exterminated, you have to be sovereign]

While Gozlan is an essayist and journalist, her prose here has a strong literary imprint in its use of striking imagery, impactful ternary structures and forceful binary oppositions. These devices vividly convey a figurative schizophrenia structuring Israeli national identity as it relates to the Shoah. Sibony, for his part, reproaches the Israeli 'establishment « de gauche »' [' "left-wing" establishment'] for filling its discourse with 'le lien sacro-saint entre Israël et la *Shoah*, laissant entendre qu'Israël en est le produit' (211) ['the sacrosanct link between Israel and the *Shoah*, implying that Israel is its product']. Here Sibony rejects the left-wing establishment's exploitation of the Shoah in its claim that without the latter, Israel would quite simply not exist (a claim which could, some would object, be viewed as a form of existential blackmail to obviate any questioning of Israel's current legitimacy).

Gozlan's and Sibony's assertions are broadly supported in our primary text for this section, *Eretz* (2010), wherein Raczymow not only recognizes Israeli politicians' instrumentalization of the Shoah, but sees it as entirely understandable:

> La Shoah est politiquement instrumentalisée? Mais je suis tout prêt à le reconnaître! Le moyen de faire autrement, du reste? Pour être sincère, je dois aussi admettre que cela ne me choque pas. Ici, en Israël, je fais corps avec tout ce qu'implique l'existence de ce pays et sa pérennité. (60)

> [The Shoah is politically instrumentalized? Well of course it is! And how could it not be? To be honest, I must also admit that this doesn't shock me. Here, in Israel, I stand solidly behind everything that the existence of this country and its permanent existence involves]

However, in contrast with his own position of understanding and even sympathy ('Le moyen de faire autrement, du reste?'), Raczymow relates his brother Alain's heated opposition to this instrumentalization within a national institution determined by political imperatives, the Israeli army:

> le commandant a levé la tête, t'a résumé l'histoire de l'État d'Israël, du peuple juif, en te demandant de temps en temps si ce qu'il évoquait trouvait le moindre écho en toi. Le point d'orgue fut: Tu sais, soldat, que le peuple juif a eu six millions de morts? Quand l'entretien – le monologue – s'est achevé, il t'a demandé si tu avais quelque chose à ajouter. Tu as pris alors ton élan et tu as récusé les gens qui s'appropriaient abusivement

les six millions. Ils appartenaient au peuple juif tout entier, et pas spécialement à l'Armée de Défense d'Israël. (112–13)

[the major raised his head, summarized for you the history of the state of Israel, of the Jewish people, asking you from time to time if what he was recalling elicited the slightest response in you. The climax was: 'Do you know, soldier, that the Jewish people has six million dead?' When the interview – the monologue – ended, he asked if you had anything to add. At that point, you took a run up and objected to people who wrongly appropriated the six million. They belonged to the entire Jewish people, and not especially to Israel's Defence Army]

Alain's spirited response to this authority figure is a pointed accusation that the IDF (Israel Defence Forces) instrumentalizes the Shoah for its own very precise political ends: in this case, the attempted moral blackmail of Alain when he refuses to continue the military operation of 'cleansing' a Palestinian village in the Occupied Territories (110).

Reference to the army evokes its cognate term war, providing a direct pathway into the final section of this chapter, where the primary text for attention is set during the Gulf War.

1.3.6. The Shoah as template for possible future destruction of Israeli

Valérie Zenatti's novel *Ultimatum (En retard pour la guerre)* (2006)[11] is set in 1991, when in the extra-diegetic real world, Iraq attacked two Israeli cities with Scud missiles, Tel Aviv, Israel's largest city, and Haifa, its main seaport, prompting fears that Israel could be drawn into the Gulf War. According to reports from Tel Aviv, the air was filled with the wail of sirens, and minutes later up to eight missiles streaked in and exploded in balls of flame. Residents scrambled for protective clothing and gas masks, issued to most of the population before the conflict began. Zenatti's novelistic restitution of this period conveys the fearful affect triggered by the attacks, with panic levels rocketing. In the novel, part of that panic stems from the memorial link made by the terrified Israeli citizens between the gas produced in this attack and the gas chambers of the Shoah. This link is at first made in a rather heavy-handed oblique manner through italicization of the nouns 'gaz' and 'chambres', with Tamar playing bitterly on the double meaning of 'chambres' ('bedroom' and 'chamber') 'On va s'enfermer parce qu'on a peur du *gaz*! On va s'enfermer dans nos *chambres* pour empêcher le *gaz* de nous tuer!' (72) ['We're going to lock ourselves in because we're scared of the *gas*! We're going to lock ourselves in our *chambers* to stop the *gas* killing us!']. Immediately afterwards, the link becomes explicit:

Nous voyons les mêmes images. Celles qui collaient à mes yeux pendant des années, quand je scrutais l'espace sombre et poussiéreux sous mon lit avant de m'endormir, le cœur affolé car sûre d'y découvrir un SS rempli d'une joie froide à l'idée de me tuer. (72–73)

[We see the same images. Those that were glued to my eyes for years, when I used to examine the dark and dusty space under my bed before falling asleep, my heart beating crazily because I was sure I'd discover an SS officer full of cold delight at the idea of killing me].

The first-person narrator attempts to resist the incipient madness that would result if the link were pursued:

je refuse de suivre Tamar sur le chemin qui mène aux forêts de bouleaux de Pologne et d'Ukraine. Je vois la folie nous y guetter, incandescente encore du sang des morts, tapie sous les fougères. Si nous cédons à la terreur que nous inspirent les deux mots associés, Gil nous trouvera tout à l'heure en train de courir dans l'appartement, échevelées et moites, le regard fiévreux, ou bien nous balançant en psalmodiant les mots terribles sur tous les tons, avec dans la voix tantôt un étonnement enfantin, tantôt les accents butés de celui qui dit non à la réalité, débordantes de détresse, miaulant comme des femmes blessées, voix démentes, voix chevrotantes de sorcières: Les chambres … le gaz … les chambres … le gaz … . Les chambres … le … (73)

[I refuse to follow Tamar along the path that leads to the birch forests of Poland and Ukraine. I see madness lying in wait for us there, still white-hot from the blood of the dead, lurking under the ferns. If we give way to the terror with which the two associated words fill us, Gil will soon find us running around in the apartment, frenzied and clammy, our gaze feverish, or rocking back and forth chanting the terrible words in every different tone, sometimes with a childlike astonishment in our voices, sometimes with the stubborn stresses of somebody who denies reality, overflowing with distress, mewing like injured women, crazy voices, the quavering voices of witches: 'The chambers … the gas … the chambers … the gas … . The chambers … the …']

Yet the affective overload of Shoah memories is such that efforts to suppress the fearful link are not entirely successful, as is seen in the broken syntax and obsessive lexical repetition in the last sentence above. Freudian slips by other characters reinforce the insidious power of those memories:

il a pu lui téléphoner pendant qu'ils étaient dans la chambre à gaz. Comment, Victor? J'ai dit « la chambre à gaz »? Ce n'est pas possible, tu te trompes. Tu as entendu ça, ma chérie? Oh mon Dieu, mon Dieu, j'ai vraiment dit ça? Quelle horreur! Je n'ai pas dormi de la nuit. (102)

[he was able to phone her while they were in the gas chamber. What's that, Victor? I said 'the gas chamber'? It's not possible, you're mistaken. Did you hear that, my darling? Oh my God, my God, did I really say that? How awful! I didn't sleep a wink that night]

Finally, however, a more combative psychological reaction is registered in the response of, ironically enough, a Shoah survivor:

Hitler ne m'a pas eue, alors personne ne m'aura! Je n'ai pas de chambre hermétique et le masque à gaz est resté dans sa boîte. On va quand même pas m'embêter avec des histoires de gaz deux fois dans le même siècle! (121)

[Hitler didn't get me, so nobody's going to get me! I don't have a sealed room and the gas mask has stayed in its box. Really, people can forget bothering me with all that fuss about gas twice in the same century!]

1.4. Endnote

The diversity of attitudes towards the Shoah and their differing links to contemporary Israeli society in *Ultimatum (En retard pour la guerre)* are mirrored in the other elements considered in the various sections of this chapter. Each element has a highly significant place in the historical foundations of Israeli nationhood, but each is discrete. Taken collectively, their diversity and lack of conceptual hierarchy obstruct attempts at synthesis. Yet a number of general observations may be made. Although the seven primary texts treating Messianism usually subject it to heavy critique, it has historical anteriority to all other foundations to Israeli nationhood. Further, it is depicted as being on the ascendant in the contemporary period, in a complex confluence with right-wing nationalism and the ideology of Greater Israel that underpins the retention of the Occupied Territories. The heroic status of the early Zionist pioneers, treated by 11 primary texts, is also subject to critique, but by a far smaller proportion – four of 11: Jacques (1983) Peskine (2000), Raczymow (2010) and Rosenthal (2005) – and is encoded as an enduring myth that on the whole serves to stimulate pride in national history. Finally, while it is the antithesis of pride-inducing, the Shoah is seen largely to vindicate the very creation of the state of Israel as the only safe haven in the world for Jews after that Judaeocide. Not surprisingly, Francophone Jewish writers are highly exercised by possible abuses of Shoah memories, which, like Messianism, feature in 11 of the 44 primary texts considered in this study. So much for the singular status of these various foundations of Israeli nationhood. But in our primary texts at least, they emerge as transversal. Indeed, in the texts taken as a whole, these historical foundations appear as resolutely rhizomatic. While the Shoah, or rather the supreme value of national survival which was the salutary moral derived from it by Israelis, is the youngest of the roots, and perhaps subject to the most problematization as such (as should be evident from sections 1.3.1–1.3.6), it also appears to be the most deeply embedded in the soil of Israeli ipseities.

Notes

1 The 1996 elections resulted in a surprise victory for the right-wing Benyamin Netanyahu.

2 This 'certain messie' is identified by Warschawski, as 'Menachem Mendel Schneersohn, dernier rabbi des Lubavitch, perçu par ses disciples comme le messie' (249) ['Menachem Mendel Schneersohn, the last rabbi of the Lubavitchers, regarded by his disciples as the messiah'].

3 Cf. Gozlan (75–76).

4 The *teudat zehut* is the Israeli identity card.

5 For a more detailed study of this novel, see Cairns (2014).

6 The most recent study – or rather studies – were conducted by Yaïr Auron in 1990 and 2008, and are detailed in Auron (see particularly p. 66).

7 It is important to note that Zertal and other New Historians' accounts of the Shoah have been questioned by other historians (the present chapter deals later on with a different form of critique of Zertal, from the philosopher Elhanan Yakira). Thus, for instance, Efraim Karsh contends: 'The "new historians" have been at the forefront of the campaign to dilute the uniqueness of the Holocaust and downplay its significance, whether by charging Israel of exploiting this tragic event for political capital, or by depicting the Palestinians as the Holocaust's "real victims", or by putting Israeli and Nazi actions and behavioural patterns on a par' (xxxviii).

8 It is hard (indeed impossible, for me at least) to translate adequately into English the French word *savonnette*; while it literally means a small bar of soap, it designates something better translated as 'wimp' or 'weakling'.

9 This article was provided to me by the author.

10 The original quotation of Derrida comes from Derrida and Roudinesco (189).

11 This novel was subsequently made into a successful film, directed by Alain Tasma and released in 2009.

CHAPTER TWO

Modern Israeli
Paradigms of Identity

While Chapter 1 considered how the primary texts inscribe key historical foundations of Israeli nationhood, Chapter 2 considers how they inscribe key elements within paradigms of Israeli identity from 1948 onwards. The first is Zionism (2.1) – which is constantly subject to resemanticization – and its enduring influence (Zionism obviously pre-dates 1948, but has changed considerably since then, and moreover continues to underpin the very existence of the state of Israel). This includes Zionism's anti-diasporic, potentially even antisemitic dimensions (2.2), and its relatively progressive gendered structures in the institution of the kibbutz (2.3), a unique creation of the Zionist state. The second element is the kibbutzim more generally, old and new (2.4). The third is the self-division of diasporic Jews (2.5). Linked to this motif is the cult of the 'New Hebrew', in reaction to antisemitic stereotypes (2.6). A further area of enquiry is the iconic but in some cases deforming role of the Israeli army in the formation of Israeli identity (2.7), including its gender equality (2.8) and thus its liberating role for young women from Orthodox families (2.9), but also its economic disadvantages and its psychological depredations (2.10). The final elements to be explored are the influence of the Francophone community in inflecting modern Israeli identities (2.11), and, in symmetry, Israel's perception of France (2.12).

First, though, a note of caution. Discussions of 'identity' are prone to overly-capacious use of the signifier, with attendant risks that are cogently flagged by Rogers Brubaker and Frederick Cooper:

> We argue that the prevailing constructivist stance on identity – the attempt to 'soften' the term, to acquit it of the charge of 'essentialism' by stipulating that identities are constructed, fluid, and multiple – leaves us without a rationale for talking about 'identities' at all and ill-equipped

to examine the 'hard' dynamics and essentialist claims of contemporary identity politics. 'Soft' constructivism allows putative 'identities' to proliferate. But as they proliferate, the term loses its analytical purchase. If identity is everywhere, it is nowhere. If it is fluid, how can we understand the ways in which self-understandings may harden, congeal, and crystallize? (1)

Brubaker and Cooper suggest various alternative terms that might stand in for 'identity', 'doing the theoretical work "identity" is supposed to do without its confusing, contradictory connotations' (14). These are: identification and categorization; self-understanding and social location; commonality, connectedness, groupness. The topoi treated by Chapter 2 cohere most with 'commonality, connectedness, groupness', since these topoi concern aspects not of individual Israelis' identity but rather of collective, national identity. Of course, as was recognized in Chapter 1, national identity is always something of a mythical construct, and that point should be heeded as we proceed – all the more so because we will be dealing with Francophone literary re-constructions of that construct.

2.1. Zionism

The scholarly literature on Zionism is so vast that it would be beyond the remit of this book to explore it. I could simply state two essential points: that the signifier 'Zionism' (along with its adjectival cognate 'Zionist') has no fixed signified, being constantly subject to resemanticization – as journalist and essayist Gozlan remarks, 'le sionisme a toujours été divisé' (30) ['Zionism has always been divided']; and that the emotions it inspires are intense. It nonetheless seems useful, in the interests of providing a historical and theoretical framework for the primary texts, briefly to present an eclectic sample of some recent non-literary contributions to the ongoing debate around the concept. Controversially, the cultural historian David Ohana has asserted the influence of Nietzsche on early models of Zionism: 'The main figures in early Zionism, whether left- or right-wing, secular or religious, pioneers of the Second and Third Aliya or ideologues of the Jewish underground LEHI and the "Canaanite" movement came under his influence before 1948' (39). Which aspects of Nietzschean thought, often (if erroneously) associated with Nazism, might have influenced the early Zionists? I would argue that those aspects were certainly not concepts like 'the blond beast', 'the Superman' or 'slave morality', even if, as Ohana rightly says, such concepts 'have been taken out of context and misused for political ends' (Wistrich and Ohana, 39). Rather, I would foreground four particular features of Nietzsche's '"philosophy of life" (Lebensphilosophie)' mentioned by Ohana: 'voluntarism, will, vitality and myth' (40). A potent example of their influence as portrayed in the primary corpus will be examined below. And while Ohana states that, 'After the establishment of the Israeli state, however, the "new Hebrew" became the "Sabra" (ideal type of the indigenous Israeli) and the passionate drive to build a "new man" made way for a more personal outlook' (39), he later concedes that 'Nietzsche would remain an important thinker for some Zionist socialists coping with the crisis of values in society, with the proper balance between individualism and collectivism within the kibbutz and with the need for a theory of will' (55). Ohana's emphasis on the socialist dimension of early Zionism is echoed by historian Diana Pinto (2010). But according to Pinto, the situation has changed radically in the twenty-first century, with the original Zionist project, which she defined as socialist and secular, being negated by the increasing influence of religious Jews on Israel (2012, 23–24). Within a psychoanalytic prism, Daniel Sibony comes to a similar conclusion about the religious turn: 'Le sionisme moderne est le passage à l'acte d'un fantasme de retour sur les lieux de l'origine' (175) ['Modern Zionism is the realization of a fantasy about returning to places of origin'].

With such contested meanings and connotations, of which these three examples provide but a tiny sample, it is hardly surprising that Zionism appears in a wide variety of guises within our primary texts. In *Les Palestiniens*, set mainly in the 1960s and published in 1968,[1] Ania Francos makes her hostility to the ideology crystal clear. It is pathologized in her claim that Zionism and antisemitism are two sides of the same illness (14); and to the trope of illness are added connotations of death in the phrase 'je maudis Théodore Herzl et sa funeste idéologie' (153–54) ['I curse Theodor Herzl and his fatal ideology']. While Israeli efforts to fertilize inhospitable land meet with her admiration, which she interestingly but wrongly posits as universal, her view of the Zionist state is replete with negative affectivity: 'l'Etat sioniste représente pour moi tout ce qui me fait horreur: un nationalisme mythique et insensé' (15) ['for me, the Zionist state represents everything I loathe: a mythical and insane nationalism']. A rejoinder to her derisive rejection of 'un nationalisme mythique' could be that all nationalisms draw on myths, as Anthony D. Smith persuasively argues in *Myths and Memories of the Nation* (1999).

An equally damning view of Zionism is found in Patricia Finaly's autobiographical *Le gai ghetto* (1970). However, the tone of the damnation differs sharply from Francos's. I have previously remarked on Finaly's 'mordant humour' (Cairns, 2011, 66), and this is what characterizes her treatment of Zionism – an approach that some readers may regard as cheap flippancy. Such a judgement needs to be balanced against the fact that Finaly was a child survivor of the Shoah who mocked virtually everything; but the sting remains. One example is the lambasting of the WIZO (here presented under the anagram ZOWI) as an organization of rich Zionists who were using their money to send impoverished, naïve Jews to the Israeli War of Independence (156). As I have previously noted, the ZOWI, a fictional representation of the WIZO (Women's International Zionist Organization), is a charitable institution with sterling feminist credentials (Cairns, in Hand and Katz, 145). Neither of these two qualities impress Finaly. Nonetheless, driven by her own money lust (she is, admittedly, penniless and on her own in the world at a very young age) she becomes involved in a Zionist youth group, for the sole reason that, in her view, it encourages her to engage in legal begging – hardly an edifying vision of Zionism (161–62). Finaly charges Zionism with both avarice (in contrast to the socialist dimension of early Zionism flagged by Ohana and Pinto above) and ruthless disregard for manipulable human beings whose lives are likely to be sacrificed in war:

> La Haute Direction était tellement heureuse d'avoir trouvé des bonnes poires pour justifier ses appointements (je ne saurais indiquer la somme exacte qu'ils touchaient par tête de pipe en partance pour la Terrre Retrouvée) qu'elle avait décidé de nous faire un comité d'accueil (164)

> [The High Command was so pleased to have found suckers to justify its salary (I couldn't say exactly how much they got per head for each poor bugger bound for death in the Re-Found Land) that it'd decided to put on a welcome committee for us]

Zionist manipulation of disempowered Jews is also insinuated in Ami Bouganim's *Le cri de l'arbre* (1983). Here, Moroccan immigrants to Israel in the early 1960s live in abject material conditions and are so looked down upon by the Ashkenazi elite that one of their number curses the day she ceded to the Zionists' advances inciting the *aliyah* (10). The same manipulative propaganda (along with malevolence) is claimed in reference to Isho's second son, who had been sent to Morocco to pursue the Zionist campaign of brainwashing among its remaining

Jews (122). The ruthlessness imputed by Finaly assumes an even darker form in Bouganim's novel in the following allegation, beginning with sardonic antonomasia, about Ben Gurion:

> l'illustre dirigeant s'était empressé de donner l'ordre à ses sbires de déposer des bombes dans le quartier juif de Bagdad pour hâter l'immigration de ses habitants (17)

> [the famous leader had rushed to give his henchmen orders to lay bombs in the Jewish quarter of Baghdad in order to speed up the immigration of its inhabitants][2]

Bouganim's novel is not as univocal as Finaly's autobiographical account, in that other characters do occasionally voice more positive views of Zionism. For example, it is predicted that one day the Moroccan immigrants will take power in Israel and teach the belligerent Ashkenazim a lesson about what true Judaism and Zionism constitute: a message of peace and fraternity (82–83). However, the main narrative thrust is towards satirical sniping at Zionism, a good flavour of which is the exposure of self-importance and orotund doctrinairism: 'il marque un temps pour souffler, et il enchaîne sur ce ton bouffi d'importance caractéristique aux doctrinaires du sionisme socialiste' (102) ['He pauses to take breath, then goes on in that tone swollen with self-importance which typifies doctrinaires of socialist Zionism']. Here the socialist dimension of early Zionism mentioned by Ohana and Pinto is implicitly denigrated as a hollow ideology bringing no social justice for the impoverished Moroccan immigrants to Israel.

If satire of Zionism is partial in Bouganim's *Le Cri de l'arbre*, it is totalizing in Paula Jacques's *Un baiser froid comme la lune* (1983). Although the satire is deadpan, amusing, indeed sometimes even laced with absurdist humour (164), Jacques's points are nevertheless serious. She presents Zionist missionaries on 1950s recruitment drives abroad as emotionally manipulative of and openly condescending towards diasporic Jews:

> Et qu'est-ce qu'un Juif en diaspora sinon un homme privé de son corps national? Veux-tu au moins tenter l'expérience? Je me charge de tous les frais, il ne t'en coûtera pas un centime (206)

> [And what is a diasporic Jew if not a man deprived of his national body? Don't you at least want to give it a try? I'll deal with all the expenses, it won't cost you a penny]

The gullible Tobias duly drags his resistant daughter Mélissa with him to Israel and obsequiously praises Zionist prejudices against diasporic Jews (216). His disillusionment with the harsh reality of life in a socialist-Zionist *kibbutz* is met with similar condescension in Albert Sebbag, who

> s'enquit, sur un ton paternel, de la manière dont on espérait quitter *Eretz*, la terre, sans préciser laquelle. Par ce raccourci propre aux sionistes, il paraissait entendu que, sur toute la planète, il n'existait pour les Juifs qu'une terre indiscutable (277)

> [inquired, in paternal tones, about how he hoped to leave *Eretz*, the land, without specifying which one. Through this shortcut peculiar to Zionists, it seemed settled that, on the entire planet, there was only one unquestionable land for Jews]

Sebbag's paternalistic pressure eventually turns into plain insult, in an ironic form of intra-antisemitism:

> Tu voulais partir? Tu pars les pieds devant comme tu le mérites puisque tu n'es qu'un sale Juif, un Juif mort pour Eretz Israël (282)

> [You wanted to leave? You're leaving feet first just as you deserve since you're nothing but a filthy Jew, a Jew who's dead as far as *Eretz Israel* is concerned]

Contrasting with the animosity of Francos and the humorous satire of Finaly, Bouganim and Jacques, Jean-Luc Allouche's evocation of Zionism in *Les jours innocents* (1984) is solemn. There is sometimes even a mournful tone deriving from the hiatus between, on the one hand, Allouche's initially passionate adhesion in the late 1960s to the religious element of the Zionist vision, viz., worldwide Jewry's return to ancient geographical roots, and particularly to Jerusalem (50),[3] and, on the other, his ultimate sense of being an irredeemable exile (131). The solemnity of his tone derives from the grim political reality of armed conflict with hostile neighbouring countries that he discovers upon arrival in Israel (72). Yet even as he becomes increasingly disenchanted he retains a certain empathy, albeit conflicted, with the buoyant new Zionist spirit sparked by Israel's reconquest of Jerusalem and its occupation of former biblical territories. His raising of the question of Palestinian rights is met by an Israeli interlocutor's bombastic determination to claim the biblical land:

> Nous sommes des Barbares, c'est vrai. Des Barbares d'un genre nouveau. Prêts à monter au bûcher pour avoir le dernier mot. Demain va naître

quelque chose de neuf entre cette terre et nous. Nous avons toujours été seuls, nous sommes seuls et nous serons toujours seuls. Notre titre de propriété sur ce sol, personne n'en possède de pareil, c'est le Livre ... (80)

[We are barbarians, it's true. Barbarians of a new type. Ready to be burned at the stake in order to have the last word. Tomorrow something new will be born between us and this land. We've always been on our own, we are on our own and always will be on our own. Our title deed on this soil, nobody else has anything like it, it's the Book ...]

The 1960s Zionist interlocutor's words suggest an enduring legacy of the 'voluntarism, will, vitality and myth' identified by Ohana (40) as aspects of Nietzsche's thought inspiring the early Zionists. Voluntarism, will and vitality permeate the thrusting determination colouring the first three sentences of the quotation (Allouche, 1984, 80), resonating with Nietzsche's statement 'Willing liberates: that is the true doctrine of will and freedom' in *Thus Spoke Zarathustra* (111). The interlocutor's mythical identification with the barbarians, and the mythical hues of the historically argued claim to the land via the Bible, illustrate within the Zionist project the creative fulcrum of myth, along with the dependency on myth of 'history'. It thereby recalls the following remarks from Nietzsche in *The Birth of Tragedy*:

> But without myth every culture loses the healthy natural power of its creativity: only a horizon defined by myths completes and unifies a whole cultural movement. [...] And now the mythless man stands eternally hungry, surrounded by all past ages, and digs and grubs for roots, even if he has to dig for them among the remotest antiquities. The tremendous historical need of our unsatisfied modern culture, the assembling around one of countless other cultures, the consuming desire for knowledge – what does all this point to, if not to the loss of myth, the loss of the mythical home, the mythical maternal womb? (135–36)

Allouche's own response to his interlocutor's heady words, however, is split between affect and reasoned cognition: 'Son cœur allait spontanément vers eux; sa tête s'y refusait' (80) ['His heart went out to them spontaneously; his head refused'].

A similarly cleft response to Zionism is found in *Un été à Jérusalem* (1986), a novel by Chochana Boukhobza with strong bases in the author's own life experiences. This time the split is figured temporally, between the earnest Zionist Sarah had been at the age of 17 and the disillusioned 20-year-old she has become after actually living in Israel (10). Her disillusionment is expressed in political and moral opposition to Israel's war with Lebanon in 1982, in which both of her conscripted brothers are fighting, and a rugged verbal exchange between the two reveals divided views on Zionism even with the IDF:

> « [...] Le virus de ce pays, c'est l'opinion de l'étranger. Mais on s'en fout des commentaires de la France et de l'Italie.
> – Sale sioniste, riposte Joseph.
> – Comment, tu t'y mets, toi aussi? Merde! On passe notre temps à se justifier devant les autres. Dites, on est assez gentils? Dites, venez voir chez nous comme on est corrects! Pendant ce temps, les autres charcutent, torturent ... (214)

> ['[...] People in this country are obsessed with what foreigners think of us. But damn the comments of France and Italy'.
> 'Bloody Zionist', retorts Joseph.
> 'What, so now you're jumping on the bandwagon too are you? Shit! We spend our time justifying ourselves to others. Hey, are we nice enough? Hey, come and stay with us to see how polite we are! And all the while, the rest are butchering, torturing ...']

No such schism appears in Sarah Frydman's *La Marche des vivants* (1997), a novel whose third-person narrative voice is univocally pro-Zionist. Going back to the Liberation period, it dramatizes efforts to secure French support for the militant Zionist underground movement known as the Stern group. This group aimed to bring about the rebirth of the state of Israel, and in Frydman's novel it denigrates as 'honteux' ['shameful'] those diasporic Jews who have assimilated to their countries of exile (54). Avrom, the protagonist representing this hard-line Zionist stance, incarnates steely positivism: 'Il faut qu'Israël renaisse de ses cendres. C'est une question de survie pour notre peuple' (143) ['Israel must be reborn from its ashes. It's a matter of survival for our people']. Other French-Jewish characters second him through the years, with Haïm anticipating in 1956 (at the time of the Suez crisis) more contemporary equations of antisemitism with anti-Zionism (see Chapter 5), based on international pro-Arab, anti-Israel armaments policies (367). Left-wing French intellectuals are depicted negatively in their anti-Zionism (see Chapter 5 again) and blatant opposition to the very existence of the state of Israel. Thus Michel Ranieri, widely regarded as a brilliant philosopher, publishes books lauded by the left-wing intelligentsia on the impossibility and even the pointlessness of the state of Israel (437). Avrom's bitter riposte – 'C'est de la merde [...] Et tous vos intellectuels sont des jean-foutre' (437) ['That's shit [...]

And all your intellectuals are utterly useless'] – elicits from Ranieri both contempt for Zionism – 'Ranieri avait dédaigné répondre à ce vulgaire sioniste' (437) ['Ranieri didn't deign to answer this vulgar Zionist'] – and the now familiar historical inversion whereby the Zionist state is posited as a fascist state (438).

Hostility to Zionism also features in Brigitte Peskine's *Buena Familia* (2000), though here it is felt not by non-Jewish French intellectuals but, rather more surprisingly, by Turkish Jews. Yet there is a Francophone hyphen between the two forms of antipathy for Zionism. In this novel, Rebecca, a Turkish-Jewish writer, is dismayed by her son Méir's decision to emigrate to Israel in the late 1940s. Dislike for any form of communitarianism had already been shown in her disinclination to live in a Jewish state at a historical juncture when the future Israel was an ideal shared by most Jews (138). The Francophone link is that as a young woman she had sided with the Alliance Israélite Universelle rather than with Zionism, and was, her older narrative self wryly admits, fanatically devoted to its cause because it emanated from France, the country of the Enlightenment and assimilation. Tempering her dislike for Zionism are two factors. The first is agreement with one implicit tenet of Zionism at the time, viz. that Christians, and the developed nation states of which they are still the historical foundations, hate Jews (139). The other also concerns hatred of Jews, this time within non-Christian, less developed nation states. Rebecca proclaims admiration for the proposal made by the Jewish philosopher Hannah Arendt for an alternative to a Jewish state, viz. a binational federation including Arabs too, but, on the other hand, Rebecca observes that Arabs also hate Jews (139) ...

Very little such equivocation is found in Paula Jacques's arch but politically hard-hitting novel *Gilda Stambouli souffre et se plaint* (2002). Set in the mid- to late 1950s, this novel portrays reluctant Egyptian-Jewish immigrants to the young Zionist state. The dominant attitude towards Zionism suggested by its free indirect style is one of mildly humorous distaste. As in Jacques's *Un baiser froid comme la lune* (1983), the Zionist Agence juive's pressure on either political or, in Gilda's case, cultural refuseniks to stay in Israel is conveyed in a report on Gilda from the French-Jewish social worker Bertha Fromkine (42). Added to this moral coercion, Gilda implies, is financial blackmail:

> Au moment de quitter Israël, j'ai été victime de cet abominable chantage qu'on appelle la « Loi du Retour ». L'argent que l'Agence juive de

Jérusalem avance gracieusement aux émigrants devient usuraire sitôt qu'ils s'avisent de vouloir quitter ce malheureux pays (45)

[Just when I was leaving Israel, I fell victim to that abominable blackmail they call the 'Law of Return'. The money the Jewish Agency of Jerusalem advances free of charge to emigrants becomes usurious if they decide they want to leave that wretched country]

The one slight attenuation to this general narrative slating of Zionism comes in the form of the character sergent Gingold. His account of antisemitic injustice in his country of origin, Russia, where he was refused admission to university qua Jew, serves to justify his turning towards Zionism: only in Israel would be free of such injustice (404).

Zionism is a more inflected percept in Michaël Sebban's *La terre promise, pas encore* (2002). This is the first in a quartet of novels set at the turn of the twenty-first century, each containing the first-person homodiegetic narrator Éli, a Jew of Algerian origin born around 1966 whose life experiences strongly resemble those of the author. Support for Zionism is assumed by the Israeli bureaucracy to be a given in immigrants, and its absence valid grounds for suspicion. When Éli is asked at the prefecture if he is Zionist and he replies, 'Pas du tout' ['Not at all'], the disarmed riposte is 'Qu'est-ce que tu viens foutre ici?' (83) ['What the hell have you come here for?']. However, another, unnamed, Israeli views Zionism with marked cynicism, and moreover claims that his view is common among Israelis. For him, it is an asinine belief which has long lost any credence and is exploited by the Jewish Agency to extort money from Americans (88). But this view is controverted by Haïm, for whom Zionism remains a reality, albeit radically different from that of the early pioneer years, and one whose future lies in Israel's economic success in the sphere of high tech (157). It is important to note, however, that Haïm lives in Tel Aviv; in *Sur la frontière* (2002), Michel Warschawski also associates this major city with Zionist modernity, but states that the latter is rejected by Jerusalem, Israel's capital city (30). In fact, Warschawski strongly dissociates Zionism and the typical twenty-first-century Jewish denizens of Jerusalem (30). For Warschawski, these deeply religious Jews of Eastern European origin are stuck in a time warp that predates Zionism (30–31). However, Warschawski also posits a complementarity within the Israeli right between notions of divine will and secular Zionism (39). One contemporary manifestation of that complementarity is the Shas party, mentioned later on by Warschawski, who contrasts its successes in the late twentieth century with a left-wing

Zionism presented as wilfully myopic to sociological, cultural and political upheavals that have radically reshaped Israeli society (222). Warschawski correctly makes broad equations of this right-wing religious Zionism with Sephardic and Mizrahi Israelis, and of the anti-theocratic Zionists with Ashkenazi Israelis (231), with the latter accorded ideological anteriority as the founding fathers of Zionism (231).

The Eastern European Jews mentioned by Warschawski are the main focus of Line Meller-Saïd's *Cela ne sera pas un rêve* (2009), which reverts to the period before Israel's creation (although it does subsequently move diegetically forward to the post-1948 period). Her evocation of them differs from Warschawski's in that her main protagonist, Léa, though part of an observant Polish family, is far less interested in religious arguments for and against returning to the biblical homeland than in the founder of Zionism's dream of a secular Jewish state. That dream is presented as a utopia rejected in Herzl's time as the ravings of a madman, but which she intuits may in fact be a fully realizable 'dream' (whence the novel's title) (14). Her long struggle to achieve *aliyah*, bitterly opposed by her father, is sustained by a Jewish youth movement whose name, *Tseire Tsion*, is at least connotationally Zionist (16). The mythos of dream and fantasy recurs almost subliminally when, after relaying Léa's parents' obstruction to her making *aliyah*, Meller-Saïd resorts to the rather unsophisticated device of capitalization: 'MAIS DANS SA TÊTE MURMURAIT TOUJOURS LE CHANT DE SIRÈNE DES MOTS-SORTILÈGES' (21) ['BUT IN HER HEAD THE SIRENS' SONG OF WORDS LIKE MAGIC SPELLS STILL MURMURED ON']. Leaving aside stylistic scruples, the reader will apprehend the almost magical property being ascribed to the pre-state Zionist project. This exaltation of Zionism obscures its downsides, one of which in particular is explored in the next section.

2.2. Zionism's anti-diasporism/antisemitism

Idith Zertal, one of Israel's New Historians (see Chapter 1), affirms the anti-diasporic character of Zionism in her comments on the Knesset's 1951 bill proposing an official day for commemoration of the Shoah and the ghetto uprisings (55). In her view, this day of commemoration didactically aimed to 'rappeler aux Juifs d'Israël, tout comme de la Diaspora, le triste sort réservé à tous ceux qui s'écartait de la voie sioniste' ['remind the Jews of Israel, and those of the diaspora, about the sad fate reserved for all those who err from the Zionist path'], and the very foundation of Israel was seen as the 'symbole d'une rédemption moderne, laïque et désaveu triomphal de l'histoire de la Diaspora' (56) ['symbol of a secular, modern redemption and a triumphant repudiation of diasporic history']. The primary text within our corpus that strongly asserts this anti-diasporic dimension to Zionism is Warschawski's *Sur la frontière* (2002), where Zionism even figures as antisemitic. One memory of his early days in Israel encapsulates this figuration, when a proudly *sabra* cousin barks the following order: 'Cesse de te conduire comme un petit youpin, tu n'es pas à Strasbourg' (213) ['Stop behaving like a little Yid, you're not in Strasbourg']. Warschawski surmises that the reason for the cousin's contempt is his (Warschawski's) tendency to apologize to strangers; but he is also at pains to stress that this is not an isolated incident. A footnote states that in January 2002 Zwi Mendel, a National Unity party member of parliament, had called the (Jewish) ambassador of the US in Tel Aviv a Yid because he had suggested spending less money on the settlements (213).

Warschawski avers that from its very inception, Zionism had opposed a certain mode of being Jewish associated with European diasporic Jews, and had created a highly derogatory caricature (which is implicitly male) of that mode: primitive, retrograde, unproductive, parasitical, passive, effeminate; in a word, degenerate (214). According to him, Zionism had wanted to rid Europe of its 'bad Jews' (214), which has uncomfortable connotations of ethnic cleansing. The notion of degeneracy in the diasporic Jew is linguistically taken up by that of regenerating Jewish immigrants to Israel, moulding them physically to the sinister point where they become 'Aryan' Jews (215–16). Some readers will consider Warschawski guilty of historical hyperbole at best, invidious libel against the young Israeli state at worst. For others, he is remembering a reality based on the state's exclusion of all that recalled Jewish weakness and vulnerability, in order to forge an empowering national *imago*. Empowerment, or alleged empowerment, is a motif treated in the next section, within the specific context of gender.

2.3. Zionism, gender and *kibbutzim*

As an incipit to this short section, it is relevant to note 'the World Zionist Organization's early granting of voting rights to women (for the second Zionist Congress of 1898, at a time when only New Zealand had national female suffrage) and the passion with which all but ultra-Orthodox members of the Yishuv advocated women's suffrage after the First World War' (Penslar, 92). Moving forward in time, it is also worth noting Gozlan's reference to a halcyon age of socialist, secular and feminist Zionism, which was incarnated in the institution of the *kibbutz* (105). However, the two primary texts that allude to the Zionist *kibbutzim*'s principle of gender equality present a rather more mixed picture, albeit for different reasons. Paula Jacques's *Un baiser froid comme la lune* (1983) depicts the ostensible advantages of the principle, but undermines them through narrative focalization on the distinctly jaundiced teenager Mélissa – who, admittedly, loathes everything to do with the *kibbutz* where she is forced to live. Thus Judith, a Hungarian immigrant in her thirties, runs a team of men with a firm hand, but her paean to the virtues of hard labour in service of both the *kibbutz* and the Israeli nation more generally singularly fails to impress Mélissa (225), who dismisses it as mere homilies from a victim of brainwashing. Narrative focalization on Mélissa's father Tobias promotes a different effect on the reader – mild amusement, set against awareness of the *kibbutz* women's immense physical strength:

> Il décida de se chercher une compagne, parmi les pionnières. Comment? La gestuelle et le maintien dénué de coquetterie du sexe dit faible (chaque femme ici aurait pu le battre à l'épreuve du bras de fer) le désarmaient (229)

> [He decided to seek out a partner for himself, among the women pioneers. How, though? The gestures and the entirely uncoquettish bearing of the so-called weaker sex – every woman here could have beaten him at arm wrestling – disarmed him]

The old-world Tobias's astonishment at these women is not limited to their physical strength but springs also from their complete sexual freedom, including the right to indulge in sexual innuendo along with men (240). Indeed, this is the dominant image of the female *kibbutz* member in Jacques's novel: that of an intrepid Amazon who does not need to conform to the gender stereotypes of diasporic existence. Such an image is also reflected in Anne Rabinovitch's novel *Chacune blesse, la dernière tue* (2012), but here it is complexified by something behind the positive image: fear, of armed conflict at least, which this institution-alized freedom from gender stereotypes paradoxically pressurizes girls and women to suppress (69). In counterpart is the complete adhesion of the *kibbutz* girls and women to the ethos of emotional control and invulnerability (72), recalling the brainwashed Judith in Jacques's novel. Images may of course be mendacious, and the female lot within the *kibbutz* hardly emerges as perfect. Literary representations of that institution, inevitably imperfect because human, more generally, not just regarding gender, form the subject of the next section.

2.4. *Kibbutzim*, old and new

Patricia Finaly's *Le gai ghetto* (1970) depicts a *kibbutz* near Tel Aviv in the early years of Israeli nationhood. Like Mélissa's in Jacques's *Un baiser froid comme la lune*, her tone is adamantly unimpressed, indeed deeply cynical. What is first stressed is the mean-minded and deformed notion of justice, presented as a typical Jewish trait, which rules the *kibbutz* and its inhabitants:

> Dès le pied sur la terre ferme on m'a filé le marché en main: un séjour en kibboutz, nourrie blanchie logée moyennant six heures de turbin. C'était donnant-donnant. Pas d'erreur, nous étions bien entre juifs (181)
>
> [As soon as I set foot on firm ground, they pitched the deal in hand: a stay in a *kibbutz*, including bed, board and laundry done for me, in return for six hours' work a day. It was a quid pro quo. No mistake, we were definitely among Jews]

Worse is to come: insinuation of an obsession with money among members of an institution that officially eschewed personal monetary gain. As soon as they hear her speaking French, which they associate with affluence, a group of male *kibbutzniks* start financially harassing her: 'Ton argent français contre mon argent, ça va? C'est pas cher et tu y gagnes ...' (181) ['Your French money for my money, okay? It's not dear and you come off better ...']. However, the dominant tenor of Finaly's whole autobiographical account is comedic (sometimes darkly so), and here the joke is finally on her – for when she demands a monthly salary slip and social security contributions from the *kibbutz*, she is summarily ejected (182). While avoiding Finaly's corrosive satire, Peskine's depiction of the early *kibbutzim* in *Buena Familia* (2000) is scarcely flattering either. Its denizens are presented as self-righteous and self-aggrandizing producers of 'magnificent' young *sabra*s (183). Yet there is also a note of self-censure in Rebecca's reflections, which expose her own attachment to material comfort and arguably bourgeois family structures (183).

A much more contemporary perspective on the *kibbutz* than Finaly's or Peskine's is provided by Raczymow's *Eretz* (2010), whose focus is initially on the 1970s but moves later to the twenty-first century. Addressing his now dead brother Ilan, who had personal experience of the institution during the 1970s, he evokes two dramatic contraventions of the socialist Zionist principles on which the *kibbutz* had been founded: that it should use only a Jewish and non-salaried workforce (51). By paying young Arab workers from Gaza for their labour, the *kibbutz* had broken its original ideological contract, and this first fracture was followed by many others (51). However, as Raczymow's diegetic move forward confirms, the *kibbutzim* still exist in twenty-first-century Israel, albeit much reduced in number and ethically etiolated:

> Élisa nous montre de loin les bâtiments où l'on élève des poulets en batterie, élevage géré par ordinateur, et qui m'évoquent bizarrement les blocs d'Auschwitz. Elle nous raconte, répondant à mes questions, le kibboutz aujourd'hui en regard de ce qu'il fut naguère, du temps de sa structure socialiste. Aujourd'hui tout est privé, et il faut payer pour tout, y compris pour les repas. « Chacun est indépendant et fait ce qu'il veut. » Elle préfère ainsi. (52)

> [Élisa shows us the buildings in the distance where battery chickens are reared, a computer-controlled rearing which seem to me oddly reminiscent of Auschwitz blocks. Answering my questions, she tells us how today's *kibbutz* compares to what it used to be not long ago, when it had a socialist structure. Today everything is private, and you have to pay for everything, including meals. 'Everyone is independent and does what he wants'. She prefers it that way]

The analogy with Auschwitz conveys in chilling terms the capitalist commodification and privatization of what was originally an idealistic socialist experiment. According to Raczymow, the only remnant of that ideal extant in the new millennium is the non-hierarchy of the tasks (57), but even that is clouded by its origin in a dying demographic (57). Raczymow's final reference to the *kibbutzim* is to one of yesteryear, and emphasizes vulnerability to Arab attack:

> Et Judith disait: Tu vois, tout ça n'est pas encore fini, loin de là. Il nous faudra encore nous battre ... Et Ilan: Mais si le kibboutz avait été construit un peu plus loin dans la vallée, il aurait été à l'abri des canons syriens! Cette logique n'était pas celle de la jeune sabra: Plus loin dans la vallée? disait-elle. Et pourquoi pas à la mer! (129)

> [And Judith said: 'You see, all this isn't over yet, far from it. We still have to fight ...' And Ilan replied: 'But if the *kibbutz* had been built a bit

further into the valley, it would have been sheltered from Syrian canons!'
The young *sabra* woman had no truck with this kind of logic. 'Further
into the valley?' she said. 'And why not into the sea!']

The young *sabra* Judith's spirit of robust resistance to such attack in itself
indexes the departure from gender stereotypes that was modelled within
the *kibbutzim*. Her final ironic exclamation is a transparent allusion
to a fixed idiom expressing an Arab wish to efface Israel's existence. In
contrast, Ilan, a French immigrant to Israel, lacks the unifocal political,
moral and psychological stability of the *sabra*. In many respects, he
is paradigmatic of the vicissitudes explored in the next section of this
chapter.

2.5. Self-division of diasporic Jews

The first of our primary texts to intimate the self-division felt by
diasporic Jews after making *aliyah* is Allouche's autobiographical *Les
jours innocents* (1984). Allouche's initial division is between his early
adhesion to Orthodox Judaism and his later flight from it (75). The
reason for his loss of faith, both in religion and in Israel, is his overriding
sense of being an exile (duplicating an original exile, from Algeria to
France), which is a second form of division:

> Il était venu chercher en ce pays des certitudes, une consolation. Mais
> l'exil n'était-il pas au cœur de la patrie? Tout, autour de lui, signifiait
> l'absence du pays à lui-même. Chaque visage trahissait le transfuge, le
> citoyen clandestin d'une nation dans les limbes de l'enfantement (75)

> [He had come seeking certainties, a consolation in this country. But was
> exile not at the heart of the homeland? Everything around him signified
> the absence of the country unto itself. Every face betrayed the defector,
> the secret citizen of a nation struggling to be born]

Here the sense of exile is presented not as a personal psychological
problem but as endemic in the Israeli nation as a whole, many of whose
citizens were originally immigrants to it. (The one demographic to which
this presentation did not apply is, evidently, the *sabra*s.) For Allouche,
Israelis are a split people – those who have made good (the pioneers), and
the destitute – in neither of whose binary parts can he locate himself (82).
What gradually alienates Allouche from Israel is its hyper-sensitivity,
earnestness and lack of personal privacy (87). Alienation does not,
though, equate to hostility: a persistent but passionless love for Israel

is evoked through the metaphor of himself as a 'spectateur anxieux et malencontreux, voyeur de son peuple, amant platonique et sans ressort' (87) ['anxious and unfortunate spectator, a voyeur of his people, a platonic and spiritless lover'].

Allouche's anguish as a diasporic Jew in Israel is entirely absent from Warschawski's subject positioning early on in *Sur la frontière* (2002), where he positively promotes the benefits of a critical perspective on the mainstream that he believes derive from diasporic identity in Israel (13). In Eliette Abécassis's novel *Sépharade* (2009), there are echoes of Allouche's exilic melancholy, but attenuated by a contrasting sense of well-being more akin to Warschawski's grounded position: 'En France, elle était en apesanteur. En Israël, d'une certaine façon, elle était à sa place' (Abécassis 159) ['In France, [Esther] was weightless. In Israel, in a way, she was in the right place']. Yet she remains a diasporic Jew:

> Elle ne pouvait s'empêcher de penser à chaque fois qu'elle aurait dû vivre dans ce pays, qu'elle le pourrait encore, si elle le voulait. Et puis elle rentrait en France et elle oubliait qu'elle n'avait pas la force de partir (158)

> [Every time, she couldn't help thinking that she should have been living in this country, that she still could, if she wanted to. And then she would go back to France and would forget that she hadn't the strength to leave]

Reflecting on the tragedy of her Sephardic ancestors, who had been condemned to exile after expulsion from Spain and Portugal in the fifteenth century, Esther's self-questioning intimates guilt-feelings about the failure to make permanent *aliyah* (160). Previous reflections on this failure had considered several negative causes – 'Était-ce par lâcheté, par indolence, par laisser-aller?' (158) ['Was it through cowardice, laziness, carelessness?'] – before lighting on the same problem as Allouche: that of exile, which for her would have been painful due to her deep attachment to France (158–59). Later on, when she has realized the marked differences between herself as an in many ways typically French woman and the tough *sabra* Israeli women, Esther's previous sense of well-being in Israel mutates into an image of entrapment – not in Israel, but in her own diasporic impossibility of complete cultural and psychic fit with either France or Israel: 'De nouveau, Esther se sentait prise en étau. Elle était israélienne en France, et française en Israël' (167) ['Again, Esther felt gripped in a vice. She was Israeli in France, and French in Israel'].

A similar existential dilemma is explored in *Eretz* (2010), where Raczymow labels both himself and his brother an 'old' Jew, marked by division and diasporism. In the case of his brother, who had emigrated to Israel, this posed a serious problem:

> Je ne les lui envie pas, cette réconciliation, cet accord avec son essence. Mon frère l'avait cherché, jadis, cet accord, à sa façon, et l'avait presque trouvé. Presque: quelque chose clochait malgré tout. Au fond de lui, il était resté comme moi un vieux Juif, divisé, diasporique (33)

> [I don't envy him that reconciliation, that harmony with his essence. My brother had previously looked for it, that harmony, in his own way, and had almost found it. Almost: despite everything, something jarred. Deep down, he had, like me, remained an old Jew, divided, diasporic]

But Jewish diasporism takes different forms in *Eretz*. A simile used to describe the rare banyan tree incidentally gives a densely ambiguous slant to the (formerly) diasporic Jew in Israel. The tree is depicted as

> un être un peu monstrueux comme des siamois ou à deux têtes ou à deux bassins collés d'où partiraient deux fois une paire de jambes, ou bien comme les Juifs mêmes en terre d'Israël qui ont réenraciné leurs branches diasporiques redevenues troncs solides et durables ... (65)

> [a rather monstrous creature like conjoined twins with either two heads or two melded pelvises from which a pair of legs comes out twice, or else like those very Jews who in Israel have re-rooted their diasporic branches, which have become solid and durable tree trunks again ...]

Use of the epithet 'monstrueux' in the first clause suggests grotesquerie, but the last clause contrastingly implies that Jewish immigrants to Israel have found new roots for their diasporic branches that are solid and enduring. Solid and enduring are adjectives that resonate positively, connoting none of the self-division witnessed above; but on the other hand, the possible implicature that even in Israel Jews *retain* 'diasporic branches', however solid, seems to undermine the very basis of Zionism, which sought to eradicate all traces of Jewish diasporism. Later on, as he again addresses his dead brother, a further twist is added to Raczymow's construction of the diasporic Jew:

> Mais si dans ton imaginaire tordu de petit Juif diasporique, quoi que tu en dises, les Arabes des territoires contrôlés par Tsahal sont comme les Juifs du ghetto de Varsovie tous promis à la mort à Treblinka, alors certes ta place dans cette armée et peut-être même dans ce pays ne coule pas de source. (77)

> [But if, whatever you may say, in your little diasporic Jew's twisted imagination, the Arabs of the territories controlled by Tzahal are like the

> Jews of the Warsaw Ghetto, who were all destined for death in Treblinka, then certainly your place in that army and maybe even in this country isn't obvious]

Derision of Ilan's diasporic 'imaginaire' seems to be implied by Raczymow's use of the adjective 'tordu'. However, for some (but by no means all) readers, that diasporic 'imaginaire' will be viewed as an ethical good, for its basis in family memories of European persecution allows activation of what Rothberg has named multidirectional memory, as Ilan links the oppression of Arabs in the Occupied Territories to the fate of Jews in the Warsaw Ghetto. Yet such a link would have annulled his place in the Israeli army, and perhaps even in Israel itself. Indeed, even without such political heresy, Ilan's status as an 'old' diasporic Jew would have been problematic within the new nation of Israel, associated with strength, resolve and force. In antithesis to the stereotype of the 'old' diasporic Jew, tormented variously by exilic melancholy, self-division and even twistedness that has been traced in this section, the next section examines the cult of the 'New Hebrew'.

2.6. The New Hebrew

On 28 August 1898, at the Second Zionist Congress in Basel, Max Nordau invented the expression 'muscular Judaism' to denote a required transformation of Jewish culture that would negate historical clichés of Jewish men strong only in intellect and replace them with physically robust and athletic male Jews.[4] Historian of religion Daniel Boyarin contends that Zionism unthinkingly adopted the European masculine idea, including its negative view of the stereotypical Jewish body (271). That negative view and its positive (however derivative) obverse of the New Hebrew are limned in many of the primary texts examined below, and in none more so than *Terre d'amour et de feu* (1965). Joseph Kessel's narrative goes back to the Yishuv, which was already striving to counter antisemitic stereotypes of weak, fearful male Jewish victims by creating a new iconography of strong, combative and valiant Jews:

> Ces colons issus des ghettos d'Europe orientale, où ils marchaient craintifs, courbés, anémiés, repoussèrent l'attaque d'un ennemi dix fois plus nombreux. Ils défendaient leur terre, celle à laquelle leurs aïeux songeaient depuis deux mille ans (29)

> [Those settlers who came from Eastern European ghettos, where they

walked fearfully, bowed down, weakened, drove back the attack of an enemy ten times bigger. They were defending their land, the land their forefathers had dreamt about for two thousand years][5]

Via a rhetorical question to reinforce the contrast, Kessel emphasizes muscularity, vigour and health over the pallid cerebrality historically associated with diasporic Jews (in this example, those living in the Jewish quarter of the Marais in Paris):

Où sont les petits Juifs malingres de la rue des Rosiers, aux têtes trop grandes, trop pensives pour des corps fragiles? Ceux de Tel-Aviv ont peut-être moins d'intelligence dans les yeux mais les muscles sont sains et les chairs brunes et fermes (83)

[Where are the sickly little rue des Rosiers Jews, heads too big, too pensive for their fragile bodies? Perhaps the Jews of Tel Aviv have less intelligence in their eyes but their muscles are healthy and their flesh is tanned and firm]

Significantly, this strength and combativity is not limited to the men. Through use of another rhetorical question to convey his quasi incredulity – 'Était-ce une femme qui venait d'apparaître?'] ['Was it a woman who had just appeared?'] – Kessel describes a boxer-like, short-haired, athletic young Jewish woman wearing '[d]es vêtements sans sexe' (49) ['sexless garments']: the female 'New Hebrew' as veritable Amazon.[6] Paula Jacques's *Un baiser froid comme la lune* (1983) also includes women in its depiction of the New Hebrews. Health and strength in Israeli men are implied metonymically via their association with the land and agriculture rather than with commerce and usury (211), the latter being urban and cerebrally coded. Israeli women are portrayed more directly as immensely strong and as reversing the gendered stereotype of the woman overly concerned with her appearance (229). Both men and women are also included in the cameo of physical vigour furnished by Allouche (1984), although this is limited to the young *sabra*s of the late 1960s/early 1970s:

ces corps aux muscles déliés et nerveux, brunis et sensuels. Il a compris quelle conjuration, quelle revanche contre l'humiliation immémoriale ces jeunes hommes et ces jeunes femmes, émergés sans mémoire de la mer, ces fruits de la terre recouvrée portaient sur leur dos cuivré (60–61)

[those sensual, tanned bodies with dynamic and agile muscles. He realized what a weight of banishing and vengeance of humiliation immemorial was borne on the copper-coloured backs of these young men and women, who had emerged without memory from the sea, these fruits of the recovered land]

Moving into still more recent times – the end of the twentieth century – Abécassis's *L'Or et la cendre* (1997) retains that bifocal lens. It presents the young female *sabra*s of Tel Aviv as tall, short-haired, energetic and tough (212): again defying gendered conventions. The (non-Jewish) male narrator through whom this vision is filtered recognizes the beauty of these women but does not neglect the young male *sabra*s, stressing how muscular and tanned they are, and endowing them with a mythical military aura. Referring to 'Les femmes-mannequins, les hommes musclés et bronzés, ces soldats mythiques comme on en voit dans les films américains' (212) ['The women models, the tanned muscular men, those mythical soldiers like you see in American films'], the narrator directly points to the will of the Israeli state to destroy Nazi Germany's stereotype of the degenerate Jew (212).

Rather than the visible muscularity of the New Hebrews, Sarah Frydman's *La Marche des vivants* (1997) stresses the self-discipline and capacity for arduous physical work characterizing their iconic avatar, the *kibbutznik*:

> Joël mettait tout son orgueil, toute sa vanité de mâle à se comporter comme eux. À se lever à l'aube, à travailler jusqu'aux heures les plus chaudes ...' (692)

> [Joël put all his pride, all his male vanity into behaving like them. Into getting up at dawn, working right into the very hottest hours of the day ...]

She thereby converges with Ohana's point cited above about voluntarism, will and vitality (Ohana, 40). Similarly, Paula Jacques's novel *Gilda Stambouli souffre et se plaint* (2002) emphasizes the astringencies and self-mastery to which *kibbutzniks* of all ages submit themselves for the greater good of their new country. This emphasis stems from the direct contrast represented by Juliette (68), who has been abandoned in a *kibbutz* by her mother. As seen in Chapter 1, Raczymow (49) compared his brother's exalted view of the *kibbutznik* to a propaganda film lauding the Soviet New Man. Similarly, Juliette likens the Israeli New Man to the 'heroes' of the Soviet Union, and the analogy is hardly flattering:

> Les juifs des kibboutz ont avec les héros de l'Union soviétique – leur seconde patrie – beaucoup de choses en commun: des faces rugueuses, des culs larges, des cuisses et des mollets musculeux, et sur toute chose

ils ont des opinions dictées par la discipline, la hiérarchie, le travail. Voilà le hic. Les juifs du kibboutz, comme les paysans du kolkhoze, sont des êtres frustes. Ils ne voient pas plus loin que leur lopin de terre. Ils ne croient qu'à ce qu'ils peuvent voir, toucher, sentir avec leurs pauvres sens animaux. (290–91)

[The *kibbutz* Jews have a lot in common with the heroes of the Soviet Union – their second country: rugged faces, big backsides, muscular thighs and calves, and on every subject they have opinions dictated by discipline, hierarchy, work. There's the snag. The *kibbutz* Jews, like the *kolkhoz* peasants, are uncouth creatures. They don't see any further than their patch of land. They believe only in what they can see, touch and feel with their poor animal senses]

For Juliette, physical robustness, muscularity, values of discipline and work all have as negative obverse a vulgarity that is at best peasant-like, at worst animalistic. Animality descends into bestiality as the narrative focalized on her presents the *kibbutzniks* as worse than pigs at the table (298).

Yaël Hassan's *Souviens-toi Leah!* (2004) also critiques the *kibbutznik*, though less humorously. Her female narrator, a Shoah survivor, sees similarities between an initially rather brutal male *kibbutznik*, Yaïr, and the Aryan SS officers with whom she had been forced to have sex:

ce type-là, derrière ces manières faussement policées et son allemand châtié, sous sa crinière blonde et son regard bleu acier, m'en rappelait d'autres ... (93)

[that guy, behind his fake civilized manners and his very proper German, beneath his blond mane and his steely blue eyes, reminded me of others like him ...]

Though no mere cypher of the Aryan 'blond beast', Yaïr does symbolize the muscular masculinity that is the Israeli ideal for men in the building of a powerful, impregnable Jewish state which would never again allow Jewish victimhood. In that brand of masculinity, emotional sensitivity is conspicuously absent. Finally, a similar portrait appears in Myriam Anissimov's autofictional novel *La Soie et les cendres* (1989), set in late 1970s Israel. The female narrator refers to the machismo of Jerusalem society with a covert dig at her male Israeli friend Yossi's ostentatious egalitarianism that appears merely to incite women to ape the bellicosity of traditionally masculine men (30). The army, which for some readers will represent the supreme institution of machismo and, more specifically, its Israeli avatar, forms the subject of the next section.

2.7. Israeli army and Israeli identity

The pivotal role of the Israeli army in the formation of Israeli identity flows chiefly from the fact that military service is compulsory for virtually all Israeli Jews, including women. Its centrality in the lives of Israelis is highlighted by a significant evolution among Israel's ultra-Orthodox Jews mentioned by Diana Pinto. Hitherto, they had insisted on exemption from any kind of military duty;[7] now, Pinto observes, even the ultra-Orthodox accept sending their sons into the army – albeit to special units – after their Talmudic studies (2012, 60). Admittedly, these special units cater for their every religious need, 'avec des plages horaires pour leurs études, de la nourriture ultra-casher, et un milieu uniquement masculin' (Pinto, 2012, 60) ['with timeslots for their studies, ultra-kosher food and an all-male environment']. But Pinto also draws attention to the Israeli army's tailoring of conditions for a scientific elite of conscripts who, having engaged in military research in security and communications, have brought considerable benefits to Israeli civil research and business (2012, 109–10). Unsurprisingly for a New Historian, Idith Zertal takes a more sceptical view, but while she claims that the Israeli army was sanctified by the Eichmann trial as saintly guarantor of the last wishes of the Shoah victims (157), she does not specify what these last wishes might have been, and indeed it is hard to fathom how she or any other historian could have been privy to such wishes.

The first of our primary texts for this section, written in the late 1960s – Ania Francos's *Les Palestiniens* (1968) – also alludes to the Shoah, but makes no link between it and the Israeli military. Rather, Francos bluntly implies brutalism through an emphatically non-sanctifying parallel between French military abuse of Arabs during the Algerian War (1954–1962) and the conduct of Israeli soldiers in the late 1960s (215). Yet this is later mitigated by recognition that these Israeli soldiers have been placed in the situation of occupiers when they are too young to exercise genuine moral responsibility (216). In striking contrast, Marc Hillel's *Tu vivras dans ton sang* (1971) mediates, via the prism of his French-Jewish immigrant narrator, a positive view of the Yishuv fighting forces in 1948 that were to become the IDF after Israel's victory in the War of Independence. In this novel, the soldiers are balanced human beings for whom fraternity is an instinctive ideal. Indeed, Major Avigdor is so relaxed in his military strategy that it is likened to the tranquil raising of chickens on the banks of the Jordan (259). Avigdor's attitude to war is humanized, his ethical reluctance to kill foregrounded and the reader incited to empathize with that first principle of survival (259).

Set rather later, in 1964, Hillel's *Les Oranges de Jaffa* (1981) paints a less rosy picture. It satirically emphasizes the state propaganda of the Agence juive, which impresses on the new North African immigrants Israel's need of their children for the country's defence (111). Lest this need be viewed as vulnerability, the Agence official asserts the glory of the Israeli army and its function as sole guarantor of Israel's security and freedom (111). North African immigrants to Israel and propaganda for the military also figure in Ami Bouganim's *Le cri de l'arbre* (1983). However, in this case the immigrants are denigrated by the authorities as uncivilized and the army's need for their children is transformed into the immigrants' need of military discipline. The army is again promoted as vital, but in more emotionally manipulative terms as the unique bulwark against either annihilation or repatriation (45). Discursive denigration of North African immigrants finds material expression in their spatial relegation to second-class positions during active combat: they are '[r] elégués à l'arrière, soldats de dernier recours, tandis que sur le front, Français, Anglais et Israéliens investissaient le Canal de Suez' (63) ['Relegated to the rear, soldiers of last resort, while on the front, French, English and Israeli soldiers surrounded the Suez Canal']. Yet these immigrants feel that the common goal of defending Israel dissolves such social hierarchy: 'La guerre effaçait les dissensions, ressoudait l'unité nationale entre Juifs orientaux et Juifs occidentaux' (63) ['The war erased conflicts, renewed the bonds of national unity between eastern and western Jews']. A Marxist analysis would dismiss this as false consciousness; a different analysis would be that it indicates a genuinely unifying effect of the army, where all social classes are united by the common goal of survival. The primacy of survival is boldly etched in Paula Jacques's *Un baiser froid comme la lune* (1983), where Tobias's critique of the massive human loss exacted by the militarization of the Israeli state (263) triggers a riposte implying no alternative to military self-defence short of death: 'Que faire, dit Zoltan, nous laisser rejeter à la mer?' (263) ['"What are we meant to do?" said Zoltan, "let ourselves be driven into the sea?"']. The cogency of that riposte is weakened by the fact that Zoltan is one of the novel's objects of ridicule.

Ridicule is also applied to the military training undergone by *kibbutz* orphans in Jacques's *Gilda Stambouli souffre et se plaint* (2002):

> pendant deux jours et autant de nuits, le groupe des orphelins va vivre une aventure merveilleuse et exaltante sur le plan du dépassement de soi.

Il s'agit, disons-le sans trémolos dans la voix, d'inculquer à ces jeunes gens les rudiments de l'art militaire. Les plus âgés d'entre eux seront appelés à remplir leur service militaire, dès l'automne prochain, les autres – notre Juliette de quatorze ans par exemple – devront patienter quelque deux ou trois années supplémentaires. [...] Tous, Juliette mis à part, ont l'intention de faire preuve d'une endurance et d'un courage démentiels. (392)

[for two days and two nights, the group of orphans is going to have a wonderful and thrilling adventure in surpassing themselves. Let's say it with a steady voice: it's a matter of inculcating in these young people the basics of military art. The oldest among them will be required to do their military service, from next autumn, the others – our fourteen-year-old Juliette, for example – will have to be patient for two or three years more. [...] All of them, apart from Juliette, intend to demonstrate crazy endurance and courage]

Derision permeates the ironic 'aventure merveilleuse et exaltante', 'sans trémolos', 'devront patienter' (as well as the non-ironic 'démentiels'). Ironic ridicule of the army also occurs in Michaël Sebban's *La terre promise, pas encore* (2002). At a holiday camp during a visit to Israel, 16-year-old Eli is informed he is to take part in a week of military preparation that was not on the official programme, the stirring explanation being that at the start of the Lebanon War, 'on voulait mettre à contribution les forces vives de la jeunesse de la Diaspora' (24–25) ['we want to make use of the strong forces of diaspora youth']. No consent given or sought, he finds himself in a military base, charged with decidedly unheroic contributions to the war effort: 'laver les chiottes et repeindre en blanc les réfectoires' (25) ['cleaning the bogs and repainting the refectories white']. Yet even in his irreverence there is recognition of that socially unifying property attributed to the army by characters in Bouganim's *Le cri de l'arbre*: 'L'armée, l'armée ... Le facteur déterminant. Le consensus national. [...] Un flic, un militaire, c'est toujours un copain, un membre de la famille' (Sebban, 2002, 85) ['The army, the army ... The determining factor. The national consensus. [...] A cop, a soldier, he's always a friend, a family member']. However, a dialogue later on reveals the emotional blackmail that can be exerted in the name of that national unity and indeed national survival represented by the army:

– Tu n'as pas honte de ne pas vouloir faire l'armée?
  – Non.
  – Et si tout le monde faisait comme toi? Nous serions tous morts.
  – Je n'y avais jamais pensé.

– C'est ça. Tu veux rester peinard dans ton coin pendant que tes copains vont se faire canarder dans les Territoires pour que tu puisses vivre en sécurité? (87)

['Aren't you ashamed of not wanting to be in the army?'
'No'.
'And what if everyone behaved like you? We'd all be dead'.
'I've never thought about it'.
'Exactly. Do you want to stay in your cushy little corner while your mates go and have potshots taken at them in the Territories so that you can live in safety?']

Later still, the ideal of unity within the army is exposed as at least partly illusory in Eli's reference to a left-wing *sabra* who risked imprisonment by refusing to serve in the Occupied Territories (175). Further, a confidence from an ex-soldier in a special Tzahal (IDF) unit reveals incomprehension of his role and a sense of sequestration that finally led him to resign (189–90). Partly offsetting these negative narrative snapshots of the Israeli military is a vignette capturing the words of an elderly French Jew whose dominant emotion is pride at having engaged in open combat defending the nascent Jewish state in the War of Independence, rather than bitterness about the serious physical wounds sustained during this action (191).

The labile trope of the army as a unifying factor in the construction of modern Israeli identity is also present in Michel Warschawski's *Sur la frontière* (2002). In fact, the Israeli army here becomes synecdoche for the Israeli populace (138). Similarly, the army's integral part in all Israelis' lives is affirmed in Valérie Zenatti's *Quand j'étais soldate* (2002) by two simple statements: 'L'armée, ici, fait partie de notre vie' (43) ['Here, the army is part of our life'] and 'tout le monde a été, est ou sera un jour à l'armée' (44) 'everyone has been, is or will one day be in the army']. Nonetheless, Zenatti does problematize aspects of that army. One is idealization of the soldier figure in the propagandist imagery targeting Israeli youth:

Les soldats et les soldates sont les héros du passé, ceux qui ont gagné la guerre d'indépendance, la guerre des Six Jours et celle du Kippour, ceux qui se font tuer au Sud-Liban. Chaque année, lors de la journée du Souvenir, on nous montre des films et des photos en noir et blanc où des soldats beaux à couper le souffle lancent un sourire lumineux et fatigué à l'objectif ou à la caméra. (43–44)

[Male and female soldiers are heroes of the past, those who won the War of Independence, the Six-Day War and the Yom Kippur War, those who get killed in South Lebanon. Every year, on Memory Day, we're shown black-and-white films and photos where breathtakingly beautiful soldiers flash a radiant, tired smile at the lens or the camera]

From the perspective of a teenager soon to do her military service, the narrator encapsulates a collective youthful optic sedulously shaped by popular cultural discourses that romanticize the army:

L'armée et les soldats, encore. Dans les rares films produits en Israël, et les nombreuses chansons qui passent en boucle à la radio. Dans chaque album de Shlomo Artzi, mon chanteur israélien préféré, il y a au moins une chanson sur un soldat [...] L'armée est, entre autres, notre collection Harlequin (44–46)

[The army and soldiers, again. In the few films produced in Israel, and the many songs played in a continuous loop on the radio. In every album by Shlomo Artzi, my favourite Israeli singer, there's at least one song about a soldier [...] The army is, among other things, our Mills and Boon series]

Despite this and her delight at joining the army (85), its harsh reality soon sinks in: she starts to fear weapons, draconian punishment for losing them or having them stolen and death while fulfilling the duty of selfless solidarity with other soldiers (120). A fellow soldier, Kineret, tries to allay her growing fear of actually having to shoot a flesh-and-blood human being by insisting that she will only ever need to use her weapon if somebody is threatening her life (146). Yet Kineret does not glorify the IDS either, stressing how the wearing of its uniform destroys one's individuality in the eyes of non-members (146). Another fellow soldier, Daniéla, is more overtly disenchanted, accusing the army of feeding them nationalistic propaganda (123–24). Ultimately, however, the narrator affirms the ethic identified in other texts discussed above: the army's centrality to the supreme good of the nation's survival. Deep affect, with the bodily dimension (see Introduction) marked by reference to new blood flowing in the narrator's veins, is expressed in her fired-up determination to contribute to that good, particularly in defence of the most vulnerable: 'Un sang neuf coule dans mes veines, comme si j'allais me battre pour cette vieille dame aux yeux doux, dont la main a tremblé sur mon bras' (248) ['New blood flows in my veins, as if I were going to fight for this old lady with gentle eyes, whose hand trembled on my arm'].

The army's crucial role in securing the nation's survival also features in Eliette Abécassis's *Sépharade* (2009), where Esther views Tzahal soldier Noam as an altruistic hero sacrificing his life for the Jewish people (161). The soldiers themselves do not endorse such heroization (164); but one particular narrative unit does emblazon the courage and valour required of Israeli soldiers in securing their country's security:

> Il avait subi l'entraînement qui permet de résister à la torture. On lui avait appris à en reconnaître les phases, a s'y habituer peu à peu sans céder à la panique. Il fallait apprendre à accepter d'avoir peur, d'avoir mal, de devenir misérable, sans cesse humilié dans son corps et son âme. [...] Rompu aux courses à travers les buissons d'épines, des heures durant, dont il revenait ensanglanté. Les tirs, les cours de langue, la géopolitique: Israël était un tout petit pays entouré d'ennemis, qui avait dû et devait encore lutter pour sa survie. (165)

> [He'd undergone training in resisting torture. He'd been taught to recognize its phases, to gradually get used to it without giving in to panic. You had to learn to accept being scared, hurting, becoming wretched, constantly humiliated in your body and soul. [...] Inured to racing for hours across thorny bushes, from which he came back covered in blood. Shooting, language classes, geopolitics: Israel was a tiny country surrounded by enemies which had had and still had to struggle for its survival]

The flipside to this at once exceptional yet normative devotion to Israel's survival through military strength emerges in Raczymow's *Eretz* (2010): the perception that any deserting soldier is a source of shame for those who know him or her (58). Bolstering the ideal of selfless dedication is the annual commemoration of all soldiers killed while defending their country, whose affective force pierces even Raczymow's sceptical carapace (67–68) to the extent that he would have liked to join in singing the Israeli national anthem. Returning to a more analytical vein, he tries to divine the reasons for his brother's growing disaffection with one of the key national institutions of Israel, the army, despite his loyalty to another, the *kibbutz*, which in fact depended on the efficacy of the former (76, 78). Ilan's disaffection had nonetheless turned into outright revolt against the politics of occupation when he was ordered to 'nettoyer' ['clean out'] a Palestinian village in Hebron suspected of sheltering terrorists (110). His request to the sergeant for an explanation having been met with contemptuous refusal (111), he complies, but upon witnessing what seems like senseless aggression towards an Arab woman (111–12), he and a handful of other soldiers mutiny. Back at the military base, the refuseniks are treated 'comme des pestiférés' ['like plague victims']: a telling simile, suggesting that revolt against military occupation could easily become contagious. When the commander tries to use the Shoah as justification for all Israeli military action, Ilan's diegetic words map on to historian Zertal's diagnosis referred to above (157):

> Tu as pris alors ton élan et tu as récusé les gens qui s'appropriaient abusivement les six millions. Ils appartenaient au peuple juif tout entier, et pas spécialement à l'Armée de Défense d'Israël (Raczymow, 112–13)

> [At that point you took a run up and you objected to people who wrongly appropriated the six million. They belonged to the entire Jewish people, and not especially to Israel's Defence Army]

But fear of condemnation by left-wing friends for defiling Zionist ideals compromises his mutiny. Where service in the IDF is concerned, these left-wing thinkers are not free thinkers; and their lack of freedom stems from the now sacrosanct principle of Jewish self-defence after the horrors of the Shoah (117). The practical corollary of that principle, namely military service, has become integrated into the national psyche as an incontestable duty. It is that sense of duty that prevents Raczymow's brother from quitting the army, despite his distress in the occupied territory of Hebron (127). And his reward is pride in symbolic recognition by the IDF, which confers a sense of national belonging absent in his French homeland (127). Despite this pride, one memory delivers a serious blow to the ethical profile of the IDF, with its implied linking of Nazi atrocities and IDF conduct during and after the Six-Day War: '« Nous passâmes devant Kuneitra, écrit mon frère. Ville déserte, barbelée depuis la guerre des Six-Jours. Je pensais à Oradour-sur-Glane' (128) ['"We went past Kuneitra", wrote my brother. "A deserted town, surrounded by barbed wire since the Six-Day War. I thought about Oradour-sur-Glane"'].[8]

From this damning reflection on the Israeli army, we will move to a contrastingly valorizing aspect of it emerging from a number of the primary texts: its gender equality.

2.8. Israeli army's gender equality

The IDF website states 'The IDF is a professional organization that considers equality a leading ethic and incorporates women in almost every mission'.[9] Noa Roei, an Israeli scholar of comparative literature and cultural analysis, echoes this point with respect to military service and underscores the latter's contribution to modern Israeli national identity: 'Israeli society prides itself on being egalitarian when it comes to compulsory military service. Both women and men have served in the Israeli army since its formation; women soldiers are part and parcel of the national ethos' (67). Only one of the primary texts suggests anything less than total equality between men and women in the IDF: Zenatti's *Quand j'étais soldate* (2002), whose narrator notes that 'Les soldates ne combattent pas dans les territoires. Les soldates ne vont pas au combat' (145) ['Female soldiers don't fight in the Territories. Female soldiers don't go into combat']. However, the narrator later affirms that very equality in saying of her pistol-revolver '*Mais c'est aussi le signe suprême qui fait de nous des soldates, un équivalent absolu des garçons*' (119–20) ['But it's also the supreme sign that makes us into soldiers, absolutely the same as the boys']. Stepping back in time, it is interesting to note Kessel's reports in *Terre d'amour et de feu* (1965) on the period immediately before the creation of the state of Israel, and more specifically on the Haganah, the Jewish paramilitary organization in Palestine that later became the nucleus of the IDF. He recounts a striking incident witnessed as a reporter in which an Arab fighter's sexism is quashed by the material reality of two young Haganah women pointing rifles at him (114). Rabinovitch's vignette of female Israeli soldiers in *Chacune blesse, la dernière tue* (2012) is far less heroizing, but still conveys the tough challenges they face and surmount:

> Dur d'être à l'armée pour une fille de 18 ans, il faut courir, apprendre à se jeter à terre, à se diriger dans la nuit.
> « Tu crois que nous sommes des héros? se moque-t-elle. Nous avons peur, comme tout le monde. » (69)

> [It's hard for a girl of 18 to be in the army: you have to run, to learn how to throw yourself to the ground, to find your way at night.
> 'You think we're heroes?' she asks, poking fun at me. 'We're scared, like everyone else']

And the toughness of what they face translates into an emotional toughness, at least in public (72). If Rabinovitch's verdict is less than glowing, one uncompromised asset for gendered equality in the IDF emerging from the primary corpus is the liberating role it plays for young women from Orthodox Jewish families, to which we will now turn.

2.9. The Israeli army and young Orthodox women

Roei has further observed of the Israeli army that 'Those with non-hegemonic identities who are also drafted, including women, Jewish men of Middle Eastern origin, Druze men, and homosexuals, frequently renegotiate their social status through their military service' (66). With respect to women, I interpret 'renegotiate' here as seeking and potentially achieving greater freedom and autonomy. This achievement is suggested in two primary texts.

The first is Hillel's *Les Oranges de Jaffa* (1981), where Rachel, a 22-year-old French immigrant to Israel from an Orthodox family, states:

> Chez nous les filles, même fiancées, ne doivent pas sortir seules. Mon père aurait préféré rester en France ... Pensez, en Israël les filles font leur service militaire ... ce serait ma perdition ... [...] L'agence juive lui a garanti que je serai dispensée d'armée, puisque je suis pratiquante (70)

> [Back home the girls aren't allowed to go out alone, even if they're engaged. My father would have preferred to stay in France ... Just think, in Israel girls do their military service ... That would be my damnation ... [...] The Jewish Agency assured him I'd be exempted from the army, since I'm a practising Jew]

However, she has decided to defy her father's wishes and do her military service once in Israel (71). As well as liberation from her family's quasi-medieval treatment of young women, she sees in military service an additional benefit – quicker integration into Israeli society:

> L'armée me permettra aussi de m'adapter plus vite. Je ne veux pas être une ... noire, comme on appelle là-bas les juifs orientaux. Noir par rapport à ceux venus d'Europe ... (71)

> [The army will also help me to integrate more quickly. I don't want to be a ... Black, as they call eastern Jews there. Black compared to those who came from Europe ...]

The stigmatization of North African Jews in Israeli society generally will be examined more fully in Chapter 3, but it would appear that the Israeli army, for all its imperfections, does allow for more mixing and mutual acceptance than in civil society of otherwise segregated social groups. Ami Bouganim's *Le cri de l'arbre* (1983) also contains an example of a young Orthodox woman (here only 18 years old) defying her father's refusal to let her do military service (47). Again the ethnic factor is brought into focus as the interlocutor condemning the young girl's filial defiance is told, 'Ecoute, camarade, nous ne sommes plus au Maroc où ...' (47) ['Listen, mate, we're not in Morocco any more, where ...']. And again the conclusion to be drawn is that even if the transversal nature of gender, age and ethnicity can produce knotty ethical dilemmas (which of those identitarian factors should be respected when their demands clash?), completing Israeli military service can be of clear benefit to young Orthodox women by providing an escape from structures of religious and patriarchal oppression.

The shape-shifting influence of the Israeli army upon individuals' identity as mediated by Francophone Jewish writers – sometimes commanding these writers' respect, at other times their reproof – should by now be patent. From the positive facets of the army, we turn finally to two more negatives.

2.10. Economic disadvantages and psychological depredations of the Israeli army

The economic disadvantages of serving in the Israeli army are represented in only one of the primary texts, Sebban's *La terre promise, pas encore* (2002), but that representation is powerful. Here an anonymous Israeli citizen crudely expresses a bitter sense of having been exploited and left penniless by the army, despite having served in an elite unit for all three years of his military service:

> Regarde, moi, j'étais Golani[10] pendant mes trois ans d'armée. Je me suis cassé le cul à faire leur putain de guerre au Liban. Quand je suis sorti de l'armée, j'avais même pas un dollar. Tu crois qu'ils m'auraient aidé, les sionistes? Si pendant ces trois ans j'avais travaillé, au moins j'aurai pu mettre du fric de côté. Je ne sais pas, cent dollars par mois. (88)

> [Look, *I* was a Golani for my three years in the army. I bust a gut fighting their fucking war in Lebanon. When I came out of the army, I hadn't a dollar to my name. Do you think they'd have helped me, the Zionists? If I'd worked during those three years, at least I could have put some money aside. I don't know, a hundred dollars a month]

Literary representations of the army's psychological depredations are much more frequent and, predictably, carry more affective charge. In Boukhobza's *Un été à Jérusalem* (1986), one example among many is the damage sustained by a sibling of conscripted soldiers rather than by the soldiers themselves. Homodiegetic narrator Sarah's feeling of isolation within and alienation from Israel, particularly from its prosecution of the Lebanese War in which her brothers are embroiled, is evinced through the simile of a lost traveller:

> Je remarque enfin, dans un cadre en plastique doré, une photo de mes frères en habit militaire. Où sont-ils? Dans les montagnes de Chouf? A Beyrouth? Plus je les détaille, plus j'éprouve un sentiment de solitude, comme un voyageur qui réalise soudain qu'il s'est trompé de destination (253)

> [I finally notice, in a golden plastic frame, a photo of my brothers in army uniform. Where are they? In the Chouf mountains? In Beirut? The more I examine them, the more alone I feel, like a traveller who suddenly realizes she's come to the wrong place]

Sarah also suffers trauma at the news of her boyfriend Henry's army death, and becomes deranged by rage at the macho military ethos that has killed him:

> Elle tourne dans le quartier, tourne sans un cri, habillée de son seul rire, et ses grandes dents blanches sont féroces, elle va mordre dans le sexe des hommes, les châtrer de ses grandes dents et ils n'iront plus à la guerre, ils ressembleront aux femmes, soumis. (254)

> [She paces up and down in the district, paces up and down without a cry, wearing only her laughter, and her big white teeth are ferocious. She's going to bite men's penises, castrate them with her big teeth and they won't go to war any more, they'll be like women, submissive]

Her mental torment is not the only collateral damage of the army's demands, for her parents endure the sorrow of their conscripted sons' absence, both literal and figurative:

> Les voici condamnés à attendre de semaine en semaine le jour de permission de mes frères qui rentrent pour se jeter dans un lit, ivres d'épuisement, et qui dorment vingt-quatre heures d'affilée comme des brutes (35)

> [So they're condemned to waiting week after week for the day's leave granted to my brothers, who come back home only to dive into bed, drunk with exhaustion, and sleep twenty-four hours in one stretch like beasts]

There is, though, more impact in Boukhobza's rendering of the psychological suffering endured by soldiers themselves, particularly in the detail of lachrymosity that chafes with their tough image:

> Ici, j'ai vu des soldats pleurer d'avoir à rentrer à leur base, perdus dans

le désert de ces trois années obligatoires, rêvant de s'y soustraire mais incapables de l'admettre (44)

[Here, I've seen soldiers crying because they have to go back to base, lost in the desert of those three compulsory years, dreaming of escaping them but unable to admit it]

Further, service in the army has caused lasting mental disturbance in her friend Roger:

J'ai eu de la chance. J'ai échappé à trois morts certaines. J'en ai bavé, crois-moi. J'en bave toujours ... La nuit. Quand mes morts se lèvent. On finit par se fiancer, tu sais, avec l'horreur (79)

[I was lucky. Three times I escaped certain death. I had a tough time, believe me. I still do ... At night. When my dead arise. You end up betrothed to it, you know, to horror]

That stasis of suffering is rendered all the more poignant by Roger's own admission that nobody in Israel really understands why they are involved in this war (79). The horror of his literally past but mentally all-too-present experience is implied by his assertion of language's inability to capture it (77) – an assertion which turns out to be a powerful preterition:

Et brutalement, il plonge. Il parle [...]. Des soldats qui vident leur chargeur au moindre frôlement suspect, abattant quelquefois un renard ou un lapin avec la rage qu'on met à tuer des hommes. [...] Du soldat qui pleure et berce dans ses bras sa jambe arrachée par une roquette. Du soldat qui rit, atteint de démence. Des chuchotements sous les tentes où des photos circulent. De l'odeur puante des latrines où l'on va vomir ses tripes comme au confessionnal. (77)

[And suddenly, he plunges in. He speaks [...]. About soldiers who fire a full round of bullets at the slightest suspect rustling, sometimes shooting a fox or a rabbit with the same rage they put into killing men. [...] About the soldier who cries and cradles in his arms his leg torn off by a rocket. About the soldier who laughs, touched by insanity. About the whispers under tents where photos circulate. About the stink of the latrines where you go to vomit up your insides like people go to the confessional]

Anne Rabinovitch's novel *Les Étangs de Ville-d'Avray* (1987) also conveys powerfully the damaging present-ness of traumatic military pasts:

Prise d'une crise subite, Amos se tord de douleur sur le lit. « Ima, hurle-t-il, Ima! »[11] Je le regarde pétrifiée. [...]

« Passez-moi le flacon de médicaments sur la table de nuit, suffoque-t-il en hébreu. Donnez-moi de l'eau. » Il tremble de tous ses membres, ses dents s'entrechoquent contre le verre. Peu à peu il s'apaise.

« J'ai été blessé à la guerre », dit-il, le teint verdâtre sous son hâle. [...] « Ils n'ont pas réussi à retirer l'obus dans ma jambe. »

J'hésite. Je ne trouve rien à dire.

« Allez-vous-en, murmure-t-il, allez-vous-en. J'ai besoin d'être seul. Je vais vous donner de l'argent pour un taxi. (87)

[Seized by a sudden fit, Amos is writhing with pain on the bed. 'Mum', he howls, 'Mum!' Paralysed, I watch him. [...]

'Pass me the bottle of pills on the bedside table', he chokes in Hebrew. 'Give me some water'. All his limbs are trembling, his teeth click against the glass. Gradually he calms down.

'I was injured in the war', he says, looking green underneath his suntan. [...] 'They didn't manage to remove the shell in my leg'.

I hesitate. I can't think of anything to say.

'Go', he murmurs. 'Go. I need to be alone. I'll give you money for a taxi']

This extract depicts ex-soldier Amos's persistent suffering not just from a physical wound sustained in the army, but also from the recurring psychological wound associated with it: terrifying flashbacks which trigger regression to a primal need for the mother. In addition, Amos's need to be alone during these flashbacks demonstrates the disabling of interpersonal relations resulting from military trauma.

Military trauma is bluntly conveyed and denounced in Sebban's *La terre promise, pas encore* (2002):

– Réfléchis. Un gosse de dix-huit ans, tu lui donnes un M16 et tu l'envoies à Naplouse faire la police et se ramasser des pierres sur la gueule. Il est traumatisé à vie. C'est normal qu'après il se casse à Goa prendre des acides et écouter de la trance dans les raves qu'ils font là-bas, dans la jungle. S'enfuir comme c'est pas possible. Ceux qui restent, c'est qu'ils ont pas le choix ou l'argent pour partir. (89)

['Think about it. A kid of eighteen, you give him an M16 and send him to Nablus to act the policeman and get stoned in the face. He's traumatized for life. It's not surprising that afterwards he heads off to Goa to take acid and listen to trance music in the raves they have there, in the jungle. An incredible need to escape. Those who stay, they stay because they don't have the choice or the money to leave']

The most poignant part of this extract is 'traumatisé à vie': the affective trauma that can be inflicted by military service is permanent, and will lead to more or less dangerous forms of escapism. Valérie Zenatti's *Quand j'étais soldate* (2002) contains a telling example of one form of psychological escapism, resorted to unconsciously by the narrator during her military service: binge eating. That she has no history of eating disorders is carefully established (109). As her bingeing increases, she locates its cause in a new sense of existential void that needs to be filled at all costs:

> Je ne comprends pas très bien cette pulsion: je n'ai pas faim, mais j'ai besoin de me remplir l'estomac sans apprécier, très vite, comme s'il y avait un vide à combler à tout prix (134)

> [I don't really understand this urge: I'm not hungry, but I need to fill my stomach without savouring the food, very fast, as if there were a hole that has to be filled at all costs]

Eventually she has a nervous breakdown and is given psychotherapy, which reveals cognitive dissonance (187). On the one hand, she is proud to be part of the Israeli army because of its crucial role in Israel's as yet short and always threatened existence, and because this confers a sense of national belonging. On the other hand, she feels oppressed by the rigidity of the military system, and the illustration she provides suggests that the system's inculcation of discipline can take absurd and counter-productive forms serving only further to diminish personal freedom and agency:

> Je sais que la discipline est indispensable, mais il me semble que, si on nous accordait un peu plus de temps, de liberté, si on ne nous obligeait pas à refaire nos lits trois fois, pour le principe, on serait d'aussi bonnes soldates. Et un peu mieux dans notre peau (188)

> [I know that discipline is essential, but it seems to me that, if we were given a bit more time, a bit more freedom, if we weren't forced to re-make our beds three times, just for the sake of it, we'd be just as good soldiers. And feel a bit better about ourselves]

Zenatti also underscores the intense distress experienced by her narrator when, travelling in army uniform in a civilian bus crossing the Occupied Territories, she becomes the target of violence from a Palestinian youth in whom she sees her mirror image (215). Her distress is based in the paradox of their human, existential similarity and the Palestinian teenager's perception of their enmity, due to her iconic army uniform.

Finally, Chochana Boukhobza's novel *Le Troisième Jour* (2010) contains what is not named as such but is a clear case of post-traumatic stress disorder resulting from military service (a similar case to those of Roger and Amos examined above, but even more extreme). Having fought and only just survived two wars (87), Daniel retains a morbid preoccupation with war and death. Immured in silence, he sometimes thinks he needs psychotherapy or psychoanalysis but never seeks it out, caught in a disjunction between the need to express his suffering verbally and his affectively (rather than neurologically) induced aphasia:

> La guerre, la mort. Il connaît. Il a donné. Largement. Il n'en parle à personne. Parfois il se dit qu'il devrait aller consulter un psy, histoire de se décharger, de se laver de toute cette merde (88)

> [War, death. He knows all about them. He's given of himself. Amply. He doesn't talk to anyone about it. Sometimes he thinks he should see a shrink, just to offload, to clean himself of all this shit]

The expletive 'merde' rawly stresses both the pain and the disgust which entrap him, worsened by a fear of the death by heart attack which this mental ill-health might prompt – as has been the case, he contends, with most Israeli men who have survived war (90). In a vicious psychological circle, fear of death is compounded by awareness of the death that might result from his recurring, apocalyptic nightmares about … death (in warfare) (135–36). So, while harmful forms of escapism (drug abuse in *La terre promise, pas encore*, binge eating in *Quand j'étais soldate*) are pursued by some as a result of traumatic experiences in the army, there is literally no escape even in sleep for others, whose condition remains mired in the realm of the pathological years after leaving that institution.

2.11. Influence of the Francophone community on modern Israeli identities

The penultimate section of this chapter bifurcates from previous sections by examining an exogamous element to modern Israeli paradigms of identity. It considers how the primary texts represent French nationals living either temporarily or permanently in Israel (Palestine in the case of Kessel) and thus influencing, even if only indirectly, those paradigms. By way of contextualization it may be instructive first to review a number of social, cultural and economic points about French nationals living temporarily in Israel. Pinto identifies the majority of frequent Franco-Jewish visitors to Israel in the twenty-first century as Sephardim (and at least two of the three authors considered in this section, Marco Koskas and Michaël Sebban, are Sephardic) who identify affectively as Israeli:

> tous ces Français qui sont des Israéliens de coeur, le plus souvent séfarades, qui ont de la famille, et possèdent souvent des appartements en Israël (30)

> [all those French people who are Israelis at heart, more often than not Sephardic, who have family and often own apartments in Israel]

French Jews' possession of apartments in Israel is revealed later by Pinto to include expensive real estate more generally acquired as second homes, their purchase being prompted, significantly, by fear that antisemitism in France may become so bad they will be compelled to move to Israel definitively and make these second homes their sole homes (184). That association of French-Jewish visitors/possible immigrants to Israel with high economic status is consolidated by the accent placed on a conversation Pinto overhears in Israel between two French-speaking men about start-up companies and computer technology (176). This implies either French contributions to Israeli high-tech developments, or at the very least the regular presence within Israel of French nationals with such skills, knowledge and contacts in booming economic sectors.

The first of our primary texts to mention French Jews in Israel, Hillel's *Les Oranges de Jaffa* (1981), is set much earlier (in 1964) than the contemporary period on which Pinto concentrates. Correspondingly, the political and economic stakes are very different. At that stage, Israel was not as economically advanced as it is in the twenty-first century, a fact reflected in the prediction that thousands of rich French (and American) immigrants will soon arrive to build factories and supermarkets (141). Mention is made of a brief but significant wave of French immigrants to Israel immediately after the state's creation, inspired by the socialist ideals of the new nation (iconicized in the *kibbutzim*) (181). Thereafter, in keeping with Pinto's findings, Hillel's novel observes Sephardic Francophone immigrants to Israel, who had come mainly from ex-French Maghrebi colonies where French was the language of administration. As Chapter 3 will go on to explore, these immigrants were usually at the bottom of the socio-economic ladder, which explains the placards in both Hebrew and French brandished by demonstrators that are recorded in Hillel's narrative:

> Quelques-uns portaient des pancartes où l'on pouvait lire, en hébreu mais

aussi en français: « Du pain pour nos enfants et du travail pour leurs pères. » (171)

['Some were carrying placards where you could read, in Hebrew but also in French: 'Bread for our children and work for their fathers']

Curiously, the Israeli officials mentioned do not seem to realize that the poor prospects offered to Maghrebi immigrants in Israel may well explain France's status as a more attractive destination (182).

The economic dissymmetry between France and Israel persists, if in somewhat altered form, within Michaël Sebban's autofictional *La terre promise, pas encore* (2002), which is set in the late twentieth century. The homodiegetic narrator Eli is French but lives for extended periods of time in Israel, where he finds it harder to make ends meet due to lower wages and higher prices than in France (74).[12] In *Lehaïm. À toutes les vies* (2004), Sebban's sequel to *La terre promise, pas encore*, that economic disparity is also one of the obstacles to Richard, a successful business man, living all the year round in Israel (79–80). In addition to the comparative economic hardships of life in Israel, *La terre promise, pas encore* implies a gruff morosity among Israelis absent among Parisians (112). Yet, despite these considerable drawbacks to living in Israel, Eli is still reluctant to return to France, due to a deep sense of emotional and existential connection to Israelis that transcends any economic or political critique (180–81).

That connection is also expressed in Marco Koskas's *Mon cœur de père* (2012), an unequivocally autobiographical narrative that recounts the author's life divided between France and Israel, where his son has done two weeks of voluntary work in a military base (9). Koskas writes of a taxi driver who has suffered a sharp drop in income in moving from France to Israel, but does not regret the move for a moment:

> Le chauffeur est un parfait francophone qui a abandonné un gros poste à L'Oréal pour revenir en Israël, où il avait grandi. Regrette-t-il d'avoir fait ce sacrifice? D'être ainsi déclassé? « Quelle question! répond-il, presque indigné. Bien sûr que non! » (131–32)

[The driver speaks perfect French and gave up an important job with L'Oréal to come back to Israel, where he'd grown up. Does he regret having made this sacrifice? The downgraded status? 'What a question!' he replies, almost indignant. 'Of course not!']

The loss of income sustained by French (or, in this case, long-term French-domiciled) Jews moving to Israel is philosophically downplayed by the implication that it is less important than the profound satisfaction of being at ease as a Jew in one's country. Koskas's account provides other interesting insights into the status of Francophone visitors to and residents in Israel. One Frenchman who has lived in Israel for 23 years is irritated by the indigenous Israelis' constant demarcation of his difference based on his French accent (10). On the other hand, it appears that attractive Parisian women exert a linguistic dominance in certain commercial contexts: 'Des Parisiennes ravissantes font aussi leurs courses dans ce supermarché, et y ont imposé le français comme langue officielle' (14) ['Beautiful Parisian women also do their shopping in this supermarket, where they've imposed French as the official language']. And various commercial contexts are important, for it is here that French tourists, if not French immigrants, wield considerable power and influence in Israel (15, 90, 120).

This section has focussed on members of the Francophone community in Israel and their attitudes towards their either partially or fully adoptive country. The final section of this chapter will reverse this purview, examining Israel's attitudes to France.

2.12. Israel's perception of France

The earliest text in our corpus to allude to Israel's perception of France is Ania Francos's *Les Palestiniens* (1968). Francos frames in terms of passion the reaction of Israeli Zionists to de Gaulle's infamous 1967 affront, which 'allait apporter des arguments aux sionistes et déclencher une campagne passionnée' (225) ['would provide Zionists with a good case and unleash a passionate campaign']. It is important to note the etymological root of the word 'passion' in suffering. Although the official reaction was anger, anger can of course arise from suffering, just as suffering is very often immanent in anger. A contrastingly positive Israeli angle on France emerges in Marc Hillel's *Tu vivras dans ton sang* (1971), but this recurs to the period immediately predating Israel's creation and to France's status as the chief facilitator of European Jewish departures to Palestine in 1948 (216).[13] Another representational zigzag occurs with Paula Jacques's *Un baiser froid comme la lune* (1983). Set in the 1950s, this novel conveys Israel's consciousness of France's active contribution to the Shoah and its prediction of a future return to antisemitic persecution in France:[14]

– Voici la terre de Jérusalem, dit-il. Je te la donne, Tobias, emporte-la avec toi. Elle te servira de porte-bonheur lorsque surviendront les persécutions.

 – En France? Tu plaisantes?

 – Là comme ailleurs, mon pauvre ami. Partout, tôt ou tard, tu l'apprendras à tes dépens. Le Vel' d'hiv', la milice, la Gestapo, tu connais pourtant? C'est ton affaire. (204)

['Here is the earth of Jerusalem', he said. 'I give it to you, Tobias, take it with you. It'll serve as a lucky charm when the persecutions start.'

 'In France? Are you joking?'

 'There as elsewhere, my poor friend. Everywhere, sooner or later, as you'll learn to your cost. The Vel' d'hiv', the Milice, the Gestapo, you must know about them? It's your business.']

Michaël Sebban's *La terre promise, pas encore* (2002) accelerates dieget-ically into the last decade of the twentieth century, conveying one young Israeli woman's fascination and admiration for French culture: 'Elle […] n'arrêtait pas de clamer à quel point la culture était un truc formidable, comment les Français en avaient fait un art de vivre' (41–42) ['She […] was constantly proclaiming what a brilliant thing culture was, how the French had made of it an art of living']. However, this youthful vision is countered in the bitter memories harboured by older Israelis of France's collaboration with the Nazis during the Second World War, thus echoing Jacques (1983, 204). Sebban's characters extrapolate from this collabo-ration to posit enduring French hatred of Jews in the late twentieth century:

– […] Mon oncle, son voisin l'a dénoncé aux Allemands pour cinquante francs.

 – C'est comme les Français. Juste bon à être collabos. Qu'ils l'avouent publiquement qu'ils ont jamais pu nous piffer. Ça sera plus clair. (109)

['[…] My uncle, his neighbour denounced him to the Germans for fifty francs'.

 'It's like the French. Fit for nothing but collaboration. They should come clean publicly that they've never been able to stand us. That'd be clearer']

Hostile reaction to a French person, albeit a Jewish visitor to Israel, is also conveyed in a young Israeli woman, but the reason for her hostility is strikingly different: dislike for the French Jew's wish to 'pouvoir jeter tous les Arabes à la mer pour redonner la joie de vivre à son peuple' (136) ['be able to throw all the Arabs into the sea to give joie de vivre back to his people']. It is significant that the young Israeli woman rejects the

French Jew's clumsy and racist attempt to express solidarity with Israel. She clearly refuses the reverse racism expressed by his remark: a reversal of the Arab metonymy about throwing all Israelis into the sea, in which murder of Israelis stands in for destruction of the state of Israel itself.

2.13. Endnote

This chapter's study of modern Israeli paradigms of identity as mediated by Francophone Jewish writers reveals above all the marked singularity of those paradigms relative to other national identities. The three predominant paradigms are interlocking and continue to exert a profound influence in the twenty-first century. The first is Zionism, represented in 12 of our primary texts – two entirely positively, four entirely negatively, and six in a more nuanced mode which balances the ideology's perceived positive properties (chiefly its decisive role in Israel's birth and continued existence) against its perceived negative properties (chiefly its manipulative propaganda). The relatively progressive gendered structures of Zionism as incarnated in the institution of the *kibbutz* are explored in two texts, in both cases, somewhat surprisingly, with some disparagement. As for the *kibbutzim* more generally, three texts scrutinize this unique (and, at least in theory, sociotropic) creation of the Zionist state, two critically, and one scathingly. The second salient paradigm in the primary corpus is in itself an ideologeme of Zionism: the cult(ivation) of Israelis' physical strength and indomitability, in negation of antisemitic stereotypes. This is represented in eight primary texts, in five cases approvingly, and in three more reservedly. Third, a metonymic component of that cult(ivation): the Israeli army, conscription to which is virtually universal among Israeli Jews, including women, military service being followed by mandatory reserve service as required. Of those 11 texts which depict the Israeli army generally, only one condemns it, and only two idealize it, the other eight being more subtle and circumspect in approach. The three texts that focus on gender equality within the army and the two that focus on its liberating role for young women from Orthodox families are, unsurprisingly, fairly upbeat. Axiomatically, the six that bring out the army's economic disadvantages and its psychological depredations paint a bleaker picture.

These paradigms are all Israeli quiddities, and the primary texts suggest modern Israel's status within the Francophone Jewish imaginary as a cultural exception among nations, in comparison with which the 'exception française', in all its admittedly diverse guises, pales into relative insignificance.

Notes

1 *Les Palestiniens* was published in revised form in 1970; all references are to that second edition.

2 While not incriminating Ben Gurion by name, cultural studies specialist Ella Shohat documents this as a historical reality: '[a] Jewish underground cell, commanded by secret agents sent from Israel, planted bombs in Jewish centers so as to create hysteria among Iraqi Jews and thus catalyze a mass exodus to Israel' (48).

3 Other primary texts referring to religious Zionism are Abécassis (1997, 80) and Koskas (2012, 106).

4 Nordau later developed the idea of steeling the body in 'Jüdische Turnzeitung' in June 1900.

5 Cf. Meller-Saïd (41).

6 Cf. Francos (1970, 209).

7 Cf. Abécassis (2000, 7–8).

8 On 10 June 1944, without any warning, the SS slaughtered 642 men, women and children at the French village of Oradour-sur-Glane, and then destroyed the village.

9 See <http://www.idf.il/1589-en/Dover.aspx>.

10 A *Golani* is a member of an elite unit of the Israeli army.

11 *Ima* means 'mum'/'mummy' in Hebrew.

12 It is important to note that income gaps in Israel are among the highest of member states of the Organisation for Economic Co-operation and Development.

13 Cf. the Introduction on France's solidarity in 1947 with Shoah survivors trying to reach Palestine in the Exodus, against the will of the British Mandate.

14 Chapter 5 considers twenty-first-century Israelis' view of France as deeply antisemitic.

CHAPTER THREE

Intra-Israeli Conflict

Chapter 3 examines how the primary corpus represents conflict between different ethnic and political demographics among Jews in Israel. Chapters 4 and 5 will each examine another type of conflict, but in all three chapters, emotions and affect (see the Introduction for a discussion of the two terms) will feature prominently. It seems self-evident that conflict arises as a result of emotions or affect pitting one individual or group against another individual or group. Yet my intention is not to reduce conflict to emotions or affect alone, for cognition plays a significant role too. As is remarked by Andrew Ortony, Gerald L. Clore and Allan Collins, who between them represent cognitive science, social psychology and cognitive psychology,

> emotions arise as a result of the way in which the situations that initiate them are construed by the experiencer [...] emotions arise as a result of certain kinds of cognitions [...] if an individual conceptualizes a situation in a certain kind of way, then the potential for a particular kind of emotion exists. (1–2)

For Ortony, Clore and Collins, emotions are 'valenced reactions to events, agents, or objects, with their particular nature being determined by the way in which the eliciting situation is construed' (12). The main, but not the only, conflict explored in Chapter 3 is between the Ashkenazic elite and what was – at least in the first three decades of Israel's existence – the Sephardic and Mizrahi 'underclass'. The principal emotions/affect expressed in literary renderings of this conflict are humiliation, resentment, anger and animosity; the eliciting condition for them is the cognitive perception of a deep injustice. For our purposes, the valenced reactions are chiefly to events and agents rather than objects, although occasionally objects can provoke strong emotions/affect if they symbolize oppression and/or condescension.

The chapter begins by considering Moroccan, and to a lesser extent Tunisian and Algerian, immigrants as the main constituents of Francophone communities in Israel (3.1). It briefly evaluates Levantinism as a potential for the queering of Israeli identity (3.2). Concentration next shifts to the Ashenazic elite's anti-Sephardic/anti-Mizrahi racism, and to protest against it as manifested in, inter alia, the Wadi Salib riots and the Panthères noires militants (3.3); then to the convergence of the oppressed working-class Sephardim/Mizrahim with the political right under Menachem Begin from 1977, and later with manifestations of the extreme right such as the Shas party (3.4). The chapter also ponders a specific, shocking reaction against this form of racism: denial of the Shoah by some Sephardim/Mizrahim, based on genuine ignorance and on the belief that the Ashkenazim want the perceived leverage of victimhood (3.5). Chapter 3 also analyses avatars of intra-Israeli conflict even within a putatively single subset of Israelis, the Sephardim/Mizrahim, where that basic commonality is overridden by barriers of differing national origins – Iraqi, Iranian, Moroccan, Romanian, Spanish, Tunisian and Yemeni (3.6). Lastly, Chapter 3 probes literary representations of a different form of schism between Israeli citizens: that between the settlers in the Occupied Territories and those who oppose or at the very least critique them and their occupation (3.7).

As a preface to the discussion of intra-ethnic differences (in both senses of the word) in Israel as mediated in the primary texts, a number of insights from various scholarly disciplines may provide helpful contextualization. Israel is arguably unique among nation states in being founded on a singular religion and ethnicity (Jewish) but having citizens whose national origin and even, to use that highly disputed term, 'race' are richly heterogeneous. This singular constellation is invoked by academic, writer and critic Éric Marty to contest widespread anti-Israeli sentiment among onlookers who are allergic to any hint of ethnic 'purity':

> Qu'y a-t-il de si insupportable à l'humanité dans l'existence d'un État juif? [...] Rien en tout cas qui puisse heurter ceux qui souffrent de la phobie à l'égard de la pureté ethnique puisque la population juive d'Israël est, on l'a dit en vertu de l'universalité originaire du peuple juif, la population la plus multiraciale qui soit. (2003, 71)

> [What is so unbearable for humankind in the existence of a Jewish state? [...] Nothing at any rate that could offend those suffering from phobia about ethnic purity since the Jewish population of Israel is, it's been

said by virtue of the original universality of the Jewish people, the most multiracial population on earth]

Psychoanalyst Daniel Sibony, for his part, draws attention to the downside of this multiracial society: its inevitable cultural frictions. First he evokes the reluctance of certain religious Moroccan Jews who in the 1950s did not want to send their children to an Israel they viewed as too secular and westernized (176). Next he evokes the inverted mirror-image of this prejudice – the disrespect of the Ashkenazi Israeli establishment for the Moroccan Jews and their (perceived) lack of cultural capital:

> Les Juifs marocains venus en Israël, sans diplômes et sans cadres, ont été laminés par un establishment normal, fier de ses qualifications, puis de ses diplômes (177)

> [The Moroccan Jews who had come to Israel without diplomas or executives were destroyed by a normal establishment proud of its qualifications, and of its diplomas]

This disrespect in particular receives prominent representation in the primary texts, as we will see presently; Sibony explains it as the Ashkenazi establishment's refusal of 'la rencontre de l'altérité, sans doute par peur de la voir resurgir en lui' (177) ['the encounter with alterity, no doubt through fear of seeing it re-emerge within themselves']. The second clause suggests the establishment's fear of being contaminated by an Otherness located in 'Arab' Jews but in actual fact discernible in its own, albeit now distant ethnic history. Such contamination would lead to it becoming the Other of the Western world; in consequence of that fear, 'les responsables israéliens des années « héroïques » (1945–1970) [...] ont écrasé la culture de ces Juifs « arabes »' (Sibony, 177) ['the Israeli leaders of the "heroic" years (1945–1970) [...] crushed the culture of these "Arab" Jews'] . Concentrating on the contemporary period historian Diana Pinto also remarks twice on intra-ethnic conflict in twenty-first-century Israel. Not between Jews, but between non-Jews in Israel and the majority Jewish population. The first example is of African refugees, mainly from Darfour, who are doomed to a marginal existence in Israel (2012, 38). The second, briefer reference is to Israel's Druze minority (2012, 83), which in Pinto's account prompts fears within the Jewish Israeli majority of eternal alterity within its state (2012, 83). More central to the present chapter, however, are the various alterities within Israeli Jewry. It is to French Jewish literary representations of these alterities that our attention will now turn.

3.1. Maghrebi immigrants to Israel as the main constituents of Francophone communities

Algeria, Morocco and Tunisia had been either part of France (Algeria) or French protectorates (Morocco and Tunisia) until independence in the 1950s/early 1960s. The language of the colonial power, French, had been the language of administration and was also commonly spoken by many of the Jews in these countries. When they were forced into exile by the antisemitism of the new Arab nationalist regimes, a substantial number of these Jews (the majority but not the totality of them Moroccan) emigrated to Israel, where they came to form the largest Francophone community – a fact reflected in a number of our primary texts.

Marc Hillel's *Les Oranges de Jaffa* (1981) registers the heavy presence of French-speaking Maghrebi Jews in a significant public-service sector of Israel: the police force (231). Ami Bouganim's *Le cri de l'arbre* (1983) also stresses the link between Maghrebi origin and use of the French language in Israel:

> Un Juif tunisien, et qu'on ne se méprenne surtout pas sur ses origines. Au Maroc, il n'a jamais mis les pieds, ni lui ni le plus lointain de ses ancêtres. D'ailleurs, pour prévenir la fatale confusion, il ne parle qu'en français (37)

> [[He is a] Tunisian Jew, and let nobody be mistaken about his origins. Neither he nor his most distant ancestors have ever set foot in Morocco. Moreover, to prevent the fatal confusion, he speaks only in French]

The neuralgic points of distinction between Tunisian and Moroccan Jews also emerge here: the Tunisian Jew spurns the 'judéo-marocain' (36) spoken by the Moroccan immigrants to Israel who surround him, and he confines himself to French so as not to suffer the indignity of being mistaken for one of them. However, at a later point, Bouganim's novel shows one factor that at least temporarily unites all three of the otherwise discrete and often mutually mistrustful groups that comprise Francophone Maghrebi immigrants to Israel. This is their common influence by Arab countries' broadcasts in French that deride Israel as a puppet state.

> Depuis que les Arabes se sont mis à traiter Israël 'd'Etat fantoche' dans leurs émissions en français, tous les francophones du pays – en d'autres termes, les Marocains et leurs rares coreligionnaires des provinces française, algérienne et tunisienne du Maroc – ne prononcent pas trois phrases sans se trouver quelque chose à qualifier de fantoche. (117)

[Since the Arabs started to call Israel a 'puppet state' in their French-language programmes, all French speakers in the country – in other words, the Moroccans and their rare coreligionists from the Tunisian, Algerian and French provinces of Morocco – don't utter three sentences without finding something to call 'puppet']

This satirizes the largely Maghrebi Francophone population of Israel in two respects. First, there is the belief of the Moroccan immigrants, whom Bouganim characterizes as comically excitable and disputatious, that they are superior to all other Francophone immigrants – as manifested in the belittling reference to Algeria, Tunisia and even the metropolis France as mere provinces of Morocco. Second, the Jewish North African population generally is presented as discursively malleable even by its political enemies (the Arab countries) and incapable of autonomous thought. This presentation seems almost to ventriloquize, no doubt again ironically, the prejudices of the Ashkenazi elite against Israel's Maghrebi immigrants. Jean-Luc Allouche's *Les jours innocents* (1984) also refers to those prejudices in recording his Algerian parents' attitude towards Israel, which in fact reveals byzantine contradictions:

Pour elle comme pour mon père, Israël était nimbé d'un halo magique, tout juste bon à être invoqué dans des prières sans âge, mais de là à y vivre! Avec ses bombes, son austérité, ses Arabes encore plus horribles que « les nôtres », ses discriminations à l'encontre des Juifs d'Afrique du Nord, dont un de mes oncles, transplanté dans une ville du Néguev, affirmait avoir été la victime, cette contrée n'était pas loin de passer à leurs yeux pour un pays de perdition, mal famé, dévolu à des esprits aventureux, pour tout dire des voyous. (49–50)

[For her and my father, Israel was surrounded by a magic halo, just about good enough to be invoked in ageless prayers, but from that to living there! With its bombs, its austerity, its Arabs who were even more dreadful than 'ours', its discrimination against North African Jews, of which one of my uncles, who'd been transplanted into a Negev town, claimed to have been a victim, this land wasn't far from striking them as a country of perdition, disreputable, reserved for adventurous spirits; in short, for hoodlums]

Eliette Abécassis's *Sépharade* (2009) too refers to discrimination against North African Jews, asserting that Israel is founded on a racist ideology which includes racism between Ashkenazim and Sephardim/Mizrahim (218). Admittedly, the source of this assertion, King Hassan II of Morocco, is hardly impartial. No more impartial is his advisors' belief that the birth of Israel constituted a rupture in the long coexistence of Jews and Muslims (218). In imputing blame to Israel for that rupture, his advisors conveniently occlude the inferior status of dhimmitude imposed on Jews in North African countries. However, this is not to deny that there were some positive shared experiences between Muslims and Sephardic Jews in those countries. One example (for others, see Chapter 4, section 4.5) is contained in the remark of a Tunisian Jew in Chochana Boukhobza's *Le Troisième Jour* (2010): 'nous, les Juifs du sud de la Tunisie, nous avons une liturgie particulière, nous chantons comme les Arabes' (53) ['we, the Jews of southern Tunisia, have a distinctive liturgy: we sing like the Arabs']. This shifting of boundaries and demarcation lines throws into question certain identitarian categories, in which identification as a Jew, as an Arab or above all as a North African Jew of Arab culture regardless of religious confession becomes blurred, or – to borrow from a different but not entirely inapt conceptual paradigm – is 'queered'.

3.2. Levantinism/queer

Rachel Harris speculates that 'Levantinism could represent fluidity; identity unbounded, with no fixed location, language or singular identity' (107). Replace the word 'Levantinism' with 'sexuality', and we could be talking about queer (which in fact increasingly extends its ambit beyond sexuality and gender to embrace questions of race and ethnicity). This is why I propose that Levantinism could be used as a conceptual tool to queer Israeli 'identity'. The queer protagonist here would map onto the 'archetypal Levantine, able to cross-boundaries [sic] and confuse binary definitions' (Harris, 115). Such a model would locate itself in a much more contemporary era than that discussed by Jacqueline Shohet Kahanoff's foundational article of 1959, 'Israel: Ambivalent Levantine' (in Starr and Somekh, 193–212), and would acknowledge but disassociate itself from the negative connotations historically attached to the terms levantin/Levantine (see Hochberg, 49). Such negative connotations are obvious in the ejaculation from Ami Bouganim's *Le cri de l'arbre* (1983):

> – L'Orient, s'esclaffe le Russe, nous sommes en Israël, pas au Maroc. Ton Orient croupit dans la misère et la saleté. L'indolence, la paresse et la veulerie n'ont pas cours ici. Que serions-nous devenus sans discipline est sans ordre? Israël ne deviendra pas un Etat levantin (196)

['The Orient', guffaws the Russian. 'We're in Israel, not in Morocco. Your Orient wallows in poverty and filth. Indolence, laziness and spinelessness aren't accepted here. What would have become of us without discipline and order? Israel will not become a Levantine state']

This new model would inhere rather in the labile, boundary-crossing potential of Israeli identities as part of a larger set of Mediterranean positionalities. As Harris points out, the French historian Fernand Braudel 'saw multiple overlapping notions of Mediterranean culture and commerce, rather than a singly defined interpretation', but, importantly, 'he highlighted the significance of regional cultures that cross traditional national boundaries' (107).[1]

In other secondary texts, historian Idith Zertal's summary of the Jewish philosopher Hannah Arendt's position also foregrounds the transcending of identitarian boundaries by the Jew, whose role was, for Arendt, to refuse all belonging (221).[2] Essayist and journalist Martine Gozlan locates a queer instance of polarized identities collapsing and apparently merging in a strange and unfixed state:

> le petit village de Silwan. C'est là qu'habite mon double. Car j'ai un nom double sur cette terre trop promise: un journaliste palestinien qui porte le même patronyme que moi (140)

> [the little village of Silwan. That's where my opposite number lives. For I have a shared name in this too promised land: a Palestinian journalist bears the same patronymic as me]

The explanation supplied – 'Mon nom a le don d'ubiquité. D'origine arabe, comme de nombreux noms de juifs séfarades, les juifs de l'Orient arabe, il est alternativement juif ou musulman' (Gozlan, 140) ['My name has the gift of ubiquity. Of Arab origin, like many names of Sephardic Jews – the Jews of the Arab Orient – it can be either Jewish or Muslim'] – locates an onomastic and cultural queerness: queerness both in the original sense of strangeness, and in the contemporary sense of eluding discrete and stable identitarian categories. Here the queerness reaches an apogee in the conflation of two figures normatively conceived as a religio-political binarism. A comment on Gozlan's Arab 'double' leads back precisely to the concept of the Mediterranean and its erosion of fixed national and cultural frontiers, producing a form of creolization: 'Nos arbres généalogiques avaient dû sombrer quelque part en Méditerranée' (Gozlan, 141) ['Our family trees must have foundered somewhere in the Meditteranean']. Finally, Diana Pinto hypostatizes this queerly Levantine ideal in one political figure (Israel's then President), even if she sombrely concludes that his ideal is hardly shared by all in contemporary Israel:

> Je ne suis pas sûre que Shimon Peres, l'homme du grand espace méditer-ranéen, qui selon lui aurait dû réunir les pays arabes et Israël dans une vaste zone économique au futur radieux, incarne toujours cet Israël à la fois planétaire et replié sur lui-même (2012, 148)

> [I'm not sure that Shimon Peres, the man of the great Mediterranean space, which in his view should have brought together the Arab countries and Israel in a vast economic zone with a dazzling future, still embodies this Israel that is at the same time global and closed in on itself]

While the potential for queering of the monolithic Israeli identity may be regarded as a positive eventuality, it requires an active reading against the grain with respect either to individual characters within, or the general ideological disposition of, certain primary texts, for whom/which fluidity and non-fixity of identity may seem to threaten cultural security. Thus in Marc Hillel's *Les Oranges de Jaffa* (1981), a young Israeli woman of Russian origin reflects that:

> Chez nous, les hommes sont toujours pressés, pressés d'aller raconter leur bonne aventure à un ami. C'est le côté phallocrate des orientaux. Ils l'ont tous, même s'ils sont nés en Bessarabie, à Cracovie ou à Londres. Ça doit être dû à la situation aux frontières qui ... (194)

> [At home, the men are always in a rush, in a rush to go and tell a friend about their great adventure. It's the phallocratic side of easterners. They all have it, even those born in Bessarabia, in Kraków or in London. It must be due to the situation at the frontiers which ...]

Her reflection, while incomplete (as conveyed by the suspension points), portrays Israeli men as feeling a need to prove themselves because of their precarious liminality, which is anathema to phallocratic monism. Jean-Luc Allouche's *Les jours innocents* (1984) also diagnoses a lesion in monism: the Eastern–Western, or the Sephardic/Mizrahi–Ashkenazi clash in Israel.

> Ainsi le nouveau citoyen probatoire avait-il besoin de Tel-Aviv [...]. Et de son agitation marchande, de son snobisme levantin emprunté à crédit sur les traites dévalorisées de la Mitteleuropa, de sa configuration trop logique, tracé au cordeau, mais bien vite pervertie par le débraillé et l'anarchie de ses habitants. Il s'émut, compatissant, de ce que recelaient de ferveur infantile cette mauvaise copie d'Occident fichée en terre d'Asie, menacée par la saleté indifférente et moite de l'Orient. (62–63)

[So the new probationary citizen needed Tel Aviv [...]. Needed its merchant bustle, its Levantine snobbery borrowed on credit on the depreciated drafts of Mitteleuropa, its overly logical shape, dead straight, but very quickly corrupted by the sloppiness and anarchy of its inhabitants. He was moved by, compassionate about the childish fervour harboured within this poor Western copy which had been driven into Asian land, threatened by the indifferent and muggy filth of the Orient]

Of particular note is Allouche's direct use of the term *levantin*. Here, in a reversal of conventionally understood Israeli hierarchies, it is the Levantine Jew, among whom the protagonist (based on Allouche, an Algerian Jew) figures, who considers himself superior ('snobisme') to the poor old Jewry of Mitteleuropa. Despite Allouche's condescension, there is a genuine sense of pathos in the last sentence. It implies a childlike, doomed passion about recreating that destroyed community of Central and Eastern European Jewry in the completely alien terrain of the Middle East, experienced as rebarbatively dirty and muggy (literally, but perhaps also figuratively). Mugginess, of course, is another indeterminate property that correlates with queer's lack of fixed identity ...

In *Sépharade* (2009), Eliette Abécassis also stresses the Sephardic/ Mizrahi–Ashkenazi clash, with the latter fearing the former's Levantinization of Israel (cf. Sibony, 177):

Obsédé qu'il était par le spectre de la « levantinisation », l'establishment judéo-européen avait refusé la culture orientale à cet État qui l'était pourtant, par sa situation géographique et sa population, constituée pour moitié de juifs d'Orient (177)

[Obsessed as it was by the spectre of 'Levantinization', the Judaeo-European establishment had rejected Oriental culture in this state which, through its geographical situation and its population, was half made up by Oriental Jews]

Interestingly, in my 2011 interview with her, the Sephardic Abécassis voiced great enthusiasm for Israel's Mediterraneanism,[3] viewing the latter as a fulcrum for dynamic synergies with France and Europe. However, in another of my 2011 interviews, Chantal Osterreicher (whose novel *L'Insouciance d'Adèle* is treated in Chapter 5) pointed to the failure of attempts formally to include Israel in a Mediterranean Union, due to the absolute veto placed on it by Arab countries.[4] A third interview in the same year revealed Ami Bouganim's serious misgivings about the very notion of Israel's Levantinization. Apropos the blurring of distinctions between Ashkenazi and Sephardic Israelis, he expressed trepidation:

je ne sais ce que ce brassage recouvre. Je crains une philistinisation des esprits. Une mauvaise levantinisation. Sans ses charmes et ses chaleurs. Le retour à une mentalité philistine[5]

[I don't know what this intermingling conceals. I fear that minds will become unsophisticated. A bad form of Levantinization. Without its charms and its warmth. The return to a philistine mentality]

Conversely, in *Eretz* (2010) Henri Raczymow expresses complete indifference to such blurring of ethnic and cultural boundaries, commenting casually of a waiter (and with echoes of Gozlan, 141), 'il est d'origine libyenne et tunisienne (nous ne pouvons déterminer s'il est arabe ou juif, quelle importance?)' (26) ['he's of Libyan and Tunisian origin (we can't tell if he's Arab or Jewish, what does it matter?)']. Admittedly, the stakes are far lower for Raczymow as a non-Israeli than for Bouganim as a long-term Israeli citizen. Finally, it is significant that in *Mon cœur de père* (2012) Marco Koskas is not only unperturbed by hybridization but positively celebrates it, pushing back the already fluid cultural and ethnic boundaries of a Levantinized Israel even further, to sub-Saharan Africa:

Gare routière de Tel-Aviv. Images traditionnelles d'Israël avec tou(te)s ces jeunes soldats(es), Uzi en bandoulière, qui regagnent leurs bases après shabbat; mélange incroyable de morphotypes, avec une nouveauté me semble-t-il: on voit maintenant des filles noires, d'origine éthiopienne, sorties de leur condition de Falacha, en uniforme couleur crème de l'armée de l'air. On en voit aussi dans les rues de Tel-Aviv en short Dolce Gabana, avec le port de tête princier qui les caractérise. (33)

[A Tel Aviv coach station. Traditional images of Israel with all those young male and female soldiers, Uzis slung across their shoulders, going back to base after Shabbat; an incredible mix of morphotypes, with something new, it seems to me: now you see black girls, of Ethiopian origin, who've left behind their Falacha condition, in the cream-coloured uniform of the airforce. You also see them in the streets of Tel Aviv wearing Dolce Gabana shorts, with that regal carriage of the head that typifies them]

His tableau of a richly multiracial Israeli society intersects with Marty's observation cited above (2003, 71). However, such openness to cultural and ethnic fluidity among Jews in Israel is the antithesis of the next section's focus.

3.3. Anti-Sephardic/anti-Mizrahi racism and protest against it

It has been established above that during the first three decades of its existence, Israel was dominated by an Ashkenazic elite who regarded Sephardic and Mizrahi Jews as inferior Jews.[6] The historical reality of this intra-ethnic racism, which has been extensively documented by cultural studies specialist Ella Shohat,[7] is reflected in a number of the primary texts, the first being Ania Francos's *Les Palestiniens* (1968). In reporting the words of an Arab Israeli, Francos might not have chosen the most immediately persuasive of sources, given the bias that many readers will assume against Jewish dominance generally in the geopolitical entity formerly known as Palestine. What cannot be denied is that his account correlates with that of many Francophone Jewish writers:

> Les Juifs d'Europe dominent le pays, ensuite viennent les Juifs d'Afrique du Nord ou du Moyen-Orient qu'on appelle « les Juifs noirs » qui font tous les travaux subalternes, n'ont aucune responsabilité politique ou militaire, et ont parfois même des difficultés pour habiter dans les quartiers résidentiels où vivent « les aristocrates Askenaz ». Il me dit que les étudiants juifs des pays arabes ne peuvent presque jamais trouver des chambres chez les particuliers à Tel-Aviv. (269)

> [The European Jews dominate the country, next come the Jews of North Africa or the Middle East who are called 'black Jews' and do all the menial jobs, have no political or military responsibility, and sometimes even face problems finding accommodation in the residential areas where 'the Ashkenazi aristocrats' live. He tells me that Jewish students from Arab countries can hardly ever find a room in privately owned Tel Aviv properties]

Francos supplements this indictment with her own eyewitness account of intra-ethnic racism among European Jews:

> Je connais bien le racisme des Juifs polonais ou russes vis-à-vis des 'Nëger'; il existe même en France, vis-à-vis des rapatriés d'Afrique du Nord qu'on appelle les 'Arabes' (269)

> [I'm very familiar with the racism of Polish or Russian Jews towards the 'Niggers'; it even exists in France, towards the North African repatriates whom people call 'Arabs']

Her Arab interlocutor's parallel between the subaltern status of Sephardic/Mizrahi Jews in Israel and that of Blacks in Western countries recurs in Marc Hillel's *Les Oranges de Jaffa* (1981). It first appears in the hesitating admission of a Maghrebi immigrant to Israel: 'Je ne veux pas être une … noire, comme on appelle là-bas les juifs orientaux. Noir par rapport à ceux venus d'Europe …' (71) ['I don't want to be a … Black, as they call eastern Jews back there. Black compared to those who come from Europe …']. It is reinforced by the litotic final sentence in the following statement on Maghrebi Jews who are about to emigrate to Israel, not through a positive choice, but for lack of any other option: 'Ce pays pourtant leur faisait peur. Les Nord-Africains n'y étaient pas très bien vus' (85) ['Yet this country frightened them. North Africans were not viewed favourably there']. A further passage more starkly exposes the racist pecking order of Israel's biopolitics:

> Avec les Polonais, les Roumains, les Tchèques, bref, les Européens, les choses n'allaient pas aussi facilement qu'avec mes malheureux Nord-Africains. Chacun connaissait quelqu'un qui connaissait quelqu'un … ce qui fait que les villes, aujourd'hui, sont peuplées de juifs blancs alors que les campagnes, les déserts, les villages-frontières sont surtout le lot des « noirs ». (97)

> [With the Poles, the Romanians, the Czechs, in short, the Europeans, things weren't as easy as with the unfortunate North Africans. Everyone knew somebody who knew somebody … Which means that today the towns are populated by white Jews while the countryside, the deserts, the frontier-villages are mostly the fate of the 'Blacks']

A later passage stresses the racist and exclusionary policies of the ruling Ashkenazi elite in Israel, of whom Mizrone, of German origin, is an egregious example.

> Mizrone, qui souffrait, comme tous les Israéliens rencontrés jusqu'ici, à l'exception toutefois de Shlomo, de « propagandite », se lança dans un intarissable monologue. Il fut question de Marocains troglodytes qui habitaient maintenant de vraies villas, de juifs malingres amenés à bord d'un tapis magique et qui s'étaient bien adaptés aux travaux de la terre, et même de juifs noirs, vraiment noirs de peau, qui se prenaient pour les fils d'Israël mais que les rabbins hésitaient à reconnaître comme tels. (134–35)

> [Mizrone, who like all the Israelis met so far, with the exception of Shlomo, suffered from 'propaganditis', launched into an endless monologue. It was about cave-dwelling Moroccans who now lived in proper houses, about sickly Jews brought over on a magic carpet and who had adapted well to working the soil, and even black Jews, really black-skinned Jews, who considered themselves sons of Israel but whom the rabbis were reluctant to recognize as such]

This exposes the Ashkenazi view that Moroccan Jews are basely primitive (with the slur of 'troglodytes' recurring on page 213 to describe an Ashkenazi nurse's view of how at least some Moroccans and Yemenis live in their countries of origin). It also reveals the prejudice of Ashkenazi rabbis against literally black Jews, whose Jewishness they would rather not recognize, and implies through use of the neologism 'propagandite' that such racist and exclusionary propaganda is a form of pathology. A later appeal made to the French Jew Pierre, which asserts a commonality between French and North African immigrants based on their shared Francophony, expresses the North Africans' fierce resentment at the inferior conditions imposed upon them by the Israeli authorities:

> Tu es Français, nous sommes d'Afrique du Nord, c'est la même chose. Ce que nous voulons, c'est nous faire entendre, nous voulons qu'on parle de nous parce que nous sommes les moins bien logés de tous les immigrants. Les tâches difficiles, les villages à la frontière, c'est pour nous (173)

> [You're French, we're from North Africa, it comes down to the same thing. What we want is to be heard, we want people to talk about us because we get the worst housing of all the immigrants. The hard jobs, the frontier villages, that's for us]

The most extreme form of racist prejudice against literally black Jews laid bare in Hillel's *Les Oranges de Jaffa* also features in Marco Koskas's *Destino* (1981). Commenting on the political efforts of Lynda to bring the plight of Ethiopian Jews to the attention of the Israeli government, the narrator conveys that government's dismissiveness: '« Qu'allons-nous faire de tous ces Noirs? »' (107) ['What are we going to do with all those Blacks?']. Ami Bouganim's *Le cri de l'arbre* (1983), however, returns to racism against Moroccan immigrants in Israel. Emphasis is placed upon their sense of humiliation, both at being treated as potentially flea-ridden and/or pestiferous upon arrival in Israel (5) and at their general sense of having been lied to by the Agence Juive: 'Une villa, qu'ils promettaient, et par famille. D'une villa, le baraquement n'était qu'une caricature' (10) ['A house, that's what they promised, and one for every family. The hut was a mere caricature of a house']. As in other works discussed above, the Ashkenazi governing class's view of them as a primitive people is relayed, and to the slur of primitivism is added potential criminality (18). Again the lexical field of blackness is mobilized, reinforcing the point that literally black Jews become the point of comparison when the intent is to insult the Moroccans (the latter being of darker complexion than the Ashkenazi, but not literally black). Thus, the supreme insult is 'Hija de la negra!' (28) ['Child of the Negress!']. The Moroccans play metaphorically on the word 'Negro' to decry their subaltern status: 'Nous sommes tous devenus des nègres' (28) ['We've all become Niggers']. Tapping into the network of associations in anti-black racism, they assert awareness of being regarded as primitive animals (33). Segregationist America is evoked:

> Ils vouaient la même passion à leur peuple, nourrissaient la même rancune à l'égard des autorités israéliennes, coupables, selon eux, d'encourager la ségrégation dont étaient victimes les Marocains (62)

> [They devoted the same passion to their people, harboured the same grudge against the Israeli authorities, who they believed were guilty of encouraging the segregation that victimized Moroccans]

In another implicit parallel with America, the Moroccans sardonically identify themselves with an even earlier group of non-Westerners oppressed and exploited by white Anglophone settlers: the Native Americans (150).

Whilst the dominant Moroccan reaction to such racism as relayed in Bouganim's *Le cri de l'arbre* is verbal expression of grievance, this novel does allude to more violent and politically agentic reaction: the Wadi Salib riots (85). These consisted in serial street demonstrations and acts of vandalism which broke out in 1959 in the Wadi Salib neighbourhood of Haifa, triggered by anger about ethnic discrimination against Mizrahi Jews. There is an eerie parallel here with the triggering factor of the riots of 2005 in Paris: police pursuit of three young men from an ethnic and religious minority, in the French case Arab Muslim, one of whom died attempting to escape, which sparked violent riots first at the site of the incident, then spreading to the rest of the country. The Wadi Salib riots were on a smaller scale, but nonetheless remarkable in Israeli history as evidence of violent reaction from a socioeconomic underclass to a state apparatus – the police. What happened in Israel was that on 9 July 1959, Israeli police shot and seriously injured a Wadi Salib resident, Yaakov Elkarif, who was drunk and creating a disturbance. This unleashed unlawful protest (including the car burning that was to feature so prominently in the French *banlieue* riots of 2005) by several hundred other Wadi Salib residents the following morning. On 11 July, further riots occurred in other parts of Israel, notably areas home to large numbers of Maghrebi immigrants, such as Tiberias, Beersheba and Migdal HaEmek. The seriality of the riots is emphasized in *Le cri de l'arbre* by radio reports 'heure après heure' ('hour after hour') that '« de graves incidents avaient éclaté entre les forces de l'ordre et des fauteurs de troubles écervelés à Kiriat Azouva, dans la banlieue de Haïfa »' (172) ['serious incidents had erupted between the forces of order and hare-brained troublemakers in Kiriat Azouva, in the Haifa suburbs']. The North African immigrants involved in these riots were branded as criminals; more seriously, their criminality became a metonymy for North African immigrants in general. This is reflected in *Le cri de l'arbre* by a bitter remark from the Moroccan immigrants: 'Au train où vont les choses, tous les Marocains se doteront bientôt de casiers judiciaires' (113) ['At this rate, all the Moroccans will soon acquire a criminal record']. Their acute sense of the Ashkenazi's contempt for them is contrasted with an alleged lack of such contempt back in Arab-dominated Morocco:

Seigneur, ce mépris! Inconnu en Orient, absent dans un mellah.[8] Une création achkénaze. Gouverner par le mépris, c'était ce que les vouz avaient emprunté à l'Occident pour venir à bout des « impulsions primitives » des Marocains (123–24)

[Lord, that contempt! Unknown in the Orient, absent from a *mellah*. An Ashkenazi creation. The Ashkenazim in Israel had borrowed governing with contempt from the West to overcome the 'primitive urges' of the Moroccans]

It is significant that the Ashkenazi mode of government by disdain is framed as slavish imitation of Western modes of biopolitical control. Later on, the previous assertion that there was no such disdain from the Arab majority back in the Maghreb is contradicted, but Arab disdain is remembered as having been far less extreme and less insulting than the Ashkenazi strain:

Constructions sauvages, instincts primitifs, mentalité d'arriérés, quel jargon! Les Arabes n'avaient jamais poussé leur mépris des Juifs jusqu'à les taxer de sauvages, ah non, jamais! (149)

[Savage constructions, primitive instincts, backward mentality. What jargon! The Arabs had never taken their contempt for Jews as far as calling them primitive, oh no, never!]

Bouganim's novel echoes Francos's statement about Algerian Jews in France being injuriously called Arabs (Francos, 1968, 269). The difference is that Bouganim's novel underlines the irony – given the long-standing tensions between Jews and Arabs in the Maghreb – of this conflation, and reveals a process whereby the Jew's hatred of the Arab (induced by

Arab military aggression and nationalist frenzy), as it is internalized, morphs into the 'oriental' Jew's self-hatred (171). A more diffuse form of irony occurs later, when the European elite's discrimination against North African immigrants in Israel is located in a historical context of European Jews' former social degradation in the ghettos, surrounded by a Christian majority just as contemptuous of them (195). Yet another form of irony, this time darkly humorous, lurks in the response given to the passionate warning issued in French by Madame Solange (a rare French woman within the diegesis) against virtual civil war in Israel if abuses of Ashkenazi power continue to perpetuate what she colourfully figures as a racist Hydra (196–97). The response is blunt and bathetic: 'Je ne comprends pas le français, déclare le fonctionnaire' (197) ['"I don't understand French", said the government official']. Here, the language barrier is not linguistic but ideological, and the government official's professed ignorance of French – which may well have been genuine – does not hide his closure to communication, since he could easily have had recourse to an interpreter. Quite simply, the representative of the Israeli state does not want to hear accusations of his state's segregationist biopolitics.

Yet *Le cri de l'arbre* is no monochrome diatribe. It does illustrate one mitigating factor in the Ashkenazi elite's unjust treatment of Israel's new Sephardic citizens:

> – Tu insultes l'Etat d'Israël, s'indigne le fonctionnaire, et il en bégaie de fureur. Qu'avez-vous fait, toi et tes semblables, pour la création de cet Etat que tu profanes en prononçant des paroles criminelles, dignes d'un Arabe? Quels sacrifices avez-vous consentis, quels efforts avec-vous investis, quels dangers avez-vous affrontés? Où étiez-vous quand bravant la malaria et les pillards arabes, les premiers pionniers assainissaient le marais, déblayaient la pierraille, fertilisaient le désert? Nous vous avons sortis de vos taudis pour vous transplanter sur une terre conquise par le sang, les larmes et la sueur de plusieurs générations d'hommes et de femmes épris de liberté. Où étiez-vous alors? (198)

> ['You insult the state of Israel', exclaimed the government official indignantly, and he was stuttering with fury about it. 'What did you do, you and your like, for the creation of this state that you defile by your criminal words worthy of an Arab? What sacrifices did you consent to, what efforts did you invest, what dangers did you confront? Where were you when, braving malaria and Arab pillaging, the first pioneers were draining the marshes, clearing the loose stones, fertilizing the desert? We brought you out of your hovels to transplant you to a land conquered by

the blood, sweat and tears of several generations of men and women in love with freedom. Where were you then?']

Here there is passion equal to if not more intense than that of Madame Solange (the Moroccan immigrants' spokeswoman), fuelled by the rancour of Ashkenazi Israelis against the North African newcomers who had contributed nothing to the Herculean heroism (see Chapter 1) of the Yishuv. In symmetry, and arguably with poetic justice, this passionate portrait of the pioneers also falls on deaf ears: 'Il nous sert « l'épopée du pionnier », répond Elkémar d'un air entendu, vous devez la connaître par cœur' (198) ['He's giving us the "pioneer epic" number', replied Elkémar with a knowing look. 'You must know it by heart']. Elkémar's cynicism is expansive and instructive. It denounces the Israeli government's priorities of supporting the socialist-based *kibbutzim*, executing ambitious public projects and giving support to the third world outside its national borders, all the while relegating its own Sephardim/Mizrahim to the status of, if not the third world (*pace* Shohat, 40), then of second-class citizens (199). In a powerfully poetic passage, the eponymous cry of the tree prophesies violent revolt on the part of these second-class citizens such that the very foundations of Israel will shake. While the tenor is poetic, the contemporary referents are material – the riots of Wadi Salib, and the implied complicity of the Maghrebi immigrants in their own pathetic pacification:

> Les émeutes de Wadi-Salib vous ont plus indignés qu'émus; quelques villas pour les meneurs, quelques kiosques aussi où brader leur vie, et la révolte était étouffée. Mais un jour viendra, et il n'est peut-être pas loin, où les enfants des femmes et des hommes que vous avez humiliés bruiront d'une telle violence que les fondements d'Israël trembleront. (211)

> [The Wadi Salib riots angered you more than they moved you; a few houses for the ringleaders, a few kiosks too where they could sacrifice their lives, and the revolt was nipped in the bud. But a day will come, and maybe it's not far off, when the murmurs of the children of the women and men you've humiliated will be so violent that the foundations of Israel will tremble]

Indeed, the sterile quietism of the Moroccans decried by the symbolic tree's cry does nothing to better their lot, and the government minister and civil servant leave their visit only with intensified disgust at the Moroccans' undignified emotionality and the sight of an epileptic Moroccan falling at the minister's feet: 'Les yeux révulsés de dégoût du ministre, le sourire narquois du fonctionnaire. Ces Marocains, décidément, ils sont atteints de toutes les tares' (213) ['The minister's eyes rolled in disgust, the government official's mocking smile. Those Moroccans, really, they've got all the defects'].

Ashkenazi disrespect for Moroccans is also depicted colourfully in Paula Jacques's *Un baiser froid comme la lune* (1983), whose temporal diegesis is roughly equivalent to that of Bouganim's *Le cri de l'arbre* (late 1950s/early 1960s):

> Dans le bas-quartier de Haiffa, réservé à une calamiteuse population, un automobiliste, juif de Russie, avait éconduit un auto-stoppeur en ces termes : « Pas de racaille marocaine dans ma voiture! » (246–47)

> [In the poorer parts of Haifa, reserved for a disastrous population, a Russian Jewish driver had turned away a hitchhiker with these words: 'No Moroccan rabble in my car!']

As with the Wadi Salib riots, there is an uncanny proleptic parallel with the Parisian riots of 2005, whose instigators – this time largely of Arab origin – were dubbed 'racaille' by the then Minister of the Interior Nicolas Sarkozy. Jacques's novel too evokes Moroccan demonstrations against Ashkenazim, but here the effect is one of unsympathetic burlesque:

> Un canari, marocain, tomba raide mort dans sa cage. Le propriétaire de l'oiseau entraîna ses clients échauffés. Les manifestants allèrent, à la manière arabe, lapider les riches demeures des Ashkenazes du mont Carmel (247)

> [A Moroccan canary dropped dead in its cage. The owner of the bird swept his heated customers along with him. The demonstrators went off, Arab-fashion, to throw stones at the rich Ashkenazi houses of Mount Carmel]

Nonetheless, the succeeding sentence, for all its archness (patent in the capitalization of 'Sages'), does directly identify social inequalities and governmental awareness of them:

> Le Gouvernement s'en émut. Il désigna une commission de Sages chargés d'enquêter sur « le malaise culturel » et les inégalités sociales frappant particulièrement les Olim[9] du bassin méditerranéen (247)

> [The government was concerned. It chose a commission of Wise Men charged with investigating the 'cultural unrest' and the social inequalities hitting immigrants from the Mediterranean Basin particularly]

What follows also reflects a greater degree of constructive political action on the part of the 'Oriental Jews':

Ils organisèrent leur propre comité. Ils distribuèrent des tracts dénonçant les promesses non tenues, les habitations insalubres, leurs conditions de sous-prolétaires, la discrimination scolaire visant leurs enfants. [...] Enfin un meeting appela la communauté, spoliée de ses droits par le pouvoir sinon par la constitution, à se soulever contre le Parlement et l'État ashkenazes. (247)

[They organized their own committee. They distributed tracts denouncing the unfulfilled promises, the housing unfit for habitation, their condition as sub-proletarians, the schools' discrimination targeting their children. [...] Finally a meeting called on the community, which had been despoiled of its rights by the powers that be, if not by the constitution, to rise up against the Ashkenazi Parliament and state]

Jacques's novel introduces yet another degree of granularity to intra-ethnic Jewish racism. When the Ashkenazi Judith tells the Egyptian-born Tobias that the Sephardim are right to revolt, he is concerned only to distinguish between Sephardic and Mizrahi Jews: 'Vous autres, prenez tous les Juifs d'Orient pour des Sépharades, dit Tobias. C'est comme si je confondais le caviar et la confiture de mûres' (247) ['"You lot, you take all Eastern Jews to be Sephardim", said Tobias. "It's as if I were to confuse caviar with bramble jam"']. His gustatory simile comically but clearly asserts a hierarchy, according to which the Mizrahi (the caviar) are far superior to the Sephardi (the bramble jam). His fine distinctions are lost on the Ashkenazi Judith, who simply lumps all oriental Jews together as equally hysterical (248).

From Bouganim's mixed economy of humour and tragic portent and Jacques's amusing but stinging satire, we move to an altogether more pensive tone in *Les jours innocents* (1984). Via third-person narrative, Jean-Luc Allouche records his identification as a Jew of Algerian origin who had lived a good part of his young life in France with the 'clan' (76) of Maghrebi immigrants to Israel. He too uses the symbolic lexicon of whiteness to designate Ashkenazi supremacy and blackness to designate Maghrebi subalternity – an ideological schema which politicizes the younger Maghrebi immigrants. Yet the fact that he has lived most of his life in a Western country, France, excludes him from integration in their social group, which spurns all Western influence:

Il accompagna, un court moment, la révolte de leurs fils, qui se voulaient noirs autant que leurs dominateurs se voulaient blancs, lui que son passage par la France mettait à l'abri et rangeait parmi les « Occidentaux » acharnés à décalquer dans ce bout d'Orient les fastes présumés de la vieille Europe et de l'entreprenante Amérique. (76)

[For a short while he supported the revolt of their sons, who liked to consider themselves black as much as their rulers liked to consider themselves white, his passage through France shielding and placing him among the 'Westerners' desperate to copy in this little bit of the Orient the presumed splendour of old Europe and enterprising America]

Whilst the older generation of original Maghrebi immigrants has lost all will to struggle, reduced by Israel to the state of 'sous-prolétaires épuisés, dépossédés d'eux-mêmes et de leur mémoire' (76) ['exhausted sub-proletarians, dispossessed of themselves and of their memory'], the younger generation is filled with rancour and antisocial impulses, exemplified by the aggressive yet poignant words of one young man:

> « Je vis ici depuis toujours, mais je me sens étranger. « Eux », les « Blancs », ils ont tout. Mon père s'est usé à nourrir huit gosses … Pourquoi veux-tu que je devienne comme lui? Pour moi, deux solutions: la rue et la prison, la prison et la rue (77)

> [I've always lived here, but I feel like a foreigner. 'They', the 'Whites', they have everything. My father wore himself out providing for eight kids … Why should I become like him? For me, there are two solutions: living on the streets and prison, prison and living on the streets]

In a vicious circle, this victim of racism himself deploys stigmatizing language against the 'white' Ashkenazi elite who have exploited his father and all other Maghrebi immigrants (77).

Such intra-ethnic conflict in Israel is evoked only once, but tellingly, in Emmanuel Moses's *Papernik* (1992), a novel which takes us forward into the late 1980s. The eponymous Papernik is an Israeli patriot horrified by French vilification of his country's politics, whereas his wife Eva is a lawyer well known for defending Palestinians. However, for all her conscious and official opposition to the racism she perceives Israel as exercising against the latter, she herself is hardly innocent of racist snobbery – against non-Ashkenazi Jews:

> ils étaient kurdes, qui faisaient qu'elle les considérait, de même que tous les Sépharades, comme des Juifs arabisés ou plutôt comme des Arabes judaïsés alors qu'elle tirait vanité de ses racines, tenant la communauté juive hongroise pour l'essence même et l'aboutissement du judaïsme véritable (177)

> [they were Kurds, which meant she considered them, like all Sephardim, to be Arabized Jews or rather like Judaized Arabs, whereas she prided herself on her roots, seeing the Hungarian Jewish community as the very essence and culmination of true Judaism]

Eliette Abécassis's *Sépharade* (2009) also reflects the perversities of intra-ethnic discrimination, this time in a form of inverted racism on the part of left-wing Ashkenazi Israelis:

> Ensuite, il y eut l'Israélien de gauche, rencontré lors d'un séjour linguistique en Israël qui ignorait tout de la religion mais était enthousiaste à l'idée de sortir avec une juive marocaine, ce qui est très correct chez les Israéliens de gauche, les *yekke*, d'origine allemande comme lui, étant donné qu'en Israël les juifs marocains forment le nid du prolétariat, la classe inferieure. (52)

> [Then there was the left-wing Israeli met during a language trip to Israel who knew nothing about religions but was enthused by the idea of going out with a Moroccan Jewish woman, which was very much the done thing among left-wing Israelis, the *yekke*, of German origin like him, given that in Israel Moroccan Jews form the core of the proletariat, the lower class]

Here the inverted racism stems from a political correctness that is ultimately patronizing towards the Moroccan 'underclass', who are treated as a lumpen ethnic proletariat to be privileged by association with a superior demographic. Such inverted racism is, though, small beer compared to the historically anterior variant of blatant racist prejudice against Moroccan immigrants to Israel that is also inscribed in *Sépharade* (177). Ashkenazi fear of contamination by oriental Jews deemed too proximate in their culture to the Arab enemy is directly imputed to the first and fourth of Israel's prime ministers, David Ben Gurion and Golda Meir respectively:

> Ben Gourion, qui détestait les juifs du Maroc, disait qu'ils n'avaient aucune éducation et que leurs mœurs étaient celles des Arabes. « Le juif du Maroc, professait-il, a beaucoup emprunté à l'Arabe marocain et je ne vois pas ce que nous pourrions apprendre des Arabes marocains. Je ne voudrais pas de la culture marocaine ici. » Il y avait aussi la fameuse phrase de Golda Meir: « Ceux-là, ils confondent leur pyjama avec un drapeau. » On parlait de *Maroco sakin*, « Marocain au couteau », et les juifs marocains étaient surnommés les *Shehorim*, « les Noirs », par opposition, bien sûr, aux Blancs. (177)

> [Ben Gurion, who loathed Moroccan Jews, said that they were ill-mannered and that their customs were those of the Arabs. 'The Moroccan Jew', he declared, 'has borrowed a lot from the Moroccan Arab and I don't see what we could learn from Moroccan Arabs. I don't want Moroccan culture here'. There was also Golda Meir's famous sentence: 'That lot confuse their pyjamas with a flag'. There was talk of

Maroco sakin, the 'knife-wielding Moroccan', and Moroccan Jews were nicknamed *Shehorim*, 'Blacks', in contrast, of course, with Whites]

The last five clauses of this extract reinforce what has pervaded the texts discussed earlier: the isomorphism of racism against Blacks in Western countries, particularly America, and the racism of Ashkenazi Israelis against North African, particularly Moroccan, Jews in Israel.

Many of Bouganim's points about the stigmatizing treatment of Moroccan immigrants to Israel are reprised in *Sépharade*. One is the shame they were made to feel about their cultural identity when they arrived in the 1950s (178). Another is their relegation to remote desert sites, where they were housed in mere tents (177). But there is fresh material too in *Sépharade*. The reader learns that this relegation was part of a calculated governmental strategy to exploit the immigrants' labour through their fertilization of the Negev Desert and construction of roads and houses within it (178). S/he also discovers that when Ashkenazi immigrants arrived they were housed in the new accommodation built by the North African proletariat, while the latter remained in their primitive huts (178–79). Although the Wadi Salib riots alluded to, if not actually named as such (179), have been evoked by Bouganim, what is new in *Sépharade* is mention of the militant Mizrahi group the Panthères noires (179), which Isaac joins along with other young Moroccan immigrants, 'marginalisés à la suite d'échecs scolaires' (179) ['marginalized after their school failures']. The Panthères noires also make a cameo appearance in Henri Raczymow's *Eretz* (2010), where their extreme disaffection is plain in the potential elision of their oppression and that of the Palestinians:

> mon frère s'acoquina avec les « Panthères noires », ces jeunes du Maroc qui refusaient de n'être ici que chair à canon et main-d'œuvre corvéable à merci, qui appelaient à manifester malgré la police qui chargeait à cheval, dont certains, même, étaient prêts à prendre langue avec les Palestiniens des territoires occupés. (130)

> [my brother teamed up with the 'Black Panthers', those Moroccan youths who refused to be just cannon fodder and labour to be ruthlessly exploited here, who called for demonstrations despite the police charging on horseback, and among whom were some who were even prepared to make contact with the Palestinians of the Occupied Territories]

As *The Jewish Week* observes, 'For nearly two years, beginning in 1971, a Mizrahi group called the Black Panthers, modelled on the black movement in America, began what many today regard as the beginning of Mizrahi civil rights' (Herschthal). However, their tactics were rather too strong-arm for many, as *The Jewish Week* goes on to indicate:

> Many Ashkenazi and Mizrahi Jews in Israel today regard the Black Panthers as violent hooligans whose implosion after only two years indicates their lack of popular support. Mizrahim have been better served, critics argue, by parties like Shas, the religious Sephardic party, which are willing to work within the system. (Herschthal)

The Jewish Week's mention of the Shas, an extreme right-wing party, and its appeal to the oppressed Mizrahim finds a counterpart in *Sépharade* (although, as its title makes clear, this novel depicts Sephardim rather than Mizrahim, the former are regarded as part of the latter in some definitions):[10] 'C'est quoi l'âme sépharade, en Israël? Les rabbins et les personnalités politiques de droite et d'extrême droite' (184) ['What is the Sephardic soul, in Israel? Rabbis and political personalities of the right or extreme right']. On the next page, the Shas party is explicitly mentioned, and its strong Moroccan contingent emphasized by Isaac: 'Nous avons le parti Shass, composé de nombreux rabbins originaires du Maroc' (185) ['We have the Shas party, made up of numerous rabbis of Moroccan origin']. Isaac also proudly mentions the leader of the Shas party: 'Notre leader s'appelle Ovadia Yossef, c'est un penseur' (185) ['Our leader is called Ovadia Yossef, he's a thinker']. What is not mentioned here is that the views of Ovadia Yossef, a former Sephardi Chief Rabbi of Israel, could be highly offensive, as when he declared that the victims of the Shoah, who were overwhelmingly Ashkenazi, had been reincarnations of 'bad' Jews.[11]

Mutual hostility between Sephardim/Mizrahim and Ashkenazim in Israel is also narrativized in Sebban's *La terre promise, pas encore* (2002), where Rav[12] Binyamin proclaims balefully:

> – La paix avec les Arabes, c'est pas un problème. On finira bien par faire la paix avec eux. On leur filera deux ou trois bouts de terrain. On se fera une petite guerre de plus pour Jérusalem, et puis ça sera fini. C'est avec nous qu'ils ne feront jamais la paix, les ashkénazes. Ils préfèrent faire la paix avec les Palestiniens que faire la paix avec les séfarades. Ils nous ont toujours pris pour des primitifs, c'est pas demain que ça va changer. Ils ont la haine contre nous, et beaucoup plus que tu le crois. (60)

> [Peace with the Arabs, that's not a problem. We'll certainly end up making peace with them. We'll give them two or three patches of land. We'll have one more little war for Jerusalem, and then it'll all be over. It's with us that the Ashkenazim will never make peace. They prefer to make

peace with the Palestinians than to make peace with the Sephardim. They've always taken us for primitives, that's not going to change any time soon. They hate us, and much more than you think]

In *Sur la frontière* (2002), Michel Warschawski posits the confluence of religious Jews and Eastern Jews (including those of Indian, Kurdish and Persian origin) suffering from social exclusion into a right-wing political formation – consummately exemplified by the Shas – as resulting from the failure of either group to meet the criteria of the 'New Jew' ideal that was coeval with the founding of the state of Israel and its modern Zionism (223). Warschawski's text also reveals disturbing details redolent of Australia's Aborigine scandal: 'Les familles yéménites n'ont pas oublié les enfants qu'on leur a enlevés dans les années 50 pour les donner en adoption à des familles ashkénazes' (225) ['The Yemeni families haven't forgotten the children who were taken away from them in the 1950s to be adopted by Ashkenazi families']. Further, he extends to Iraqi Jewish immigrants (226) the humiliating experience of delousing upon arrival in Israel, which *Le cri de l'arbre* had shown being inflicted on Moroccan immigrants (Bouganim, 1983, 5). But Warschawski concurs with the other authors considered above in imputing Ashkenazi contempt to Moroccan Jewish immigrants particularly: 'Les Marocains, surtout, n'oublient ni ne pardonnent le mépris dont ils ont été l'objet' (226) ['The Moroccans, especially, neither forget nor forgive the contempt in which they were held']. The use of 'surtout' is ambiguous, but seems to imply that of all the forms of maltreatment meted out to Mizrahi immigrants generally in Israel, this was the most enduringly traumatic. It was certainly the most politically significant in its long-term effects for, as Warschawski goes on to state, one of the reasons Moroccan Jews rallied around the right-wing Begin was that he did not scorn them (226). The other reason was that he was, like the majority of them, a religious Jew. These two factors – the absence of contempt for Moroccan immigrants, and the absence of contempt for religious Jews – is also the reason Warschawski advances for the eventual electoral victory of the right over the socialists (in 1977) (226). Eight years later, in *Eretz* (2010), Henri Raczymow broadly echoes Warschawski's point: 'les travaillistes avaient été chassés un jour du pouvoir au profit du Likoud de Begin par le vote protestataire du « petit peuple sépharade »' (141) ['Labour was one day driven from power, losing ground to Begin's Likud, by the protest vote of the "little Sephardic people"']. This ostensibly counterintuitive rejection of the left by a deprived and exploited underclass and that underclass's support for the right are explored in greater detail in the next section.

3.4. Convergence of oppressed working-class Sephardim/Mizrahim with the political right

Bouganim's *Le cri de l'arbre* (1983) is the first of our primary texts to touch on this convergence. This he does in characteristically ironic and sardonic vein:

> Elkémar ne pouvait alors se douter qu'une quinzaine d'années plus tard, les Marocains, surtout eux, porteraient au pouvoir le plus vouz des vouz, le plus morbide d'entre eux, et que les plus exaltés scanderaient sur un air vengeur: « Begin, Roi d'Israël! » (97)

> [Elkémar couldn't have guessed then that some fifteen years later, the Moroccans, they above all, would bring to power the most Ashkenazic of the Ashkenazim, the most morbid of them all, and that the most excited among them would chant vengefully 'Begin, King of Israel!']

The founder of Likud in 1973 and Israel's sixth prime minister from 1977 to 1983, Menachem Begin was of (Russian) Ashkenazi origin, but strategically gathered mass electoral support from disaffected Sephardim and Mizrahim as well as from religious Jews.[13] Warschawski's tone in *Sur la frontière* (2002) is more sober than Bouganim's but makes the same point about this unexpected political development, and elaborates on it helpfully (223). Warschawski gives a clear exposition of the reasons for Begin's ascent to power in 1977, and extends his analysis to the continuing support of at least religious Jews for the right-wing Benjamin Netanyahu, who became leader of Likud in 1993, then prime minister from 1996 to 1999, and again in 2009:

> Les Juifs marocains ont aimé Begin, non seulement parce qu'il ne les méprisait pas, mais aussi parce qu'il allait à la synagogue et savait citer les textes sacrés; les religieux ont respecté Netanyahu parce que son courant politique n'a jamais exprimé publiquement de mépris face à la tradition. C'est ainsi que religieux et Juifs arabes ont pris le pouvoir des mains des travaillistes pour le donner à la droite. (226)

> [The Moroccan Jews loved Begin, not only because he didn't look down on them, but also because he went to synagogue and could quote the sacred texts; the religious respected Netanyahu because his political movement never publicly expressed contempt for tradition. This is how religious and Arab Jews took power from the hands of Labour to give it to the right]

An important point here is the rejection of the left and support for the right by both an ethnically oppressed class – the Sephardim/Mizrahim

– and a religious class that felt marginalized by the secular ethos of Israel's governing class until the late 1970s. Of course, in many cases this specific ethnicity and religious observance were found in the same individual. More arresting, perhaps, is the recurring *topos* of contempt, and the key point for section 3.4's purview is that Begin differed from Ashkenazi type in not looking down upon Moroccan Jews. Eliette Abécassis's *Sépharade* (2009) also stresses the signal importance of the dignity which the rise of the right in Israel restored to Sephardic Jews (she limits herself to the latter, but the same was true extradiegetically of Mizrahi Jews): 'Lorsque la droite l'avait emporté en Israël, portant le coup de grâce aux travaillistes au pouvoir depuis la création de l'État, les sépharades avaient enfin relevés la tête' (181) ['When the right won in Israel, giving the deathblow to Labour, which had been in power since the creation of the state, the Sephardim had at last held their heads high']; 'avec Begin, je t'assure que les choses vont changer. Maintenant, crois-moi, nous allons redresser la tête avec fierté' (181) ['with Begin, I assure you things are going to change. Now, believe me, we're going to raise our heads with pride']. And with that restored pride comes a will to avenge their humiliation at the hands of the European Ashkenazim who had previously held power:

> « Aujourd'hui, nous allons enfin régler nos comptes avec l'establishment judéo-européen. Nous avons déjà du pouvoir. Nous sommes devenus majoritaires. Nous avons un président sépharade en Israël, Itzhak Navon » (182)
>
> [Now, we're finally going to settle our scores with the Judaeo-European establishment. We already have power. We've become the majority. We have a Sephardic president in Israel, Itzhak Navon]

Despite this triumphalist tone, the Sephardim and Mizrahim did not suddenly cease to suffer from social inequalities in Israel, and their resentment of the Ashkenazim certainly did not disappear. This is starkly illustrated in the next section, which though short contains affectively explosive material.

3.5. Denial of the Shoah by some Sephardim/Mizrahim

In *Sur la frontière* (2002) Warschawski recalls a deeply disturbing memory from the 1980s. While working at a drug rehabilitation centre he was asked to organize an activity for Israel's Shoah commemoration day. Significantly, he first recalls that the vast majority of the people at the centre were Sephardim (224). This establishes the continuing social inequalities between Ashkenazim and Sephardim(/Mizrahim), since a disproportionately high number of drug addicts come from socially disadvantaged backgrounds. The enduring grievance of the Sephardim *vis-à-vis* the Ashkenazim becomes dramatically clear in an audience member's astonishing intervention some 15 minutes into Warschawski's speech:

> « Michel, tu es un type cultivé et on sait que tu n'es pas idiot. De plus on croyait vraiment que toi, tu nous respectais. Alors pourquoi nous raconter toutes ces salades sur six millions de Juifs assassinés? Ne nous dis pas que tu y crois! » La plupart des autres hochèrent la tête, d'accord avec lui. Complètement abasourdi, je répliquai: « Et toi, qu'est-ce que tu crois? » Ils m'ont répondu à l'unisson: « Les Ashkénazes veulent nous faire croire que ce sont eux les victimes et pas nous. Mais on refuse de tomber dans le panneau. » (224)

> ['Michel, you're a cultured guy and we know you're not a fool. Also, we really believed that *you* respected us. So why spin us all these yarns about six million murdered Jews? Don't tell us you believe it!' Most of the others nodded their heads, agreeing with him. Completely stunned, I retorted, 'And you, what do you believe?' They replied in unison: 'The Ashkenazim want to convince us that they're the victims and not us. But we won't fall for it']

Such negationism from Jews was not an isolated incident: it occurred year after year, even after the members of the centre had been exposed to the abundant documentary proof of the Nazi Judaeocide held at Yad Vashem (224). The Sephardim clearly felt victimization to be their own unfortunate preserve. It seems not inapt here to invoke Michael Rothberg's model of competitive memory in *Multidirectional Memory*, where different social or ethnic groups compete for recognition of their 'true' status as the worst-treated of all victims. The paradox in applying Rothberg's model to this case is that the Sephardim claimants denied the possibility of Ashkenazi memory of the Nazi Judaeocide since, according to the Sephardim, there had never been any Nazi Judaeocide to remember. Their resentment of the Ashkenazim is so intense that it blinds them to empirical evidence that Ashkenazi Jews had indeed been victims of the most infamous genocide in recorded history.

This resentment illustrates the cataclysmic affect by which relations between Israeli citizens of Eastern and Western origin have been striated. But this is not the only ethnic dichotomy registered in the primary texts.

For even within one of the two parts of the Ashkenazi–Sephardim/
Mizrahim binary, viz. the Sephardim/Mizrahim, tensions emerge
forcefully, as our next section demonstrates.

3.6. Intra-Israeli conflict between Iraqi, Iranian, Moroccan, Romanian, Spanish, Tunisian and Yemeni Jews

This further fissuring of basic Jewish ethnicity into intra-ethnic
antipathies is succinctly conveyed by a (di)stichomythic passage in
Ami Bouganim's *Le cri de l'arbre* (1983), where the interlocutors are
Moroccan immigrants to Israel:

> – Je n'ai tout de même pas quitté les Arabes pour me retrouver avec des
> Espagnols?
> – Hé, ç'aurait pu être pire! Des Roumains, par exemple, ou encore des
> Iraniens. (14)

> ['Surely I didn't leave the Arabs just to end up with Spaniards?'
> 'Hey, it could've been worse! Romanians, for example, or even
> Iranians']

This brief extract exposes the Moroccan immigrants' prejudices against
Iranian, Romanian and Spanish Jews. Shortly afterwards, the reader
discovers the Moroccans' contempt (ironically, given their own justified
resentment of Ashkenazi contempt for them) for Iraqi Jews, whom they
deem uncivilized:

> Quelque temps après, les Juifs irakiens débarquaient, vêtus de tuniques
> rayées que les âmes condescendantes originaires des pays civilisés
> assimilèrent méchamment à des pyjamas:
> – *Iraki-pyjama!* (17)

> [Some time after, the Iraqi Jews landed, wearing striped tunics that
> the condescending souls who'd come from civilized countries spitefully
> labelled pyjamas:
> 'Iraqi-pyjama!']

In the snap judgement made by the Moroccan immigrants, the new Iraqi
immigrants' arrival in attire associated with bed dress means that they
are an indolent people (18). Next in the firing line of social demotion are
Yemeni Jews, considered by the Moroccans to be naive and backward:

> Les Yéménites, eux, confirmés dans leur naïve foi par les aigles en acier
> qui s'étaient présentés un beau matin pour les transporter du rêve à la

réalité, gardaient, vaille que vaille, leur sourire mystique ... que d'anciens prirent pour le sourire béat d'enfants attardés dans l'Histoire. (18)

[As for the Yemenis, strengthened in their naïve faith by the steel eagles which had turned up one fine morning to transport them from dream to reality, somehow or other they kept their mystical smile ... which some once took to be the blissful smile of children left behind in History]

Strict ethnic demarcation operates even between the Moroccan and Tunisian immigrants, despite the fact that their countries of origin are highly proximate and they may be physically indistinguishable from each other (37; see quotation on p. 102 above).

These diverse intra-ethnic tensions, indeed hostilities, are consummately expressed in a slapstick sketch evoking the daily conflagrations between the heterogeneous community of immigrants cooped up in the 'réserve' ('reservation') that is their so-called home (64). Despite the humour, the last sentence of this sketch – 'Les querelles domestiques sont âpres entre ces déshérités de la terre promise' (64) ['Domestic quarrels are bitter among the disadvantaged of the promised land'] – drives home a sombre point. The roots of this endemic intra-ethnic strife are the socioeconomic degradation and marginalization of most non-Ashkenazi immigrants to Israel: a shared misfortune which blinds them to their shared common heritage.

Moving away from these intra-ethnic distinctions, the final section of this chapter investigates French Jewish writers' mediations of a different form of conflict among Israelis: that between settlers in the Occupied Territories and those Israelis who oppose or at the very least criticize them.

3.7. Settlers in the Occupied Territories and opposition to them

Two secondary texts provide a helpful material context for such literary mediations: Gozlan's and Pinto's. Gozlan traces the dramatic contours of internecine Israeli conflict since the 1990s:

La guerre des juifs aux juifs s'est manifestée avec un éclat noir à la face du monde, le 4 novembre 1995, avec l'assassinat du général Itzhak Rabin [...] Tué parce qu'il voulait échanger les territoires occupés depuis 1967 contre la paix avec les Palestiniens. Un mois avant le meurtre, on distribuait dans les synagogues de Jérusalem le texte d'une antique malédiction inspirée par les sectes kabbalistes (déviations constamment rejetées par le judaïsme traditionnel): « Nous demandons aux Anges du Mal de tuer le maudit Itzhak, fils de Rosa, le plus vite possible, en raison de sa malveillance envers le peuple élu. » (13–14)

[The Jew-on-Jew war became apparent to the world in a sombre explosion, on 4 November 1995, with the assassination of General Yitzhak Rabin [...]. Killed because he wanted to exchange territories occupied since 1967 for peace with the Palestinians. A month before the murder, people were distributing in Jerusalem synagogues the text of an ancient curse inspired by Kabbalist sects (deviations constantly rejected by traditional Judaism): 'We ask the Angels of Evil to kill the accursed Yitzhak, son of Rosa, as quickly as possible, because of his ill will towards the Jewish people']

Here the conflict is very clearly located between Israelis seeking peace with the Palestinians and those determined to retain the territories won in the Six-Day War of 1967, the latter being depicted as religious extremists. Gozlan's tableau should be nuanced by recognition that, while religious extremism is an important component in arguments endorsing retention of the Occupied Territories, it is not the only one. Some members of the settler community are less inspired by religion than by right-wing political ideology, as is evinced in the words Gozlan cites from a former head of Shin Bet (Israel's internal security service) in 2012, Yuval Diskin:

Les mouvements d'extrême droite sont de plus en plus violents: la menace d'assassinats politiques ne peut plus être écartée. Les extrémistes n'hésiteraient pas à tirer sur leurs frères juifs si on tentait aujourd'hui d'évacuer les colonies de Cisjordanie (15)

[The extreme-right movements are increasingly violent: the threat of political assassinations can no longer be ruled out. The extremists wouldn't hesitate to shoot their Jewish brothers if an attempt were now made to evacuate the West Bank settlements]

The interviews conducted by Gozlan provide valuable insights into views on the Occupied Territories, both of Israelis living within them (the 'settlers') and Israelis living outside them. One of the settlers interviewed is Raffi, a member of 'le Bloc de la Foi, le Goush Emounim' (Gozlan, 77) ['Bloc of the Faithful, Gush Emunim'], whose niece had been stabbed by a Palestinian and who had settled in Kedumim 'pour affirmer l'éternité des nouvelles frontières d'Israël' (Gozlan, 78) ['to assert the eternity of Israel's new frontiers']. Interestingly, Raffi was born in France, whereas his ideological opposite, Dror, was born in Israel (Gozlan, 81). For Dror, the very idea of a 'colonie' ['colony/

settlement'] is discriminatory (Gozlan, 81). On the anti-occupation side of the fence, Gozlan also mentions Hagit Ofran, codirector of 'La Paix maintenant', who has received death threats (81). Others advocating surrender of the Occupied Territories evoked by Gozlan are religious Jews for whom the sacrifice of young Israeli soldiers' lives contravenes Judaism's belief in the sanctity of life and its preservation (84). Their concerns are countered by their opponents, 'le second Israël' with the claim that Jewish lives would be in far greater danger if the settlements were abandoned (84). A proponent of this other face of Israel is Avishaï, a former member of the elite commandos of Tzahal, now director of the military *yeshiva* of Paduel that trains religious soldiers (95). His position is tightly predicated on arithmetical justice:

> On a donc décidé de montrer aux Palestiniens que plus personne ne serait tué car, désormais, les juifs seraient là. Pour chaque juif tué, il y aurait une colonie (Gozlan, 94)

> [So we decided to show the Palestinians that nobody else would be killed because, from now on, the Jews would be there. For every Jew killed, there would be a settlement]

More briefly, but illuminatingly, Pinto reports on different rationales for retaining and living in the Occupied Territories. One is identification with a reappropriated biblical past (2012, 112). Another, in sharp contrast, is linked with current economic difficulties experienced by young Israelis, who are attracted to cheaper housing in the Territories (Pinto, 2012, 158).

After the secondary texts, how do the primary texts represent the settlers and their occupation? Marco Koskas's *Destino* (1981) goes back to the very beginning of the occupation: the end of the Six-Day War in 1967, when abandonment of houses and gardens in Jericho prompted Israeli jubilation (71). An apocalyptic picture of Jericho at the time is painted through focalization on an employee at the Dead Sea Hotel, a mysterious female character who witnessed the invasion. What emerges is a tableau of the Israelis' absolute military might and triumph in occupying deserted homes:

> They came. Elle ne se souvenait pas de Lynda mais elle pouvait décrire comme si cela se passait sous ses yeux l'arrivée des soldats juifs debout sur la tourelle des tanks ou grimpés à la cime des arbres, investissant la cité en traversant ses murs, faisant ployer les portes les plus lourdes de leur seul souffle guerrier et vrillant le silence de brèves rafales qu'ils tiraient depuis les fenêtres des maisons désertées. (73)

[They came. She didn't remember Lynda but she could describe it as if it were happening before her very eyes: the arrival of Jewish soldiers standing on tank turrets or at the tops of trees they'd climbed, taking over the city by crossing its walls, making the heaviest of doors give way under their warrior breath alone and piercing the silence with brief bursts of gunfire from the windows of deserted houses]

The symbolic imprint of the Jew on the conquered territories is literalized in one striking image: 'elle se souvenait encore des soldats rampant, déterrant les cailloux qu'ils estampillaient un à un de l'étoile de David' (73–74) ['she still remembered the soldiers crawling, unearthing pebbles that they stamped one by one with the Star of David']. The most salient features of this witness bearing are the joyous, even altruistic initial mood of the victorious Israeli soldiers and the spectral, almost lunar-like silence of the land they have conquered:

> Elle [...] poursuivait son évocation par le souvenir encore vivace d'un soldat d'Israël, noir de peau, debout sur un side-car, qui appelait les sourds à venir se faire soigner l'oreille et promettait la réfection miraculeuse de leur bouche à ceux qu'un bec-de-lièvre disgraciait [...] Mais à mesure qu'ils essaimaient la ville ils en mesuraient la vacuité, rideaux de fer baissés, persiennes tirées, vitrines barbouillées. Et en même temps qu'ils se rendaient compte du silence absolu qui y régnait, l'ordre leur était donné de disséminer des postes à transistors aux quatre points cardinaux pour ranimer par la polyphonie la grande muette qu'ils avaient conquise (74)

> [She [...] carried on her reminiscence with the still vivid memory of an Israeli soldier, black-skinned, standing on a side-car, who was calling on the deaf to come and get their ears treated and promising a miraculous repair job to those rendered unsightly by a harelip [...] But as they swarmed through the town they weighed up its emptiness, metal shutters lowered, blinds drawn, windows daubed. And as they took in the absolute silence that reigned there, they were given orders to distribute transistor radios to the four points of the compass in order to bring back to life the great mute they had conquered through as much noise as possible]

Views on the settlers within the Occupied Territories from a much later period (the new millennium) are reflected in Michaël Sebban's *La terre promise, pas encore* (2002). The narrator Eli's attitude as a French, long-term though non-permanent resident of Israel is conveyed when in the Golan Heights he finds himself surrounded by a hetero-geneous group of Jews, including Haredim (ultra-Orthodox Jews), girls in miniskirts and high heels, soldiers on leave or on patrol and elderly people. The experience is intensely spiritual:

> Je les regarde flotter autour de moi et pour un instant j'oublie tout ce qui me sépare d'eux. L'agressivité qui pourrait s'emparer de leur regard s'ils se tournaient vers moi. Et je comprends, à cet instant, que je les aime (180)

> [I watch them drifting around me and for a moment I forget everything separating me from them. The aggression that could take over their gaze if they turned towards me. And I realize, at that moment, that I love them]

This sudden effusion of love from a narrator normally characterized by wryness and dryness seems to issue from a sense of ethnic cohesion with or belonging to them, of what Brubaker and Cooper might call 'groupness', even in recognition of their individual differences. Another cause, however, is the implicit pathos of their quest to find something they did not have outside the Occupied Territories:

> Comprendre pourquoi ils me ressemblent. Comment, envers et contre tout, ils vivent au rythme du sang, de la mort, et continuent de rire et de manger des glaces. C'est pour cela que j'hésite tant à rentrer en France. Je me fous éperdument de la politique. Personne ne sait ce qui se passera ici demain et j'ai choisi d'être avec eux. Ces gens qui me ressemblent, qui sont venus chercher ici ce qu'ils n'avaient pas ailleurs. Là. Sur la promenade. Ils sont tous moi. Ce sont tous des moi, différents et identiques. (181)

> [Understanding why they are like me. How, in relation to and against everything, their daily lives are dominated by blood and death, yet they continue to laugh and eat ice cream. That's why I hesitate so much about going back to France. I really couldn't give a damn about politics. Nobody knows what will happen here tomorrow and I've chosen to be with them. These people who are like me, who came here to seek out what they didn't have elsewhere. There. On the promenade. They're all me. They're all different and identical me's]

Like Sebban, Esther Orner in *Une année si ordinaire* (2004) also reflects twenty-first-century views on the occupation. While references to the Occupied Territories in this diary account of one year during the Second Intifada are few, they are affectively dense. The first stoutly defends the efforts of the military at that point in time to combat terrorism in the Territories, and relays a pathematic response to the collateral damage inevitably flowing from the situation:

> L'armée est dans les territoires en train de continuer et d'achever l'opération

« Rempart » (implicitement contre le terrorisme). Malheureusement ça ne se fait pas sans morts dans le souci de protéger les populations civiles. Et aux nouvelles comme chaque jour les horaires des enterrements. (121)

[The army is in the Territories, continuing and completing operation 'Defensive Shield' (against terrorism, though it's not spelt out). Sadly, given the concern to protect the civil populations, this can't be done without loss of life. And, like every other day, the burial times are announced on the news]

Another reference in close succession imputes murderous intent to Palestinians resisting the settlers (recalling the Palestinian stabbing of the niece of Raffi, who was interviewed by Gozlan): 'Une accalmie jusqu'à ce que Tsahal se retire des territoires et que nos cousins reconstituent leur infrastructure meurtrière' (122) ['A lull until Tzahal withdraws from the Territories and our cousins reconstitute their murderous infrastructure']. Finally, Orner depoliticizes the motives of one section at least of the settlers, those of Adora, hinting at the same sort of economic factors adduced by Pinto (2012, 158):

Les « colons » d'Adoura disaient on n'est pas venu ici pour des raisons idéologiques, mais pour le calme, la beauté du site. Et peut-être parce qu'ailleurs ils n'auraient pas pu se payer de maisonnettes (2004, 137)

[The 'settlers' of Adora say people haven't come here for ideological reasons, but for the peace, the beauty of the site. And maybe because they couldn't have afforded to buy a small house elsewhere]

No such advantages to life in the Occupied Territories feature in Michaël Sebban's *Le Cadenas du marché Yéhouda* (2008), which stresses rather its tensions and dangers. When at a checkpoint before entering Hebron he is given to understand that he should have a gun for self-defence (25), narrator Eli ponders how Jews living there manage to survive psychologically (25–26). He also renders the profound physical and mental pressures produced at the checkpoints, particularly for the soldiers obliged to staff them:

Un *checkpoint* c'est différent, parce que cela donne l'impression d'être un sas. Une cabine de décompression, un atelier de stérilisation. L'index du soldat tendu sur la gâchette, la tension permanente de ses muscles, son regard à l'affût du sac à dos qui pourrait contenir une ceinture explosive. Tous veulent partir le plus vite possible de ce foutu péage. L'horreur arrive si vite, et personne ne veut en être. (163)

[A checkpoint is different, because it feels like it's an airlock. A decompression chamber, a sterilization unit. The soldier's forefinger on the trigger, the permanent tension of his muscles, his gaze on the lookout for the rucksack that could contain an explosive belt. Everyone wants to leave this damn tollbooth as quickly as possible. Horrible things happen so quickly, and nobody wants to be caught up in them]

Henri Raczymow's *Eretz* (2010) is less rawly emotive and more forensic in approach, systematically examining the question of the Occupied Territories from various perspectives. The first is that of settlers in Gilo, five kilometres from Jerusalem, who in fact consider themselves not to be living in the Occupied Territories but rather in a post-1967 reunited and liberated Jerusalem (29). Significantly, Raczymow informs us that Gilo is home to a high proportion of Moroccan Jews (30). This could be seen to reflect the confluence of factors identified above: Moroccan immigrants' disaffection with the rest of (internationally recognized) Israel, their support for right-wing parties and ideologies, and their greater religiosity. The latter in particular is picked up on and linked with a further feature not normatively ascribed to the settlers – something akin to pacifism:

> Les gens du cru n'ont pas l'air belliqueux au demeurant. Ils paraissent même très pacifiques. Ils sont religieux, voilà tout. Orthodoxes. [...] Ce sont des gens comme vous et moi, ce ne sont pas des *haredim* (comme ceux de Jérusalem, en habits noirs et chapeau noir) (30–31)

> [The locals don't actually look hawkish. They even seem very peaceable. They're just religious, that's all. Orthodox. [...] They are people like you and me, they're not Haredim – like the men in Jerusalem, in black clothes and black hat]

While their bearing of arms may appear flagrantly to contradict pacifism, it is pointed out that these arms are intended not for attack of the enemy but defence of their own lives, lives righteously lived in the land given to them, so they believe, by god (32) – a belief also noted by Pinto above (2012, 112). A rather different slant is found in Raczymow's later observations about the people of Gilo. For if, on a micro level, they seem peaceable, on a macro level they are pessimistic about peace with the Palestinians, with whom they refuse any kind of dialogue:

> il n'empêche qu'ils ont en commun ce qu'il faut bien appeler une idéologie – ne disons pas fanatique, ne disons pas fasciste (comme on dirait en France), ce serait mal venu, disons de droite, voire d'extrême droite –, favorable au « Grand Israël », pessimistes quant à une paix possible, refusant tout dialogue avec les Palestiniens, avec les plus modérés des

Palestiniens, jugeant que c'est leur droit – droit divin! – de conserver les
« colonies. » (38–39)

[they nevertheless have in common what has to be called an ideology
– let's not say a fanatical ideology, let's not say a fascist ideology (as
would be said in France), that would be inapt; let's say a right-wing,
indeed extreme right-wing ideology – that supports 'Greater Israel',
is pessimistic about the chances of peace, rejects all dialogue with the
Palestinians, [even] with the most moderate of Palestinians, judging that
it's their right – a divine right! – to keep the 'settlements']

Diegetically recurring to the early 1970s, Raczymow sketches a historical
context of the mentality of the Occupiers as, precisely, not one of
occupation of another people's land, but of liberation of what used to
be theirs and had been confiscated by others (108; cf. Pinto, 2012, 112).
But cracks in this official mentality of righteousness are discerned in his
brother, now an Israeli citizen:

Quant à mon frère, crâne, il faisait semblant d'être ici très à l'aise, et
comme chez lui. Il entendait probablement me faire croire qu'il était
tout naturel, et légitime, pour un soldat en arme de l'Armée de Défense
d'Israël, de se promener le soir dans les ruelles d'une ville arabe, annexée
ou pas. Il n'en était rien bien sûr. (108)

[As for my cocksure brother, he pretended to be very at ease here, very
at home. He probably intended to make me believe that it was entirely
natural, and legitimate, for a soldier with an IDF weapon to take an
evening stroll in the alleyways of an Arab town, annexed or not. Of
course, it was nothing of the sort]

No such doubts occur to the Israeli Judith, another witness bearer, who
insists on the legitimacy of the separation walls as defence against the
settlers being fired at by Palestinians:

Nous sommes obligés de construire ce mur devant Bethléem et Beit Jala,
disaient-ils, car *ils* nous tirent dessus. *Ils* ne nous aiment pas, comment
veux-tu faire la paix avec *eux*? Il n'y aura jamais la paix (129)

['We have to build this wall between Bethlehem and Beit Jala', they said,
'because *they* fire at us. *They* don't like us, how do you expect us to make
peace with *them*? There'll never be peace']

However, Judith's adamant defence of the settlers is far from standard,
and the primary corpus reveals a spectrum of attitudes towards them
which includes growing unease, partial critique and outright opposition.
Unease is forcefully conveyed in *Les jours innocents* (1984), where

Jean-Luc Allouche expresses a sense of guilt at receiving hospitality from his old Arab friend Farid while on Farid's television screen Jews can be seen repressing the Palestinians in the West Bank (165). It is true that he attempts to provide mitigating circumstances:

> Je prends mon courage à deux mains et tente de lui expliquer notre propre besoin de dignité, de recouvrer un coin dans le monde où n'être plus des invités, plus ou moins tolérés, en bout de table du festin des peuples (165)

> [I take my courage in both hands and try to explain to him our own need for dignity, our need to recover a corner of the world where we're not simply more or less well tolerated guests, at the end of the feast table of peoples]

But this does not erase his guilty feelings, which resurface in a memory of his own unwilling complicity in the occupation as a soldier following orders:

> Je ne lui ai pas raconté comment, vigile à Jérusalem, je devais chaque matin vérifier, à mon tour, l'identité des ouvriers de Gaza venus construire les bâtiments de l'université et comment je devais fouiller ces hommes qui avaient le visage de mon père et du sien, mettre la main dans leur pita, le pain arabe creux, pour y chercher une bombe. J'eus la chance d'être très vite transféré vers un autre poste de garde. (165–66)

> [I didn't tell him about how, when I was a watchman in Jerusalem, every morning it was my turn to check the identity of workers from Gaza who'd come to construct the university buildings and how I had to frisk those men whose faces looked like my father's and his father's, had to put my hand into their pitta, the hollow Arab bread, to search for a bomb within it. I was lucky enough to be very quickly transferred to another guard-duty post]

In *Un été à Jérusalem* (1986), Chochana Boukhobza's homodiegetic narrator Sarah expresses not so much guilt about, as outright opposition to the settlers, the occupation and what she sees as its cause – an adamantly religious conception of Israel:

> l'Israël antique qui s'obstine à reconstituer l'univers biblique, et qui bravant la guerre, s'acharne à édifier sur ces mêmes collines, des colonies ceintes de fils barbelés (43)

> [the ancient Israel which persists in reconstituting the biblical world, and which, braving the war, tries desperately to build on those same hills settlements encircled by barbed wire]

Set in 1982, during the Lebanon War, the novel also conveys the minority view of an Israeli soldier, Roger, who is equally opposed to the occupation: 'il m'avait tenu sur le sionisme et la condition des Arabes en territoires occupés des discours qui n'étaient pas au goût du jour' (75) ['He'd said things to me about Zionism and the situation of the Arabs in the Occupied Territories that were out of step with the times'].

Whilst Michaël Sebban's *La terre promise, pas encore* (2002) does not express such overt political opposition to the settlers, they are nonetheless critiqued, this time for their paranoia, and through the scathing voices of anonymous Israeli citizens:

> – Regarde un village arabe, c'est inscrit dans le paysage. C'est bâti sur le flanc de la colline.
>   – Leurs implantations, ils les foutent toujours sur le sommet.
>   – C'est pas des colons, c'est des paranos. (122)

['Look at an Arab village, it fits within the landscape. It's built on the side of the hill'.
    'Their settlements, they always stick them at the top'.
    'They're not settlers, they're paranoid']

La terre promise, pas encore also mediates an Israeli willingness to relinquish the Occupied Territories not for political or ethical reasons, but through simple scorn for their squalor:

> Gaza, Jéricho, qu'ils se les gardent. Ils veulent leur autonomie, qu'ils se démerdent. J'y ai été à Gaza, pendant l'Intifada. C'est immonde, ils ont même pas d'égoûts. J'irais même pas y pisser. Mais après, faut pas qu'ils comptent sur nous pour leur filer à bouffer. (100)

[Gaza, Jericho, they can keep them. They want their autonomy, let them bloody well get on with it. I've been to Gaza, during the Intifada. It's filthy, they don't even have sewers. I wouldn't even go there to piss. But afterwards, don't let them count on us to feed them]

For all its condescension, this blunt statement indicates clear non-opposition to a Palestinian state comprising the currently Occupied Territories, and thus to their surrender by Jewish Israelis. There is, admittedly, a certain aggression in the final sentence, which suggests that an independent Palestinian state might try to be parasitical upon Israel. But the essential point is the basic lack of support for the settlers.

Unlike Sebban's polyphonous novel *La terre promise, pas encore*, Michel Warschawski's *Sur la frontière* (2002) presents the author's own monolithic perspective on the Occupied Territories and the settlers:

one of unqualified censure. The first reference alludes to what in the immediate wake of the Six-Day War of 1967 he condemns as Israel's 'politique de plus en plus ouvertement colonialiste' (65) ['increasingly overtly colonialist policy']. The adjective 'colonialiste' and its cognate 'colonial'[14] are often applied to Israel at other points in Warschawski's text. Later on, he seems optimistic that a younger generation will in adulthood comprise a majority that opposes the occupation (135). All is not positive in his account, however: quite the contrary. While Warschawski's tone is neutral in the following observations, their context makes it plain that he deplores the political consensus to retain the Territories that developed after the assassination of Rabin, who had been moving towards their surrender in exchange for peace:

> Après l'assassinat de Rabin, le clivage gauche-droite a cessé d'exister. La colonisation de la Cisjordanie et de Gaza est devenue l'une des composantes du nouveau consensus, le débat ne portant que sur l'aspect quantitatif de cette colonisation. C'est d'ailleurs ce qui permet de comprendre comment tant d'électeurs et de militants travaillistes ont pu voter Sharon quelques années plus tard. (229)

> [After Rabin's assassination, the left-right split ceased to exist. The colonization of the West Bank and Gaza became one of the components of the new consensus, with debate bearing only on the quantitative aspect of this colonization. What's more, this is what explains how so many Labour electors and activists felt able to vote for Sharon a few years later]

However, the left-right split that Warschawski claims has disappeared is fully present in Valérie Zenatti's *Quand j'étais soldate* (2002), set at the turn of the millennium. Zenatti's homodiegetic narrator finds herself in the awkward position of having moderately left-wing political views that are critical of the settlers and the occupation whilst at the same time doing her military service in an institution regarded as right-wing. Her own opposition to the settlers and occupation is implicit in her enthusiastic response to author and journalist Yonatan Geffen, who for his part expresses his opposition directly (107). Her comments on television reports are dispassionate in being confined to the facts presented, but the figures of those injured do imply a situation of unequal force in favour of the Israelis in the Occupied Territories:

> J'ai allumé la télé. [...] Des émeutes dans les territoires, à Jénine. Violence des pneus en feu, violence des frondes et des pierres, violence de nos

soldats, en face, qui tirent des balles en caoutchouc. Quinze blessés côté palestinien. Trois blessés côté israélien (107)

[I turned on the TV. [...] Riots in the Territories, in Jenin. Violence of burning tyres, violence of revolts and stone throwing, violence of our soldiers, on the opposite side, firing rubber bullets. Fifteen Palestinians injured. Three Israelis injured]

Much later on, condemnation of the occupation is finally implied via three single words – 'bouchent', 'masquent' and 'mal' – in the following passage:

Des militants qui veulent la paix maintenant, et qui savent que, pour cela, il faudra donner aux Palestiniens le droit de vivre comme ils l'entendent. Et d'autres qui proclament leur attachement à la Terre, à la Bible, qui se bouchent les oreilles et masquent leurs yeux pour ne pas savoir que trois millions de Palestiniens vivent – mal – à Gaza, dans les collines de Judée et de Samarie. (204–05)

[Activists who want peace now, and who know that, for this to come about, Palestinians will have to be given the right to live as they see fit. And others who proclaim their attachment to the Land, to the Bible, who turn a deaf ear and a blind eye, to avoid acknowledging that three million Palestinians live – in bad conditions – in Gaza, in the hills of Judea and Samaria]

Soon after this political coming out, the narrator overtly voices her opposition to Israeli domination of the Palestinians and her belief that Israelis should withdraw from the Occupied Territories. She also remarks that only after such a withdrawal will Israel be able to start seriously tackling its other problems of social inequality among Israeli citizens, including the privileging of religious over non-religious students (210–11). Yet despite her conviction that withdrawal from the West Bank is a moral imperative, she remains unable to answer the strident question, 'Et Jérusalem, tu en fais quoi de Jérusalem?' (211) ['And Jerusalem, what would you do with Jerusalem?']. Here, analysis of her own response consummately illustrates, even as it denies it, the inevitable intermingling of affect and politics:

Mon cœur se serre. Je ne peux pas imaginer cette ville coupée en deux. Les sentiments n'ont rien à voir avec la politique mais tout de même ... La moitié d'un corps peut-elle survivre sans l'autre? (211)

[I feel a pang of anguish. I can't imagine this city cut into two. Feelings

have nothing to do with politics, but even so ... Can one half of a body
survive without the other?]

Her response is, it has to be said, somewhat limp: 'Je ne sais pas ... On
trouvera une solution intelligente ...' (211) ['I don't know ... We'll find
an intelligent solution ...'].

Despite failure of nerve about the fate of Jerusalem, this young
soldier pursues her dissection of the Occupied Territories more generally
(211–12). Her conviction that they must be surrendered is based on
both external and internal concerns: continued occupation will only
further damage Israel's standing on the worldwide stage, and, worse
still, it will – or she believes at least that it should – lead to intolerable
shame among Israelis themselves. For her part, and as a typical Israeli
who has never set foot in these Territories, she determines to learn more
about them than can be gleaned through the filtered information (and,
it is implied, possibly disinformation) purveyed by television images
(213). She thus embarks on a bus journey through the Territories during
which she sees half-built houses in Palestinian villages, is warned
about their inhabitants' habit of throwing stones at buses suspected of
bearing Israeli Jews and finally utters in pared down, affectively dense
prose the wrenching conclusion 'Pauvreté, tristesse, haine' (214). The
hatred is directed by the Palestinians against the Israeli bus passengers,
viewed collectively as colonizers. By the end of the novel, the narrator's
confusion about Jerusalem is addressed by a close friend whose opinion
she does not challenge:

> Il dit qu'il faut tout rendre, tout donner aux Palestiniens, y compris la
> partie de Jérusalem qu'ils réclament. Il pense que la vie n'a pas de prix,
> que c'est le seul slogan valable (235)

> [He says that we have to hand everything back, give everything to the
> Palestinians, including the part of Jerusalem that they're demanding. He
> thinks that life is priceless, that this is the only valid slogan]

From hesitant, passive opposition to the Occupied Territories, she has
ultimately moved to confident, active and public demonstration against
them:

> nous allons parfois manifester avec les « femmes en noir » qui réclament
> le retrait d'Israël des territoires palestiniens. Elles portent le noir en signe
> de deuil, et se font copieusement insultées par les contre-manifestants de
> droite, tous les vendredis (239)

> [sometimes we go and demonstrate with the 'women in black' who are

demanding Israel's withdrawal from the Palestinian territories. They wear black as a sign of mourning, and get masses of insults from the counter-demonstrators on the right, every Friday]

A later novel by Zenatti, set in 2004 during the Second Intifada, places the pathematic motif of the settlers and the Occupied Territories centre stage. The first-person narrator of *Une bouteille dans la mer de Gaza* (2005), Tal, is a young (17-year-old) Israeli woman. The novel consists largely in an email exchange between Tal and Naïm (or 'Gazaman', his virtual pseudonym), a young Palestinian living in Gaza. (The exceptions are the opening pages and the occasional intercalations of first-person narrative alternating between Tal's and Naïm's voice.) Tal strives for a balanced account that recognizes the injustices endured by Palestinians living in Gaza, but also implicitly reproves their joy at news of the murder of Israeli civilians by Palestinian militants (30–31). For some time, Naïm meets Tal's emails only with implacable irony and derision. Offended by his sexist condescension – 'ta petite tête' (47) – she eventually loses her calm, voicing indignation at his failure to acknowledge that many Israelis, like her own family, have always agitated for a Palestinian state, which obviously equates to Israeli surrender of the Occupied Territories (64–65). On a far smaller scale, Michaël Sebban's *Le Cadenas du marché Yéhouda* (2008) also presents Israeli opposition to the occupation, in a vignette where a group of young protesters who demonstrate against it ritually receive an amicable, resigned response from the soldier on duty:

> Et tous les jours le soldat de garde leur dit bonjour, ça va les gars, vous voulez un café, non merci on a du boulot, bon alors à demain, salut à la prochaine. Puis il rentre dans sa cabine en se redisant chaque fois que ces gars-là sont sympas mais un peu dérangés, et que si on ne l'avait pas envoyé passer son temps à contrôler des cartes d'identité, des plaques d'immatriculation et des coffres de bagnole, il aurait bien d'autres choses à faire que de venir gueuler des conneries. (165)

[And every day the soldier on guard duty says hello to them, you okay guys, do you want a coffee, no thanks we've got work to do, fine okay see you tomorrow, bye seen you soon. Then he goes back into his booth thinking every time that those guys are nice but a bit crazy, and that if he hadn't been sent to spend his time checking identity cards, registration plates and car boots, he'd have lots of other things to do than come and shout bullshit]

The main point here is the ineffectual nature of the protest. And while the narrator Eli concedes the protesters' good intentions, his conclusion on them is extremely patronizing: in his view they are motivated by a Manichean optic, engaging in a childish game of cops and robbers/ cowboys and Indians:

> Ce sont des enfants, voilà tout. Des gosses qui voient le monde avec leurs yeux de gosses. Le gendarme et le voleur, les cow-boys et les Indiens et le happy end où tout le monde applaudit en essuyant une larme (165)

> [They're children, that's all there is to it. Kids who see the world through kids' eyes. The cop and the robber, the cowboys and the Indians and the happy ending where everyone claps and wipes away a tear]

The poignancy here, of course, is that there is no such happy ending in the Occupied Territories.

That lack is borne out two years later by *Eretz* (2010), where Henri Raczymow depicts a persisting occupation and a persisting opposition to the settlers by a significant proportion of Israelis. Danit typifies the latter:

> J'interroge Danit sur les colons. Je voudrais en avoir le cœur net. Ces gens la mettent simplement en colère. Le mieux, pour elle, serait de créer deux États, fermer la frontière et laisser se débrouiller ces soixante mille fanatiques au-dehors. (55)

> [I question Danit about the settlers. I'd like to be clear in my own mind about them. These people quite simply make her angry. In her view, the best thing would be to create two states, to close the frontier and to let those sixty thousand fanatics get on with things on their own outside it]

However, as in Zenatti's *Quand j'étais soldate* (2002), the sticking point is the fate of Jerusalem:

> Il faut que je l'interroge sur Jérusalem. Que je lui demande brutalement si selon elle il faut rendre le Mur aux Arabes, comme c'était le cas avant 1967. Ou bien s'il faut négocier au coup par coup chaque parcelle des territoires conquis alors. Tu prends ça, je prends ça … C'était justement la question de Jérusalem qui était la plus épineuse et complexe … (55)

> [I have to question her about Jerusalem. To ask her bluntly if in her view the Wall should be given back to the Arabs, like before 1967. Or if every bit of the territories conquered then needs to be negotiated as we go along. You take this, I take that … It was precisely the question of Jerusalem which was the most thorny and complex …]

No response from Danit is forthcoming, for a third interlocutor diverts the discussion away from the surrender of the Territories towards France and whether or not its Arab population influences French society and politics. Two points arising from *Eretz* will be considered in greater detail in further chapters: in Chapter 6, the central importance of Jerusalem; and in Chapter 5, the imbrication of Israel, Arab–Jewish conflict and France.

3.8. Endnote

The apodictic point to emerge from this chapter is that intra-Jewish conflict is rife in Francophone Jewish writers' representations of Israel. The main form of such conflict depicted is an ethno-cultural one that had serious socioeconomic consequences: the original Ashkenazi establishment's altericidal refusal of Sephardic/Mizrahi difference, which it construed as dangerously oriental.[15] Those consequences – stigmatization of Sephardic/Mizrahi Jews (who formed the bulk of Francophone communities in Israel) and their relegation to the bottom of the socioeconomic heap – placed them in a position of disempowerment against which some reacted with physical violence, as evidenced in the Wadi Salib riots and the militant action of the Panthères noires movement. The proxemics of this chapter reveal the reflection of such trends in eleven of our primary texts. Modern Israeli culture has involved efforts by the Ashkenazi elite to subject immigrants (largely North African) to a process of ideologico-cultural deculturation. The queering of hegemonic models of Israeli identity theoretically offered by Levantinism remains a potential discernible in five of our primary texts, but a localized and limited one characterized by anfractuosity. Instead, the development that is most 'queer' in the original sense of 'strange' has been the compact of oppressed, largely working-class North African immigrants with the right wing from the late 1970s (as sketched out in three of the primary texts). This compact is queer/strange insofar as in traditional political models, the socialist left is seen as the more natural home of oppressed groups. This in its turn has exacerbated conflicts between the Israeli left and right wings – the latter in alliance with religious proponents of Greater Israel (see Chapter 6) – over the highly charged political question of the Occupied Territories. Finally, the question of the Occupied Territories in itself has since 1967 sparked a further form of conflict, reflected in seven of the primary texts: that between the settlers and their supporters on the one hand and their

Israeli opponents on the other. Observation of these various dynamics has performed an incursion into some of the myths about unified Israeli national identity that were scrutinized in Chapters 1 and 2.

Notes

1 Harris refers to Braudel's *Memory and the Mediterranean*.

2 Zertal refers to Arendt's 'La tradition cachée'.

3 For a more equivocal view, see Bernfeld (171, 177–78).

4 Interview conducted 30 December 2011.

5 Interview conducted 31 December 2011.

6 Even *Ha'aretz*, usually regarded as a left-wing, anti-racist newspaper, seems to have participated in such racism. In April 1949, Arieh Gelblum commented of Jewish immigrants from Algeria, Libya, Morocco, and Tunisia that: 'We face a people whose primitiveness is paramount, [whose] level of education borders on total ignorance, and, all the more grave, [there is] a total lack of talent to absorb anything intellectual. In general, they are only a bit higher on the economic ladder than the Arab inhabitants, the Africans, and the Barbarians in their place [of origin]; in any case, this is a level that is even lower than what we are acquainted with among the Arabs of *Eretz-Israel*'.

7 Shohat's study is of Sephardim in Israel, but it does in fact also apply to Mizrahim in Israel; see note 9 below.

8 A *mellah* was the Jewish quarter in a Moroccan town.

9 The *olim* are Jews who make the *aliyah*.

10 As stated in the Introduction, Sephardic Jews are of Spanish or Portuguese descent, tracing a lineage back to the people expelled from Spain and Portugal in 1492, and Mizrahi Jews are of Middle Eastern or North African descent. However, those Jews expelled in 1492 subsequently migrated in large numbers to North Africa, and so, according to some definitions, came to form part of the Mizrahim.

11 See 'Israeli Rabbi Stirs Uproar by Saying Holocaust Victims were Reincarnated Sinners', www.CNN.com, 6 August 2000.

12 A *rav* is a senior rabbi.

13 Steven J. Zipperstein ascribes to Begin an even wider appeal and influence: 'he set in motion a working coalition – North Africans (eventually augmented by post-Soviet Jews), economic liberals, national-religious [*sic*], secularists and home-grown rightists – that has dominated Israeli politics, on and off, for decades now' (74).

14 See the Author's Note within the Acknowledgements and Author's Note section.

15 This refusal will be seen by some as refusal of the Ashkenazi self within its purported Other. Thus, Aziza Khazzoom argues: '[t]he two past centuries of Diaspora Jewish history in Europe and the Middle East can be conceptualized

as a series of orientalizations. Through this history, Jews came to view Jewish tradition as oriental, developed intense commitments to westernization as a form of self-improvement, and became threatened by any elements of Jewish culture that represented [their own] Oriental past' (482); and Gil Z. Hochberg opines 'that the fear of the Orient, as captured in the various racist expressions of the Zionist founders, is not only about "influence." More accurately, it is a fear of identification: the fear of being identified *once again* with the Orient, the Arab, Asia' (13).

CHAPTER FOUR

Arab–Israeli Conflict

Chapter 4 investigates Francophone Jewish writers' representations of the second and by far the most notorious of the three forms of conflict considered in this monograph: the Israeli–Palestinian/Jewish–Arab conflict (4.1). As in Chapter 3, affect is prominent in literary mediations of the conflict, the main intense emotions felt by the Israeli Jews depicted being fear (of threats to their country and their own lives) and anger (about the existence of those threats). As in Chapter 3 again, the eliciting conditions for these emotions are cognitive apprehension of a reality – the threat – and perception of its profound injustice, given the millennia of persecution that Jews had already suffered before the creation of the state of Israel in 1948, most particularly in its immediate history with the death of six million European Jews in the Nazi genocide. After considering representations of the conflict itself, I will focus on representations of some of its collateral damage: the acute psychological tension induced by Israel's vulnerability to attack and by its need for constant military vigilance (4.2); the severe trauma experienced by survivors of suicide bomb attacks and by those close to their victims (4.3). Less bleakly, Chapter 4 also examines literary renderings of an intermittent aspiration to dialogue and mutual comprehension between the two enemy sides (4.4); of nostalgia felt by Sephardic/Mizrahi Jews for a time and place when Jews and Arabs (allegedly) lived together peacefully, even amicably: elegiac memories of Jewish–Arab friendships in pre-Israeli personal history (4.5); and, cognate with this, the ideal of fraternity between Arabs and Jews as (Semitic) brothers (4.6). In the first and longest section (4.1), attention to the primary texts' mediations of the Arab–Israeli conflict will be preceded by eclectic insights from disciplines outside literary analysis. Inevitably, these insights vary greatly in their political positioning, and each will no doubt prove contestable for at least some readers.

4.1. Israeli–Palestinian/Jewish–Arab conflict

Psychoanalyst Daniel Sibony posits a history of primal venom between Jews and Arabs that antedates the Israeli–Palestinian conflict by many centuries but partly explains it:

> Dans le monde arabe, déjà avant l'islam, le rejet des Juifs (vindicte ou mépris) était une tradition. Depuis l'islam, cette vindicte s'est exercée au fil des siècles sur les Juifs des pays arabes, quand ils y étaient. Aujourd'hui, il n'y en a presque plus, elle est donc sans objet palpable. Mais elle se reporte sur Israël, considéré comme présence juive souveraine sur une terre arabe. De fait, le « retour » des Juifs sur leur terre « possédée » réactive les sources de cette vindicte. (69)

> [Already before Islam, in the Arab world rejection of Jews (condemnation or contempt) was traditional. Since Islam, this condemnation has over the centuries targeted Jews in Arab countries, when they lived there. Now, there are almost none left, so it has no tangible object. But it is transferred onto Israel, considered to be a sovereign Jewish presence on Arab land. De facto, the 'return' of Jews to their 'possessed' land reactivates the sources of this condemnation]

For Sibony, the current Middle Eastern conflict lays bare this originary hatred (69). In his view the hatred is mutual, although historically Jews have never been in a strong enough position to act upon it (69–70). Sibony traces the roots of this enmity further, to a form of textual parasitism for which unconscious shame is felt by Muslim Arabs, and in place of which animus takes a psychic grip:

> Le monde arabe souffre de « quelque chose » dont sa vindicte envers les Juifs est le symbole. [...]
>   Ce problème peut se formuler cliniquement en termes d'entre-deux-groupes ou collectifs: qu'en est-il lorsque l'un d'eux assoit son Texte fondateur (l'arabe) sur celui de l'autre (l'hébreu) qu'il absorbe, sachant que par la suite cette absorption est passée sous silence ou mise sur le compte de Dieu (c'est l'Ange qui a tout dit à Mohamad)? et que plus tard, après plus d'un millénaire, le Texte absorbé revient, se présente comme ayant sa vie propre et autonome? Qu'en est-il du trauma que cela réveille chez le groupe absorbant? (71–72)

> [The Arab world suffers from 'something' for which its condemnation of Jews is the symbol. [...] This problem can be formulated clinically in terms of intermediate groups or collectives: what happens when one of them bases its founding Text (Arabic) on the other's (Hebrew), which it absorbs, knowing that afterwards this absorption is passed over in silence

or put down to God (the Angel told Muhammad everything?) and that later on, after more than a millennium, the Text that's been absorbed returns, presenting itself as if it has its own autonomous life? What about the trauma that this awakens in the absorbing group?]

So for Sibony the psychoanalyst, the Middle Eastern conflict represents (inter alia) a return of the Hebrew repressed in a geographical space previously dominated by Arabs (72). Two further psychoanalytically based contentions about the conflict from Sibony merit attention. One posits Jewish narcissism and weights the conflict in favour of the Arabs:

> Car les Juifs aussi se sont dits les premiers, les élus: mais eux n'ont jamais eu la force – politique, militaire – d'imposer cette certitude narcissique; ni le projet. Les Arabes ont eu cette force, à partir du VIIe siècle. Armés du glaive et du Livre, ils ont déployé leur plénitude originaire. (241)

> [For the Jews too said they were the first, the elect: but they have never had the strength – political, military – to impose this narcissistic certainty; nor the intention. The Arabs had that strength, from the seventh century. Armed with the sword and the Book, they displayed their innate richness]

The other asserts internal weakness on both sides, and appears to equalize them:

> Dire que le conflit est identitaire et symbolique signifie que deux identités y cherchent à faire co-exister leurs failles internes, et déjà à les reconnaître: Israël a dénié la faille juive essentielle, en produisant son « homme nouveau », humainement infirme; et le monde arabe n'a jamais connu sa faille si ce n'est en se cognant sur le mur des réalités. (239)

> [To say that the conflict is about identity and is symbolic means that two identities seek through it a coexistence of their internal weaknesses, and already to recognize them: Israel has denied the essential Jewish weakness, through producing its 'new man', who in human terms is disabled; and the Arab world has never been aware of its weakness except when it has bumped up against the wall of reality]

These contentions may provide readers with an interesting psychological lens through which to view the raging affect saturating what others may regard as a 'merely' politico-religious conflict, albeit one of devastating magnitude.

Psychology and politics are conjoined in the findings of Halperin, Canetti-Nisim and Hirsch-Hoefler (2009). Drawing on ethnographic research in Israel, they come to the following conclusions about three of the most powerful emotions alluded to by Sibony and which constantly fuel the conflict: anger, fear and hatred. Their conclusions bear not so much on dramatic forms of the conflict such as rocket attacks and air strikes as on tensions within the Jewish and Arab polities, and the political disempowerment of the latter:

> Four population-based surveys have unequivocally shown that hatred is an antecedent of greater levels of political intolerance. In line with our hypotheses, this finding was substantiated when other negative emotions – fear and anger, or threat perception – were controlled for. Anger was conducive to political intolerance only when hatred mediated the relationship. Fear, however, was conducive to political intolerance only when both threat perception and hatred mediated the relationship. The role of hatred in inducing political intolerance was more substantial during a period of heightened existential threat (115–16)

As we will see, the primary texts strongly suggest that the existential threat felt by Jewish Israelis is key to the denial of Palestinian rights.

The analyses of essayist and journalist Martine Gozlan seem more purely political, but they too are subtended by affect. One example is her claim that Israel views the advocacy of physical mediation between it and the Palestinians as an offence (a word which cannot help but connote emotion) to its sovereignty (154–55). Another is her teasing out of the conflict's highly emotive stakes for Jewish Israelis due to memories of the Shoah:

> Les juifs se scindent en deux factions: celle qui voit un reflet du déporté juif à travers le Palestinien, et déteste le soldat considéré alors comme un oppresseur; celle qui voit dans le Palestinien un reflet de ce qui pourrait amener le juif à devenir un déporté, et donc aime le soldat, considéré dans ce cas comme un défenseur. (209)

> [Jews split into two factions: one which sees in the Palestinian a reflection of the Jewish deportee, and hates the soldier who is thus seen as an oppressor; and one which sees in the Palestinian a reflection of what could lead the Jew to become a deportee, and thus loves the soldier, who in this case is considered a defender]

The first primary text to evoke the conflict is *Terre d'amour et de feu* (1965), which recurs to the early twentieth century. Differing at least initially from Sibony's thesis of primal venom, Joseph Kessel's narrative portrays peaceful coexistence of Arabs and members of the Yishuv, and emphasizes the non-belligerence of the ordinary Palestinian peasants who formed the majority of the Arab population in Palestine at the time (24). Into this prelapsarian idyll he introduces the post-First

World War eruption of riots that nearly became a civil war (24). Kessel's explanation of this sudden change in Arab–Jewish relations in Palestine is that ordinary Arabs came to be manipulated by the ideological force of nationalism embraced by the Arab elite (24–25). Kessel argues that this elite, accustomed to absolute control of a passive peasantry, viewed the freedom of the Jews as a threat to their own power and so used propaganda to convince their peasantry that the Jews should be exterminated before they could take everything from them (25–26). The success of such propaganda is the reason adduced by Kessel for growing attacks on 'les colonies juives' (26).[1] The second section of *Terre d'amour et de feu* focuses on the War of Independence (1947–1949). Kessel stresses the extreme military disadvantage of beleaguered Jews against the six Arab nations which had refused to accept both the UN resolution approving the creation of a Jewish homeland in Palestine and the declaration of the state of Israel in May 1948 (94–95). He then goes on to extol the dogged battle waged by the Haganah, the Irgun (see Chapter 1, section 1.2) and the Stern group, culminating in an entirely unpredictable and, in Kessel's rhetoric, entirely glorious victory. Two further points in Kessel's account are of note. One is his reporting of the words of a Jewish combatant who insisted on the former friendship of the Palestinian Arabs and Jews, and on the sole responsibility of the Arab Legion in the exodus of the former (121). The second is Kessel's stress, arguably manipulative, on the humanitarian mercy shown by Jewish soldiers on an elderly Arab woman too infirm to join the exodus:

> Et sa voix exténuée, sa voix sans âge – voix de toutes les vieilles abandonnées – se mit à dévider, en arabe, l'interminable litanie des bénédictions coraniques pour ces jeunes guerriers juifs qui la nourrissaient. Et elle souriait, d'un sourire édenté, incrédule, d'outre-tombe ... (137)

> [And her exhausted voice, her ageless voice – the voice of all abandoned old women – started to reel off, in Arabic, the endless litany of Koranic blessings for those young Jewish warriors who fed her. And she smiled, a toothless, incredulous smile, from beyond the grave ...]

Published only three years after Kessel's account, the explicitly pro-Palestinian, anti-Israeli stance of Ania Francos's *Les Palestiniens* (1968) offers a sharp contrast:

> Ce livre n'est pas un dossier impartial faisant part égale aux opprimés et aux oppresseurs. C'est un livre partial: ma sympathie va aux Palestiniens. Israël n'est pas un pauvre petit paysan seul au monde, il a eu pour parrain

l'impérialisme anglo-américain qui n'a cessé de veiller sur lui depuis sa création; il ne manque pas d'avocats pour justifier sa cause. (12)

[This book is not an impartial record giving equal place to the oppressed and the oppressors. It's a partial book: my sympathies lie with the Palestinians. Israel is not a poor little peasant all alone in the world, it's been sponsored by the Anglo-American imperialism that has constantly looked after it since its creation, it doesn't lack advocates to justify its cause]

Two elements command attention here. First, in the original text of 1968, the word 'paysan' had been 'pays' ('country'); the change in the 1970 edition (from which all quotations are drawn) considerably ups the emotional ante through its denial of Israel's vulnerability. Second, Francos associates Israel with imperialism, a link which recurs in the tribute paid to her by a Palestinian: 'On se moque totalement du Dieu de vos ancêtres: pour nous, l'important est votre activité anti-impéri-aliste' (135) ['We couldn't care less about your ancestors' God: for us, what matters is your anti-imperialist activity']. But whereas the Anglo-American imperialism rejected by Francos is a historical reality, some would contend that it is a category error to cast as imperialism Israel's occupation of Gaza and the West Bank, which was undertaken partly for religious and partly for nationalist reasons rather than to exploit the natural resources of another country for economic gain. This possibility does not seem to occur to Francos, who is simply concerned to dissociate herself completely as a Jew from all Israelis, as is illustrated in her comment about a member of the PLO in Gaza:

Il dit « Yehoud », les Juifs, non les Israéliens et cela me gêna. Par la suite, tous mes interlocuteurs, connaissant mes origines, s'efforcèrent de dire les Israéliens (52)

[He says 'Yehud', the Jews, not the Israelis and that bothered me. Afterwards, all those who spoke to me, aware of my origins, tried hard to say 'the Israelis']

Ten years after *Les Palestiniens*, Francos published the autofictional *Sauve-toi Lola* (1978). Here she has changed her position substantially, from one of unconditional sympathy for the Palestinians to one of cynicism, even bitterness on the part of her alter-ego Lola about having devoted herself to a cause through irrational feelings of guilt:

Ces chers Palestiniens – dont lui se foutait comme de l'an quarante – mais dont moi, avec mon culpabilisme, j'avais porté des années la cause (« Et

Kadia », comme ils disent du côté de Damas) comme une croix. [...] Et je me dis: « S'il me parle des Palestiniens, je lui fous une baffe. » (44)

[Those dear Palestinians – who he couldn't have given a damn about – but whose cause I, with my guilt obsession, had borne for years ('And Kadia', as they say in Damas) like a cross. [...] And I think: 'If he mentions the Palestinians, I'll give him a slap']

Francos's position has undergone not a complete reversal but rather a disillusionment with Manichean judgements. Her words may signal a self-referential irony, given that in *Les Palestiniens* she had consistently lambasted Israelis but represented Palestinians respectfully. Thus there is flagging of Lola's irritation at the simplistic abuse of highly sensitive lexis pertaining to the Shoah within the context of the Israeli–Palestinian conflict:

Avouez, Lola, que vous aviez vous aussi une overdose de Palestiniens, d'Israéliens, de Juifs et d'Arabes. Avouez surtout que vous ne supportiez pas non plus ces mots utilisés à tort et à travers: génocide, ghetto de Varsovie, Oradour, solution finale (365)

[Admit it, Lola, you too had had an overdose of Palestinians, Israelis, Jews and Arabs. Above all, admit that you too couldn't stand those carelessly used words: genocide, Warsaw Ghetto, Oradour, final solution]

The pathological nature of her irrational feelings of guilt about Palestinians is implied towards the end of the novel in the neologism 'culpabilitalgie': 'ma culpabilitalgie, je me sentais une fois de plus responsable du sort réservé aux Palestiniens' (366) ['my guiltalgia, once again I felt responsible for the fate reserved for Palestinians'].

A similar disowning of responsibility by diasporic Jews for the suffering of Arabs may be discerned in Marcel Cohen's *Miroirs* (1980). In the following extract about Jews visiting the Western Wall (see Chapter 6), the rejection is both reflective and righteous:

Faut-il préciser que nous étions là sans réelle joie, que l'anonymat des villes grises signifiait mieux notre espoir de venir un jour à bout du passé. Simplement nous étions là. Pour le reste nous ne nous sentions pas responsables (156)

[Do I need to spell out that we felt no real joy about being there, that the anonymity of the grey towns was a better signifier of our hope of one day leaving the past behind. We were simply there. For the rest, we didn't feel responsible]

Responsibility for the suffering of the Arabs is not so much disowned by as simply alien to another diasporic Jew in Paula Jacques's *Un baiser froid comme la lune* (1983). Tobias, an Egyptian Jew and thus familiar with Arabic, is staying at a *kibbutz* when he notices

> les fondations rases d'un village arabe dont les habitants, lui avait-on dit, étaient partis de leur bon gré. Il s'étonnait un peu que l'on pût détruire des maisons et songeait qu'il lui aurait été agréable d'échanger quelques mots dans la langue sympathique (211–12)

> [the razed foundations of an Arab village whose inhabitants, he'd been told, had left willingly. He was rather surprised that people could destroy the houses and thought that it would have been nice to exchange a few words in that pleasant language [i.e. Arabic]]

Having fallen asleep when he was meant to be protecting the *kibbutz*, he is subject to a stern reprimand that underscores the *kibbutz*'s sense of being an enclave surrounded by not just hostile but life-threatening Arab countries – and this still in the late 1950s, when 'Il n'était pas rare de retrouver la citerne d'eau potable empoisonnée, un tracteur incendié, un promeneur à la gorge tranchée' (212) ['It wasn't uncommon to find the drinking water tank poisoned, a tractor set on fire, a walker with their throat cut']. Entirely unlike the *ingénu* Tobias is Jean-Luc Allouche in his autobiographical *Les jours innocents* (1984). Displaying keen political awareness and nuanced ethical engagement, he makes a critical assessment of the situation in France during the events of 1968, when the PLO was starting to gain support from left-wing students – for dubious reasons, it is implied:

> Je n'ignorais pas la juste revendication du peuple palestinien, mais déjà s'annonçait l'obtuse dénégation d'Israël chez ces étudiants acerbes, bavards, et au fond indifférents sinon en mal d'investissement idéologique, eux qui venaient tout juste de rater le soutien à l'indépendance de l'Algérie. [...] ils approvisionnaient en canettes de bières les révolutionnaires arabes assoiffés, asséchés, après leurs longues harangues approximatives, qui auraient eu tort de ne pas exploiter cette formidable conscience de boy-scouts christo-marxistes. (52)

> [I wasn't unaware of the Palestinian people's just demand, but already the obtuse denial of Israel was emerging among those caustic, talkative students who were basically indifferent if not lacking in any ideological investment, those who had just missed out on being able to support Algerian independence. [...] they provided stocks of beer cans to the Arab revolutionaries who were thirsty and dry after their long,

rambling harangues, and who would have been wrong not to exploit that tremendous boy scout, Christian-Marxist conscience]

His concern as an Algerian Jew for dialogue with Arab students is patent, but ultimately unfruitful, as is illustrated by an abortive effort:

« Tu ne penses pas que tout nous rapproche? Qu'en concédant, chacun de son côté, quelque chose, on pourrait trouver une solution? Je suis favorable à une reconnaissance de l'entité palestinienne, mais pourquoi vous obstinez-vous à reprendre ce slogan de la liquidation de l'Etat d' Israël? [...] »

   Sa conviction fut-elle entamée? Je n'eus pas le temps de le savoir, car, déjà, se rapprochaient quelques pucelles de la section lettres classiques. Enhardi par ce renfort qu'il ne pouvait décevoir, il me répliqua, le regard perdu vers un poster de Yasser Arafat: « De toute façon, nous avons Arafat pour résoudre notre problème! » (53)

['Don't you think that everything draws us together? That if each side conceded something, we could find a solution? I support recognition of the Palestinian entity, but why do you persist in once again taking up this slogan of the liquidation of the state of Israel? [...]' Had his conviction been weakened? I didn't have the time to find out because, already, maidens from the classical literature department were approaching. Emboldened by these helpers whom he couldn't disappoint, he retorted, his gaze lost towards a poster of Yasser Arafat: 'Anyway, we've got Arafat to solve our problem!']

Towards the very end of *Les jours innocents* Allouche recounts his final attempt, driven by vicarious guilt, to reduce the gulf that has widened between Jews and Arabs over the Palestinian question and the Occupied Territories. When his Arab friend Farid ripostes that Jews cling to obsession with their own misfortunes, Allouche's efforts – intersecting with the second part of Gozlan's sentence cited above (209) – to explain the Jewish fear of renewed victimhood after the Shoah again result in failure, due to Farid's and his fellow Arabs' adamant anger about the occupation (165).

   The homodiegetic narrator of Chochana Boukhobza's *Un été à Jérusalem* (1986), a young French Jew named Sarah, is initially less equivocal than Allouche but becomes increasingly divided. In an ironic jibe she roundly condemns the Israeli Prime Minister Begin's prosecution of war against Lebanese Arabs in 1982: 'Je m'exclame, ironique: « Et papa, il soutient encore Begin? Il estime que nous avons eu raison de faire le Liban? »' (18) ['I exclaim ironically, "And dad, does he still support Begin? Does he think we were right to go into the Lebanon War?"'].

She also shows a sensitivity, often painful for her, to the inferior status of Arabs within Israel and awareness of both their hurt pride about this status and their actual dignity (21). However, she cannot ignore the distress provoked by the Arab–Israeli conflict on the opposite 'side', among Israeli Jews. Indeed, she has her own anxieties about her brothers, Danny and Joseph, who are trapped in military conflict whilst completing their compulsory military service:

> les deux communiqués radio qui annonçaient plusieurs dizaines de blessés et trois morts victimes d'une embuscade à Beyrouth. La journaliste, voix fade, presque lunaire, n'avait pas dévoilé l'identité des soldats. Jusque dans ce bus étanche qui roulait fenêtres fermées sur le ruban d'asphalte, l'actualité nous poursuit. La guerre entre de partout. Énervés, les voyageurs avaient commenté l'incident, et ils se tournaient les uns vers les autres en soupirant. Une femme s'était mise à geindre et ses mains tremblaient au-dessus de sa robe bleue. Comment arracher Danny et Joseph à ce conflit? (46–47)

> [the two radio statements announcing several dozen wounded and three dead, victims of an ambush in Beirut. The journalist, with a dull, almost lunar voice, had not revealed the identity of the soldiers. Even in this sealed bus driving with closed windows on the asphalt strip, current events pursue us. War gets in from everywhere. The edgy passengers had commented on the incident, and were turning towards each other with sighs. A woman started to groan and her hands were trembling over her blue dress. How to tear Danny and Joseph away from this conflict?]

In this passage even Sarah, the peacenik, feels hounded and invaded by a minatory force, the reporter's lunar voice adding to the haunted, desolate quality of the scene. The passages referenced above illustrate the affective damage caused by the Arab–Israeli conflict for the two adversaries taken separately. The extract below brings the adversaries together, and stages a *mise en abyme* of the larger military conflict being played out on the macro level. It brings home the tensions and mutual mistrust experienced by both sides on a daily, ostensibly minor level, and the habitual swing of the power pendulum in favour of the Jewish Israeli – but at high psychological cost, since his/her power is precariously based on a domination springing from existential threat (cf. Halperin et al., 116). In this extract, an Israeli soldier is disappointed by an Arab vendor's refusal to accept his price for a copper ewer. Having glimpsed the submachine gun that the soldier is obliged to carry, the Arab issues a verbal provocation that unleashes a scene of panic, anger and reprisals:

« Tu n'as pas besoin de « ça », toi qui vas mourir dans quelques jours au Liban. »

Saisi au collet, insulté, l'homme s'enfonce dans le magasin, poussé par les soldats. L'un d'entre eux, vingt ans à peine, tient en respect les voisins qui veulent intervenir.

« Restez où vous êtes. Ne bougez pas. Sinon, je tire! »

Galopade dans les ruelles. La police en uniforme beige écarte des badauds, ordonne aux marchands de rejoindre leur place, mais des sarcasmes fusent, des protestations montent, et un gosse lance des amandes et des raisins secs comme s'il jetait des pierres.

« Taisez-vous! Taisez-vous! Vérification de papiers. Rangez-vous contre le mur. Dépêchez-vous! » (186)

['You don't need "that". In a few days you're going to die in Lebanon'.

Grabbed by the collar, insulted, the man sinks into the shop, pushed by soldiers. One of them, barely twenty years old, keeps at bay the neighbours who want to intervene.

'Stay where you are. Don't move. If not, I'll shoot!'

Stampede in the alleys. The police in beige uniform move away the onlookers, order the traders to go back to their places, but sarcasms come thick and fast, protests mount, and a kid launches almonds and raisins as if he were throwing stones.

'Shut up! Shut up! Identity card check. Stand against the wall. Hurry up!']

The easy escalation of verbal or visual threat into material violence and counter-violence is reiterated:

Des incidents éclatent un peu partout. A Jéricho, à Bethléem, dans les faubourgs d'Hébron, à Gaza, à Ramallah. Il suffit d'un rien, un mot déplacé, un regard haineux, un mot malencontreux, et l'on se saute à la gorge avec l'alibi donné par la tension. On brûle des pneus, on casse des vitres, on lance des pierres. Alors durant deux heures, les soldats dressent des barrages sur les routes et effectuent des contrôles. (187)

[Incidents break out pretty much everywhere. In Jericho, in Bethlehem, in the suburbs of Hebron, in Gaza, in Ramallah. The slightest thing suffices, a careless word, a look of hatred, a clumsy word and people leap at each other's throats with the excuse provided by tension. Tyres are burned, windows are broken, stones are thrown. So for two hours, soldiers put up roadblocks and carry out checks]

Equally, the heavy civilian losses on both sides of the border with Lebanon are dramatically emphasized (233), the pervasive imagery of death lending a tragic tone to this novel.

Set in the late 1970s, Myriam Anissimov's *La Soie et les cendres* (1989) shows none of Boukhobza's ambivalence or melancholy: its tone is resolutely satirical, and it appears to narrativize elements of Sibony's thesis. For homodiegetic narrator Hannah, an event supposedly promoting communication between Israeli and Arab public figures is stage-managed (167) and hypocritical (168). In this scene there is no genuine dialogue, and the die is cast in advance against Israel:

> Il n'y eut, en fait, aucune discussion, car les hôtes secrets en provenance du Liban n'y tenaient pas. Cependant, la largeur de leurs vues les autorisait à rencontrer, pour leur propre édification, des citoyens du « soi-disant État d'Israël », comme ils dirent d'une voix où ne perçait aucune colère, mais plutôt le dédain. Finalement, expliquèrent-ils, les choses tenaient en peu de mots. Pourquoi devaient-ils payer pour les fautes de Hitler? Que les Juifs russes retournent en Union soviétique, les Polonais en Pologne, et ainsi de suite. Le partage de 1948 lui-même n'était qu'une vaste rigolade mais, comme chacun pouvait le constater, ils avaient toute la patience du monde, et les données démographiques jouant en leur faveur, ils prédisaient au « soi-disant État » la même fin tragique et ridicule que celle du Royaume des Croisés. En attendant, ils considéraient le recours à la violence à la fois payant et légitime. (172–73)

> [In fact there was no discussion, as the secret guests from Lebanon didn't want any. However, their broadmindedness allowed them to meet, for their own edification, citizens of the 'so-called state of Israel', as they said in a voice that showed no anger, but rather disdain. After all, they explained, things could be summed up briefly. Why should they pay for Hitler's mistakes? The Russian Jews should return to the Soviet Union, the Polish to Poland, and so on. The 1948 partition was nothing but a huge joke but, as everyone could see, they had all the patience in the world, and the demographic facts were playing in their favour, they predicted the same tragic and ridiculous ending for the 'so-called state' as for the kingdom of the Crusaders. In the meantime, they considered recourse to violence both worthwhile and legitimate]

The condoning of physical violence against Israel is of particular note, but later on Hannah is subject to verbal violence also. Her civil question as to why the whole of the Arab world had in 1947 refused the partition of Palestine into two states, one Jewish, the other Arab (189) prompts only verbal abuse from her Arab host Djamilah:

> « [...] Vous appelez ça une question? Si c'en est une, elle n'est pas innocente! C'est plutôt une insulte, une provocation! Vous venez dans ma maison, me planter un couteau dans le dos! » (189)

[Do you call that a question? If it is, it's not innocent! It's more an insult, a provocation! You come into my house and stick a knife in my back!]

Hannah's doomed efforts to engage in serious historico-political discussion '– Admettez tout de même que la Ligue Arabe a attaqué l'État d'Israël au lendemain de sa fondation! C'est pendant les combats de la guerre d'Indépendance qu'environ 600 000 Palestiniens se sont enfuis' (189) ['You can't deny, though, that the Arab League attacked the state of Israel the day after it was founded! It was during combat in the War of Independence that around six hundred thousand Palestinians fled'] – meet with blank denial, and an exhortation that all Jews in Israel 'return' to the Soviet Union (190), which ignores the fact that Israeli Jews in the 1970s had multiple national origins.

Violence assumes murderously material forms in Chochana Boukhobza's novel *Sous les étoiles* (2002), which recounts a typical micro-element of the larger Arab–Israeli conflict. Newly arrived in Israel, a visitor hears about a grimly banal event:

Des touristes américains commentaient l'émeute dans la Vieille Ville. Le bilan était lourd: deux soldats lapidés et deux jeunes Palestiniens tués par balle (197)

[Some American tourists were talking about the riot in the Old Town. The death toll was heavy: two soldiers stoned and two young Palestinians shot dead]

The words of an old Yemeni Jew happy to be living in Jerusalem partly counterbalance this – but only partly, for his happiness is compromised by the growing threat of arbitrary death (197–98). Apprehension of that threat is, however, also conveyed from an Arab perspective, where it leads immediately to minor vandalism and verbal violence:

Les sept avions qui fonçaient vers le nord, en direction du Liban, furent bientôt des points d'argent dans le ciel, puis disparurent tout à fait. Les gens se regardèrent. Le Sud-Liban serait encore bombardé, en représailles à l'attentat commis la veille contre l'autobus dans le centre-ville de Jérusalem. Une pierre fut projetée vers le ciel. D'autres suivirent. Des imprécations s'élevèrent. (274)

[The seven aeroplanes charging towards the north, heading for Lebanon, were soon silver specks in the sky, then vanished completely. People looked at each other. South Lebanon would soon be bombed, in retaliation for the attack committed the day before on the bus in Jerusalem town centre. A stone was thrown into the sky. Others followed. Curses rose up]

The violence inscribed in Michaël Sebban's *La terre promise, pas encore* (2002) assumes both verbal and material forms. To take the verbal first: if Anissimov's *La Soie et les cendres* lampooned the Arab countries' contemptuous wish for Israel's death during the late 1970s, Sebban's novel, set during the Second Intifada, relays vitriolic contempt on the part of ordinary Israelis about Western institutions (foreign media and the United Nations) which regard them as fascists:

> – Les journalistes étrangers, c'est tous des enculés. Ils nous font passer pour ces fachos, mais ils viennent ici, c'est pas à Ramallah qu'ils peuvent boire du whisky et mater les filles en minijupe. C'est comme l'ONU, ils ont fait leur club à Gaza. Interdit aux Palestiniens. Comme ça, ils peuvent boire de l'alcool tranquillement et se bourrer la gueule entre eux. (49)

> [Foreign journalists, they're all arseholes. They make us out to be fascists, but they come here, since they won't be able to drink whisky and ogle girls in miniskirts in Ramallah. It's like at the UN, they've set up club in Gaza. Out of bounds for the Palestinians. That way, they can drink alcohol in peace and get pissed among themselves]

This bitterness about the UN in particular hyphenates with Gozlan's words cited above on offence (154–55). A further instance of such bitterness about the international community's involvement in the conflict targets its perceived favouring of the Palestinians: 'Ils reçoivent plein de fric, les Palestiniens. L'Europe, les Arabes, les Américains, les organisations humanitaires, tout le monde leur en file' (53) ['They get loads of money, the Palestinians. Europe, the Arabs, the Americans, the humanitarian organizations, everyone gives to them']. But the political discourse of the novel is not monochrome, for it includes dialogue revealing unpalatable arrogance in the unnamed, often reactionary Israelis whose exchanges are italicized:

> – *Les Arabes, on veut pas les foutre à la mer. On veut juste qu'ils nous laissent tranquilles. Ils peuvent vivre ici s'ils en ont envie, mais il faut qu'ils reconnaissent qui c'est les patrons.*
> – *Ils ont raison, et nous aussi. On leur a piqué leur pays, on leur a piqué leurs baraques. Et maintenant on y est. Alors, que le plus fort gagne!*
> – *Si c'était nous qui étions dans des camps de réfugiés, tu crois qu'ils gueuleraient, les goys? Rien du tout. Mon oncle, son voisin l'a dénoncé aux Allemands pour cinquante francs.* (109)

> ['We don't want to chuck them into the sea, the Arabs. We just want them to leave us alone. They can live here if they want, but they have to recognize that we're the bosses'.

'They're right, and so are we. We nicked their country from them, we nicked their shacks from them. And now we're here. So, may the strongest win!'

'If it were us in refugee camps, do you think they'd be kicking up a stink, the goys? Not at all. My uncle, his neighbour denounced him to the Germans for fifty francs']

Partial mitigation of such arrogance is made in the last interjection's provision of background: traumatic memories of the Shoah and an enduring sense of existential threat (cf. again Halperin et al., 116).

The second form of violence portrayed by Sebban, this time material, takes the form of a Palestinian suicide bomber's attack that leaves 14 Israelis dead and 140 injured (147–48). In this context, the ordinary Israeli citizens whose dialogue is relayed below envisage no possibility of peace:

> – Alors? Il n'y aura jamais la paix. On s'est fait niquer.
> – Mais on n'avait pas le choix.
> – Évidemment qu'on n'avait pas le choix, mais on s'est quand même fait niquer.
> – Il fallait bien qu'on le crée notre État. On n'avait pas le choix.
> – Bien sûr, mais on a créé en même temps les Palestiniens.
> – Tu crois?
> – J'en suis sûr. Crois-moi, si on avait fondé un État en plein milieu du bush australien, on aurait eu sur le dos l'Organisation de libération de l'aborigénie. (205–06)

['So? There'll never be peace. We've been screwed over'.
'But we had no choice'.
'Of course we had no choice, but we've still been screwed over'.
'We had to create our state. We had no choice'.
'Of course, but at the same time we created the Palestinians'.
'You reckon?'
'I'm certain. Believe me, if we'd set up a state right in the middle of the Australian bush, we'd have had the Organization for the Liberation of Aboriginals on our backs']

The last interjection asserts a point commonly occluded: Jews' lack of choice over where to found their homeland, desperately needed after the Shoah, without prejudice to other occupants other than in the land promised to them by the British Balfour Declaration and subsequently approved as theirs by UN vote.

In *Sur la frontière* (2002), Michel Warschawski's stance is diametrically opposed to Sebban's. Warschawski polemically condemns a

figure widely regarded as a noble martyr to the goal of peace between
Arabs and Israelis: Yitzhak Rabin. Referring to the Oslo agreements,
Warschawski avers that less than six months after the signing of the
statement of principle, Rabin had started to sabotage it,

> d'abord en annonçant qu'il n'avait pas l'intention d'en respecter le
> calendrier (« Il n'y a pas de dates sacrées », annonçait-il dès février 1994),
> puis en estimant que le retrait de la Bande de Gaza pouvait n'être que
> partiel (203)

> [first by announcing that he didn't intend to respect the time schedule
> ('There are no sacred dates', he announced as early as February 1994),
> then by reckoning that withdrawal from the Gaza Strip could only be
> partial]

In Warschawski's analysis the disappearance of the pacifist movement,
which he accuses of blind confidence in Rabin, cleared the way for the
colonizers and the extreme right, leading ultimately to Rabin's assassination and the end of the entire Oslo process (207). Also in his line
of fire is 'le dispositif connu sous le nom de « bouclage »' (207) ['the
mechanism known as "cordoning off"'], which he contends ended any
freedom of movement for Palestinians in the Occupied Territories (208).
Rejecting the more positive line expressed in 1995 by Naomi Hazan,
a Meretz member of parliament for whom sealing off was the first
step towards a Palestinian state (209), Warschawski protests that 'Le
bouclage est un système qui impose aux Palestiniens la séparation, et
une séparation imposée unilatéralement se traduit en néerlandais par
apartheid' (209–10) ['Cordoning off is a system that imposes separation
on Palestinians, and a unilaterally imposed separation is translated in
Dutch as *apartheid*']. Italicization of the loaded term 'apartheid' (see
Chapter 5 for more on apartheid) evinces Warschawski's will to present
Israel as a structurally racist state. Few more stinging indictments of his
elective home country (he emigrated to Israel from France in 1965) are
imaginable.

Valérie Zenatti's *Quand j'étais soldate* (2002) also criticizes the
Israeli government's role in the Arab–Israeli conflict, though much less
virulently. One example is the intervention of Daniéla, who opposes the
consensus of most of her fellow female conscripts to the army:

> Quelle vérité? Celle à laquelle vous voulez croire, pour ne pas vous poser
> des questions sur l'uniforme que nous portons, sur ce qu'il représente
> pour les Palestiniens, par exemple (124)

[Which truth? The one you want to believe in, so you don't have to ask yourself questions about the uniform we wear, about what it represents for the Palestinians, for example]

But counterbalancing such voices are the motile impressions of the homodiegetic narrator herself who, while increasingly opposed to her country's government, does on more than one occasion stress the plight of Israeli civilians:

Il y a quelque temps, un Palestinien s'est jeté sur le chauffeur d'un bus de cette ligne, la 400, et a précipité le véhicule dans le ravin. Bilan: seize morts et une immense frayeur qui s'est abattue sur le pays tout entier' (158)

[A while ago, a Palestinian threw himself on the driver of a bus on this line, the no. 400, and pushed the vehicle into the ravine. The result was sixteen dead and a huge wave of fear that hit the whole country]

Another, highly emotive passage dramatizing a bus attack also accentuates the suffering of Israeli civilians:

Tout le monde est à terre dans le bus, y compris moi. Nous sommes balancés de droite à gauche et de gauche à droite pour éviter les projectiles. Chaque impact de pierre m'atteint douloureusement, comme si on me frappait. J'entends une détonation. Je ne saurai pas qui a tiré, s'il y a eu un mort, ou un blessé. J'éclate en sanglots et les autres passagers tentent de me rassurer. Je n'ai pas envie de leur expliquer que ce n'est pas la peur qui fait couler mes larmes. (215)

[Everyone's lying on the floor in the bus, me included. We're tossed from right to left and from left to right to avoid the missiles. The impact of every stone hits me painfully, as if I were being beaten. I hear a bang. I couldn't say who fired, if anyone was killed or injured. I burst into tears and the other passengers try to reassure me. I don't want to explain to them that it isn't fear that's making me cry]

No direct cause of her tears is given, but the reader can easily infer it from the song lyrics that succeed this passage – 'Et nous serons plongés pour toujours dans la haine et la violence' (216) ['And we'll be plunged into hatred and violence forever'] – her tearfulness reinforcing her despair at the seeming intractability of the conflict.

In *Une année si ordinaire* (2004) Esther Orner oscillates far less *vis-à-vis* the conflict than Zenatti's narrator, but does report another Israeli's ambivalence *vis-à-vis* the Palestinians:

> Le chauffeur de taxi [...] a dit que nous n'avions pas une position franche avec « nos cousins ». La paix oui, mais. La lutte contre le terrorisme oui, mais. Il faudrait trancher dans un sens ou dans un autre (56)

> [The taxi driver [...] said that we don't have a clear-cut position with 'our cousins'. Peace yes, but. The fight against terrorism yes, but. We should come down on one side or the other]

And while on the whole Orner's position is plainly pro-Israeli, this does not preclude sensitivity to the human suffering experienced by both sides in the conflict, be it emotional or physical. Sensitivity to emotional suffering is patent in the following:

> Cette semaine j'ai lu *Le verger* de Tamouz. Une histoire terrible entre deux frères d'un même père. Une mère musulmane, turque. Une mère juive, russe. Ils aiment la même femme qui est muette. La parabole est évidente. Et l'histoire se passe bien avant la création de l'Etat. Situation toujours aussi brûlante. (66)

> [This week I read *The Orchard* by Tamouz. A terrible story about two brothers from the same father. One Turkish Muslim mother. One Russian Jewish mother. They love the same woman, who is mute. The parable is obvious. And the story is set well before the creation of the State. The issue is still just as burning]

Later on, however, a report concluding on a bitterly terse remark and conjoining affective and physical suffering – indeed, death – focuses squarely on Israeli victims:

> A Hedera, une fête de Bat Mitsvah. Un Palestinien surgit vers la fin tire à bout portant. Six morts, la plupart des Russes du sud de la Russie, des Boukhariens ou des Géorgiens, un musicien des Hébreux noirs de Beer Sheva. Une femme se précipite sur la reine de la soirée, une petite fille de douze ans, la cloue au sol avec un tu ne vas tout de même pas mourir le jour de ta Bath Mitsvah. Et la petite fille est sauvée, mais quel souvenir va-t-elle emporter de ses douze ans. (76)

> [At Hedera, at a Bat Mitzvah party. Towards the end, a Palestinian suddenly appears and fires at point-blank range. Six dead, mostly Russians from the south of Russia, Bukharans or Georgians, a musician from the black Hebrews of Beersheba. A woman throws herself onto the queen of the evening, a little girl of twelve, nails her to the ground with a 'no way are you going to die on your Bat Mitzvah day'. And the little girl is saved, but what a memory of her twelfth birthday she's going to take away with her]

Bitterness also colours the following, which implicitly laments the banalization of terrorist attacks ('bien sûr') and the media's resort to litotes to attenuate the shocking:

> Et bien sûr un attentat à Jérusalem. On ne sait pas encore combien de blessés. Espérons qu'il n'y aura pas de morts, à part le terroriste qui a dû se faire sauter. A nouveau dans la rue King George et la rue Jaffa. Au début on annonce un ou deux blessés, et plus on écoute et plus les chiffres montent. Sans doute certains graves. On sait ce que veut dire – moyens et graves. (79)

> [And of course an attack in Jerusalem. We don't know yet how many are wounded. Let's hope there'll be no dead, apart from the terrorist, who must have blown himself up. Again in King George Street and Jaffa Street. To start with, they announce one or two injured, and the longer you listen the more the figures increase. No doubt some of them are seriously injured. We know what moderately and seriously mean]

The relentless cataloguing of multiple terrorist attacks against Israeli civilians is a salient feature of *Une année si ordinaire*, whose very title condenses bitter irony: for this year, which we learn is October 2001–October 2002, is antinomic to normality, being part of the Second Intifada. The psychological tension and dysfunction produced by the politico-military conflict will be addressed below; here, it is worth noting Orner's recording of their somatization in unprecedented outbreaks of colds, influenza, angina and other ailments, which she views as the result of 'une grande tristesse' (82) ['a great sadness']. It is also worth noting Orner's vindication of affect in discussions that, ostensibly, are purely political:

> Rien ne me sort autant de mes gonds dans une discussion « politique » que d'être traitée comme quelqu'un qui ne réfléchit pas car trop émotionnelle. Je revendique le droit de réagir aussi avec mes tripes. Au diable le pseudo-rationalisme. D'ailleurs c'est une manière commode de clouer le bec à celui qui ne pense pas comme vous. (128)

> [Nothing makes me fly off the handle in a 'political' discussion as much as being treated like someone who doesn't reflect because they're too emotional. I demand the right to have a gut reaction too. To hell with pseudo-rationalism. I might add that it's a convenient way of shutting up someone who doesn't think like you]

This reflects philosopher Elisabeth de Fontenay's answer (cited in the Introduction) to Stéphane Bou's provocative question '« Viscéral, la philosophe assume ce mot?' (13) ['Visceral, you the philosopher accept this word?']. Regarding Israel, Fontenay's 'attachement émotionnel, profondément ancré, est en même temps un engagement réfléchi historique et politique' (14) ['deeply rooted emotional attachment is at the same time a reasoned political and historical commitment']. Literary scholar Bruno Chaouat anticipates the sort of (rhetorical) questions that many readers may pose about de Fontenay's assertion:

> N'est-il pas singulier, voire dangereux, pour une philosophe, gardienne en principe du discours de la raison, de légitimer un engagement politique par l'affect? Le pathos en politique, n'est-ce pas le retour du fascisme, la passion et l'enthousiasme qui exaltent, magnétisent les foules, leur font perdre la tête et adorer les idoles? (2011, 196)

> [Is it not odd, even dangerous, for a philosopher, in theory the guardian of rational discourse, to legitimize a political commitment through affect? Is pathos in politics not the return of fascism, the passion and enthusiasm that thrill and magnetize crowds, make them lose their heads and adore idols?]

My response to these questions is that affect and pathos are the essence of much political participation, particularly political speeches and audience response to them, and certainly not just those from fascist politicians. To gain votes, all politicians seek to 'move' the electorate, to engage people at a personal and thus inevitably at an affective level. Orner is lucid on this point and on the muffling effect that 'pseudo-rationalisme' can have.

No amount of pseudo-rationalism is likely to diminish the brute impact of a tableau in Michaël Sebban's *Le Cadenas du marché Yéhouda* (2008) depicting a Palestinian bomb attack:

> L'explosion a déchiré l'air chaud et ouvert une brèche dans le ciel. Elle a fait voler en éclats la vitrine du magasin d'en face, les chaises de la terrasse, et plusieurs passants. Le temps s'est arrêté, transpercé par une déflagration venue de nulle part. Silence. Quelques instants ont passé, l'atmosphère s'est remplie d'une odeur insupportable de métal calciné et de corps brûlés. Et la vie a repris son cours, vite, très vite. Comme pour rattraper ces instants qui venaient d'échapper à l'horloge, un vacarme assourdissant a envahi la rue. Les sirènes de la police et des ambulances, les cris des blessés et des passants, la course effrénée de tous dans tous les sens. (9)

> [The explosion ripped through the warm air and opened up a hole in the sky. It blew to pieces the window of the shop just opposite, the terrace chairs and several passers-by. Time stopped, pierced by a detonation that

came from nowhere. Silence. A few moments went by, the atmosphere filled up with an unbearable smell of charred metal and burnt bodies. And life resumed its course, quickly, very quickly. As if to make up for those moments that had just escaped time, a deafening din invaded the street. Police and ambulance sirens, screams of the injured and of passers-by, a mad rush in all directions]

Perhaps more chilling is what follows: when sirens, helicopters and paramedics arrive, it is merely 'Le scénario habituel qui succède à un attentat' (9) ['The usual scenario that follows an attack'], the adjective 'habituel' (much like Orner's 'bien sûr') indicating that this sort of scene has become normal. The narrator's habituation to such horror is reinforced by his inattention to television coverage of the attack, due to the predictability of its source and motivation (10). Palestinian attacks are framed from the perspective of an Israeli soldier in Eliette Abécassis's *Sépharade* (2009). Noam's sense of Israel being encircled by enemy Palestinian groups leads him to reject a form of rationalism he associates with the West (165), which recalls Orner's rejection of 'pseudo-rationalisme' (2004, 128). On the other hand, another of Esther's boyfriends, this time a French Gentile 'fascinated' by Jews, persists in needling her with a simplistic levelling of the two sides in the conflict:

« D'un côté comme de l'autre … » Et c'était le mieux qu'elle pût espérer de lui. D'un côté les Israéliens, de l'autre les terroristes palestiniens. Non. Impossible. [...] Quand il y avait du terrorisme dans un autre pays, on ne disait pas: « d'un côté comme de l'autre ». Lorsqu'il y avait eu des attentats dans le métro parisien, personne n'avait dit: d'un côté les terroristes, de l'autre les Français, les torts sont partagés, personne n'a raison, les choses sont compliquées. (Abécassis, 2009, 290)

['On the one side/on the other …' And this was the best she could hope for from him. On the one side the Israelis, on the other the Palestinian terrorists. No. Impossible. [...] When there was terrorism in another country, people didn't say 'On the one side/on the other'. When there'd been attacks in the Paris metro, nobody had said: on the one side the terrorists, on the other the French, the wrongdoing is shared, nobody is right, things are complicated]

Rather than on this public, politico-military level, Chochana Boukhobza's *Le Troisième Jour* (2010) treats the Arab–Israeli conflict on a private, (inter)personal plane. Striking in the following extract is the refusal of the (unnamed) Palestinian woman to acknowledge the existence of the Jewish woman (the homodiegetic narrator Rachel)

– the negative obverse of the Levinasian imperative to acknowledge and respect in all its alterity the 'face' of the Other:

> Elle n'a pas répondu à mon sourire. Elle me regardait comme si j'étais transparente, comme si je n'étais rien. Elle s'adressait à cette transparence pour écouler son raisin. J'avais oublié qu'en principe nous étions ennemies. Qu'il y a entre nous le manque de paix, les pneus brûlés des enfants de Gaza, les tirs de nos soldats à Hébron, à Jénine et Ramallah, les jets de caillasse des adolescents masqués sur tout ce qui porte l'uniforme de Tsahal, sur toutes les voitures, civiles ou militaires, des Israéliens. (66)

> [She didn't respond to my smile. She looked at me as if I were transparent, as if I were nothing. She was addressing this transparency in order to sell her grapes. I'd forgotten that in theory we were enemies. That between us there is the lack of peace, the Gaza children's burnt tyres, our soldiers' shooting in Hebron, Jenin and Ramallah, the masked teenagers' stone throwing at anything in a Tzahal uniform, at all Israeli cars, whether civil or military]

The only acknowledgement made by the Palestinian woman is when she exhorts Rachel to admire the fine fruit she is selling: 'Manière de dire que même si nous étions supposées nous haïr, ce n'était pas une raison pour renoncer à la beauté' (66) ['A way of saying that even if we were supposed to hate each other, that was no reason to give up on beauty']. And the encounter between the Palestinian woman and another Jewish woman who suddenly appears on the scene scantily clad is infused with deep animus:

> Et l'une et l'autre se jugeaient en silence, l'une se disait: malheureuse, t'es prisonnière de ton connard de mari et de ta foutue tradition, l'autre qui ruminait, espèce de sale pute à moitié nue, Juive de malheur, ta vue m'offense les yeux et souille mon âme. (67)

> [And the two women silently judged each other, one thinking, 'You poor woman, you're a prisoner of your stupid bastard husband and of your bloody tradition'; the other one brooding, 'Filthy half-naked whore, wretched Jewess, the sight of you offends my eyes and sullies my soul']

In these two encounters the Arab–Jewish conflict is played out on a private, gendered level, but is no less palpable than the more dramatic avatars of conflict on a wider, geopolitical scale. A further scene of private interaction, this time between Rachel and a six-year-old Palestinian boy charged by his father with protecting her in the Old City of Jerusalem, directly foregrounds the hatred of the Palestinian boy for the Israeli woman, whom he automatically equates with his people's enemy (243–44).

Rachel's response makes it clear that the Palestinian child's hatred is not reciprocated, but does express anger, invoking the more enlightened affect and cognition of his father *vis-à-vis* the Arab–Israeli conflict (244). The implacable hatred of the Palestinian child for the Jew is reprised and pluralized later on in the novel. Here it is observed by Ilan, a Tzahal colonel who, for all his weapons, finds that hatred frightening:

> Il connaît bien les Palestiniens et les yeux des enfants, qui te donnent les foies, même armé jusqu'aux dents. Il était devant eux durant l'Intifada. Il a vu les pierres voler, les pneus brûler, la fumée qui tournoyait en grandes gerbes noires dans le vent. (55)

> [He's well acquainted with the Palestinians and with the children's eyes, which give you the jitters even when you're armed to the teeth. He'd faced them during the Intifada. He'd seen stones flying, tyres burning, smoke swirling in great black wreaths in the wind]

He is also psychologically scarred by the equally intense animosity of Palestinian teenagers:

> Il n'a pas oublié les adolescents masqués qui se jetaient vers les chicanes, en hurlant « Allahou akbar », prêts à mourir devant les soldats qui tentaient de les contenir, qui reculaient, puis s'accroupissaient, qui visaient, tiraient; des soldats qui s'effondrent, qui demandent à être mutés, qui n'en peuvent plus de se faire lapider et de se battre contre des mômes. (355)

> [He hasn't forgotten the masked teenagers who charged towards the chicanes, yelling 'Allahu akbar', ready to die in front of the soldiers who tried to contain them, who moved back, then knelt down, who aimed, fired; soldiers who break down, ask to be moved to a different posting, who can't take any more of having stones thrown at them and of fighting kids]

The last two clauses express the moral discomfiture felt by Israeli soldiers at having to fight those they deem to be no more than children. Free indirect speech evokes Ilan's partial empathy with the Palestinian insurgents' despair:

> Les soulèvements ont été jugulés; mais le désespoir? Tant que les conditions de vie dans les camps ne seront pas améliorées ... Tant que les hommes ne trouveront pas de travail chez eux ... (355)

> [The uprisings have been crushed; but the despair? As long as living conditions in the camps aren't improved ... As long as the men can't find work back home ...]

His empathy is well informed, for he appreciates the causes of the increased hatred for Jews felt by Palestinians seeking work in the Occupied Territories: their sense of impotence and humiliation (355). In symmetry, however, there is evocation both of the Israeli soldiers' complete lack of autonomy, and of their resulting sense of solitude – posited with sad irony as the sole factor uniting Israelis and Palestinians (355–56).

That melancholic tonality resonates in Henri Raczymow's *Eretz* (2010). Although the diegetic present is 2009, there are many incursions into the past via periodic focalization on Raczymow's dead brother Alain, who had emigrated from France to Israel with high humanitarian hopes of a socialist, secular state in which Arabs and Jews would live together as brothers (11). These hopes were to be painfully dashed as Palestinian hatred of Jews became manifest. A settler in the Occupied Territories explains that it is the Palestinians who insist on different colours for Palestinian water cans and Israeli water cans, because they believe that Jews poisoned wells in medieval Western Europe and that Jews now poison the world in general (29). But a countervailing view is given as the author comments on the settlers in Gilo (38–39). In Raczymow's assessment, it is the settlers' belief that they have a literally god-given right to retain this biblical land which is the main obstacle to peace with the Palestinians. Later on, indignation at the settlers' defensiveness seeps through his otherwise measured prose:

> Nous sommes obligés de construire ce mur devant Bethléem et Beit Jala, disaient-ils, car *ils* nous tirent dessus. *Ils* ne nous aiment pas, comment veux-tu faire la paix avec *eux*? Il n'y aura jamais la paix … Et Anne et moi aurions eu bien envie de leur dire: Mais vous êtes chez eux! Vous avez pris leur terre et vous ne les aimez pas non plus! Et vous les enfermez derrière un mur! À leur place, je serais comme eux, je ne vous aimerais vraiment pas! (129)

> ['We have to build this wall in front of Bethlehem and Beit Jala', they said, 'because *they* fire at us. *They* don't like us, how do you expect us to make peace with *them*? There'll never be peace …' And Anne and I would so much have liked to say to them: 'But you're in their home! You took their land and you don't like them either! And you shut them up behind a wall! In their place, I'd be like them, I really wouldn't like you!']

Raczymow does strive for balance, implying the potential myopia of sympathizers of both sides in a remark about the neutral Viennese accommodation he and his partner Anne have chosen:

Ce palais est bien ce qu'il nous fallait. Logés chez les Juifs, nous eussions pensé aux « pauvres » Arabes. Chez les Arabes, aux Juifs que nous trahissions. Bref, culpabilité des deux côtés. (98)

[This historic building is just what we needed. If we'd stayed with Jews, we'd have been thinking about the 'poor' Arabs. If we'd stayed with Arabs, about the Jews we were betraying. In short, guilt on both sides]

However, in his memories of his brother, reasoned balance gives way to violent vacillation between opposing viewpoints:

Tu n'avais que mépris pour ces jeunes et pauvres Palestiniens qui venaient travailler six mois en Israël, notamment chez toi, au kibboutz, le temps d'avoir assez d'argent pour vivre six autres mois pendant lesquels, chez eux, à Gaza, ils ne faisaient rien. Pourtant, d'un autre côté, ta critique d'Israël était tout aussi virulente que la mienne [...]. (106)

[You had nothing but contempt for those young and poor Palestinians who came to work for six months in Israel, more particularly in your home, at the *kibbutz*, for just enough time to get just enough money together to be able to live for the other six months during which, back home, in Gaza, they did nothing. Even so, on the other hand, you were as virulently critical of Israel as I was]

Violent vacillation between opposing viewpoints forms the very structure of Valérie Zenatti's *Une bouteille dans la mer de Gaza* (2005), set in 2004 during the Second Intifada. Much of this novel's form can be described as digitalized epistolary, since (as stated in Chapter 3) it consists largely in email communication between the 17-year-old Israeli Tal and the young Palestinian Naïm. Tal renders concisely the pathos of the situation for ordinary Israelis: 'Ce sont des jours de ténèbres, de tristesse et d'horreur. La peur est revenue' (7) ['These are days filled with gloom, sadness and horror. Fear has returned']. After a bomb explosion at a café causing six Israeli deaths, she is haunted by thoughts of one of the dead in particular, a 20-year-old bride-to-be onto whose fate she projects herself in horrified imagination (11). Raised by irenicist parents, Tal is distressed partly because of the gulf between her ideals of peace and reconciliation and the bloody reality of numerous bomb attacks in Jerusalem over the last three months (16). Yet she avoids homogenizing Palestinians, attempting instead to view them as differentiated individuals rather than a monolithic enemy (22). And while she recognizes all the myriad factors that separate them, she hopes that if she and her Palestinian interlocutor try to get to know each other, the future of their respective peoples might be less sanguinary and hate-ridden (31).

But her hopes for peace are clouded by other painful memories, such as the assassination of Yitzhak Rabin, which she had actually witnessed at a peace rally and which is powerfully evoked in the passage:

> Puis les visages de tous les adultes se sont déformés, comme dans un film d'horreur. On aurait dit que leurs joues, leur front, leur menton devenaient liquides, et ce liquide lui-même se noyait dans quelque chose d'invisible. [...] Maman a dit: « C'est la fin du monde. Le début de l'Apocalypse ».' (45–46)

> [Then all the adults' faces lost their shape, like in a horror film. It was as if their cheeks, their forehead, their chin were becoming liquid, and this liquid was drowning in something invisible. [...] Mum said 'It's the end of the world. The start of the Apocalypse']

Incensed by Naïm's sneering rejection of all her efforts to engage in constructive dialogue, when he knows that her family have always campaigned for a peaceful resolution to the Israeli–Palestinian conflict, Tal finally goes on the verbal offensive, asking where the Palestinian peace activists are, why the Intifada had erupted just when the Israelis were ready to give the Palestinians their own state, and why Palestinian terrorists kill women, children and even babies – deftly conceding that while he might say the Israeli army does the same thing, at least there are Israelis who protest against this killing of innocents (65). Through a series of aggrieved questions, she then strives to inspire in him if not empathy for, then at least some cognition of the distress induced in, Israeli civilians by the conflict and the daily dangers it entails for them:

> Est-ce que tu penses, parfois, que nous non plus ne vivons pas une situation normale? Que ce n'est pas normal que des parents tremblent comme des feuilles parce que leurs enfants prennent le bus ou vont au café? Est-ce que tu sais que les parents d'Efrat lui ont interdit de sortir avec sa sœur le soir? Comme ça, s'il y a un attentat quelque part, ils ne perdront qu'une fille et pas deux! Tu trouves normal que des parents pensent à ça? Et est-ce que tu sais que dans mon lycée il y a trois filles et deux garçons qui ont été blessés dans des attentats, à qui il manque un bras, une jambe, ou qui ont d'horribles cicatrices? (65–66)

> [Do you ever think that the situation we're living in isn't normal either? That it's not normal for parents to shake life a leaf because their children take the bus or go to a café? Do you know that Efrat's parents won't let her go out with her sister in the evening? That way, if there's an attack somewhere, they'll only lose one daughter and not two! Do you find it normal that parents should think about that? And do you know that

in my school there are three girls and two boys who've been injured in attacks and have a missing arm, a missing leg, or horrible scars?]

Mired in this suffering and longing for an end to the conflict, including the creation of a Palestinian state, Tal metaphorizes the situation as a nightmarish maze from which there is no exit (80). That sense of entrapment is more explicit in the following words to Naïm:

> J'aurais aimé trouver une formule magique pour que tu aies ton État comme moi j'ai le mien et pour qu'on vive en paix. Tranquilles. En interdisant les informations, les nouvelles, les flashes spéciaux. « Les radios et les télévisions allumées en permanence », je connais bien. C'est à la fois un bourdonnement et un martèlement, on se sent prisonnier des voix et des images. (93)

> [I'd have loved to find a magical solution so that you could have your state as I have mine and we could live in peace. In peace and quiet. Banning the news, the special news flashes. 'Radios and televisions that are constantly on' are very familiar to me. It's at the same time a buzzing and a hammering, you feel like a prisoner of the voices and the images]

Naïm's initial antagonism gradually cedes to respect for Tal, and later to intense concern when he discovers that she has been wounded in a Palestinian bomb attack. One of the consequences of such attacks, less dramatic than death or physical mutilation but still of serious import, forms the subject of the next section.

4.2. Acute psychological tension caused by Israel's vulnerability to attack

This tension is salient in a number of the primary texts. Chronologically, the first is Chochana Boukhobza's *Un été à Jérusalem* (1986), set during the 1982 Lebanon War. Having returned to Israel after several years in France, homodiegetic narrator Sarah intuits the tension from the chance remarks of strangers. A bridegroom explains the haste with which he and his bride have married as a will to enjoy together whatever moments possible of a life which could end at any moment, concluding 'C'est un pays où l'urgence est une qualité nécessaire' (64) ['This is a country where urgency is a necessary quality']. A taxi driver

> maudit l'insécurité qui sévit désormais sur les collines, le terrorisme des gars de Bethléem qui imitent les Palestiniens en plaçant des bombes sur les marchés ou dans les autobus. (159–60)

[curses the insecurity that is now rife in the hills, the terrorism of the guys from Bethlehem who imitate the Palestinians by placing bombs in markets or buses]

And a remark rather closer to home made by her boyfriend Bernard in France the last night before her departure for Israel – though 'mi-figue mi raisin' (162) ['half in jest half in earnest'] in tone – is sobering in content, conveying diasporic Jewry's constant anxiety about the ever-present possibility of Israel's annihilation (an anxiety also directly expressed by Jean-Luc Allouche and Myriam Anissimov in my 2011 interviews with them; see Chapter 7):

> « Israël, c'est l'objet du délit pour chaque Juif. Chaque été nous n'avons qu'une hâte, vérifer si le corps n'a pas rendu l'âme. Et chaque année nous revenons piteux, avec un démenti. Nous devrions être poursuivis pour préméditation de meurtre! » (162)

> [Israel is the object of criminal offence for every Jew. Every summer we're in a hurry to do one thing alone, check that it hasn't come to its mortal end. And every year we come back ashamed, with a negative answer. We should be prosecuted for premeditating murder!]

This anxiety is voiced in high-octave tones by Sarah Frydman's *La Marche des vivants* (1997). The attack by neighbouring Arab countries on Israel at its very birth in 1948 produces in French-domiciled Avrom a state of nervous tension that includes multiple emotions, including delirious excitation, as well as insomnia (262). Twenty-five years later, in 1973, a similar scenario occurs when Israel is again attacked by Arab countries, and Egypt and Syria's assault sparks the Yom Kippur War on the Jewish Day of Atonement. Avrom the invincible is visibly traumatized, blanching and uttering, 'Impossible …, dit-il. Impossible … pas aujourd'hui!' (737) ['"Impossible …", he said. "Impossible … not today!"']. Less dramatic than the outright warfare depicted by Frydman are the triggers to psychological tension registered in Chochana Boukhobza's *Sous les étoiles* (2002), set in Jerusalem in 1999, but the effects on one of its characters, Benbassar, of everyday violent conflict between Israelis and Palestinians are hardly anodyne:

> Il ne choisit pas la route de Hébron, qui était la plus belle, la plus courte, mais la plus dangereuse. Les accords de paix avec les Palestiniens tardaient à être conclus et les jets de pierres se poursuivaient sur les véhicules israéliens. […] Grisé par la vitesse, se débattant contre ses souvenirs, il entra dans Jérusalem une demi-heure plus tard. (183–84)

[He didn't choose the Hebron route, which was the prettiest and the shortest, but the most dangerous. There were delays in concluding the peace agreements with the Palestinians and the throwing of stones on Israeli vehicles continued. […] Intoxicated by the speed, battling against his memories, he entered Jerusalem half an hour later]

Even the need to see calming natural objects such as trees, plants and flowers is qualified as frenetic, underscoring the extreme mental pressures of everyday life for Israelis (184). Focalization on Benbassar reiterates that quotidian quality to Israelis' fear of injury and death from Palestinian bombs: 'Israël vivait chaque jour un peu plus dans la peur du sang versé, dans la peur des êtres déchiquetés par des bombes' (185) ['Every day, life in Israel was a little more clouded by fear of spilt blood, fear of being torn to pieces by bombs']. From this wide-lens narrative angle, Boukhobza returns to the close-up, emphasizing again Benbassar's state of nervous tension provoked, ironically, by Israeli's security and defence measures:

Il avait les nerfs à vif ces derniers temps et tout l'exaspérait, les contrôles de sécurité aux points névralgiques de la vieille cité, les soldats postés sur les remparts qui surveillaient les mouvements de la foule, les Jeep garées sur le bas-côté de la route avec, au volant, un homme qui somnolait ou attendait que la radio de bord lui crachote un ordre. À quand la paix? pensa-t-il en frissonnant. L'idée qu'il se faisait de l'avenir l'emplissait d'angoisse. (184)

[He'd been on edge recently and everything infuriated him, the security checks at the sensitive spots of the old town, the soldiers stationed on the ramparts keeping watch on the movements of the crowd, the Jeeps parked on the verge of the road with, at the steering wheel, a man dozing or waiting for the radio on board to spit out an order. When would peace come, he wondered, trembling. His view of the future filled him with anguish]

Reverting again to a wide-lens narrative angle, Boukhobza renders the troubling moral and psychological dilemma faced by Jerusalemites in the face of attacks by Palestinian children (cf. Boukhobza, 2010, 355):

Dans certaines ruelles, c'étaient les enfants qui attaquaient. Des gamins âgés d'à peine six ans surgissaient des voûtes, brandissaient des pierres, hurlaient « Yahoud, Yihia Palestina. » Les Israéliens étaient impuissants contre les enfants. Se défendre, c'était appeler la colère des adultes qui se rassemblaient en criant qu'on massacrait leurs petits. Ignorer les insultes, c'était attirer leurs quolibets. (186)

[In some alleyways, it was the children who attacked. Kids of barely six suddenly appeared from archways, brandishing stones, yelling, 'Jew, long live Palestine'. The Israelis were powerless against children. To defend themselves was to summon the anger of the adults who gathered together shouting that their little ones were being slaughtered. To ignore the insults was to incur their gibes]

The hazards of Jerusalem in particular are also foregrounded in Michaël Sebban's *La terre promise, pas encore* (2002), when a friend warns the narrator Eli, 'Fais gaffe à Jérusalem. C'est vraiment dangereux' (163) ['Be careful in Jerusalem. It's really dangerous']. But Eli's offhand response in fact extends the hazards to the whole of the country rather than just the particularly intense point of its capital city:

Je n'y pense pas. À n'importe quel moment, dans ce pays, un mec peut se faire sauter avec dix kilos d'explosif et anéantir tout ce qui vit à vingt-cinq mètres à la ronde. Il pourrait être là dans ce bar, assis tranquillement dans un coin en train de siroter une bière, et ... BOUM. Plus de branchés en train de boire dans des verres en cristal. Plus de rap cool. (163–64)

[I don't think about it. At any moment, in this country, a guy can blow himself up with ten kilos of explosives and destroy everything living within a twenty-five metre radius. He could be here in this bar, sitting quietly in a corner sipping a beer, and ... BOOM. No more trendy types drinking from crystal glasses. No more cool rap]

Eli's personal insouciance here is offset by his reporting of huge agitation and screams from direct witnesses of a bomb attack (147). In *Sur la frontière* (2002), Michel Warschawski also makes laconic but cogent testimony to the sense of relentless threat experienced by Israelis, via lexis connoting the Second World War: '*Dans un pays qui est à la fois un ghetto et un bunker assiégé*' (17) ['In a country which is both a ghetto and a besieged bunker']. And in *Une année si ordinaire* (2004), Esther Orner conveys one oppressive aspect of this bunker-like existence in Israel: the constant surveillance needed to avoid death in a terrorist attack (27). Simple but poignant details are foregrounded, such as aversion to mobile phones due to the fear of realizing that a loved one has just died through their sudden silence at the end of the line after the sound of an explosion (pp. 30–31). The tension produced by that surveillance in the most banal of situations also emerges in other apparently simple actions like taking a bus:

Comment écrire après ce massacre. Un en chasse un autre. Jeudi à Afoulah, samedi soir à Jérusalem, dimanche midi à Haïfa. Comment vivre, comment continuer. Demain, je dois me rendre à Jérusalem et pour la première fois, je me demande si j'y vais. Si d'habitude assise dans l'autobus j'ai des appréhensions tout en sachant qu'il faut continuer, là j'ai les jambes coupées. (50–51)

[How can I write after this slaughter. One gives way to another. Thursday in Afula, Saturday night in Jerusalem, midday on Sunday in Haifa. How can I live, how can I go on. Tomorrow, I have to go to Jerusalem and for the first time, I wonder if I'll go. If usually I'm apprehensive when sitting in the bus but knowing I have to go on, now I'm knocked sideways]

The normally simple act of using public transport becomes a frightening ordeal as not only buses but trains too become possible targets for bomb attacks (75). Generalized mistrust makes not just travel a tense experience: even the most apparently innocent of pleasures such as a walk by the sea can be infected by fear of suicide bombers (97–98). Indeed, such fear can become an enduring state of mind (194), spawning a bunker mentality strikingly captured in the imperative of the last sentence here:

Si j'accompagnais Maya jusque chez elle, c'était pour remplacer la marche que je n'ose plus faire au bord de l'eau. La digue, la plage me semblent des cibles. Tout est devenu cible. Terrons-nous. (114)

[If I accompanied Maya right back to her home it was in order to replace the walk by the water's edge that I no longer dare take. The sea wall, the beach seem to me to be targets. Everything has become a target. Let's hole ourselves up]

Whilst fear of suicide attacks is justified by their regular occurrence, the cognitive aspects of that fear are not always rational, such are the psychological distortions produced by living through the Second Intifada:

j'étais au café Bialik apeurée et assise à l'intérieur. J'avais refusé de m'asseoir à la terrasse comme si ça changeait quelque chose et comme si ça avait à voir avec un raisonnement rationnel. (114)

[I was at café Bialik, frightened and sitting inside. I'd refused to sit on the terrace as if this could make any difference, as if it were something kind of rational reasoning]

These distortions have erased any sense of personal liberty: 'Tel-Aviv seule ville ou même à deux heures du matin je me sentais en sécurité. Cette liberté est bafouée' (137) ['Tel Aviv, the only city where I used to feel safe even at two in the morning. That freedom is being scorned']. A cognate of liberty, liberation – or rather its negation – is also caustically contemplated *vis-à-vis* the terrorists:

> Hier jeudi un lycéen assassiné à Ofra. Peu importe qui a revendiqué ce crime qui devrait « libérer » nos « cousins ». Ne devraient-ils pas se libérer d'abord de leur fanatisme et utiliser enfin leur créativité pour autre chose que le meurtre gratuit?' (162)

> [Yesterday, Thursday, a schoolboy was murdered in Ofra. It matters little who said they carried out this crime meant to 'liberate' our 'cousins'. Should they not first of all liberate themselves from their fanaticism and finally use their creativity for something other than gratuitous murder?]

The deleterious psychological effects on Israeli civilians of bomb attacks also feature in Michaël Sebban's *Le Cadenas du marché Yéhouda* (2008), where Eli's eyewitness experience takes on a sinister, surreal quality:

> L'explosion a déchiré l'air chaud et ouvert une brèche dans le ciel. Elle a fait voler en éclats la vitrine du magasin d'en face, les chaises de la terrasse, et plusieurs passants. Le temps s'est arrêté, transpercé par une déflagration venue de nulle part. Silence. (9)

> [The explosion ripped through the warm air and opened up a hole in the sky. It blew into pieces the window of the shop just opposite, the terrace chairs, and several passers-by. Time stopped, pierced by a detonation that came from nowhere. Silence]

Unsurprisingly, Eli later concludes that 'Vivre en Israël est un combat de tous les instants' (79) ['Living in Israel is a battle every moment']. Several narrative fragments of Anne Rabinovitch's *Chacune blesse, la dernière tue* (2012) bear this conclusion out, showing continuation through the night of the daily struggle against death. The first concerns the West Bank:

> Le retour de nuit, sur cette route déserte, éclairée par des réverbères solaires, les zones verdâtres au niveau du sol.
>   « C'est pour piéger les terroristes », explique Mardochée qui accélère à fond. La journaliste s'est endormie, inconsciente du danger. (52)

> [The return at night, on that deserted road, lit by solar lamps, greenish zones at ground level.
>   'It's to trap the terrorists', explains Mardochée, who accelerates as fast as he can. The journalist has fallen asleep, unaware of the danger]

The second concerns a besieged *kibbutz* ten kilometres north of Gaza, where children are gripped by fear:

Tout en marchant, Mati parle de la guerre, des enfants qu'il faut réveiller en pleine nuit pour les emmener dans l'abri: « Je ne veux pas traverser cette flaque d'eau … » Pas une lumière dans le kibboutz, et pendant la dernière alerte, une jeune fille a eu si peur qu'elle a tenté de se jeter dans la citerne. (68)

[While walking along, Mati talks to me about the war, about the children who have to be woken up in the middle of the night to be taken to the shelter: 'I don't want to cross that puddle …'. Not a single light is on in the *kibbutz*. During the last alert, a young girl got so frightened that she tried to throw herself into the cistern]

A further sequence hauntingly sets interpersonal desire against a background of insidious external menace:

Je la sens marcher près de moi, en haut de la dune je me tourne, elle est blonde comme la steppe, mais dans ses yeux: la mer. L'instant glisse dans l'oubli, la caresse muette, le danger peut-être, au bout de la plage, des pêcheurs s'approchent, ils viennent de Gaza, ils passent et leur peur est plus grande que la mienne. Les vagues s'échouent sous les corps, je roule avec Nurit sur le sable, au milieu des coquillages et des crabes minuscules. La chair, si douce. Une pastèque pour la soif.
    Quelques barques au loin.
    Dans le ciel, le bourdonnement d'un hélicoptère. (70–71)

[I can feel her walking close to me. At the top of the dune I turn round. She's as fair as the steppe, but in her eyes: the sea. The moment slips into oblivion, the mute caress, the danger, perhaps, at the end of the beach. Fishermen approach, they come from Gaza, they pass by and their fear is greater than mine. The waves run aground beneath bodies, I roll with Nurit on the sand, surrounded by shellfish and tiny crabs. The flesh, so soft. A watermelon for thirst.
    A few boats in the distance.
    In the sky, the drone of a helicopter]

With danger and war as their backdrop, the lyrical intensity and eroticism are disorientingly charged with a high-voltage tension. But tension is inescapable even in more ordinary circumstances: 'Toutes les heures, les informations à la radio [...]. La tension permanente, le sentiment de vivre sur un volcan' (74) ['Every hour, the radio news [...]. Permanent tension, the sense of living on a volcano']. Perhaps the most memorable rendering of that tension is a sequence where it escalates into fear, panic and even delirium:

À travers les vignes chargées de raisins mûrs, à quelques kilomètres au nord de Gaza, des balles sifflent à mes oreilles. Seulement la peur, des hommes tirent sur la plage déserte. Saisi de panique, je me mets à courir, je cours pieds nus dans les ronces que je ne sens plus me déchirer, je m'enfonce dans le sable, le kibboutz n'est plus très loin mais il n'a jamais semblé aussi inaccessible. J'entends le bruit sourd du départ d'une roquette, puis le sifflement perforant du projectile qui trace dans l'air son sillon et atterrit à cinquante mètres de moi. J'oublie tout, dévoré par une énergie soudaine, je gravis encore une dune et puis une autre, devant mes yeux glissent le rêve et l'illusion que je ne connaîtrai plus, comment survivre dans une terre dénuée de paix, il fallait s'y attendre, autant mourir brûlant de soleil, prêt à m'affaisser à chaque pas, je guette ce grand éclatement dans mon corps, je les entends se rapprocher en criant, tout s'éclaire et je m'effondre d'un seul coup. (112–13)

[Across the vines heavy with ripe grapes, a few kilometres away to the north of Gaza, bullets whistle past my ears. Only fear, men are shooting on the deserted beach. Gripped by panic, I start to run. I run barefoot in the brambles that I no longer feel shredding me up, I dive into the sand. The *kibbutz* isn't very far away, but it's never seemed so inaccessible. I hear the dull sound of a rocket being fired, then the piercing whistle of the missile drawing its furrow in the air and landing fifty metres away from me. I forget everything. Consumed by a sudden energy, I climb one more dune and then another, before my eyes the dream and the illusion that I'll never experience are slipping away. How is it possible to survive in a land deprived of peace? I should have expected it, might as well die burning in the sun. Ready to collapse with each step, I lie in wait for this great explosion in my body. I hear them coming closer, shouting, everything is lit up and all of a sudden I collapse]

This disturbing scene in which the homodiegetic narrator's very life is threatened by rocket fire forms a bridge to the next section.

4.3. Severe trauma of bomb attack survivors and those close to victims

Michaël Sebban's *La terre promise, pas encore* (2002) refers to a newspaper report about the effect on a young child of its mother's murder by a Palestinian terrorist:

En première page de *Yediot*, la photo en gros plan d'en enfant de cinq ans qui pleure à l'enterrement de sa mère. Sa mère a été abattue par un Palestinien alors qu'elle rentrait dans la colonie où elle habitait, au nord-est de Jérusalem. Des larmes coulent sur la joue de l'enfant. Je tourne les pages. Des publicités pour des vacances à Eilat, les dix conseils d'un sexoloque. (153)

[On the first page of *Yediot*, the close-up photo of a five-year-old child crying at his mother's funeral. His mother was shot by a Palestinian while returning to the settlement where she lived, north-east of Jerusalem. Tears flow down the child's cheek. I turn the pages. Adverts for holidays in Eilat, ten tips from a sexologist]

The cursory reference and its follow-up by mention of trivial newspaper items underscore the pathos of the child's pain by presenting it as nothing out of the ordinary for the average Israeli. In Valérie Zenatti's *Une bouteille dans la mer de Gaza* (2005), at 17 Tal is little more than a child herself, and an ordinary Israeli who is eyewitness to a bus bombing. The severe trauma resulting from this experience is rendered in terse but moving language, and reinforced by her difficulty in summoning any kind of language for her Palestinian friend Naïm: 'Malheureuse, anesthésiée, vidée, c'est moi, aujourd'hui. Je n'ai pas les mots, je ne les trouve pas, ils me manquent désespérément pour t'écrire' (107) ['Unhappy, deadened, emptied, that's me, today. I don't have the words to write to you, I can't find them, I lack them desperately']. Tal feels marked for life by the atrocity she witnessed, and again stresses the inadequacy of language to convey it or its psychological impact on her:

Un bus est entré dans mon champ de vision.
  Il n'en est pas ressorti. Il n'en ressortira jamais.
  Je ne peux pas, je ne peux pas écrire ce qui s'est passé la seconde suivante, et toutes les secondes qui ont suivi.
  Je ne peux pas. Je ne peux pas. Je ne peux pas. Les mots n'ont aucun sens.
  Terrible? C'était plus que terrible. Affreux? C'était plus qu'affreux. Cauchemardesque?
  Non, l'enfer. L'enfer comme surgi d'un endroit invisible pour s'abattre au milieu de la rue. (108–09)

[A bus entered my line of vision.
  It hasn't come out of it. It will never come out it.
  I can't, I can't write what happened the following second, and all the seconds that have followed.
  I can't. I can't. I can't. Words have no meaning.
  Terrible? It was more than terrible. Dreadful? It was more than dreadful. Nightmarish?
  No, it was hell. Hell, as if it had suddenly appeared from an invisible place to swoop down in the middle of the street]

In the emphasis placed on the hiatus between the media coverage of such bomb attacks and their reality for those directly affected, the sensorium of suffering emerges:

> Tu crois que tu sais tout parce que tu allumes ta télé chaque fois?! Mais la télé, Ouri, elle ne te fait pas sentir l'odeur, elle ne te fait pas entendre le silence, la seconde de silence qui suit l'explosion, la seconde où tout le monde est hébété, pétrifié! Et les cris, après, les plaintes, les pleurs, les gémissements, ils pleurent tous comme des gosses, les blessés, même ceux qui ont cinquante ans! (112)

> [You think you know everything because you turn on the TV every time? But Ouri, the TV doesn't make you smell the odour, it doesn't make you hear the silence, the second of silence that follows the explosion, the second where everyone is dazed, paralysed! And the screams, afterwards, the groans, the tears, the moans: they all weep like kids, the injured, even the fifty year olds!]

Particularly shattering is the auditory shock: 'J'ai entendu des cris, j'ignorais que les humains pouvaient produire de tels sons' (129) ['I heard screams, I didn't know human beings could produce such sounds']. Various traumatic symptoms of her own are conveyed – a sense of void, fragility, vertigo, nausea: 'Je pleurais de me sentir si vide, en vie mais vide, fragile comme une coquille d'œuf, creuse, un gouffre à l'intérieur qui me donne le vertige, la nausée' (115) ['I cried at feeling so empty, alive but empty, as fragile as eggshells, hollow, a chasm inside that made me feel giddy, nauseous']. Here, the asyndeton drives home Tal's fractured mental state after the bomb attack. After psychiatric treatment in hospital, she continues to experience psychosomatic symptoms and becomes a recluse:

> Je n'ai pas remis les pieds dehors depuis qu'on m'a ramenée de l'hôpital [...]. J'ai des vertiges, du mal à marcher, je veux rester dans mon lit. On m'a dit que j'étais en état de choc, que ça allait passer, que c'était toujours comme ça pour ceux qui assistaient à un attentat. (116)

> [I haven't set foot outside since I was brought back from hospital. [...] I get giddy, find it hard to walk, want to stay in bed. People told me I was in a state of shock, that it would pass, that it was always like that for those who were caught up in an attack]

The last clause here is significant in generalizing her experience to all witnesses of bomb attacks. A sense that her very being has been dismantled is succinctly conveyed (128), involving a complete inability to concentrate on anything unrelated to the bomb attack and its resulting carnage (128). And in a final anagnorisis Tal discovers the true nature of her desolate situation: 'je suis une boule de mercure qui s'est divisée en minuscules petites boules affolées' (129) ['I'm a ball of mercury that's been divided into tiny little terror-stricken balls']. Part of the key to her slow but eventual return to, if not 'normal' life (for life is never normal in Israel), then a functioning life, is renewed dialogue with her Palestinian 'Other'-cum-friend, Naïm. Aspiration to such dialogue more generally is the subject of our next section.

4.4. Aspiration to dialogue and mutual comprehension between Israelis and Palestinians

Jean-Luc Allouche's *Les jours innocents* (1984) registers the failure of this aspiration in his own case:

> Il fréquenta quelques condisciples arabes, isolés dans la masse des étudiants, en butte à l'indifférence hostile de la majorité d'entre eux. Jamais l'amitié ne versa entre eux dans la complicité vraie; une réserve non confessée les cantonnait dans le discours politique. Ils n'échangèrent que rarement une confidence ou un aveu. (83)

> [He spent time with a few Arab fellow students, who were isolated in the mass of students, exposed to the hostile indifference of the majority of them. Friendship never lapsed into real complicity; a non-avowed reserve confined them to political talk. Only rarely did they exchange a confidence or a confession]

There is one exception to this Arab rebuff:

> Parfois, il courait avec l'un d'eux, fils d'une grande famille palestinienne, les rues [...]. Il aimait plus que tout le regard approbateur des commerçants, au fond de leurs boutiques, leur accueil courtois et compassé. (83–84)

> [Sometimes, he'd run around the streets [...] with one of them, the son of a great Palestinian family. What he liked more than anything was the approving gaze of the shopkeepers, at the back of their shops, their courteous and formal welcome]

At these moments, hope of reconciliation between Arabs and Jewish Israelis is rekindled (84). But again it is dashed when his Arab friend makes a verbal ambush born of resentment about sociocultural inequalities between the two types of Israeli citizen:

« Qui suis-je? Un bâtard! Un étranger sur ma propre terre! Vous, vous dites que vous revenez dans votre pays. Mais, moi, j'y demeure depuis toujours. A l'école, vos maîtres m'ont enseigné la Bible, vos poètes de Russie ou de Pologne, et deux sourates du Coran. Oui, deux sourates du Coran! (84)

[Who am I? A bastard! A foreigner in my own land! *You* say that you're returning to your country. But *I've* always lived here. At school, your teachers taught me the Bible, your Russian or Polish poets, and two *surah* from the Koran. Yes, two *surah* from the Koran!]

This leads to a series of questions to which, depressingly, there seems no answer:

Comment reconnaître les droits de l'un sans rendre caducs ceux de l'autre? Comment échapper à cette lutte inexpiable de deux peuples persuadés, chacun, de sa bonne foi? Que pouvait l'amitié dans ce nœud inextricable? (84)

[How could we recognize the rights of one without invalidating those of the other? How could we escape that inexpiable struggle of two peoples each convinced of their own honesty? What power did friendship have in this inextricable knot?]

Yet three pages from its end, Allouche's autobiographical narrative contains a detail of deep ethical significance, as he remarks of his old Arab friend:

Je ne lui ai pas dit que c'est par lui, pour lui que, sous la brutalité de l'affrontement politique, j'ai toujours essayé de lire le visage du Palestinien dans sa vérité. (165)

[I didn't tell him that it was through him, for him, beneath the brutality of political confrontation, that I've always tried to read the Palestinian's face in all its truth]

The Levinasian undertones are resonant, and offer a renewed, if highly fragile hope for dialogue and mutual comprehension between Israeli Jews and Arabs.

In *Sur la frontière* (2002), Michel Warschawski also registers his sudden cognizance in July 1967 of the human dignity of the Arab 'Other', which he argues was denied by Jews in the newly occupied Territories:

Et c'est à ce moment que je vois le regard soumis et humilié du commerçant arabe, à qui j'essaie de marchander une peau de mouton avec l'arrogance de tous les colons du monde. Comme un coup de poing en pleine figure, je prends conscience que cette fois l'opprimé c'est lui et que, moi, je me trouve de l'autre côté de la frontière, celle où se trouvent les forts, où se trouve le pouvoir. Et cette place je refuse de l'assumer, immédiatement, spontanément. (36)

[And it's at that moment that I see the submissive and humiliated gaze of the Arab tradesman with whom I'm trying to haggle over a sheep skin with the arrogance of all colonialists across the world. Like a punch in the face, I become aware that this time *he's* the oppressed one and *I'm* on the other side of the frontier, where the strong, and power are positioned. And I refuse, immediately, spontaneously, to take up that position]

In the simile of the punch in the face, that cognizance is inscribed as a brutal coming-to-consciousness. He insists that this reaction was in no sense ideological or political, for he continued to believe that the Arabs were responsible for the war (36). But despite this belief he refuses to side with the occupying forces; what is naturalized as his personal compassion for the occupied people (36) again offers a fragile hope for dialogue and mutual comprehension between the two opposed sides. Warschawski's purview widens out to track the various political efforts that have been made in this direction, notably the creation of the AIC by Matzpen[2] and left-wing Palestinian activists, whose aim was to circulate suppressed information on both sides of the demarcation line (156).

Valérie Zenatti's *Une bouteille dans la mer de Gaza* (2005) is, as a whole, a performative instance of aspiration to dialogue and mutual comprehension between the two adversaries in the Israeli–Palestinian/ Arab–Jewish conflict. The aspiration is evident in one of Tal's early missives to her Palestinian interlocutor Naïm:

Je me dis, naïvement peut-être, naïvement certainement à tes yeux, que, si des gens comme toi et moi essaient de se connaître, l'avenir aura des chances d'avoir d'autres couleurs que le rouge du sang et le noir de la haine. (30)

[I tell myself, perhaps naively, certainly naively in your eyes, that if people like you and me try to get to know each other, maybe there's a chance that the future will have colours other than the red of blood and the black of hatred]

This aspiration is reinforced in future-oriented terms by another appeal: 'L'avenir, ton peuple, le mien, notre guerre, tu ne crois pas qu'on peut en parler, toi et moi?' (33) ['The future, your people, mine, our war, don't you think we can talk about them, you and me?']. While it takes some time for Naïm to overcome his cynicism, even animosity, the two do eventually come to care for each other. Admittedly, this is due to Tal's tenacity, based on the conviction that they are not two peoples condemned in perpetuity to hate each other (70). Yet there is no saccharine happy ending in which the two young people from the opposite sides physically meet and stand as symbol of reconciliation between their respective peoples. Zenatti's novel avoids such glibness; her fictional construct Tal maturely reflects on her epistolary dialogue:

> je ne pense pas mieux connaître les Palestiniens – ça ne rime pas à grand-chose de dire ça, à moins de s'installer là-bas pendant plusieurs mois et de partager leurs vies. Je pense connaître Naïm. (152)

> [I don't think I know the Palestinians any better – it doesn't make much sense to say that, unless you go and live there for several months and share their lives. I think I know Naïm]

Chochana Boukhobza's *Le Troisième Jour* (2010) also portrays an attempt to cross the Israeli–Palestinian divide and foster solidarity with the Other. Despite being accused of treachery for his criticism of settlers in the Occupied Territories (254), Rachel's brother Avner gives illegal asylum in his home to a Palestinian worker (255). His act has had a high personal cost: harassment by the military and civil police, trouble at work and ostracism by some Jerusalemites (255). Avner is not, though, acting in the name of abstract justice, for he actually likes Ahmed as an individual. Ahmed, in his turn, does not abuse Avner's goodwill, refusing the offer to take Avner's own bedroom (256). It is telling that Avner's altruistic gesture of friendship with a deprived Palestinian worker is rare in our primary texts – and that it puts him on the wrong side of Israeli law. The friendship between Jew and Arab to which Avner aspires is examined in the next section, but in the primary texts it is a friendship that either precedes the creation of the state of Israel in 1948 or is located geographically outside that state.

4.5. Jews, Arabs, Nostalgia

Some of our primary texts are traversed by mnemic systems evoking a pre-Lapsarian period of peace and even friendship between Jews and Arabs. However, the putative memories in question are not always to be taken at face value. In some cases it is doubtful whether these memories are meant to be taken as accurate, and/or whether they truly belong to the narrating subject. Nostalgia implies a bittersweet longing for something once possessed, then lost but retained in memory. However, nostalgia may be culturally mediated, and transformed into a pseudo memory, via a process of autosuggestion and wish fulfilment.

The first such text is Joseph Kessel's *Terre d'amour et de feu* (1965), which evokes an originally idyllic coexistence in Palestine of ordinary indigenous Arabs and Jewish settlers who have bought land there:

> Les colons israélites étaient trop peu nombreux pour inquiéter en quoi que ce fût la population indigène. Le sol qu'ils cultivaient avait été acheté un bon prix [*sic*]. Ils ne manifestaient aucune intention belliqueuse et leur seul souci était de faire rendre le plus possible à des terrains jusque-là restés en friche.
>
> D'autre part le fellah, le paysan de Palestine, était le plus doux des musulmans. Tranquille, accueillant, se contentant de peu; rien ne le prédisposait à la bataille. (24)

> [There were too few Israeli settlers to worry the indigenous population in any way. The soil they cultivated had been bought for a good price. They showed no aggressive intentions and their only concern was to produce as great a yield as possible from those plots of land that had previously been fallow.
>
> Moreover the *fellah*, the Palestinian peasant, was the gentlest of Muslims. Peaceful, welcoming, happy with little, he was not predisposed to battle in any way]

Kessel even affirms a gradual perception by the Arabs of positive benefits in the Jewish settlers' agricultural and technological advances (26–27). But a note of latent condescension towards the Arabs creeps in as Kessel's compares the two parts of this peaceful coexistence:

> deux civilisations, l'une endormie d'un sommeil qui semblait éternel, l'autre encore mal formé mais qui réunissait toutes les armes de l'avenir, deux mondes, deux ordres de vie: celui d'hier et celui de demain. (27)

> [two civilisations, one in what seemed like an eternal sleep, the other as yet poorly developed but uniting all the weapons of the future; two worlds, two orders of life: one of yesterday and one of tomorrow]

In Kessel's account the Arabs lived passively, in the past, whereas the Yishuv was active and future-oriented. Moving forward in time to 1960s Israel, Ami Bouganim's *Le cri de l'arbre* (1983) evokes a strong nostalgia in Moroccan Jews for their old life in the home country, where, apparently, Jews and Arabs had mutually respected the ethnic Other: 'Je menais la belle vie là où j'étais, moi! Respecté des Juifs, honoré par les Arabes, et tout mon avenir devant moi!' (8) ['*I had a good life where I was! Respected by the Jews, honoured by the Arabs, and my whole* future ahead of me!']. While this nostalgia occludes the actual, inferior state of dhimmitude imposed on Jews in Arab countries,[3] Bouganim's novel both implicitly acknowledges this state later on and minimizes it via comparison with the discrimination at the hands of the Ashkenazi elite now experienced in Israel by these Moroccan Jews (149; cf. Chapter 3). Further, the novel includes concrete memories of genuine friendship and social commingling between Arabs and Jews in Morocco:

> Au Maroc, le mellah se prolongeait dans la casbah, et la casbah dans le mellah, les murailles entre Juifs et Arabes étaient tombées depuis longtemps. Nous invitions nos voisins arabes à nos fêtes, ils nous invitaient aux leurs; nos saints se confondaient dans une même vénération, nos mendiants se mêlaient dans une même misère, nos fous dans une même folie. Ils avaient leurs dignitaires, nous avions les nôtres, et nous respectant mutuellement, nous avions appris à vivre ensemble. (207–08)

> [In Morocco, the *mellah* extended into the *casbah*, and the *casbah* into the *mellah*, the walls between Jews and Arabs had fallen a long time ago. We invited our Arab neighbours to our parties, they invited us to theirs; our saints were confused in the same reverence, our beggars mixed in the same poverty, our madmen in the same madness. They had their dignitaries, we had ours, and respecting each other mutually, we had learnt to live together]

Nathalie Azoulai's *Les Manifestations* (2005) paints a much more problematizing picture. The Sephardic Jew Anne refers to similar memories of social commingling in North Africa, in this case Arab and Jewish women. But she is more lucid about the risks of false or at least euphemized, mediated memories, and fully aware of Jews' official status of inferiority in Arab-majority countries:

> Et, bizarrement, je me sens presque plus proche de ces femmes arabes qui se rappellent un temps où la haine n'existait pas [...]. En ce temps-là, nous dansions avec elles, tout le monde dansait ensemble. Enfin, j'aime à le croire. Je sais pourtant que l'histoire ne dit pas ça non plus, que dès qu'on cherche, on trouve la haine qui s'avance masquée, les dhimmis [...]. (124–25)

> [And, strangely, I almost feel closer to these Arab women who recall a time when hatred didn't exist [...]. Back then, we danced with them, everyone danced together. At least, that's what I like to think. Nonetheless, I know that history doesn't tell us that either, that as soon as you look, you find hatred advancing under a mask, the *dhimmi*s [...]]

The danger inherent in nostalgia – distorted anamnesis – is succinctly conveyed in Chochana Boukhobza's *Le Troisième Jour* (2010), where it gives rise to mental imbalance:

> J'ai compris que mon père était fêlé et que sa folie était très particulière, qu'elle était le résultat de sa naissance en terre d'islam. Qu'il soit un sioniste convaincu ne changeait rien à son problème. Il portait en lui un terrain secret mais tenace, un terrain où Juifs et Arabes pouvaient s'entendre, faire des affaires, continuer à se parler. (223)

> [I realized that my father was nuts and that his madness was very specific, that it was because he'd been born in an Islamic land. Whether he was a committed Zionist or not made no difference to his problem. He carried within him secret but tenacious ground, ground where Jews and Arabs could get on with each other, do business, carry on speaking to each other]

In this novel of 2010 Boukhbobza is decidedly charier of nostalgia than in *Un été à Jérusalem* of 1986. The earlier novel's reference to elderly Tunisian immigrants to Israel had elegiacally recalled former peace between Jews and Muslims in Tunisia:

> Ils viennent d'un pays où durant des siècles, le juif a vécu en paix avec le musulman [...] c'est en Tunisie qu'ils ont vécu leurs plus beaux jours. Israël ne représente que ce sol trop sacré où ils sont venus mourir et qui rabattra sur eux la dalle d'une tombe. (192)

> [They come from a country where for centuries the Jew lived in peace with the Muslim [...] it was in Tunisia that they'd been happiest. Israel only represents this overly sacred soil where they've come to die and that will close a tombstone down on them]

Quite why Israel's sacrality meant death to this former happiness in a predominantly Muslim country is not spelt out. But the implication is that Israel, as hypostasis of Judaism, had posed such a religious gulf between Jews and Muslims that Arab–Jewish fraternity mutated from a then entirely realizable ideal into a now melancholic memory. Yet not all of the primary texts represent that ideal as moribund, as the next and final section of this chapter demonstrates.

4.6. Ideal of Arab–Jewish fraternity

Ania Francos's *Les Palestiniens* (1968) gives significant space to Arab articulation of this ideal of fraternity:

> Comme je souriais, Ibrahim Makhos, pensant que je pouvais être choquée, se lança pendant quelques minutes, avec sa fougue habituelle, dans un long discours pour m'expliquer que nous étions tous cousins, que nous descendions tous d'Abraham, que les Arabes étaient sémites, ne pouvaient donc pas être antisémites, et que les premiers à donner de l'argent après la « guerre des six jours » pour les réfugiées, avaient été les Juifs syriens. Je renonçai à lui expliquer que je n'étais malheureusement pas sa cousine vu que je n'étais certainement pas sémite et que je ne descendais pas d'Abraham. Le docteur Zouayer, le Premier ministre, m'expliqua lui aussi qu'il se souvenait avec émotion des voisins de ses parents, des Juifs syriens qui, avant 1948, vivaient en parfaite amitié avec lui: 'Nous étions des frères, disait-il, et maintenant, regardez à quoi l'entreprise sioniste a abouti'. (260–61)

> [As I was smiling, Ibrahim Makhos, thinking that I might be shocked, and with his usual enthusiasm, launched for a few minutes into a long speech explaining to me that we were all cousins, that we were all descended from Abraham, that Arabs were semites, so couldn't be antisemitic, and that the first to give money for the refugees after the 'Six-Day War' had been Syrian Jews. I gave up on the idea of trying to explain to him that unfortunately I wasn't his cousin given that I certainly wasn't semitic and didn't descend from Abraham. Doctor Zouayer, the prime minister, also explained to me that he remembered with emotion his parents' neighbours, Syrian Jews who, before 1948, lived in perfect friendship with him: 'We were brothers', he said, 'and now look what the Zionist venture has led to']

The second sentence of this extract implies Francos's scepticism about this ideal, or at least about its genetic underpinnings. One narrative cameo in Chochana Boukhobza's *Sous les étoiles* (2002) initially seems free of such scepticism, depicting a hard-won but now genuine friendship between an Israeli boss (Benbassar) and one of his Palestinian workers (Mahmûd). Given the family meals and village events at which Mahmûd now warmly hosts Benbassar, it would seem that this friendship, while not entirely without reserve on Mahmûd's part, has become at least potentially fraternal (188). Yet the narrator, like Francos, dons no rose-coloured spectacles: despite the friendship, Mahmûd is fully aware that Benbassar's duties as an Israeli citizen include those of reservist in the army, which could lead to conflict or worse between him and Mahmûd's village. And as Mahmûd declares that he would defend his family first even if it meant killing Benbassar, the ideal of fraternity between them starts to seem like a romantic illusion (188). Benbassar's appeal to the model of two armed individuals refusing to killing each other as the route to more generalized peace is summarily dismissed by Mahmûd: '« Tu es généreux et fou. Mais les bonnes résolutions volent en éclats au moment du danger »' (188) ['You're generous and mad. But good resolutions go up in the air in times of danger']. Benbassar nonetheless clings to his ideal of peace through authentic fraternity, explicitly calling Mahmûd his brother:

> « Si nous sommes déterminés à faire respecter nos vies ... la vie ... les autres nous suivront! Dis-le à tes fils, comme moi je le répète à mes amis ... Dis-le, crie-le, mon frère, que la paix ne tient qu'à nous ». (189)

> [If we are determined that our lives ... life ... should be respected ... the others will survive! Tell your sons this, as I repeat it to my friends ... Tell it, shout it out loud, my brother, that peace depends only on us]

But ultimately even Benbassar, with a sense of nausea, concedes Mahmûd's point, and the conversation between them is closed. Pessimistic though this scenario is, there is a crumb of comfort in Mahmûd's comment that Benbassar's lack of interest in conflictual Arab–Jewish politics and in the possession of disputed land has made him into a more peaceable man (236).

Fraternity in the sense of friendship and mutual support between a Jewish and an Arab Israeli features in Esther Orner's *Une année si ordinaire* (2004):

> J'arrive chez moi, je rencontre Abed que je dois régler pour le nettoyage des escaliers. Il propose de me porter mes sacs, il insiste et me rappelle qu'à la guerre du Golfe je lui avais ouvert ma chambre étanche. Et on se quitte sur des vœux que toute cette violence puisse un jour s'arrêter. (120)

> [I get home, I meet Abed, whom I must pay for the stair cleaning. He offers to carry my bags, insists and reminds me that during the Gulf War I'd opened up my sealed room to him. And we leave each other with the wish that all this violence will one day stop]

Given Mahmûd's words in Boukhobza's *Sous les étoiles* about potentially killing his Israeli friend in order to protect his own people, Orner's subsequent reflections on such killing may appear naive, but she does try level-headedly to assess the political stakes of the situation:

Je ne peux m'imaginer que lorsque l'on a ce genre de relations, ils puissent vous tuer comme c'est arrivé si souvent. Chaya, le frère d'Esther une amie d'enfance et tant d'autres. Certains avec beaucoup de regrets ont dû renvoyer de fidèles et excellents ouvriers. Mais Ahmed et Abed sont des Israéliens. Ils ne sont pas fous. Les Arabes israéliens même s'ils sont palestiniens ne nous attaqueront pas comme vient de le dire un député arabe qui ne représente qu'une petite partie de son peuple et dont la haine d'Israël atteint des sommets. (120)

[I can't imagine that when you have that sort of relationship, they can kill you as has happened so often. Chaya, the brother of Esther, a childhood friend, and so many others. Many have very regretfully had to let go faithful and excellent workers. But Ahmed and Abed are Israelis. They're not mad. Arab Israelis, even if they're Palestinians, won't attack us as was claimed by an Arab member of parliament who only represents a small part of his people and whose hatred for Israel reaches record levels]

As its title suggests, level-headed political assessment is rare for the eponymous character of Olivia Rosenthal's *Les Fantaisies spéculatives de J. H. le sémite* (2005). Rosenthal's postmodern novel does depict a situation of fraternity between a Jew and a Palestinian, but with the crucial proviso that this is a fantasized fraternity existing only in the mind of the Franco–Jewish narrator. The reason for J. H.'s fantasy is his guilty conscience as a Jew about Israeli treatment of Palestinians (70). His quixotic impulses lead him to imagine welcoming a hypothetical Palestinian friend into his Jewish family, making of him, effectively, a brother (69). Indeed, he explicitly addresses him as a brother in the letter he decides to write to this as yet unknown Palestinian (69). However, he comes regularly to veer between wildly idealistic dreams of Arab–Jewish fraternity on the one hand and, on the other, paranoia about how his adoptive Palestinian brother might turn dangerously against him as a cypher for the Jewish enemy (77). In the latter, paranoid phases of his fantasy life, his anticipation of recriminations from fellow Jews parodies the condemnation as self-hating by Jews who champion Palestinian rights (87–88). Thus Rosenthal represents the convoluted network of constraints produced by perceptions of Israel that tend to inhibit even imagined configurations of Jewish–Arab fraternity.

4.7 Endnote

The distribution of material in this chapter demonstrates that Francophone Jewish writers dwell at far greater length on the Israeli–Palestinian/ Jewish–Arab conflict itself rather than on any of its by-products, however important the latter may be. These by-products include the psychological tension the conflict induces in Israelis, which is depicted in eight of the primary texts, and the severe trauma suffered by Israeli survivors of suicide attacks, which appears in two of the primary texts. Possible mitigators of that conflict receive relatively limited coverage, too. Efforts at dialogue and mutual comprehension between the two enemy sides appear in four primary texts; four also consider the nostalgia felt by (mainly Sephardic/Mizrahi) Jews for peaceful and even amicable coexistence; and the ideal of fraternity between Arabs and Jews as (Semitic) brothers is also treated by four works. In comparison, the Israeli–Palestinian/Jewish–Arab conflict receives massive coverage, appearing in no fewer than 18 primary texts. Most of these 18 at least attempt to acknowledge the suffering on both sides, with only three confining themselves to an Israeli perspective alone (Anissimov, 1989; Sebban, 2008; Abécassis, 2009), and only two to a Palestinian perspective alone (Francos, 1968; Warschawski, 2002).

Francophone Jewish writers overwhelmingly relay a psychic division in Israeli Jews which is summed up by two orthogonal sentences in Valérie Zenatti's *Une bouteille dans la mer de Gaza* (2005):

> Tout ça, c'est de la faute aux Palestiniens, qui ne veulent pas la paix, qui nous haïssent, qui ne rêvent que de nous tuer. Non, c'est notre faute à nous, qui leur refusons, depuis des années, le droit à un État, mais de quel droit leur refuse-t-on ce droit? (129)

> [All that, it's the fault of the Palestinians, who don't want peace, who hate us, who dream only of killing us. No, it's *our* fault, for years we've been refusing them the right to a state, but what right do we have to refuse this right?]

The dialectic of these two sentences juxtaposes contrasting processes of affect (Jewish Israeli fear of murder by hate-filled Palestinians) and cognition (Jewish Israeli cognitive awareness of denying Palestinians the right to self-determination). But whereas in Hegelian dialectic the thesis and antithesis should result in a synthesis, no such resolution of the two opposed elements transpires here. In their failure to produce any resolution, these two processes condense the sempiternal intractability of the Arab–Israeli conflict.

Notes

1 A similar (though not identical) analysis was made *in situ* by the non-Jewish Albert Londres, who visited Palestine in 1929: 'Plus la situation des Juifs s'affirmait en Palestine, plus les privilèges féodaux des chefs arabes se trouvaient menacés. Les temps étaient venus d'arrêter l'*invasion juive*. Il fallait, pour cela, exciter les fellahs (les serfs) que les Juifs, dans l'ordinaire de la vie, ne gênaient pas outré mesure' (190) ['The stronger the Jews' situation in Palestine became, the more the feudal privileges of the Arab chiefs were threatened. The time had come to arrest the *Jewish invasion*. For that, they had to whip up feeling among the *fellah*s (the serfs) who, in everyday life, were not unduly bothered by the Jews').

2 Matzpen was a revolutionary socialist and anti-Zionist organization active from 1962 until the late 1980s.

3 Bruno Chaouat pertinently recalls Albert Memmi's cynicism: 'Comme le rappelait Albert Memmi dans les années soixante-dix, « la fameuse vie idyllique des Juifs dans les pays arabes, c'est un mythe! »' (2007, 160, citing Memmi, 50) ['As Albert Memmi reminded us in the 1970s, "the legendary idyllic life of Jews in Arab countries is a myth!"'].

CHAPTER FIVE

Arab–Israeli Conflict
Turned Franco–Israeli Conflict

Chapter 5 studies the third nexus of conflict limned in the primary texts: that produced between Israel and France by what is perceived as the latter's systematic anti-Israeli/anti-Zionist bias regarding the Israeli–Palestinian question. This is a bias with potentially very close links to antisemitism. Indeed, at the start of the twenty-first century, the (non-Jewish) philosopher, political scientist and historian of ideas Pierre-André Taguieff suggested that anti-Israeli/anti-Zionist sentiments have spawned a new form of antisemitism. Referring to a rise in antisemitic attacks without precedent in post-Second World War France, he avers:

> Cette récente vague de judéophobie est inséparable d'un discours idéologique légitimatoire et mobilisateur dont la diffusion est planétaire, où l'on reconnaît certains héritages de mots et de thèmes provenant des diverses traditions antijuives, mais aussi de noveaux motifs d'accusation, centrés sur « Israël » et « le sionisme », érigés en mythes répulsifs. Pour aller à l'essentiel, disons que sa forme argumentative générale est la suivante: « Les Juifs sont tous des sionistes plus ou moins cachés; or le sionisme est un colonialisme, un impérialisme et un racisme; donc les Juifs sont des colonialistes, des impérialistes et des racistes, déclarés ou dissimulés ». C'est à travers une représentation du « sionisme » comme incarnation du mal absolu que s'est constituée une vision antijuive dans la seconde moitié du XXe siècle. (12)

> [This recent wave of Judaeophobia cannot be separated from a mobilizing and legitimizing ideological discourse present across the world, in which one recognizes certain legacies of words and themes coming from diverse anti-Jewish traditions, but also new grounds for accusation, centring on 'Israel' and 'Zionism', which are set up as repulsive myths. To cut to the

chase, let's say that the general form of argument is as follows: 'Whether they declare or hide it, Jews are all Zionists; well, Zionism is a form of colonialism, imperialism and racism; therefore Jews are colonialists, imperialists and racists, whether they declare it or hide it'. It is through a representation of 'Zionism' as the incarnation of absolute evil that an anti-Jewish vision has been formed in the second half of the twentieth century]

It is also worth noting the recollection of historian and J-Call[1] member Élie Barnavi about his two years (2000–2002) as ambassador of Israel to France:

> Jamais, même aux pires heures de la guerre du Liban, Israël n'avait été l'objet d'une attaque aussi massive et vicieuse, sans rapport aucun avec la critique normale, parfois justifiée, dont tout gouvernement est la cible légitime. (Barnavi and Rosenzweig, 16)

> [Never, not even during the worst points of the Lebanon War, had Israel been subjected to such a massive and vicious attack, bearing no relation whatsoever to the normal, sometimes justified, criticism which can target any government]

The period 2000–2002 coincided with the beginning of the Second Intifada (which, as noted in the Introduction, is generally thought to have begun in 2000 and ended in 2005), and many of the primary texts focus on French Jews' experience of that paroxysmal period. The various vectors of the anti-Israeli/anti-Zionist bias portrayed in the corpus include the French media (5.1); the French political class (5.2); the French intellectual class, including some of its Jewish members (5.3); the French education system (5.4); and French civil society (5.5). A counter-discourse within the corpus will also be scrutinized. Warschawski is alone in claiming that Israel is a colonialist state, even a state based on apartheid; however, certain other writers show the perception that those living in the Occupied Territories are colonialists (5.6). Chapter 5 then analyses the common assertion of a causal link between French hostility towards Israel and the increase of antisemitism in twenty-first-century France (5.7); the alleged reproduction of the Israeli–Palestinian conflict and its acting out within the French *banlieues* as a form of geopolitical psychodrama (5.8); and, as a consequence of this reproduction, twenty-first-century Israeli's view of France as a deeply antisemitic country in which the Republican model of integration is defunct (5.9).

As in Chapter 3, the principal emotions expressed in literary renderings of this third form of conflict are humiliation, resentment, anger and animosity; the conditions eliciting these emotions are, as in Chapter 3 and Chapter 4, the cognitive perception of a deep injustice. However, the cognitive structure to the emotions treated in the present chapter is more pronounced than in the preceding two, given the conceptual filtering of the emotions that is required to understand fairly complex postulates. These postulates are the importation of a Middle Eastern conflict into a French context – which is, strictly speaking, a metaphor (and a contested one at that) – and the modulations to identification with Israeli Jews experienced by French Jews in the face of such an importation. These modulations include split loyalties to France as French citizens, and to Israel as diasporic Jews for whom Israel represents, inter alia, a spiritual hypostasis and a safe haven should antisemitism in the Hexagon become intolerable.

5.1. French media

Before examining the primary texts' representation of this perceived anti-Israeli bias in the French media, I will outline a number of relevant reflections from non-literary discursive fields. The first comes from academic, writer and critic Éric Marty. In the context of France's reaction to the Second Intifada, Marty points to 'les innombrables falsifications, erreurs, malveillances, bévues chaque jour assénées sur tous les médias quels qu'ils soient' (2003, 28) ['the countless falsifications, errors, spiteful outbursts, daily blunders in all the media irrespective of type']. For Marty, media disinformation represents a loss of freedom against which at least some of the French polity has an intensely negative reaction (2003, 29). Marty posits a cynically selective reporting of events which contributes to a deformation of reality in the Middle East (2003, 31–32), and accuses the French media of overt anti-Israeli propaganda in reference to Arab wars of aggression against Israel in 1948, 1967 and 1973 (45). He also engages in telling discourse analysis of the media:

> Il y a ces mots qui ne cessent de revenir, comme si le Docteur Mabuse contrôlait la totalité des médias français et y avait inscrit le chaos de la falsification comme principe ordonnateur du langage: « déporté » pour expulsé, « collabo » pour informateur, « colonie » pour présence juive sur les Territoires, « colon » même lorsqu'il s'agit d'un enfant de six ans, « apartheid » ou « quasi-apartheid » à propos d'un pays où l'égalité de droits entre citoyens israéliens, juifs, arabes est la loi, à l'exception du

service militaire pourtant nullement réservé aux seuls juifs puisque les Druzes et les Bédouins le font. (2003, 57)

[There are those words that keep coming back, as if Doctor Mabuse controlled the whole of the French media and had written into it the chaos of falsification as a governing principle of language: 'deportee' for someone who's been expelled, 'collaborator' for an informer, 'colony' for the Jewish presence in the Territories, 'colonialist' even for a six-year-old child, 'apartheid' or 'virtual apartheid' about a country where equality of rights between Arab, Jewish and Israeli citizens is the law, except for military service which nonetheless is in no way reserved for Jews alone since the Druze and Bedouins do it]

Marty's other examples of the French media's bias against Israel are too numerous to quote in their entirety, but pages 31–32, 45, 243, 260 and 261 of *Bref séjour à Jérusalem* may be of particular interest for readers who wish to pursue his analysis.

Psychoanalyst Daniel Sibony concurs with Marty in asserting the French media's systematically anti-Israeli distortion of events in the Middle East. And like Marty, he engages in discourse analysis, which in Sibony's case exposes a conceptual circularity and ultimate vacuity:

Un journaliste français déclare: La seconde Intifada « est une réaction totalement spontanée aux menaces des Israéliens et à leur riposte militaire disproportionnée ». – Leur riposte à quoi? À l'Intifada. Donc la cause de celle-ci est la dureté de la riposte … qu'elle provoque (233)

[A French journalist declares that the Second Intifada 'is a totally spontaneous reaction to the Israelis' threats and to their disproportionate military riposte'. 'Their riposte to what?' To the Intifada. So, the cause of the Intifada is the harshness of the riposte … that it provokes]

But his main quarrel is with the visual medium of television, which he charges with a martyrological representation of Arabs and a corresponding anti-Israeli prejudice subtended by anti-American prejudices (276). Literary scholar Bruno Chaouat, who also has expertise in the Israeli–Palestinian conflict, likewise singles out the particular distortions of French television's coverage of that conflict, and points cogently to their deleterious effects on the psychic health of French Jews (2007, 161). French televisual partiality is further identified by journalist Charles Cohen, who cites media sociologist Benjamin Ferron on the Arab–Israeli conflict:

« *Les médias télévisés induisent une compréhension simplifiée et binaire du conflit: les bons d'un côté, les méchants de l'autre. Une vision manichéenne qui creuse plus encore cette opposition entre chaque camp* », constate Benjamin Ferron, chercheur et auteur d'une thèse sur les stratégies médiatiques des mouvements sociaux dans le conflit israélo-palestinien. (65)

['The TV media induce a simplified and binary understanding of the conflict: the goodies on the one side, the baddies on the other. It's a Manichean vision which just makes the gulf between the two camps all the deeper', notes Benjamin Ferron, a researcher and author of a thesis on the media strategies of social movements in the Israeli–Palestinian conflict]

Interestingly, Cohen extends the claimed partiality beyond television to include social network sites (65). Equally interesting is his citation of political scientist Jean-Yves Camus:

cette situation tendue est assez spécifique de la France ». *La raison?* « *Le conflit fait écho à des problèmes de fond 100% franco-français qui dépassent le strict cadre du conflit* ». (66)

['this tense situation is quite specific to France'. Why? 'The conflict reflects problems that are 100 per cent Franco-French and that go beyond the precise limits of the conflict']

Cohen asserts that the Arab–Israeli conflict is the mirror, and the outlet, for unresolved structural problems peculiar to France, such as the postcolonial question – notably the Algerian War and its memory, which is now projected onto the Arab–Israeli conflict (66). While Cohen does not spell it out, the inference to be drawn is that France salves a guilty conscience about its own colonial abuses during the Algerian War of Independence (1954–1962) by casting Israel as a colonial culprit, thus deflecting attention away from French wrongdoing.

Before appraising the primary texts, I would like to consider one strikingly dissonant voice in the secondary texts: that of political scientist Pascal Boniface. In his *Est-il permis de critiquer Israël?* (2003), Boniface's dissent is not merely from the postulate of anti-Israeli bias in the French media (53), but also from the postulate of such an anamorphic tendency in the French political class and French civil society. He trenchantly expresses his opposition to the then Sharon government of Israel, which is of course his absolute right. More questionable is a disingenuous blind spot that limits many of his analyses. For in frequently asking why the French are apparently so much more sensitive to antisemitism than to Islamophobia or anti-Arab racism, Boniface occludes France's historical guilt about its publicly recognized collusion in the Shoah[2] – which is, patently, the prime reason for that greater sensitivity. In a book of 238 pages, the first time Boniface makes even a fleeting reference to Vichy is on page 100. What some readers at least will find perturbing is the document that motivated the writing of Boniface's book and is included within it as an annex. This was an internal note for the Parti Socialiste sent by Boniface in April 2001, in the run-up to the French elections, to François Hollande and Henri Nallet:

> Il vaut certes mieux perdre une élection que son âme. Mais, en mettant sur le même plan le gouvernement d'Israël et les Palestiniens, on risque tout simplement de perdre les deux. Le soutien à Sharon mérite-t-il que l'on perde 2002? (238)

> [It's certainly better to lose an election than your soul. But in putting the Israeli government and the Palestinians on the same level, you quite simply risk losing the two. Is support for Sharon worth losing 2002?]

Boniface's appeal to the Parti Socialiste to place electoral considerations above any reasoned assessment of the Israeli government could be seen somewhat to diminish his ethical credibility in the debate.

After this eclectic set of views of a broadly social sciences orientation, let us now turn to appraisal of just how the accusation of French media bias against Israel is treated in Franco-Jewish literature. Sarah Frydman's *La Marche des vivants* (1997) goes back to a much earlier historical point than most of the other primary texts: the immediate post-Second World War period. The first hint of anti-Israeli bias comes in a comment on a brief article published by *Le Monde* on 3 October 1946:

> Le billet du *Monde* était comme à l'accoutumée méchant, et terriblement mesquin à y bien réfléchir. Ce qui comptait, c'était que l'un des plus brillants philosophes français, que l'une des plus remarquables femmes de ce siècle prissent fait et cause pour la renaissance d'Israël ...
> *Un communiqué du Comité hébreu de libération nationale nous apprend que la cause de la Nation hébraïque vient d'enregistrer deux adhésions sensationnelles: M. Jean-Paul Sartre et Mme Simone de Beauvoir.*
> [...]
> *Avec l'entrée en lice de l'existentialisme, l'imbroglio palestinien va-t-il enfin trouver une solution prochaine?* (214)

> [The short article in *Le Monde* was nasty, as usual, and come to think of it terribly petty. What mattered was that one of the most brilliant French philosophers, that one of the most remarkable women of this century was fighting for Israel's rebirth ...

'A press release from the Hebrew Committee of National Liberation informs us that the Hebrew Nation's cause has just got two sensational pledges of support: Monsieur Jean-Paul Sartre and Madame Simone de Beauvoir'.

[...]

'With existentialism entering the lists, is the Palestinian mess at last going to find a solution some time soon?']

While 'méchant, et terriblement mesquin' may constitute excessive censure, it does appear that *Le Monde* had trivialized support for the creation of a Jewish state from two prominent French philosophers, presenting it as merely an intellectual game about a confused little situation in foreign climes. In the historical context – less than two years after the Shoah was revealed – this is, to put it mildly, an insensitive editorial line. One year later, following the UN's vote in favour of the creation of this Jewish state in Palestine, more overt anti-Zionist opposition from a particular section of the French press – the Christian right wing – is decried:

> une certaine presse française, digne héritière de Maurras, qui se baptisait *Témoignage chrétien*, n'était pas contente, et s'interrogeait, pincée: Mais que vont devenir nos lieux saints?
>
> – Ils ne se demandaient pas ce qu'étaient devenus les lieux saints du temps des Arabes! Et surtout, ils ne se demandent pas comment les Arabes et les Anglais ont respecté nos lieux saints à nous, juifs! ... grogna Avrom furieux. (259)

> [a certain section of the French press, a worthy heir of Maurras, which was baptised *Christian Testimony*, was not happy, demanding stiffly, 'But what will become of our holy sites?'
>
> 'They didn't ask themselves what had become of the holy sites during the time of the Arabs! And, most importantly, they don't ask themselves how the Arabs and the English respected the sites that are holy to we Jews!' grumbled Avrom, furious]

Many years later, Myriam, one of the novel's main protagonists, takes to task the journalist Joël, representative of a profession whose anti-Zionism she sees as rooted in a basic antisemitism (759 and 760). For Myriam, French journalists lack intellectual and moral probity and are willing to communicate only with Israel's militant Arab enemies:

> – Vous avez surtout besoin d'un scoop, riposta Myriam. Et peu vous importe d'analyser une situation dans son intégrité. Peu vous importe la vérité ... Ce que vous savez faire, c'est vous refiler, d'un journal à l'autre,

d'un magazine à l'autre, les mêmes versions d'un fait bien dramatisé, bien sanglant. Jamais deux versions différentes. Jamais une analyse en profondeur … Deux ou trois gros titres bien accrocheurs, surtout en ce qui concerne Israël, et alors, là! c'est le pied! Votre seul interlocuteur valable, c'est un hezbollah bien gras, rempli de haine … (759–60)

['What you need more than anything is a scoop', retorted Myriam. 'And you're not bothered about analysing a situation fully. You don't care about the truth … What you're good at is passing from one newspaper to another, from one magazine to another, the same versions of a well-dramatized, nicely bloody fact. Never two different versions. Never an in-depth analysis … Two or three eye-catching headlines, especially about Israel, and then, hey! It's great! Your only recognized representative is an oily, hate-filled Hezbollah …']

When Joël asks if she is not exaggerating, Myriam ripostes with wounded but eloquent passion. Her referential arsenal is powerful: the bombing and shooting attack on the Jewish Goldenberg restaurant in Paris on 9 August 1982, which was later attributed to the militant Palestinian group Abu Nidal Organization; and the French antisemitism (which in her view explains French anti-Zionism) of the notorious Dreyfus Affair at the turn of the century:

– Absolument pas! Ce n'est pas pour rien que tes confrères ont failli se faire lyncher par la foule rassemblée devant Chez Goldenberg! Pour ma part, je les tiens pour directement responsable de ce qui s'est passé! Ils jouaient cyniquement la carte gouvernementale … Ils savaient qu'en attaquant les juifs, et seulement les juifs, ils vendraient leurs sales torchons pourris … Et ils feraient de l'audimat! Au fond, je me suis souvent demandé pourquoi cette haine contre Israël? Mais la réponse est là! toute trouvée! C'est la continuité de ce vieux fond d'antisémitisme indécrottable que l'on trouve en France, et qui date de l'affaire Dreyfus! (760)

['Absolutely not! It's no coincidence that your colleagues nearly got lynched by the crowd gathered in front of Goldenberg's restaurant! I for one hold them directly responsible for what happened! They were cynically supporting the government … They knew that by attacking Jews, and Jews alone, they'd sell their rotten rags … And that they'd get good ratings! In fact, I've often wondered about this hatred for Israel. But the answer's staring us in the face, we've found it! It's the continuation of that hopeless old pit of antisemitism that you find in France, that goes back to the Dreyfus Affair!']

While less strident than Myriam's, the condemnation of the French media made by Esther Orner in *Une année si ordinaire* (2004) is intensely morally freighted:

> Ce matin en regardant « Thé ou café », j'ai vu les nouvelles en France égales à elle-même – les Israéliens ont répliqué par des tirs sur le Q. J. [*sic*] de la sécurité palestinienne à l'attentat dans un quartier ultra-religieux. Autant d'images d'un côté que de l'autre. Pas une image sur Ramallah en liesse. Puis un communiqué sur Ofra en « territoire occupé ». Comprendront-ils un jour qu'une fois de plus ils collaborent avec les forces du mal? (102)

> [This morning, while watching *Tea or Coffee*, I saw the news in France, true to form – the Israelis have responded to the attack in an ultra-religious area by firing on the HQ of the Palestinian Security Council. As many images from the one side as from the other. Not one image of Ramallah, which is in jubilation. Then a press release on Ofra in 'the occupied territories'. Will they ever come to understand that once more they're collaborating with the forces of evil?]

Such direct authorial indictment of anti-Israeli bias in the French media is absent from *Les Manifestations* (2005). Rather, Nathalie Azoulai implies the bias through the words of her Jewish protagonist Anne, but also represents the opposite view in those of the non-Jewish Virginie:

> – Il n'y a pas eu de massacre à Jénine.
>   – Comment peux-tu dire une chose pareille? C'était dans toute la presse!
>   – Dans quelle presse?
>   – Partout, dans les magazines, les quotidiens …
>   – Mais toute la presse est partisane …
>   – Anne, tu peux accuser un journal, deux journaux, mais tous les journaux, ça commence à faire beaucoup, non?
>   – Je te dis que Jénine, c'est une cinquantaine de morts dont plus de quarante terroristes, ce n'est pas ce qu'on appelle un massacre. (121)

> ['There was no massacre at Jenin'.
>   'How can you say such a thing? It was all over the press!'
>   'In which press?'
>   'Everywhere, in the magazines, the daily newspapers …'
>   'But the entire press is partisan …'
>   'Anne, you can accuse one newspaper, two newspapers, but all newspapers, that starts to look a bit much, don't you think?'
>   'I'm telling you, Jenin was about fifty dead, more than forty of them terrorists. Not what you'd call a massacre']

However, it is Anne's view that there was no Israeli massacre of Palestinians at Jenin which has prevailed in more recent investigation. Of pertinence here are the words – particularly *'un peu hâtivement'* ('rather hastily') – of Luc Rosenzweig, himself a former journalist for *Libération* and then *Le Monde*, on the Jenin case:

> *certains journaux, comme* Le Monde *et* Libération *ont été mis en cause, en particulier dans la presse communautaire juive, pour avoir un peu hâtivement accrédité l'idée, claironnée par les dirigeants palestiniens, que les soldats de Tsahal se seraient livrés à Jénine à des massacres de grande ampleur'* (Barnavi and Rosenzweig, 124)

> [certain newspapers, like *Le Monde* and *Libération*, were called into question, particularly by the Jewish community press, for having rather hastily given credence to the idea, trumpeted by the Palestinian leaders, that the Tzahal soldiers had carried out large-scale massacres at Jenin]

Chantal Osterreicher's *L'Insouciance d'Adèle* (2006) deploys the same technique as Azoulai, dialogue between a Jew (Adèle) and a non-Jew (her boyfriend), to suggest the bias of French television in the early twenty-first century. In one exchange it is implied that a bomb attack on Israeli civilians is of such little interest that it merits literally only three seconds of air time (87). But the French media's minimization of bomb attacks on Israeli citizens is not the only charge made in *L'Insouciance d'Adèle*. Adèle's cousin Jocelyne, who decides to make *aliyah* with her husband, insists on the French media's essential hostility to Israeli Jews: 'Aujourd'hui, les médias ne s'en prennent ni aux Juifs de France et de Navarre, juste aux Juifs d'Israël' (123) ['Today, the media don't lay into the Jews of France or of Navarre, just into the Jews of Israel']. In Jocelyne's opinion, the general public's hostility towards Israel is due to an ignorance created by the limited and distorted perspective of the French televisual and print media (123). As a pendant to this anti-Israeli stance, Jocelyne posits a French media *doxa* of pro-Palestinianism:

> Les Français ont peur. Ils savent ce que c'est un attentat. Ils en ont déjà eu. Ils font tout ce qu'ils pensent être bon pour éviter qu'il ne s'en produise sur leur territoire. Mais au lieu de condamner de front la terreur, par le biais des médias, ils banalisent le terrorisme palestinien, évitent de montrer des images d'Israël ou des victimes d'attentats pour ne pas sensibiliser la population, à la place, montrent des enfants palestiniens dans la misère, et c'est vrai qu'ils souffrent et que c'est une catastrophe pour ceux qui vivent sous l'égide de l'Autorité palestinienne, corrompue jusqu'au trognon. (123–24)

[The French are frightened. They know what attacks are like. They've already had them. They do all they think fit to avoid any more happening on their territory. But instead of condemning terror head-on, through the media they trivialize Palestinian terrorism, avoid showing images of Israel or of victims of attacks in order not to make the population aware of them, and in their place, they show Palestinian children in poverty, and it's true that they're suffering and that it's a catastrophe for those living under the aegis of the Palestinian Authority, which is corrupt to the core]

Along with its factual omissions and focus on negative aspects of Israel, Jocelyne further points to the French media's semantic abuses (cf. Marty, 2003, 57):

Tout est dans la sémantique, les termes utilisés, les omissions d'infos, des focus sur les côtés sombres d'Israël, le fait de ne pas nommer le terrorisme par son nom et de ne pas dire, par exemple, qu'il est inculqué aux enfants palestiniens jusque dans les écoles. (122)

[It's all in the semantics, the terms used, the omission of information, the focus on the grim sides of Israel, the not calling terrorism by its name and not saying, for example, that it's instilled in Palestinian children even at school]

In the face of this mainstream media disinformation, French Jews in *L'Insouciance d'Adèle* need to turn to Jewish community radio for information about attacks on Israelis, for lack of such information from the mainstream French media – an ironic need, given republican France's dislike of 'communautarisme' (roughly translatable as identity politics):

« Il y a eu combien de morts?
– Quinze environ. Et plus de cinquante blessés, dont une dizaine de graves. Et en Israël, quand ils disent « grave », c'est qu'ils sont tout près de la mort.
– Où as-tu eu toutes ces informations?
– Sur la radio juive. À la télé, ils n'en ont presque pas parlé. (89)

['How many dead were there?'
'About fifteen. And more than fifty wounded, about a dozen seriously. And in Israel, when they say "seriously", it means practically dead'.
'Where did you get this information?'
'On the Jewish radio. On the TV, they barely mentioned it']

Finally, Marco Koskas's *Mon cœur de père* (2012) also remarks scathingly upon the French media's biased reporting of Palestinian attacks against Israelis. Like Éric Marty and Sarah Frydman, he singles out *Le Monde*:

Hier il y a eu un attentat à Jérusalem, à un arrêt d'autobus de la rue de Jaffa. *Le Monde* d'aujourd'hui précise tout de suite que c'était contre un autobus « qui relie Jérusalem à la colonie de Maal Adoumim », comme si c'était moins grave, et moins criminel. En plus c'est inexact, Maal Adoumim étant une ville nouvelle, limitrophe de Jérusalem, capitale de l'État d'Israël, et elle compte 40 000 habitants. (145)

[Yesterday there was an attack in Jerusalem, at a bus stop in Jaffa Street. Today *Le Monde* immediately specifies that it was against a bus 'that connects Jerusalem to the colony of Ma'ale Adumim', as if that were less serious, and less criminal. On top of that it was inaccurate, since Ma'ale Adumim is a new town, bordering Jerusalem, capital of the state of Israel, and has 40,000 residents]

And with echoes of the inference to be drawn from Charles Cohen's words (66), Koskas interprets French media prejudice against Israel as displacement of French guilt about its past colonial wrongs in ex-colonies of the Arab world:

Ce terme de « colonie » montre bien que ce qui travaille encore et toujours les médias français, ce n'est pas le conflit israélo-palestinien lui-même, mais le passé colonial de la France. Toujours pas débarrassés de ce poids, les Français projettent sur Israël leur culpabilité à l'égard du monde arabe. (145)

[This term 'colony' really shows that what *still* bothers the French media is not the Israeli–Palestinian conflict itself, but France's colonial past. Still not rid of this weight, the French project onto Israel their guilt about the Arab world]

The postcolonial argument is pursued by Koskas in an unpublished article entitled 'Peut-on encore être un écrivain juif en France?':

Si l'on peut encore être publié en tant qu'auteur juif en France, c'est seulement à certaines conditions. D'abord se déclarer clairement anti-israélien, tout au moins critique à l'égard d'Israël. Les nouveaux stéréotypes médiatiques, systématiquement hostiles à l'état juif, ont sonné le glas de l'époque précédente.[3] La victimologie palestinienne y est sans doute pour quelque chose, et l'accroissement exponentiel de la population musulmane en France également. Sans conteste, par son importance, la clientèle arabe locale dicte aux médias français d'autres priorités.

[If you can still be published as a Jewish author in France, it's only on certain conditions. First of all clearly declaring yourself to be anti-Israeli, at the very least critical of Israel. The new media stereotypes, system-atically hostile to the Jewish state, have sounded the death knell of the previous era. No doubt Palestinian victimology has something to do with it, as well as the exponential growth of the Muslim population in France. By its importance, the local Arab clientèle unquestionably dictates other priorities to the French media]

However, in Koskas's account, of all the French media it is television whose anti-Israeli bias is the most totalizing:

> Aujourd'hui, si je suis encore publié par un grand éditeur français, je n'ai pourtant aucune chance de passer le barrage de la télé, en raison de mes positions pro-israéliennes. Aucune antenne ne me sera ouverte pour dire que j'ai quitté la France parce que mon fils ne peut pas marcher dans les rues avec une kippa sur la tête, sans risquer de se faire agresser.

> [Nowadays, while I'm still published by a big French imprint, I nonetheless have no chance of getting through the barrier of TV, because of my pro-Israeli position. No channel will be open to me to say that I left France because my son can't go down the street with a *kippa* on his head without risking being attacked]

In this judgement, he concurs with the emphases of Sibony, Chaouat and Cohen/Ferron that prefaced this section's analysis of the primary texts.

5.2. The French political class

Returning briefly to *Le Monde*, impugned by Marty, Frydman and Koskas above, it is interesting to note that it in fact published an article by Marty (2000) which seems to subvert the rule they predicated of an anti-Israeli/pro-Palestinian bias in the French media. For in publishing this article, *Le Monde* allowed Marty to reach a wide readership in his condemnation of that same bias, and also in his extension of it beyond the media to the French political class. French journalist Luc Rosenzweig, for his part, refers to a reputation for virulent anti-Israeli bias within one restricted but highly powerful part of the French political class – its diplomatic service:

> *Parmi les institutions de la République, le Quai d'Orsay passe pour avoir été et continuer d'être systématiquement hostile au projet national juif hier, à l'Etat d'Israël aujourd'hui.* (Barnavi and Rosenzweig, 55)

> [Among the institutions of the Republic, the Quai d'Orsay[4] is generally thought to have been and still to be systematically hostile to the national Jewish project in the past, and to the state of Israel today]

Similarly, philosopher Elisabeth de Fontenay rebukes not the French political class as a whole but a specific sector of it – the French left (with which she had formerly sympathized):

> force est pour moi de constater désormais qu'antisionisme, antisémitisme et antijudaïsme font chez certains, chez beaucoup, et plus à gauche qu'à droite, excellent ménage. (30)

> [henceforth I have no choice but to note that anti-Zionism, antisemitism and anti-Judaism are highly compatible in certain people, and in rather more people on the left than on the right]

One instance of these prejudices on the French left is highlighted: its failure to denounce the offensive recycling by Arab and Muslim media of mendacious tracts like *The Protocols of Zion* (Fontenay, 33–34). Another is the refusal of the far left, because of Israel's second Lebanon War and its Gaza War, to join the demonstration against the prolonged torture and murder of French Jew Ilan Halimi (189). When asked by Stéphane Bou, '*Mais vous ne pensez pas qu'un antisionisme de gauche peut se développer sans céder un pouce sur la critique de l'antisémitisme?*' (Fontenay, 191) ['But don't you think that a left-wing anti-Zionism can develop without giving an inch on criticism of antisemitism?'), Fontenay pays respect to legitimate criticism of Israel (192), but on the condition that

> on ne minimise pas, en la traitant de péril *rhétorique*, la violence palestinienne exploitée par certains États arabes et par les islamistes: l'insécurité menace ce petit pays depuis sa fondation. (192)

> [people don't minimize, by treating it as a *rhetorical* danger, the Palestinian violence that is exploited by certain Arab states and by Islamists: since its foundations, this little country's security has been threatened]

An anti-Israeli stance in the French left is also located by journalist and essayist Martine Gozlan:

> Des centaines d'articles écrits depuis vingt ans dans deux journaux – *L'Événement du jeudi* puis *Marianne* – pour lesquels la sécurité vitale d'Israël ne pouvait se conjuguer qu'à travers la nécessité tout aussi vitale de rendre justice aux Palestiniens. Nous avions dénoncé le procès intenté par le gauchisme et l'islamisme à l'existence de l'État hébreu, autant que le rejet par l'extrême droite israélienne des droits de la Palestine à devenir un État. (12)

> [Hundreds of articles have been written over twenty years now in two

papers – *L'Événement du jeudi* then *Marianne* – for which the essential security of Israel could only be combined with the equally essential need to give justice to the Palestinians. We had denounced the fundamental challenge issued by leftism and Islam to the Jewish state's right to exist, as much as we had denounced the extreme right Israeli rejection of the rights of Palestine to become a state]

Whilst Gozlan's final clause attempts to provide a counterbalance and thus to avoid ascription of right-wing bias either to herself or to the two print media to which she has contributed, *L'Événement du jeudi* and *Marianne*, what is relevant for the present study is her positing of leftism and political Islam as allied in their opposition to the very existence of Israel.

The alleged anti-Israeli bias of the French political class emerges in a number of our primary texts. Again, the first in chronological terms of publication is Sarah Frydman's *La Marche des vivants* (1997). This novel relays an early instance (from the immediate post-Second World War period) of such bias against what was then not yet Israel but the aspiration to create a Jewish homeland in Palestine – with the bias being ascribed to pro-Arab interests rooted in French colonialism:

> De même n'accordait-il qu'une confiance méfiante à tous ceux de ses amis politiques résistants de fraîche date qui se proclamaient « amis des juifs » et qui, dans l'ombre, travaillaient contre la création de l'État d'Israël pour ne pas déplaire à leurs amis arabes. (152)

> [Equally, he could only put distrustful trust in all those last-minute resistance-fighter friends of his who claimed to be 'friends of the Jews' and who, behind the scenes, were working against the creation of the state of Israel in order not to displease their Arab friends]

The pro-Arab, anti-Jewish sentiments of these last-minute resisters are also ascribed to the Quai d'Orsay (cf. Barnavi and Rosenzweig, 55) by the character Samuel Merlin, talking a few days after the UN vote in favour of the creation of the state of Israel:

> – Le Quai d'Orsay n'a qu'une seule position, et elle est invariable. Ne pas heurter la susceptibilité arabe. [...] Les diplomates en poste au Proche-Orient n'en ont rien à fiche de l'État d'Israël, ce qui compte pour eux, c'est leurs petits copains arabes ... qui n'hésitent pas au chantage: la France s'oppose à Israël, ou il y aura des troubles en Afrique du Nord ... (261)

> [The Quai d'Orsay has only one position, and it never changes. Don't offend Arab sensitivities. [...] The diplomats posted in the Middle East

don't give a damn about the state of Israel. What matters for them are their little Arab friends ... who don't hesitate to use blackmail: either France opposes Israel, or there'll be trouble in North Africa ...][5]

Twenty years later, in June 1967, that same pro-Arab/anti-Israeli policy is asserted:

> Tandis que les pays arabes obtiennent de l'Union soviétique toutes les armes dont ils ont besoin, pour ne pas déplaire à ses amis arabes, la France, seul fournisseur d'armes d'Israël, prononce l'embargo sur toute vente d'armes aux adversaires potentiels. (638)

> [While the Arab countries obtain from the Soviet Union all the weapons they need, France, which is the only supplier of weapons to Israel, pronounces an embargo on any sale of weapons to potential enemies, in order not to displease its Arab friends]

But Frydman's critique of the French political class is not just of its collective institutions; it can also be *ad hominem*, as when elision of antisemitism and anti-Zionism is imputed to Couve de Murville (French Minister of Foreign Affairs from 1958 to 1968 and Prime Minister from 1968 to 1969): '– Couve de Murville est un antisémite, dit Joël [...] Pardon ... Un antisioniste ...' (689) ('"Couve de Murville is an antisemite", said Joël [...] "Sorry ... An anti-Zionist ..."').

Nathalie Azoulai's *Les Manifestations* (2005) is set in a much more recent period: the start of the twenty-first century, when the political complexion of France was in many ways very different, particularly with respect to the political left. Bruno Chaouat provides an excellent analysis:

> En effet, ce roman est un règlement de compte avec ce que Régis Debray appelle la « gauche divine » [...] Le roman d'Azoulai suggère judicieusement, me semble-t-il, qu'Israël et les Juifs qui lui sont restés fidèles durant la seconde *intifada* ont fait les frais du manichéisme de la gauche divine, qui les a relégués dans le camp du Mal radical. [...] De fait, la gauche divine aura privilégié la figure d'Anne Franck, battue en brèche par la figure d'un Israël martial. [...] Le roman d'Azoulai apparaît ainsi comme le procès impitoyable de la métaphysique qui sous-tend la gauche divine fondée sur une mystique de l'indignation et de l'empathie. (2007, 168–69)

> [Indeed, this novel is a settling of scores with what Régis Debray calls the 'divine left' [...] Azoulai's novel judiciously suggests, it seems to me, that Israel and the Jews who remained faithful to it during the second Intifada have borne the brunt of the divine left's Manichaeism, which has

relegated them to the camp of radical Evil. [...] Effectively, the divine left has privileged the figure of Anne Frank, which has been given a pounding by the figure of a military Israel. [...] Azoulai's novel thus appears as the merciless indictment of the metaphysics which underlies the divine left, based on a mysticism of indignation and empathy]

Azoulai's critique of the French left's growing tendency towards antisemitism disguised as anti-Zionism is welcomed by Fontenay who, referring to *Les Manifestations* along with two other books, states

Je puis vous dire que ces trois livres m'ont beaucoup marquée et que je leur suis reconnaissante de m'avoir permis de faire l'expérience d'une solitude partagée (190)

[I can tell you that those three books really left their mark on me and that I'm grateful to them for allowing me to experience a sharing of my loneliness]

In Azoulai's novel, two exemplars of this growing tendency on the French left are the non-Jewish Virginie and Alain, and their left-wing Jewish friend Emmanuel and his cousins. Anne's bitterness about the latters' sheep-like pursuit of hipness and their concomitant denunciation of Israel is expressed forthrightly in an apocalyptic warning:

– Vous êtes dans la mouvance, vous voulez nager dans ce courant-là, mais sans cesse un autre courant vous emporte ailleurs, vous maintient à distance du banc, de tous ces autres que vous voulez rejoindre, parmi lesquels vous voulez vous fondre à tout prix. Vous êtes juifs et ce courant s'appelle Israël mais personne ne le sait, personne ne veut le savoir. Comme il y a eu la solution finale de Hitler, il y aura la solution finale contre Israël, ce pays ne peut pas durer, il s'épuisera. Rien n'y fera, pour les Européens, c'est le Palestinien le juste, seulement lui. Alors vous vous faites les bons juifs de gauche mais vous serez comme tous les autres, sur les mêmes listes, raflés comme les autres, dénoncés comme les autres, rien ne vous sauvera, surtout pas votre esprit critique, encore moins votre bonne conscience progressiste. (231)

[You're in that sphere of influence. You want to swim with that current, but another current is always carrying you elsewhere, keeping you at a distance from the shoal, from all those others you want to join, all those you want to blend into at any price. You are Jews and that current is called Israel but nobody knows it, nobody wants to know it. Just as there was Hitler's final solution, so there'll be a final solution against Israel. This country can't last, it will wear itself out. Nothing can be done. For the Europeans, it's the Palestinian alone who is righteous. So you turn yourself into good left-wing Jews but you'll be like the others, on the same lists, rounded up like the others, denounced like the others. Nothing will save you, especially not your critical mind, even less your good progressive conscience]

Antinomy between support for Israel's existence/Zionism and the French left is also captured, succinctly but effectively, in Marco Koskas's *Mon cœur de père* (2012). Referring to his French-raised son's response to two Israelis, Koskas remarks:

> Fiston est sidéré qu'ils soient à la fois universitaires et religieux, de gauche et néanmoins sionistes. Il me chuchote à l'oreille: « Mais alors c'est pas des gens de gauche? ... » Car il ne reconnaît pas en eux les stéréotypes de la gauche d'aujourd'hui, toujours hostile à Israël. (188–89)

> [Sonny is staggered that they're at once academics and religious, left-wing but Zionist. He whispers in my ear 'But they're not left wing, then?' For he doesn't recognize in them the stereotypes of today's left, always hostile to Israel]

However, Koskas does not restrict indictment of anti-Israeli sentiments to the French political left. His unpublished article 'Peut-on encore être un écrivain juif en France?' takes the long view, positing twenty-first-century French animus for Israel as beginning with the (moderately) right-wing de Gaulle's infamous insult (see the Introduction). Interestingly, Koskas correlates this souring of Franco–Israeli relations with a conjunction of French guilt about its colonial past and the resurgence of an antisemitism that had been repressed since the fall of Vichy:

> Ce n'est pas un hasard si De Gaulle devient hostile à son ancien allié israélien après l'achèvement de la décolonisation. Deux représentations du peuple juif se succèdent alors dans l'imaginaire gaulliste; la victime du nazisme est devenue un guerrier triomphant. Du même coup, les interdits qu'a créés la Shoah s'avèrent trop contraignants, comme s'ils avaient empêché un certain antisémitisme cérébral de s'exprimer librement depuis la Libération; comme si enfin, il était urgent de se défausser de sa culpabilité coloniale sur l'état d'Israël, aux prises lui aussi avec d'acerbes nationalismes arabes.

> [It's no accident if de Gaulle becomes hostile to his former Israeli ally after the completion of decolonization. At that point two representations of the Jewish people succeed each other in the Gaullist imagination; the victim of Nazism has become a triumphant warrior. By the same token, the taboos created by the Shoah prove too restrictive, as if they'd prevented a certain type of cerebral antisemitism from expressing itself

freely since the Liberation; as if, finally, it was vital to dump your colonial guilt on the state of Israel, which was also grappling with bitter Arab nationalisms]

5.3. French intellectuals

The transformation of the Jewish victim of Nazism into triumphant Israeli warrior in the citation from Koskas above echoes a point previously made by Marty. Marty had observed that transformation in the work of renowned French intellectual Étienne Balibar, presented anonymously in the main text as 'un philosophe' ('a philosopher') but identified in a footnote supplying further information (2003, 47–48). Balibar's stance as viewed through Marty's prism is broadly paradigmatic of many French intellectuals and artists represented in the primary corpus as systematically hostile to Israel. One instance is *Une année si ordinaire* (2004), where Esther Orner refers with sad resignation to the negative vision of Israel purveyed by Israeli film director Gittaï and its warm reception by French cinema critics:

> Gittaï [qui] dans son dernier film *Kedma* démontre que la violence est inhérente à Israël [*sic*]. Daphna l'écoutait, et elle m'a dit je suppose qu'il a perdu tout crédit à tes yeux, tu ne t'y attendais pas. Effectivement et ça m'a rendu [*sic*] triste. Et surtout lasse. L'attitude envers Israël n'est jamais neutre. Et quant à Gittaï, il a trouvé un créneau pour conquérir la France. On dit qu'il n'y est pour rien. Il serait récupéré. Je veux bien. On ne peut récupérer, vérité de La Palice, que ce qui est récupérable. (160)

> [Gittaï [who] In his last film, *Kedma*, Gittaï shows that violence is inherent to Israel [*sic*]. Daphna was listening to him, and she said to me, 'I suppose he's lost all credit in your eyes, you weren't expecting that'. Indeed, and it's made me sad. And above all weary. Attitudes towards Israel are never neutral. And as for Gittaï, he's found a niche to conquer France. It's said that this has nothing to do with him. That he's been recuperated. Fair enough. You can only recuperate, as La Palice rightly said, that which is recuperable]

While not absolving Gittaï for projecting Israel as an inherently violent country, Orner does imply that this has been exploited by the French intellectual class for its own ends. However, Orner is scrupulous in making three exceptions to the implied rule of French intellectuals' anti-Israeli prejudices. One is the implication that five French academics broke a boycott on Israel by attending a colloquium on Proust held in

Israel (50). Another is commendation of Éric Marty's dissent from the prevailing opposition of French intellectuals to Israel (144). The final is a similar lauding of the writer, journalist and politician Françoise Giroud for bringing attention to what is commonly ignored by other French intellectuals – the deaths of Israeli civilians in the Second Intifada (170–71). Nonetheless, the making of these three very limited exceptions tends merely to reinforce the rule.

No such exceptions to that general anti-Israeli rule among French intellectuals are found in Nathalie Azoulai's *Les Manifestations* (2005). In this novel, Anne finds that her passionate love for Israel places her in an isolated and troubling position, unlike that of (inter alia) certain Jewish publishers whom she views as fundamentally self-aggrandizing:

> ces éditeurs qui s'abritent derrière leur patronyme pour publier des pamphlets, en ayant ainsi le sentiment d'être plus libres-penseurs que les autres, plus dégagés, regardez-moi, tout juif que je suis, je critique, donc je suis libre, ni communautaire, ni apeuré comme vous autres … (135)

> [those publishers who shelter behind their patronymic to publish satirical tracts, each thereby feeling more of a freethinker than the next, more casual, look at me, I might be a Jew but I criticize, therefore I'm free, not limited to the community or fearful like the rest of you …]

Another French intellectual demonstrating an antipathy for Israel that distresses Anne is the highly acclaimed Jean-Luc Godard, whose film *Ici et ailleurs* (1976) had been firmly pro-Palestinian and anti-Israeli. When Anne finally steels herself to read a recent article by Godard about the Palestinians, her first impression is that this artistic and intellectual idol has distorted a complex historical moment:

> Et elle, elle lit les paroles de l'idole qui se dit clairement « palestinien de cœur », comme ça, d'entrée en jeu, c'est le titre de l'article, c'est une formule. Il raconte la souffrance palestinienne, ceux qui sont tombés à la mer au moment de la guerre de 1948, ce ne sont pas les juifs qu'on a jetés à la mer, non, ce sont les Palestiniens. (178)

> [And as for her, she's reading the words of the idol who clearly pronounces himself to be a 'Palestinian at heart', just like that, straight off. It's the title of the article, it's a formula. He tells the story of Palestinian suffering, of those who were driven into the sea during the 1948 war. It wasn't the Jews who were driven into the sea, no, it was the Palestinians]

As she reads on, her verdict becomes more damning – that in fact Godard has not only distorted but actively falsified the Middle Eastern conflict, and that he has done so with impunity as a revered left-wing intellectual whose dogma is akin to a religious credo (180). The left-wing intellectual is later denigrated as engaging in endless uniform condemnation of Israel, rather than any form of reasoned debate about it:

> Les mêmes mots sonnent à mes oreilles, les territoires, Sharon, ce connard de Bush. Je me demande pourquoi ils discutent encore de ça, puisqu'ils ont l'air tous d'accord. Ce n'est même pas un débat, c'est un dodelinement. Les intellectuels de gauche aiment ça, discuter pendant des heures sur le reste du monde en se targuant d'avoir inventé la Révolution et les Droits de l'homme. (229)

> [The same words are ringing in my ears: the territories, Sharon, that stupid bastard Bush. I wonder why they're still discussing it, since they all seem to agree. It's not even a debate, it's just head nodding. Left-wing intellectuals love that, discussing the rest of the world for hours while priding themselves on having invented the Revolution and the Rights of Man]

As a coda to this section, it is worth citing a remark from *Eretz* (2010) by Henri Raczymow about his and his partner's experience in sixth-*arrondissement* Parisian circles:

> les intellectuels de gauche qu'ils avaient jusque-là fréquentés (et ils étaient légion sur leur territoire germanopratin) les blessaient toujours davantage dans leur antisionisme tranchant, qu'ils prenaient à tort ou à raison pour un pur antisémitisme. (143)

> [the left-wing intellectuals (and they were legion in their Saint-Germain-des-Prés territory) they'd kept company with until then upset them more and more with their cutting anti-Zionism, which they took, rightly or wrongly, for pure antisemitism]

The fact that Raczymow himself could be described as a left-wing French intellectual, and like Orner a cognitively scrupulous one at that (as is evidenced by the concession 'qu'ils prenaient à tort ou à raison'), renders all the more acute the injury inflicted by a numerically minoritarian but culturally powerful class in France.

If the various primary texts considered in this section depict French intellectuals as a collective institution that fails in its duty impartially to pursue conceptual and ethical truths, the French educational institution appears in other literary mediations equally remiss (even if the conceptual standards expected of it are less exacting) in fulfilling such a duty, as the following brief section evinces.

5.4. The French education system

Anti-Israeli bias in the French education system is depicted in two of the primary texts. The first is Nathalie Azoulai's *Les Manifestations* (2005), where the non-Jewish Virginie evokes the palpable animus of her fellow school teachers for Israel, and their condemnation – in which she starts to participate – of French Jews who defend it:

> J'ai si souvent entendu Anne me parler de son attachement à Israël, de ce que ce pays représentait pour elle, que ça me gêne lorsqu'en salle des profs j'entends les commentaires des autres. Je ne mêle pas ma voix mais je suis bien obligée de reconnaître que, récemment, je me suis un peu plus exprimée que d'habitude. J'ai condamné Sharon avec les autres, j'ai été choqué par les images des camps de réfugiés et par tous ces enfants jetés dans la violence, j'ai approuvé Jean-Paul lorsqu'il a dit que les juifs français défendaient trop aveuglément Israël, qu'ils devaient se montrer plus objectifs, que c'était un pays comme un autre, qu'on n'avait pas le droit de traiter les gens ainsi. (77–78)

> [I've so often heard Anne telling me about her attachment to Israel, about what this country represented for her, that I feel uncomfortable when I hear the comments of the others in the teachers' common room. I don't join in the talk but I have to admit that, recently, I've expressed my views a bit more than usual. I've condemned Sharon along with the others, I've been shocked by images of the refugee camps and by all those children thrown into violence, I've agreed with Jean-Paul when he's said that French Jews are too blind in their defence of Israel, that they should show more objectivity, that it's one country like any other, that they don't have the right to treat people like that]

The second is Marco Koskas's *Mon cœur de père* (2012), which records the author's discovery that new-style history textbooks used in schools are describing Israel in incriminating terms:

> Sur Facebook, ce matin, je lis que les nouveaux manuels d'histoire décrivent Israël sous le jour le plus noir: colonialisme, occupation, etc. Après les médias, c'est au tour de l'école de fausser la réalité de ce pays magnifique. (198–99)

> [On Facebook this morning I read that the new history text books describe Israel in the most negative terms: colonialism, occupation, etc. After the media, schools are now taking their turn in distorting the reality of this magnificent country]

This is also a theme taken up in his article 'Peut-on encore être un écrivain juif en France?', which asserts that 'Certains manuels scolaires sont déjà contaminés par l'hostilité gaullo-hesselienne à l'égard de l'état juif' ('Certain school textbooks are already contaminated by Gaullo-Hessselian hostility towards the Jewish state'). In *Mon cœur de père*, Koskas ponders the cause of what he reproves as falsification of history, concluding that it occurs

> Sans doute pour se délester du poids de la Shoah, qui a rendu l'antisémitisme illégal et intellectuellement intolérable. Aujourd'hui c'est cette illégalité qui est en train de devenir intolérable à la société, et non la Shoah elle-même. (199)

> [No doubt to offload the weight of the Shoah, which made antisemitism illegal and intellectually intolerable. Now it's this illegality that is becoming intolerable to society, and not the Shoah itself]

5.5. French civil society

So far, this chapter has examined variants of anti-Israeli/anti-Zionist (sometimes shading into antisemitic) sentiments in very specific sectors of French society. This final section examines a rather looser category: French civil society. Elements of French civil society may overlap with the other sectors, but broadly speaking it can be correlated with ordinary French citizens who have no special political, intellectual or professional/institutional status. The following incipit foregrounding general statements by two intellectuals on the issue may appear counterintuitive in a section dealing with ordinary French citizens, but is intended to provide a conceptual prism through which to consider the often more affectively driven primary texts' treatment of the issue.

In 'De l'antisémitisme à venir', a chapter of *De quoi demain: dialogue* (2001) focusing mainly on France, the pre-eminent philosopher Jacques Derrida argues that 'il faut en effet redoubler de vigilance devant un endoctrinement anti-israélien qui évite rarement l'antisémitisme' (191) ['indeed one has to be extra vigilant faced with an anti-Israeli indoctrination that rarely avoids antisemitism']. Éric Marty enumerates the diverse ideological, political and economic strands of such indoctrination:

> Et plus encore étais-je dans l'inquiétude de savoir que cette trahison d'Israël, ce reniement, cet accueil fait à une idéologie de masse au nom de l'« amour des pauvres » s'opéraient pour les plus incertaines raisons:

« politique arabe » de la France, tiers-mondisme, poujadisme, populisme, excitation mimétique, intérêts pétroliers, sidération devant le spectacle des foules en furie ou en liesse après le carnage, sentimentalisme du dénuement, orientalisme de bazar, retour de l'énigme de l'identité juive dont la rareté était problématique, gêne et embarras devant cette identité devenue opaque, y compris pour bien des juifs, pression d'une importante communauté musulmane en France, désinformation mécanique liée au simple phénomène des médias de masse, changement cyclique de l'opinion après l'intense intérêt porté à la question de la Shoah, prestige du keffieh sur la jeunesse, lâcheté des journalistes sur place qui savent qu'ils peuvent taper sur Israël impunément [...], lâcheté de l'opinion en France même qui a fait sienne la loi d'être toujours du côté des « faibles », c'est-à-dire de s'ouvrir un crédit illimité de bonne conscience, etc. (2003, 50)

[And I was even more worried to learn that this betrayal of Israel, this denial, this welcoming of a mass ideology in the name of 'love for the poor' operated for the most uncertain of reasons: France's 'Arab policy', third-worldism, Poujadism, populism, mimetic excitement, oil interests, amazement faced with the spectacle of crowds furious or jubilant after carnage, sentimentality about poverty, pop orientalism, a return to the enigma of Jewish identity whose rarity was problematic, unease and confusion about this identity that had become unclear, including for many Jews, pressure from a sizeable Muslim community in France, cyclical changing of opinion after the intense interest paid to the question of the Shoah, the *keffiyeh*'s cachet among young people, the cowardice of journalists on the ground who know they can lay into Israel with impunity [...], the cowardice of public opinion in France itself which has adopted the law of always siding with the 'weak', i.e. opening up a limitless credit in good conscience, etc.]

The length of this quotation is justified by its exceptional ideational range. One salient factor in these disparate components of contemporary French hostility to Israel is a theoretically noble but often superficial, even hypocritical sympathy for the poor and the weak: in a word, the oppressed (a romantically invested category previously identified with the working class). Later Marty essays yet another – but persuasive – explanation for such hostility: the French republican ideal of universalism as opposed to particularism, and its corresponding antipathy for any organism, be it a local community or a nation, based on particularisms such as ethnicity (2003, 60–61). Looking beyond the specifically French republican conception of universalism, Marty sees in Israel an equally valid if very different version of universalism which the French model cannot comprehend:

Comment comprendre ces juifs, en qui tout l'univers affleure puisque toutes les races sont représentées par le nom d'Israël, dans le nom d'Israël et par son peuple composé de Noirs, de Blancs, d'Orientaux, de Slaves, de Méditerranéens et autres, et qui en même temps circonscrit l'appartenance au nom à des conditions fort strictes? Comment comprendre le cosmopolitisme, ethnique, culturel, linguistique, comment comprendre ce cosmopolitisme essentiel du nom d'Israël et du peuple d'Israël, lui qui ne fut jamais, comme Rome, comme Londres ou comme Paris, le foyer d'un empire? Comment comprendre la diversité pure de cet universel, diversité non seulement historique, liée à la diaspora de l'ère chrétienne, mais presque originelle, associée à la dispersion des tribus d'Israël? (2003, 61)

[How can one understand these Jews, in whom the whole universe surfaces since all races are represented by the name of Israel, in the name of Israel and by its people composed of Blacks, Whites, Orientals, Slavs, Mediterraneans and others, and which at the same time confines within strict limits belonging to the name? How can one understand the linguistic, cultural, ethnic cosmopolitanism, how can one understand this cosmopolitanism which is essential to the name of Israel and to the people of Israel, which was never, unlike Rome, London or Paris, the centre of an empire? How can one understand the pure diversity of this universal, a diversity which is not only historic, linked to the diaspora of the Christian era, but almost originary, associated with the dispersal of the tribes of Israel?]

No such appreciation of Israel's universalism and multi-ethnicity occurs to the non-Jewish characters Paula and Felix in Anne Rabinovitch's *Les Étangs de Ville-d'Avray* (1987). When the homodiegetic narrator is banned qua Jew from her old friend Paula's house by Paula's husband Felix after the 'bouleversement' (98) provoked in France by the 1982 Lebanon War, the narrative tone contracts to a terse, compressed minimum, but betrays deep melancholic affect:

Paula ricanant rue des Rosiers après l'attentat. Paula me reprochant de jeûner le jour du Kippour. Les Israéliens dans Beyrouth. Les flics devant les synagogues. Envie de pleurer.
   Paula fragile, émouvante dans sa volonté de toucher la vérité. Notre amitié avait résisté aux années, aux conflits, aux jalousies. Elle sombrait dans une querelle raciste sordide. (98)

[Paula sniggering in the rue des Rosiers after the attack. Paula criticizing me for fasting on Yom Kippur. The Israelis in Beirut. Cops in front of the synagogues. Wanting to cry.

Paula fragile, moving in her will to get at the truth. Our friendship had withstood the years, the conflicts, the jealousies. Now it was sinking in a sordid racist quarrel]

Here it is clear that Paula's anti-Israeli feelings do tangibly shade into antisemitism. Reproaching her Jewish friend for observing an important ritual of Judaism may be minor on the scale; far more grave is Paula's sniggering after a bombing and shooting attack at the Jewish Goldenberg restaurant in Paris on 9 August 1982 that left six Jews dead and 22 wounded (cf. Frydman, 760).

While Rabinovitch's sobriety in *Les Étangs de Ville-d'Avray* is absent from the tone of Emmanuel Moses's *Papernik* (1992) – which is humorously ironic, even bordering on lampoon at points – Moses too depicts anti-Israeli sentiments in French civil society, albeit of a less obviously offensive variety. During their stay in Paris the Israeli Papernik's wife Eva, a defence lawyer for Palestinians, arranges meetings within their own home of 'un organisme dénommé le Bureau Méditerranéen pour la Paix' (52). What is meant to be an opportunity for dialogue between Israelis, Arabs and French citizens degenerates into a forum for Israel bashing:

Aucun des Israéliens invités à prendre part à ces réunions, pour autant que le Bureau pour la Paix les eût effectivement conviés, ce dont Papernik doutait fort, n'avait jamais franchi le seuil de l'appartement, laissant ainsi le champ libre aux Arabes et aux Français – loin de s'en tenir à la neutralité commandée par leur rôle, ceux-ci s'étaient dévoilés des défenseurs ardents de la cause palestinienne – qui avaient d'emblée perverti la nature de ces séances prétendument vouées au dialogue et à la compréhension mutuelle entre les deux peuples en les transformant en une plate-forme destinée à déverser leur bile et leur aversion contre son pays et son peuple. (53)

[None of the Israelis invited to take part in these meetings, if the Bureau for Peace had in fact invited them, which Papernik strongly doubted, had ever set foot in the apartment, so leaving the field open to the Arabs and the French – far from sticking to the neutrality required by their role, the latter had turned out to be ardent defenders of the Palestinian cause – who had from the outset corrupted the nature of these sessions, which were supposedly devoted to dialogue and mutual understanding between the two peoples, by transforming them into a platform intended for pouring out their bile and their aversion for his country and his people]

Chochana Boukhobza's *Sous les étoiles* (2002) differs from both *Les*

Étangs de Ville-d'Avray and *Papernik* in its non-French setting, but converges with them in alluding to anti-Israeli prejudices in France via focalization on the French character Chauvet's prejudices: 'Avec les Israéliens ... Son bureau de Paris l'avait prévenu: des hommes sans éducation, arrogants, colériques' (24) ['With the Israelis ... His Paris office had warned him: ill-mannered men, arrogant, quick-tempered']. In ironic contrast, in Michaël Sebban's *La terre promise, pas encore* (2002) arrogance is exuded not by Israelis but by a French woman living in Israel. The latter loudly condemns the Israeli state as an imperial capitalist yoke around the Palestinian people's neck (171). She also guilelessly admits to the root of her mission to rend asunder this yoke: shame about her grandfather's role under the Vichy government, which has prompted a desire for penitence on her part (171–72). She thus recalls some of the reasons we have seen advanced by Marty for French hostility to Israel: 'une idéologie de masse au nom de l'« amour des pauvres »' and 'changement cyclique de l'opinion après l'intense intérêt porté à la question de la Shoah' (2003, 50). It has to be said that the woman's credibility is somewhat undermined by her partial agreement with Eli's remark that she is completely mad – 'C'est vrai que j'ai été délirante en France' (172) ['It's true I was crazy in France'] – and by her cheerful admission that she used to think she was the wife of Christ.

In *Une année si ordinaire* (2004), Esther Orner recounts two rather more serious experiences of animus against Israel, both expressed by French friends. Madeleine's words during a phone call are relayed via indirect speech: 'Quant à elle, elle ne mettra probablement plus les pieds ici. Et pourquoi? Car elle est contre Israël' (175) ['As for her, she probably won't set foot here again. And why? Because she's against Israel']. In her diatribe, Madeleine rejects any contemporary sympathy for or even tolerance of Israel deriving from the Shoah and French guilt about it: 'Et puis ça suffit de remettre toujours l'holocauste (et non pas la Shoah) sur le tapis. Fini le passé' (175) ['And stop this constant bringing up of the Holocaust (and not the Shoah) for discussion. The past is over']. In so doing, she too appears to substantiate Marty's postulate of a 'changement cyclique de l'opinion après l'intense intérêt porté à la question de la Shoah' (2003, 50). Shortly afterwards, Orner relays a phone call from another, very close French friend who is less trenchant but leaves her more pessimistic about the future of their friendship, for she had at least appreciated Madeleine's honesty (175). The cause of the pessimism is the lack of open and honest communication between them about the Israeli–Palestinian conflict:

Hier à mon retour de Beer Sheva, une de mes amies les plus chères me téléphone de Paris. Pas un mot sur la situation. On en avait convenu.

Elle est pour les « autres ». Mais pas franchement. Elle n'est pas contre nous, mais pour les faibles. On a parlé longuement. Et « l'affaire » sous-tendait toutes nos paroles. Nous avons été « correctes ». Je me demande jusqu'à quand notre amitié tiendra. Elle en souffre déjà. Et je suis triste. (183)

[Yesterday on my return from Be'er Sheva, one of my dearest friends phoned me from Paris. Not a word about the situation. We'd agreed on this.

She is for the 'others'. But not openly. She isn't against us, but for the weak. We spoke at length. And 'the matter' underlay all our words. We were 'polite'. I wonder how long our friendship will hold out. It's already suffering from it. And I'm sad]

The friend's support for 'les faibles' once more resonates with one of Marty's observations about the causes of hostility to Israel: 'une idéologie de masse au nom de l'« amour des pauvres »' (2003, 50). Damage to friendship caused by anti-Israeli prejudices in French civic society are at the heart of Nathalie Azoulai's *Les Manifestations* (2005), where they become most apparent in the first-person narrative voice of the non-Jewish Virginie. At an early point in the novel Virginie is less overtly hostile than equivocal towards Israeli, tending more to sympathy with her young *beur* (second-generation French Arab of North African) pupils, who identify with the Palestinians (77). But later on Virginie's stance towards Israel becomes one of revulsion, inscribed through metonymy, as her erstwhile friend Anne, Jewish and pro-Israeli, becomes in Virginie's unconscious a substitute for Israel itself, and an object of disgust (133). However, such revulsion for Israel is also ascribed to the French in general, via reflections from Anne:

ils disent Tsahal comme on murmure le nom d'un monstre, prononciation déjà épouvantée mais qui se répète à l'envi, Tsahal a tué, Tsahal a bombardé, Tsahal a détruit, Tsahal, Tsahal. (90)

[they say Tzahal the way you murmur the name of a monster, an already appalled uttering but repeated over and over again: Tzahal has killed, Tzahal has bombed, Tzahal has destroyed, Tzahal, Tzahal]

French civil society's revulsion for Israel is equally troubling for the Jewish characters in Chantal Osterreicher's novel *L'Insouciance d'Adèle* (2006), where it is expressed both in what are meant to be convivial social situations and within the workplace. At a party, the eponymous protagonist Adèle overhears crudely expressed anti-Israeli sentiments from drunken young men who entirely ignore the rocket/bomb attacks on Israeli civilians:

> « Ce qui est aberrant, c'est de voir que ces territoires, ils les occupent de manière totalement illégale. Ils n'ont rien à foutre là-bas. Et tous les jours ils détruisent des baraques avec leurs putains de tanks, dit l'un d'eux, la voix traînante.
> – Ils se considèrent toujours comme les victimes. N'empêche que l'Etat d'Israël s'est construit sur une purification ethnique. Et maintenant, le pays vit sous un régime d'apartheid, avec un boucher à la tête du gouvernement, dit un autre avec plus de verve.
> – Ils sont dans l'illégalité, reprend le premier. Ils envahissent des territoires qui ne sont même pas à eux. L'Amérique leur a toujours tout donné. Ils ont tout, et les Palestiniens, ils n'ont rien. (58)

[‘What's absurd, is seeing that they occupy those territories totally illegally. They've got no bloody business being there. And every day they destroy shacks with their fucking tanks’, said one of them in a drawl.

‘They still think they're the victims. All the same, the state of Israel was built on ethnic cleansing. And now, the country's living under an apartheid regime, with a butcher heading the government’, said another with more vigour.

‘They're acting illegally’, the first one starts up again. ‘They invade territories that don't even belong to them. America has always given them everything. They have everything, and the Palestinians, they have nothing’]

Adèle's cousin Jocelyne has an even more unpleasant experience at a party with her husband Dan:

> J'étais à une fête du boulot de Dan la semaine dernière. Il racontait que pour plonger, il aimait aller à Eilat en Israël. Deux types, en entendant en Israël, lui sont tombés dessus. En en rien de temps, ils traitaient Dan de colonisateur et de violateur de droits de l'homme contre un peuple opprimé. Classique. (85)

[I was at a party for Dan's work last week. He was saying that he loved to go to Eilat in Israel for diving. Two guys, hearing ‘in Israel’, laid into him. In no time at all, they were calling Dan a colonialist and a violator of human rights against an oppressed people. It's classic]

Within the workplace, Jocelyne – who is no blind zealot for Greater Israel (see Chapter 6), and does in fact allude to the settlements in Israel as illegal – witnesses the expression, albeit less personalized, of similar prejudice:

> Au boulot, quand on aborde le sujet d'Israël, je me rends compte que mes collègues pensent qu'Israël est un vaste champ de bataille peuplé de religieux fanatiques et de soldats sanguinaires. J'évite d'en parler maintenant. C'est une pure perte d'énergie. (22)

> [At work, when people start to talk about Israel, I realize that my colleagues think Israel is a huge battlefield full of religious fanatics and bloodthirsty soldiers. I avoid talking about it now. It's a complete waste of energy]

Later on, Jocelyne reveals that Dan also faces anti-Israeli animosity directly within his French workplace – a cultured one at that, composed of 'professionnels' (123) – and that his efforts to educate those who in fact know nothing about Israel other than what they are fed by the media, denounced here as propaganda, prove futile (122). The accretion of stress and distress experienced by Jocelyne and Dan is the cause of their final decision to emigrate to Israel, despite Jocelyne's love for and sense of belonging to France (123). As she expresses in briskly practical terms, that love and sense of belonging are outweighed by the unprecedented number of French antisemitic acts that to her mind masquerade as anti-Zionism, despite newspaper editors' rejection of this charge (123). Further, she is sickened by accusations that Dan is a colonizer through mere association with Israel. His calumniators would presumably not demur in extending their framing of Israel as a colonizing state to framing it as an apartheid state. Such a framing is the topic of the next section.

5.6. The accusation of Israeli colonialism/apartheid

These accusations have already emerged in certain quotations above; here, I will focus on them squarely, but preface study of their treatment in the primary corpus by brief consideration of two polarized academic viewpoints. Idith Zertal advances an aetiology of what she clearly reproves as occupation of foreign territories by a colonialist state (a reproof common within the whole micro-discipline formed by the New Historians among whom she numbers). For Zertal, since the Shoah the Israeli state has been determined to promote Jewish self-preservation at all costs, and has regarded retention of the Occupied Territories as non-negotiable (275–76). In this credo, anything less would be akin to a weakening of Israel and thus of Jewry generally, with Israel being hypostatized as the most important locus of Jewry in the world. Marty also refers unreservedly to 'les Territoires', but without the qualifier 'occupés', and takes issue with what he regards as misuse of the term 'apartheid' in application to Israel:

> On a fait état d'un apartheid dans les Territoires sous le prétexte qu'il y aurait des routes réservées aux juifs tout comme en Afrique du Sud il y avait des bus réservés aux Blancs. La différence est toute simple: s'il y a des routes réservées aux juifs, c'est que les autres leur sont interdites sous peine de prendre une balle ou une pierre en pleine tête. (2003, 83)

> [There has been mention of apartheid in the Territories on the pretext that, allegedly, there are roads reserved for Jews just as in South Africa there were buses reserved for Whites. The difference is quite simple: if there are roads reserved for Jews, it's because the other roads are out of bounds to them, on pain of taking a bullet or a stone in the head]

His explanation of the need for roads reserved for Jews is bluntly impactful. Later on, the charge of apartheid is again vigorously rebutted, first via the use of rhetorical questions which invalidate the word's application to Israel:

> De quoi parle-t-on? De quel apartheid? Y a-t-il mise à l'écart d'une race? Dans ce cas comment expliquer qu'un million et demi d'Israéliens arabes jouissent des mêmes droits que les juifs sur le territoire d'Israël, puissent faire l'amour avec des juives et éventuellement le font? (256)

> [What are we talking about? About which apartheid? Is one race being kept out of things? In that case, how do you explain that a million and a half Arab Israelis enjoy the same rights as Jews in the territory of Israel, can have sex with Jewish women and possibly do?]

Marty refers to the French author and journalist François Masperos's observation that there are roads reserved for 'colons' ('colonialists'), but contests the implied negative charge with a further rhetorical question: 'Est-ce pour affirmer une supériorité raciale et pour ne pas entrer en contact physiquement avec l'autre que ces routes ont été construites?' (2003, 256) ['Is it in order to assert a racial superiority and to preclude physical contact with the other that these roads were built?'] His answer is lapidary:

> Non, c'est pour ne pas être tué. C'est que si les « colons » empruntaient les mêmes routes que les Arabes, ils seraient systématiquement massacrés. (256)

> [No, it's in order not to be killed. It's because if the 'colonialists' took the same roads as the Arabs, they'd be systematically slaughtered]

Some of our primary texts, such as Sebban's *Lehaïm. À toutes les vies* (2004) and Zenatti's *Quand j'étais soldate* (2002), contain Jewish characters who believe or used to believe that Israelis living in the Occupied Territories are colonialists; and in Osterreicher's *L'Insouciance d'Adèle* (2006), the word 'apartheid' is used by a non-Jewish character to denounce Israel (85). However, Michel Warschawski's *Sur la frontière* (2002) is the only primary text in which a Jew (Warschawski himself) applies the word 'apartheid' to Israel: 'Le bouclage est un système qui impose aux Palestiniens la séparation, et une séparation imposée unilatéralement se traduit en néerlandais par *apartheid*' (209–10) ['Cordoning off is a system that imposes separation on Palestinians, and a unilaterally imposed separation is translated in Dutch as *apartheid*']. It could be argued that this definition of the word 'apartheid' is a disingenuously narrow one that cannot fail to connote the structural racism of South Africa from 1948 to 1994. But as Marty has opined, the separation of Jews and Arabs imposed unilaterally by the Jews in Israel is for reasons of security rather than race. Warschawski again uses the word 'apartheid' in reference to the Camp David summit of July 2000:

> les négociateurs palestiniens découvrirent à leur grande surprise que le gouvernement israélien voulait faire du système d'apartheid, c'est-à-dire de la parcellisation des territoires, du contrôle des frontières et des ressources naturelles, le statut définitif et la solution ultime à la question nationale palestinienne. (210)

> [The Palestinian negotiators discovered to their great surprise that the Israeli government wanted to make the apartheid system, i.e. dividing up of the territories, control of the frontiers and of natural resources, the definitive status and the ultimate solution to the national Palestinian question]

Warschawski here appears to have redefined 'apartheid' as division of territories and control of both frontiers and natural resources; and again this definition lacks the egregious racism characterizing the South African regime with which apartheid is most widely associated.

Nonetheless, such perceptions of Israel as a racist state guilty of human rights abuses are represented as common in France by the primary texts. It is to the hostility spawned by such perceptions and to their disturbing correlative for French Jews that the next section turns.

5.7. French hostility towards Israel/increases in French antisemitism

A causal link between French hostility towards Israel and an increase in French antisemitism figures in four of our primary texts. The following extract, set in Paris, from Michaël Sebban's *La terre promise, pas encore* (2002), provides a stark example:

> Je suis sorti de la synagogue vers une heure du matin. Trois beurs m'ont interpellé.
>   – Eh! Le juif!
>   – C'est à moi que tu parles?
>   – Ouais, c'est à toi. T'es juif, hein?
>   – Oui et alors?
>   – T'es fier d'être juif?
>   – Oui.
>   – Sale bâtard! Vous êtes des assassins. Vous massacrez les Palestiniens parce que vous êtes les plus forts, mais vous êtes que des enculés.
>   – T'as qu'à y aller en Palestine si tu veux te battre. Vas-y!
>   – Enculé de juif!
>   Le mec s'est approché de moi et m'a craché au visage. (204)

> [I left the synagogue around one in the morning. Three French Arabs shouted at me.
>   'Hey! Jew!'
>   'You talking to me?'
>   'Yeah, to you. You're a Jew, right?'
>   'Yes, and?'
>   'You proud of being a Jew?'
>   'Yes'.
>   'Filthy bastard! You're murderers. You slaughter the Palestinians because you're stronger than them, but you're nothing but arseholes'.
>   'You only have to go to Palestine if you want to fight. Go there!'
>   'Arsehole Jew!'
>   The guy approached me and spat in my face]

The link is also made on several occasions in Sebban's *Lehaïm. À toutes les vies* (2004). On the first occasion, it comes from homodiegetic narrator Eli:

> Je pressentais les regards qui allaient de nouveau se poser sur moi, les réflexions sur les juifs et Israël. J'étais de retour à Paris, capitale de l'antisémitisme. (165)

> [I predicted the renewed staring at me, the comments on Jews and Israel. I was back in Paris, the capital of antisemitism]

Another iteration of the link comes from Ethan, a militantly left-wing Israeli who had demonstrated against the occupation in his home country (175), but gradually been shocked by what he witnessed during his studies in Paris:

> Je ne fréquentais que des intellectuels du 6ᵉ arrondissement. [...] Cela ne me dérangeait pas de participer avec eux à des manifestations contre les colonies en Judée et en Samarie. Au contraire. Et puis Sharon est arrivé au pouvoir et j'ai compris. Dieu sait que je déteste Sharon mais grâce à lui, j'ai compris. Je les écoutais parler entre eux et petit à petit ils ont commencé à déverser leur haine sur les Juifs. (176)

> [I only kept company with intellectuals of the sixth arrondissement. [...] I didn't mind joining them in the demonstrations against the colonies in Judea and Samaria. On the contrary. And then Sharon came to power and I realized. God knows I hate Sharon but thanks to him, I realized. I listened to them talking among themselves and gradually they started to pour out their hatred on Jews]

In Nathalie Azoulai's *Les Manifestations* (2005), while watching an anti-Israeli demonstration in Paris, Anne makes the link in similarly pointed, indeed dramatic terms, and implies the emotional manipulation of French parents in particular:

> D'abord, il y a la pitié, la charité qu'on éprouve pour les enfants dans la guerre – les bons parents qui voient les photos pensent un jour ils vont aussi nous prendre nos enfants, après les petits Palestiniens ce sera le tour des nôtres de se vider leur sang pour qu'ils s'abreuvent et décuplent leurs forces; les prisonniers torturés, toutes ces familles maintenues dans la misère par l'occupant. Ensuite, il y a la politique, ce peuple qui résiste à l'impérialisme depuis soixante ans, et plus loin, au fond, là où les gens ne posent pas leurs regards, où rien ne s'appesantit, il y a ce choix, plutôt les Arabes que les Juifs. (279)

> [First, there's the pity, the charity that people feel for children in the war – the good parents who see the photos think that one day they're going to take our children away from us too, after the little Palestinians, ours in turn will have their blood emptied so that they can drink it and increase their strength tenfold; the tortured prisoners, all those families kept in poverty by the occupier. Next, there's politics, this people which has been resisting imperialism for sixty years, and further on, right at the heart of it all, which people don't look at, where nothing is dwelt on, there's this choice, we'd rather have Arabs than Jews]

Olivia Rosenthal's eponymous narrator in *Les Fantaisies spéculatives de J. H. le sémite* (2005) makes the link by reference to the empirical fact of 'la multiplication des actes antisémites depuis la reprise des hostilités entre Israël et les Palestiniens' (60) ['proliferation of antisemitic acts since the resumption of hostilities between Israel and the Palestinians']. Finally, it is worth noting that in his unpublished article 'Peut-on encore être un écrivain juif en France?', Koskas implies the link in a wry play on words that supplements the logic of the preceding four primary texts, by suggesting that even if it disguises itself as righteous condemnation of Israel, contemporary antisemitism in France can draw a straight historical line back to (at least) Vichy: 'Chaque jour apporte son eau de Vichy au moulin de l'antisémitisme ordinaire, plus ou moins maquillé en israélophobie' ('Every day brings its Vichy water to the mill of ordinary antisemitism, disguised to a greater or lesser degree as Israelophobia'). Whatever the validity of this historicizing claim, a number of the primary texts examined in the next section suggest that this (alleged) politically correct cover is often conjugated with reference to disadvantaged demographics in contemporary France.

5.8. Acting out

The hostility to both Israelis and French Jews manifested by youths of North African origin in the quotation from Sebban (2002, 204) above pinpoints generational specificities among French Arabs in their attitudes towards the Israeli–Palestinian conflict that are also highlighted by psychoanalyst Daniel Sibony (249). Sibony posits a form of 'violence « mimétique »' ('mimetic violence'), by which he seems to mean – although he does not put it in these terms – young French Arabs mirroring the Israeli–Palestinian conflict in a form of compulsive acting out, and never working through, that targets French Jews (257–58). Although Éric Marty does not refer to generational specificities, he too uses the adjective 'mimétique' ('mimetic'): of the outbreak of the Second Intifada in 2000, he recalls 'l'effervescence mimétique négative contre Israël qui, dès les premiers jours de l'Intifada, s'est répandue en France comme une flambée brûlante et obscure' (2003, 27–28) ['the negative mimetic agitation against Israel which, from the very first days of the Intifada, spread in France like a dark burning blaze']. Nine years later, the material ravages of that acting out (viz., the explosion of antisemitic attacks in France, although of course it cannot be assumed that all such attacks were made by young French Arabs) were asserted by journalist Aurélia Blanc:

> Lorsque le Proche-Orient s'embrase, les agressions explosent: 924 en 2002 (deuxième Intifada), 815 en 2009 (opération « Plomb durci »), presque deux fois plus qu'en temps ordinaire » ... (2012b, 62)

> [When things flare up in the Middle East, attacks [in France] explode: 924 in 2002 (second Intifada), 815 in 2009 (Operation 'Cast Lead'), almost double compared to normal periods]

Her fellow journalist Charles Cohen cites political scientist Marc Hecker:

> des expressions comme 'importation du conflit' ou 'Intifada des banlieues' ont émergé depuis une dizaine d'années, période où les actes antisémites en France, corrélés à l'actualité proche-orientale, sont montés en flèche. (2012, 64)

> [expressions like 'importation of the conflict' or 'Intifada of the *banlieues*' have emerged over the last ten years or so, a period when antisemitic acts in France, linked to current events in the Middle East, rose sharply]

In his *Intifada française? De l'importation du conflit israélo-palestinien* (2012), Hecker puts the case concisely and rightly identifies the French *banlieue* as being the arena in which this 'importation' is most obvious: 'Le conflit israélo-palestinien est, en quelque sorte, devenu une affaire française. Il suffit de se rendre en banlieue pour s'en rendre compte' (9) ['The Israeli–Palestinian conflict has, in a way, become a French matter. You only have to go to the *banlieue* to realize this'].

Michaël Sebban's *Lehaïm. À toutes les vies* (2004) dramatically enacts the mimesis posited by Sibony and Marty. Set in 2003, the novel follows the trajectory of Éli, who has moved back to France from Israel and is teaching philosophy at a secondary school in, precisely, a Parisian *banlieue*. When a group of Arab pupils discover he is Jewish one of them asks aggressively why he slaughters Palestinians (30). The question captures the elision of French Jews with Israeli Jews that seems to be a major cause of the rise in antisemitic attacks in France during the Second Intifada noted by Blanc and Cohen. Eli's ensuing exchange with a group of pupils triggers what seems to be a cognitive breakthrough – but only for one of the pupils, Karim:

> – T'y as été en Palestine?
> – Non.
> – Alors comment tu sais que les feujs massacrent les Palestiniens?
> – Parce que je vois la télé.
> – Dis-moi, quand à la télé ils parlent de ta téci,[6] tu crois ce qu'ils disent?

– Ils racontent que des conneries sur nous. Quand ils viennent ici les journalistes, ils se croient au zoo. Ils veulent qu'on pose devant les blocs avec les pitts. La dernière fois avec Kader et Amokrane on leur a niqué une caméra.

– Alors si tu les crois pas pour ta téci, pourquoi tu les crois pour la Palestine?

Karim éclate de rire.

– Ouah! Comment il t'a eu le prof de philo! Il est trop fort. Tu parles avec lui, il te retourne le cerveau. C'est trop chanmé! (30)

['Have you been to Palestine?'
'No'.
'So how d'you know that Jews slaughter Palestinians?'
'Because I watch the telly'.
'So tell me, when they talk about your housing estate on the telly, do you believe what they say?'
'They only talk bullshit about us. When the journalists come here, they think they're at the zoo. They want us to pose in front of the blocks with pit bulls. The last time with Kader and Amokrane we broke their camera'.
'So if you don't believe them about your estate, why d'you believe them about Palestine?'
Karim bursts out laughing.
'Wow! He really took you in, the philosophy teacher! He's too much. You talk with him, he does your head in. It's wicked!']

That breakthrough is further evidenced, although in rather undesirable form, when Karim's respect for the teacher he knows to be Jewish leads him to react violently to the blending of anti-Israeli sentiments with blatant antisemitism. Karim asks when Éli will return a CD he has lent him and Éli apologizes, saying he needs time to think about its contents; Karim's friend then sneers that Éli will never return the CD: 'Les feujs, c'est tous des voleurs. T'as pas vu qu'ils nous ont volé la Palestine' (204) ['Jews, they're all thieves. Haven't you seen how they stole Palestine from us'). Karim begins to attack the erstwhile friend in defence of Éli, who manages to stop injury being inflicted (204), Karim contenting himself with spitting and yelling '– *Ya hra*! La prochaine fois que tu dis du mal de M. S., j'te défonce la gueule' (204) ['Piece of shit! The next time you bad-mouth Mr S., I'll smash your face in']. But Karim represents an exception that again proves the rule – and not just among these French teenagers of Arab origin, one of whom argues that he is simply repeating what a teacher has said: '– Mais c'est pas moi qui l'a dit, m'sieur, que les juifs y'z avaient volé la Palestine, c'est le prof d'histoire-géo' (205) ['But it wasn't me, sir, who said the Jews stole Palestine, it was the history and geography teacher'].

Sebban also depicts the response by some elements of the French-Jewish community to this antisemitism: a highly organized plan of action. To optimize logistics, the plan includes recourse to an Israeli guest, whose speech urges adoption of an aggressive policy of self-defence:

> – Il n'est pas dans notre nature d'être offensifs ou provocateurs, cela ferait le bonheur de nos ennemis. Nous voulons seulement nous organiser et nous défendre. Il faut que nos adversaires sachent que nous ne les laisserons pas faire ce qu'ils veulent. Vous autres, les Juifs de la diaspora, avez encore des peurs que nous en Israël n'avons plus. Il faut que chaque antisémite de ce pays apprenne que les Juifs savent se battre et qu'ils rendent les coups qu'on leur donne. Votre survie est à ce prix. (182)

> [It's not in our nature to be offensive or provocative, our enemies would be all too happy about that. We simply want to organize and defend ourselves. Our enemies need to know that we won't let them do what they like. You diaspora Jews still have fears that we don't have any more in Israel. Every antisemite in this country needs to learn that Jews know how to fight and that they return blow for blow. That's the price of your survival]

Significantly, only half the audience applaud the Israeli demagogue's speech. On a personal as opposed to a community level, of note is a letter written by Éli that he hopes to have published by the left-wing newspaper *Libération*. Here he strongly suggests the importation to France of the Second Intifada (cf. Cohen, 2012; Hecker, 2012):

> « Les Juifs! Ils dominent la France. » « Les Juifs! Ils ont volé la Palestine. » Il ne sert à rien de feindre la naïveté. Ces phrases s'entendent tous les jours dans les banlieues parisiennes. N'importe quel observateur attentif de la banlieue française sait qu'elles sont prononcées par quelques beurs qui quelquefois n'hésitent pas à passer à l'action et à agresser rabbins et synagogues. Elles sont aussi prononcées par quelques-uns de mes élèves et j'ai pu en discuter avec eux. (218)

> ['The Jews! They dominate France'. 'The Jews! They stole Palestine'. There's no point pretending to be naïve. Those sentences are heard every day in the Parisian *banlieues*. Anyone who observes the French *banlieue* closely knows that they are said by some French Arabs who sometimes don't hesitate about resorting to action and attacking rabbis and synagogues. They're also said by some of my pupils and I've been able to discuss it with them]

Éli diagnoses the underlying cause of this importation as the disintegration of the French republican model:

> Le modèle républicain français permettait d'endiguer toute forme de discrimination avec une seule proposition: la République ne connaît ni Juifs, ni Arabes, ni Noirs. Elle ne connaît que des citoyens. Peu importe que la haine du Juif existe, la France en rend ses manifestations impossibles. [...] La barrière républicaine à toute forme de racisme ou de discrimination ne fonctionne plus. Cette barrière qui protégeait la France de toute recrudescence du racisme ne protège plus rien, elle est tombée. La possibilité des manifestations antisémites de ces derniers mois n'est que le fruit de la vacuité d'un certain idéal républicain. La transposition dans les rues de Paris du conflit israélo-palestinien n'est pas une erreur, c'est la conséquence de l'échec du modèle d'intégration français. (218–19)

> [The French republican model used to allow the containment of any form of discrimination with a single proposal: the Republic does not recognize Jews, Arabs or Blacks. It only recognizes citizens. It matters little that hatred of Jews exists, France makes all demonstrations of it impossible. [...] The republican barrier to all forms of racism or discrimination no longer works. This barrier, which used to protect France from any resurgence of racism, no longer protects anything. It has come crashing down. The possibility of the antisemitic demonstrations we've seen these last few months springs merely from the emptiness of a certain republican ideal. The transposition into the streets of Paris of the Israeli–Palestinian conflict is no mistake, it's the result of the failure of the French model of integration]

This long disquisition, which *Libération* never actually publishes, presents a grim tableau of France as a now antisemitic country where the republican model of integration is utterly defunct.

Limning of the importation of the Israeli–Palestinian conflict to France is equally grim in Nathalie Azoulai's *Les Manifestations* (2005). One example is found in the first-person narration of the Gentile teacher Virginie (the 'Il' in the following passage being a gifted but antisemitic pupil of North African descent):

> il prend la parole pour dire qu'il n'ira pas à la manif, qu'avec tous ces enfants palestiniens tués tous les jours, c'est deux poids deux mesures, il ne suit pas, il est indigné. Je réponds immédiatement sur les confusions à ne pas faire, sur le fait qu'ici, c'est la France, pas le Moyen-Orient, que les juifs français ne sont pas des Israéliens, qu'en république on ne profane pas les tombes, que, bien sûr, toutes les formes de racisme sont scandaleuses. (239)

[he intervenes to say that he won't go to the demo, that with all those Palestinian children being killed every day, it's double standards. He doesn't follow, he's indignant. I immediately reply about the need to not confuse different things, about the fact the fact that this is France, not the Middle East, that French Jews are not Israelis, that in the Republic you don't desecrate graves, that, of course, all forms of racism are scandalous]

Another example is found in the first-person narration of the Jewish Anne, whose teenaged son Tom is seriously injured by a group of *beurs* for not wearing the Palestinian *keffiyeh* – recalling Marty's reference to the 'prestige du keffieh sur la jeunesse' (2003, 50):

Tom se promenait avec sa bande de copains dans le quartier de la Bastille, une altercation a commencé avec d'autres gamins. La plupart de ses copains portent des keffiehs, c'est la mode, ma mère ouvre des yeux ronds, et les autres ont commencé à demander à Tom pourquoi lui, il n'en portait pas. C'était des beurs qui demandaient. Il n'a pas répondu, quelqu'un a donc dit à sa place, c'est qu'il doit être feuj, un sale feuj! Et là, ça a dégénéré, ils se sont battus, Tom et un autre, et voilà. (Azoulai, 300)

[Tom was walking along with his gang of friends in the Bastille area, and an altercation with other kids started. Most of his friends are wearing *keffiyeh*s, it's the fashion, my mother opens her eyes wide, and the others started to ask Tom why *he* wasn't wearing one. It was French Arabs who were asking. He didn't answer, so someone said in his place, it must be because he's a Jew, a dirty Jew! And then it degenerated, they started fighting, Tom and another boy, and there you have it]

Finally, in Eliette Abécassis's *Sépharade* (2009), the importation transpires in a conversation between members of a Jewish family about the situation in France:

– L'antisémitisme. Tu sais ce qu'ils disent, dans les banlieues? « Hitler c'est mon cousin, c'est bien ce qu'il a fait. » Et d'autres: « Oui, ils ont de l'argent, ils tiennent les médias, ils sont partout, ils tuent les Palestiniens. »
   – Nous c'est pour ça qu'on est partis, dit Colette. Dans les écoles, les élèves demandaient à sortir du cours lorsque le prof abordait la Shoah.
   – C'est de pire en pire. Maintenant, il y a un nouveau jeu: on entoure un enfant. S'il est juif, on le tabasse. Le mot « juif » est à lui seul une injure. Une fille a été passée à tabac dans le couloir du métro par deux Arabes qui avaient vu son étoile de David. Tous les jours, on lit dans la presse des histoires comme ça. (328–29)

['Antisemitism. Do you know what they say, in the *banlieues*? "Hitler's my cousin, what he did was right". And others say "Yes, they've got money, they control the media, they're everywhere, they kill Palestinians"'.

'That's why *we* left', said Colette. 'In the schools, pupils were demanding to leave the class when the teacher started to talk about the Shoah'.

'It's getting worse and worse. Now, there's a new game: a child is surrounded. If he's Jewish, he's given a beating. The word "Jew" itself is an insult. A girl was beaten up in the metro passage by two Arabs who'd seen her Star of David. Every day, you read stories like that in the press']

The advice from one member of the family, Colette, is that the others should follow her example and emigrate to Israel. Colette's view as an Israeli citizen that France is a profoundly antisemitic country leads us to the next and final section of this chapter.

5.9. Israelis' view of France as deeply antisemitic

A number of the primary texts represent France as being, in Israel's view, a particularly antisemitic country. In Michaël Sebban's *La terre promise, pas encore* (2002), two anonymous Israeli characters engage in an exchange where Vichy France's complicity in the Shoah is viewed as an atrocity whose Judaeophobia persists in contemporary France:

> – *Si c'était nous qui étions dans des camps de réfugiés, tu crois qu'ils gueuleraient, les goys? Rien du tout. Mon oncle, son voisin l'a dénoncé aux Allemands pour cinquante francs.*
> – *C'est comme les Français. Juste bon à être collabos. Qu'ils l'avouent publiquement qu'ils ont jamais pu nous piffer. Ça sera plus clair.* (109)

['If it was us in refugee camps, do you think they'd be kicking up a stink, the goys? Not at all. My uncle, his neighbour denounced him to the Germans for fifty francs'.

'It's like the French. Fit for nothing but collaboration. They should come clean publicly that they've never been able to stand us. That'd be clearer']

That Israeli perspective is reprised in Sebban's sequel to this novel, *Lehaïm. À toutes les vies* (2004). When Ethan, an Israeli who has spent some years in Paris, is asked if he is going to leave France, he replies in the affirmative, adding: 'J'ai du mal à l'admettre mais c'est en découvrant l'antisémitisme que j'ai compris' (192) ['It's hard to admit but it was when I discovered antisemitism that I understood']. Esther Orner's *Une année si ordinaire* (2004) conveys the Israeli view of France as a bastion of antisemitism via reference to increased Jewish immigration from France to Israel (97). Orner here takes the long view, demonstrating critical awareness of the historicity of antisemitism in France, and – notwithstanding its new ideological avatars – of its Christian repressed element within a secular republic. Finally, in *Eretz* (2010), Henri Raczymow at first alludes to rather than asserts Israeli perceptions of France as an incubator of antisemitism, by reporting the leading if hesitant question posed by an Israeli (Itsik) and his own response to it:

> Les nombreux Arabes qui vivent en France ont-ils une influence sur la société française, sur sa politique? [...] Je tente, pédagogiquement, de dissocier société et politique. Sur la politique de la France, les Arabes, me semble-t-il, n'ont pas d'influence. Sur la société, leur influence me semble au contraire importante. Dans les quartiers populaires où résident beaucoup de Juifs et beaucoup d'Arabes, les familles juives sont contraintes de mettre leurs enfants dans des écoles privées juives, sous peine de harcèlements. Dans ces quartiers, il n'y aura bientôt plus d'élèves juifs dans les collèges publics. (55–56)

> [Do the numerous Arabs living in France have an influence on French society, on its politics? [...] I try, like a good teacher, to separate society and politics. On the politics of France, it seems to me that the Arabs have no influence. On society, their influence seems to me on the contrary to be considerable. In working-class neighbourhoods where many Jews and Arabs live, Jewish families have to put their children into private Jewish schools, under pain of harassment. In those neighbourhoods, there will soon be no more Jewish pupils in state schools]

The reaction to this effort at scrupulous analysis, which posits French politics as free from Arab-inspired antisemitism and certain working-class areas of France as the converse, is affectively loaded – 'Itsik semble frissonner d'horreur' (56) ['Itsik seems to shudder with horror']. Raczymow's conclusion generalizes this individual Israeli's response to many of his compatriots: 'Mais cela conforte sa vision de la France, qui est celle, comme je le verrai au cours de mon séjour en Israël, de beaucoup d'Israéliens' (56) ['But this reinforces his vision of France, which is one held by many Israelis, as I'll see in the course of my stay']. That generalization is elaborated in subtly critical terms, whereby Raczymow again implies rather than asserts, this time, that the Israeli vision of France as incubator of antisemitism is, if not groundless, somewhat exaggerated:

> Car ici, tout le monde pense que la France est un pays dangereux pour les Juifs. Chaque Israélien qui projette de visiter la France se voit mettre

en garde contre des situations qui pourraient lui être fatales. Et chaque Israélien qui revient de France a toujours une anecdote quasi sanglante à raconter. Cela a trait aux Arabes de France. Les Israéliens ne sont pas loin de considérer la France comme un énième pays arabe, qui leur est évidemment très hostile. Beaucoup des Juifs de France qui font ici leur *alya* pensent la même chose. Et même ceux qui ne font pas leur *alya*: la vision de la France qu'ils transmettent à leur parentèle israélienne est apocalyptique. Je surprends Élisa, femme « de gauche », ex-kibboutznik de l'Hashomer Hatsaïr, en lui disant que je ne risquais rien en France. Ça l'étonne beaucoup. Elle n'est pas loin de penser qu'à Paris et dans les banlieues on est à la veille d'une Nuit de cristal et qu'il faut qu'Anne et moi prenions nos précautions, notamment en préparant sérieusement notre *alya*. (56–57)

[Because here, everyone thinks that France is a dangerous country for Jews. Every Israeli who plans to visit France is warned about situations that could be fatal for them. And every Israeli who returns from France always has an almost bloody story to tell. This relates to French Arabs. The Israelis are not far off considering France as yet another Arab country, which of course is very hostile to them. Many French Jews who make *aliyah* here think the same thing. And even those who don't make *aliyah*: the vision of France they pass on to their Israeli relations is apocalyptic. I surprise Élisa, a woman 'of the left', an ex-*kibbutznik* of Hashomer Hatsaïr, by telling her that I ran no risk in France. This astonishes her. She's not far from thinking that in Paris and the *banlieues* we're on the eve of *Kristallnacht* and that Anne and I must take precautions, particularly by seriously preparing our *aliyah*]

5.10. Endnote

The alertness to exaggeration in Raczymow's last sentence above shows a cognitive prudence rare in discourse on the (alleged) importation of the Arab–Israeli conflict into France. It is important to recall that this importation, directly inscribed in three of our primary texts, is axiomatically a metaphor: the physical conflict between Israelis and Palestinians is not a product that can be literally imported, and the conflict between Jews and Arabs in France is nowhere near as physically violent or as widespread as that between Israelis and Palestinians. But that the metaphor indicates something affectively real in French society is an assertoric statement. Many French Jews do feel targeted, often physically (see the Introduction on the bodily dimension of affect), in diverse spheres of French society by an anti-Israeli, pro-Palestinian stance liable to conflate Israelis with all Jews, and by a resulting swell in antisemitism (narrativized in four of the primary texts). These spheres include the French media, particularly television (five primary texts); the French political class, particularly the diplomatic service and the left wing (three); the French intellectual class (again, three); the French education system, in its text books and (some of) its teachers (two); and French civil society (seven). Indictment of Israel as a colonialist or even an apartheid state is registered in four of the primary texts, and twenty-first-century Israel's view of France as a deeply antisemitic country emerges in four.

The acting out of the Arab–Israeli conflict in France portrayed in the primary literature incites passions underpinned by such different ideological positions that any Archimedean point is difficult to achieve. A tentative move towards it might observe that the whole (psycho)drama is overdetermined by sociohistorical factors unique to France: France's colonial past in the Maghreb, and France's present status as a postcolonial, multi-ethnic society which (as observed in the Introduction) is home to both the largest Jewish and Arab populations in Europe. Identifications, whether autonomic or conscious, inevitably occur: French Arabs with Palestinians, and (frequently though not invariably) French Jews with Israelis. Identifications are almost always based on an opposition to the Other, which can, as in this case, have tinderbox effects.

Notes

1 J-Call is a grouping of Jewish European citizens who are 'deeply attached to Israel's existence and security' but also 'consider that only the end of occupation and the creation of a viable Palestinian state will guarantee the long-term sustainability of Israel as a democratic state with a Jewish majority, and restore its deserved position among nations' (see http://en.jcall. eu/who-we-are). Opposed to the stance of J-Call are the signatories of Raison Garder, who declare, inter alia, that 'L'idée d'une paix imposée à Israël sous la pression, voire l'intervention de puissances, est un déni de la démocratie et du droit international, aux relents néo-colonialistes. Elle bafoue le libre choix des citoyens de la démocratie israélienne et constitue un dangereux précédent pour toutes les autres démocraties' (http://www.dialexis.org/php/index.php) ['The idea of a peace imposed on Israel through the pressure or even the intervention of powerful countries is a denial of democracy and of international law that smacks of neo-colonialism. It scorns the free choice of the citizens of democratic Israel and constitutes a dangerous precedent for all other democracies'].

2 This guilt was acknowledged in a public speech by President Jacques Chirac in 1995.

3 In 'l'époque précédente', Koskas refers to a period from the late 1970s when, he avers, Jewish authors were 'fashionable' in France.

4 The Quai d'Orsay is the French Diplomatic Service.

5 Cf. Rosman (32).

6 The word 'téci' is *verlan* for 'cité', meaning a housing estate in a deprived urban area of France. *Verlan* is a form of slang that reverses the syllables of words, sometimes fairly approximately: hence, *feuj* for *juif*, *keuf* for *flic*, and *téci* for *cité*, and indeed *verlan* for *l'envers*.

CHAPTER SIX

The Metaphysics and *Poesis* of Israel

Chapter 6 treats *topoi* that this monograph has either not treated so far or has mentioned only in passing. In their aesthetic and affective complexion, they appear to be more 'purely' literary than the ostensibly more 'purely' political material of the preceding chapters. Yet the aesthetic and affective density of these topoi often have important political substrata. The first topos to be discussed is the potency and ambivalence of Jerusalem as a mesmerizing, hypostatic but conceptually elusive site of affect, and/or as aporetic ideal (6.1). Linked to the first, the second topos is the image of Israel as marked by madness (6.2). Third is the force, be it quasi-mystical or political, of the Hebrew language (6.3). Fourth is the frontier trope, interpreted pluralistically and in terms of liminal positionings between the state of Israel and the Arab-Muslim world; between Israelis and Palestinians; between diasporic Jews and Israelis; between religious and secular Israelis; and between Ashkenazi and Sephardi/Mizrahi Israelis (6.4). Penultimately, Chapter 6 will consider the frontier between Israelis living within internationally recognized Israeli boundaries and those living in the Occupied Territories (6.5). Finally, attention will devolve to the figurative and biblically derived frontier between Israel's consumption and ejection of its people (6.6). Unsurprisingly, affect will figure prominently in this chapter, and the range of emotions will be wider than those observed in the primary texts analysed in Chapters 3, 4 and 5, all of which examined a particular form of conflict. While conflict is not absent from the topoi examined in Chapter 6, when it does arise it tends to be less with an exterior enemy than with contradictory, even belligerent impulses within the private self or within the national ipseity. Equally, while cognition is certainly not absent from the experiences considered in Chapter 6, its role is less obvious than in Chapters 3, 4 and 5, with imagination and poesis taking a more central position.

6.1. Jerusalem

To some extent this section forms a mini-ecology in the sociological sense of the study of relationships between a human group (here, Israeli Jews) and their physical and social environment (here, Jerusalem) – but all as mediated through French-language literary texts. Before examining these texts, it is useful to ponder the status of Jerusalem in a selection of non-literary discourses: those of historian Idith Zertal; academic, writer and critic Éric Marty; essayist and journalist Martine Gozlan; historian Diana Pinto; and historian Catherine Nicault.

Zertal observes an official link made between Jerusalem and one of the most vital constituents of Israeli collective memory, the Shoah:

> La loi Yad Vashem instituait également le lien crucial et exclusif entre la mémoire de la Shoah et l'État d'Israël, entre la Shoah et Jérusalem, le seul endroit digne d'accueillir cette mémoire, d'après le récit officiel israélien. (120)

> [The Yad Vashem law also instituted the crucial and exclusive link between memory of the Shoah and the State of Israel, between the Shoah and Jerusalem, the only place worthy of housing this memory, according to the official Israeli narrative]

Within the material entity that is Jerusalem, a far smaller material entity is ascribed great symbolic importance going beyond its primary religious significance: 'Le Mur des Lamentations, considéré comme un vestige du mur extérieur du Second Temple de Jérusalem' ['The Wailing Wall, considered to be a relic of the exterior wall of the Second Temple of Jerusalem'], which has become 'un symbole national et un important site religieux juif' (Zertal, 128) ['a national symbol and an important Jewish religious site']. The Zola Levitt Ministries website states of the Wailing Wall (also known as the Western Wall or, more rarely, as the *Kotel*):

> This is the holiest shrine of the Jewish world. The Western Wall is part of the retaining wall supporting the temple mount built by Herod in 20 B.C. After the destruction of the Second Temple in 70 A.D., Jews were not allowed to come to Jerusalem until the Byzantine period, when they could visit once a year on the anniversary of the destruction of the Temple and weep over the ruins of the Holy Temple. Because of this, the wall became known as the 'Wailing Wall'.[1]

Quoting Élie Wiesel, Zertal brings out a religious power of the Western Wall felt even by non-religious Jews:

La conquête de territoires abritant les lieux saints mentionnés par les Écritures juives et les tombes mythiques des ancêtres transforma la guerre des Six-Jours en une expérience religieuse transcendante; la terre et les pierres devenaient des entités sacrées. « Même ceux d'entre nous qui se conçoivent comme des libres penseurs parlent d'une expérience à caractère essentiellement religieux », écrivait Élie Wiesel après avoir visité le Mur des Lamentations « libéré » dans le secteur oriental, arabe, de Jérusalem. (161)

[The conquest of territories sheltering the holy places mentioned by the Jewish Scriptures and the mythical tombs of ancestors transformed the Six-Day War into a transcendent religious experience; the earth and the stones became sacred entities. 'Even those of us who see ourselves as freethinkers talk of an essentially religious experience', wrote Élie Wiesel after visiting the Wailing Wall that had been 'liberated' in the eastern, Arab sector of Jerusalem]

Marty also presents the Western Wall as a site of intense affect and pathos (2003, 55). In many of the primary texts, it is not just the Wall but Jerusalem as a whole that inspires in even secular Israelis emotions isomorphic with religious affect. This goes some way to explaining why Jerusalem emerges within the primary texts as such a potent and magnetic force.

On a drier, demographic level, Marty asserts that

contrairement à ce que l'on croit, Jérusalem, par exemple, est depuis longtemps, si l'on se fie aux premières statistiques fiables (1844, le fisc ottoman), une ville plus juive que musulmane; au début du siècle il y a deux fois plus de juifs que d'Arabes. (2003, 73)

[contrary to what is believed, if you go on the first reliable statistics (1844, Ottoman tax office), Jerusalem has, for example, long been more of a Jewish than a Muslim city; at the start of the century there were twice as many Jews as Arabs]

Nonetheless, Gozlan argues that it is precisely the Arab imprint on Jerusalem that makes it so emotionally and sensually potent for Sephardic and Mizrahi Jews:

Le juif oriental, lui, aime d'instinct ce qui lui ressemble, la mélodie dans laquelle il a grandi et qui le fait toujours danser. L'espace en boucles successives où d'autres se perdent mais où lui, fils de Tunis, de Tanger, de Bagdad, de Tripoli, de Téhéran, se repère parfaitement, avec ses émotions ondoyantes accordées aux modifications de la lumière [...]. Il la respire en amant, cette Jérusalem arabe. (133)

[The oriental Jew instinctively loves what resembles him, the melody in which he's grown up and which still makes him dance. The space made up of successive loops where others get lost but where he, son of Tunis, Tangiers, Baghdad, Tripoli, Tehran, gets his bearings perfectly, his rippling emotions in harmony with changes in the light [...]. He breathes it in like a lover, this Arab Jerusalem]

Yet Gozlan does not depict Jerusalem as uniformly seductive; for her, its aesthetic appeal is compromised by its ultra-Orthodox community's uniform darkness of both dress and spirit (183). Her exasperated apostrophe to the Haredim conjures up the other, colourful side of Jerusalem: 'Et alors? Ne voyez-vous pas ces ocre et ces roses, ces bosquets émeraude, tous ces blancs étincelants?' (185) ['So what? Can't you see those ochres and pinks, those emerald groves, all those brilliant whites?'].

Pinto combines Gozlan's focus on the Haredim of Jerusalem – drawing attention to the sombre sartorial code expected of women in the community, and the duty to cover their own natural hair (2012, 55) – with Zertal's and Marty's focus on the signal importance of the Western Wall in Jerusalem. Her own view of the ambition of reconstructing the Temple is deeply critical:

Nous sommes en pleine psychose collective, car la reconstruction du Temple implique bien sûr la destruction du Dôme du Rocher, construit au-dessus du mont par un islam qui voulait s'approprier les Lieux saints. La menorah ainsi que le commentaire qui l'accompagne sont l'oeuvre de l'Institut du Temple, une organisation créée en 1987. Son but: reprendre aux musulmans le mont du Temple, reconstruire le Temple détruit par les Romains et revenir aux rituels du judaïsme prérabbinique. (2012, 84)

[We're deep in collective psychosis, as reconstruction of the Temple of course implies destruction of the Dome of the Rock, built above the Mount by an Islam that wanted the holy places for itself. The *menorah* and the commentary accompanying it are the work of the Temple Institute, an organization created in 1987. Its goal is to recapture the Temple Mount from the Muslims, to rebuild the Temple destroyed by the Romans and to return to the rituals of pre-Rabbinic Judaism]

The ambition is presented as highly politicized, pitting Jews against Muslims but also Jews against Jews (Pinto, 2012, 89). This conflict is not the only one marking a Jerusalem described by Pinto in a terse ternary structure as 'Jérusalem la conflictuelle, la complexe, la confinée' (2012, 133) ['Jerusalem the conflictual, the complex, the confined'].

For her, Jerusalem is so fraught with memories (of, one infers, former religious conflicts over the millennia) that celebration of difference and the mixing of cultures is unfeasible. But what is most striking and most pessimistic is Pinto's use here of Jerusalem as synecdoche for the whole of Israel (2012, 175).

Before turning to the primary texts, I would like to flag up an image within them that is remarked upon by two of the secondary texts and is present in the quotation above from Zertal (161). Jerusalem's 'pierres' are mentioned with remarkable frequency within the primary corpus, and a whole micro-*poesis* develops around them. Their prominence may appear unremarkable given that much of the stone in Jerusalem, such as the stone of the Western Wall, is ancient and regarded by many as sacred. But the Jerusalem stone poeticized in the primary texts is not always ancient or sacred, and is often mediated phenomenologically, on more sensory and aesthetic grounds. This is partly true also of the two secondary texts, which foreground qualities of clarity, colour and harmony. Gozlan comments appreciatively, 'Toujours cette odeur de pins et la clarté nocturne de la pierre de Jérusalem, teintée de rose par les réverbères' (180) ['Always that smell of pine and the nocturnal clarity of Jerusalem stone, tinted pink by the street lights']. In response to her interviewer Jacques Salomon's question apropos Jerusalem stone, 'N'est-ce pas ce qui unifie finalement la ville?' ['Isn't this what ultimately unifies the city?'], Nicault[2] says:

> Architecturalement parlant, c'est indéniable. C'est une loi anglaise qui a contraint les constructeurs d'utiliser cette pierre à l'extérieur des bâtiments. Cela a perduré car on a compris le parti-pris esthétique qui en ressortait. C'est une très belle parure dont la ville s'est dotée. (Salomon, 59)

> [Architecturally speaking, it's undeniable. An English law required all builders to use this stone on the outside of buildings. That has lasted because people understood the aesthetic bias behind it. It's a very beautiful finery with which the city has endowed itself]

Further attention will be paid to the qualia of Jerusalem stone as expressed by narrators or characters in the primary texts. It will in fact inform analysis of one of the other common motifs mentioned above: the Western Wall, and phenomenological responses to it. Chronologically, this motif first appears in Joseph Kessel's *Terre d'amour et de feu* (1965), in the following extract, where 'dernier' refers to the 'Mur des Pleurs' (42):

Je ne parlerai ici que du dernier, puisque c'est le réveil juif en Palestine qui fait l'objet de cette étude et que, en vérité, les larmes qui coulent depuis des siècles, auprès des suprêmes vestiges tu Temple, ont fécondé les vallées désertes de la Judée et de Galilée. (42)

[I'll only talk here about the latter, since it's the Jewish revival in Palestine which is the subject of this study and because, truth to tell, the tears that have flowed for centuries, by the supreme vestiges of the Temple, have fertilized the desert valleys of Judea and Galilee]

The lachrymose conceit underscores the supreme spiritual importance accorded by religious Jews to the destruction of the Second Temple, and thus to the Wall which was historically part of it. Yet in Kessel's typically triumphalist idiom, the tears shed at the Wall over this loss have been transformed into a positive, irrigating force that has rendered fertile land belonging biblically to the Jews of Palestine. In *Les Palestiniens* (1968), Ania Francos also suggests the intense affect inspired by the Western Wall, but encodes it more as a cathexis consisting in melancholy and loss:

appuyée à la fenêtre, regardant les grands blocs de pierre polie rongée par les baisers et les pleurs puis par le moisi et l'herbe, j'avais le cafard non parce que je pensais que ce Mur appartenait à mon patrimoine culturel – c'est sur les ruines du ghetto de Varsovie que je pleure – mais parce que ce Mur d'à peine 50 mètres de long, au nom duquel on s'était tant battu depuis cinquante ans, me semblait un symbole absurde. (153)

[leaning on the window, looking at the great blocks of polished stone eroded by kisses and tears and by mould and grass, I felt depressed not because I thought that this wall belonged to my cultural heritage – it's over the ruins of the Warsaw Ghetto that I cry – but because this wall barely fifty metres long, in whose name people had fought so much for fifty years, seemed to me an absurd symbol]

Note here the attention to stone signalled above: here, it is a stone made smooth over many years by human gestures springing again from embodied emotional expression – kisses and tears. Marcel Cohen's *Miroirs* (1980) too refers to the stone of the Western Wall, with the stone as integral to the identity of the Western Wall and endowing them with a trans-spatial, trans-epistemological force:

Ne délimitant aucun lieu, aucune certitude, le Mur renvoyait indéfiniment aux grands espaces du monde. [...] Ici, l'intelligence était à jamais désarmée puisque, face à la pierre, le juif avait choisi d'honorer sa blessure la plus profonde. (157)

[Delimiting no place, no certainty, the Wall referred us indefinitely to the great spaces of the world. [...] Here, intelligence was forever disarmed since, faced with the stone, the Jew had chosen to honour his deepest wound]

Shortly before this, Cohen also ascribes to the Western Wall an almost mystical mnemonic force:

Si près maintenant du Mur des lamentations, du signe même de l'expulsion, comment ne pas reconnaître le poids traîné depuis l'enfance, tout ce qui, déjà, décidait à ma place. [...] Certes, j'étais gêné de n'envisager le Mur qu'à ce niveau élémentaire, mais empêchera-t-on que les cris cherchent un point d'ancrage? C'est cette pensée qui me travaillait maintenant: les cris venus s'évanouir là, siècle après siècle, comme l'océan à bout de force sur la grève. (155)

[So close now to the Wailing Wall, to the very sign of expulsion, how could I not recognize the weight I've dragged around since childhood, everything that, already, was deciding things for me. [...] Of course, I was uncomfortable about viewing the Wall only at this basic level, but can one prevent cries from seeking an anchoring point? This was the thought that now exercised me: the cries that had come here and vanished, century after century, like the exhausted ocean on the shore]

In their reference to cries, the second and third sentences here are replete with an affect that saturates literary depictions of the Western Wall.

Jean-Luc Allouche's *Les jours innocents* (1984) refers not to this most iconic of walls but to Jerusalem walls more generally, which in their renaissance symbolize the Israeli recovery of Jerusalem in the Six-Day War (50). Allouche's portrait of Jerusalem is in general more holistically attentive to its natural form and surroundings. Indeed, the sensorium of Jerusalem is richly evoked in several passages. In the following passage, he contrasts the daytime spent in Tel Aviv with the more mysterious, sensuous and emotive return to Jerusalem at night:

Mais, à la nuit, il regagnait Jérusalem, s'épurait au long de la route escarpée, bordée de pins et de cyprès, dans la senteur tenace de la résine, des miasmes de la vallée côtière et des bruissements mondains de la métropole. Il n'était pas tout à fait dupe de l'outrance symbolique de cette ascension routière, mais il y cédait, avec une émotion sollicitée et entretenue à plaisir. (64)

[But at night, he would return to Jerusalem, purifying himself along the steep road bordered by pine and cypress trees, in the lingering scent of resin, the fumes of the coastal valley and the social murmurings of the metropolis. He wasn't entirely taken in by the symbolic extravagance of this road ascent, but he yielded to it, with an emotion that he sought out and sustained for the sake of it]

As well as emphasis on the draw of Jerusalem's natural and cosmic beauty – another example of which is 'les nuits froides et étoilées de Jérusalem' (73) ['the cold, starry nights of Jerusalem'] – that contribute to his growing exaltation, he is also fascinated by its religio-cerebral interiors:

> il rôdait encore dans les quartiers orthodoxes; il épiait les chambres d'étude, les ombres noires qui s'y agitaient hors du temps et d'elles-mêmes, sans lui jeter un regard. (73)

> [he still roamed around the orthodox quarters; he spied on the study rooms, on the black shadows bustling around in them outside of time and of themselves, not even looking at him]

Similarly to Allouche, in her *Un été à Jérusalem* (1986), whose very title foregrounds the centrality of Israel's capital city, Chochana Boukhobza often conveys a sense of Jerusalem's natural elements as being dramatic and supremely powerful over its human denizens:

> A Jérusalem, les crépuscules sont précoces. Il est à peine quatre heures, mais déjà dans l'air on devine une sorte de rémission, comme une trêve que le ciel accorde aux hommes. (22)

> [In Jerusalem, dusk comes early. It's hardly four o' clock in the afternoon, but already you foresee in the air a sort of remission, like a truce accorded by the heavens to men]

Its people too are dramatic, with a form of violence and even lack of reason produced by the tensions of their daily life. This psychological excess contributes to the mesmerizing power of the city, which homodiegetic narrator Sarah feels has repossessed her after years away in France:

> Je suis seulement intriguée par l'éclat de violence qui flamboie dans les yeux des gens, cette même déraison qui habite le regard de ma mère. Elle n'a rien de prophétique, cette extravagance. De petits enfers quotidiens l'ont forée. Jérusalem m'a reprise (23)

> [I'm just intrigued by the spark of violence gleaming in people's eyes, that same insanity that inhabits my mother's gaze. There's nothing prophetic about it, that extravagance. Little daily experiences of hell have forged it. Jerusalem has taken hold of me again]

A second reference to madness ascribes it to the city itself, which for Sarah defies logic and once more exerts a mesmerizing influence in the myriad details of the sensorium which it stimulates:

> Jérusalem est hors des limites de ma logique. Elle danse en moi par des détails insignifiants d'une banalité extrême. Des buissons rabougris qui se cramponnent aux fissures d'un mur. Une qualité de lumière. Une qualité de silence. Le vent qui se lève le soir et vous gèle la peau brûlée par la chaleur de midi. Les robes de grossesse des femmes, d'une lenteur criarde, ornées de fleurs et de dentelles. (35–36)

> [Jerusalem is beyond the limits of my logic. It dances in me through insignificant details that are extremely banal. Shrivelled bushes clinging to cracks in a wall. A certain quality of light. A certain quality of silence. The wind which rises in the evening and freezes your burning skin in the midday heat. Women's maternity dresses, suggesting a striking slowness, trimmed with flowers and lace]

The two cryptic sentences that immediately follow reinforce the sense of Jerusalem's unfathomable affective grasp: 'Jérusalem est embarrassante. On l'imagine fragile, elle vous oppresse' (36) ['Jerusalem is uncomfortable. You think she's fragile, [but] she oppresses you']. It is later implied that part of that grasp may be to do with the again unreasonable, even mad (cf. section 6.2. below), yet infinite desire and hope incarnated by the city. Sarah observes of her mother:

> Et dans ce désir fou qu'elle a de la vie, je reconnais Jérusalem et son attente, je retrouve l'espérance que cette ville irradie et qui devient pour tous les pèlerins la clef de l'infini. (45)

> [And in that mad desire she has for life, I recognize Jerusalem and her expectation, I recover the hope this city radiates and which becomes for all pilgrims the key to infinity]

It is important to note that the pilgrims mentioned here may be existential rather than religious pilgrims. Pilgrimage is about a quest for something that may or may not be found, and so about a certain degree of mystery. Mystery permeates the following mediation of Jerusalem:

> Un pas devant l'autre sous le soleil, voir la ville s'élargir et grandir démesurément, dans une enfilade de ruelles, d'avenues, qui mènent sans répit à d'autres ruelles, comme si le coeur battant de Jérusalem était enfoui dans un lieu souterrain. (127)

> [One step in front of the other beneath the sun, seeing the city expand and grow inordinately, in a series of alleyways, of avenues, that lead

relentlessly to other alleyways, as if the beating heart of Jerusalem were buried in an underground place]

Mystery is also to do with secrets, and it is secrecy that stamps the scents penetrating what I have posited as a seminal figural presence in our primary texts' evocations of Jerusalem – its unique stones:

> Et j'ai ressenti le parfum secret de Jérusalem, celui qui se faufile dans les fins d'après-midi et vous donne le sentiment que quelque chose de très solennel effleure les pierres. (79)

> [And I experienced Jerusalem's secret perfume, the one that slips into the late afternoon and gives you the feeling that something very solemn is lightly touching the stones]

Another variant on Jerusalem's mystery in *Un été à Jérusalem* is its ultra-Orthodox Méa Shéarim quarter. That mystery relative to the rest of Jerusalem – a form of otherworldliness, even extraterritoriality – inheres in its Haredi inhabitants (cf. Gozlan, 183–85; Pinto, 2012, 55):

> Ils glissent dans le soleil telles des ombres surgies de nulle part et allant on ne sait où, farouches, méfiants, défendant rageusement les textes de la loi coincés sous leurs aisselles. (135)

> [They glide in the sun like shadows that have suddenly appeared from nowhere and are going who knows where, unsociable, mistrustful, furiously defending the texts of the law that are stuck under their armpits]

Yet in *Un été à Jérusalem* the whole of Jerusalem has something sibylline about it, and this is partly linked to the poetics of stone mentioned above. One instance is the following, where the stones of the city along with the sky are anthropomorphized, both displaying a stealthy indifference to the human tragedy they witness and to the oxymoronically ecstatic madness it prompts:

> Jérusalem ne mène à rien. Les pierres ne disent mot. Le ciel se tait, splendidement. Les hommes s'agitent dans la poussière âcre, mangent goulûment, oublient de rire, s'évertuent à blasphémer contre la mort, mais leurs paroles naissent mutilés. Et la mort passe, royale, et la mort fauche les jeunes gens. On les porte en terre dans la révolte des mères qui sombrent lentement dans une folie extatique. (136)

> [Jerusalem leads to nothing. The stones don't say a word. The sky holds a splendid silence. Men bustle about in the acrid dust, eat greedily, forget to laugh, try their best to blaspheme against death, but their words are born mutilated. And death passes, regal, and death mows down young people.

They are carried into the earth amidst the revolt of their mothers, who slowly sink into an ecstatic madness]

A passage shortly after this dwells on the quality, provenance and texture of Jerusalem stone, which through human manipulation collectively becomes the formidable walls of the city – to which Jerusalemites cannot remain indifferent, any more than they can to the city itself (142). Part of the mystery of Jerusalem is linked to its insidious seduction. To begin with, Henry had been disappointed by the city; but its stone, along with its unique light, had stealthily begun to work its charm on him (114; 144–45) to such an extent that he now claims, '« Jérusalem éclipse la beauté de ses femmes' (146) ['Jerusalem eclipses the beauty of its women'].

Eliette Abécassis's *La répudiée* (2000) gives prominence both to Méa Shéarim, home to its homodiegetic narrator Rachel, a young ultra-Orthodox woman, and to the Western Wall as privileged place of internal (if relative) liberty for her. In Méa Shéarim, unworldliness reaches a form of paroxysm, for the quarter's uniqueness sets it apart even from the rest of an already uncanny city. Méa Shéarim is mediated almost literally as an otherworldly place: 'Nous habitons Jérusalem mais en fait nous n'y sommes pas. Nous sommes ailleurs. Nous ne sommes nulle part. Nous sommes à Méa Shéarim' (8) ['We live in Jerusalem but we're not really there. We're somewhere else. We're nowhere. We're in Méa Shéarim']. In a richly textured passage, the ultra-Orthodox quarter is described as, again, marked by secrecy, enclosure, labyrinthine qualities (as well as a distinctly gendered spatiality in which only Haredi men circulate freely):[3]

> Entre la vieille ville et la ville nouvelle, c'est un quartier aux maisons basses, aux cours entrelacées, entrées infinies, tunnels confidentiels, petites chambres, mansardes ou caves, balcons de fer forgé, intérieurs, extérieurs, enclaves secrètes. Entrez, venez parmi nous, vous verrez les Hassidim au pas pressé, dans les yechivas où l'on étudie la nuit. Entrez donc, voyez ces hommes aux papillotes, aux lévites et aux barbes noires. Entrez la tête couverte, mais entrez, car l'on ne cesse d'entrer ici, cour après cour, couloir après couloir, boutique et arrière-boutique, entrez donc, et vous sauterez de l'autre côté du miroir de ce pays que l'on n'ose nommer. (8)

> [Between the old and the new town, it's a quarter with low houses, interlacing courtyards, infinite entrances, private tunnels, little rooms, attics or basements, wrought-iron balconies, interiors, exteriors, secrets enclaves. Enter, come in among us, you'll see the Hassidim who walk

along hurriedly, in the *yeshiva*s where people study at night. Do enter,
see these men with sidelocks, Levites and black beards. Enter with your
head covered, but enter, for people never stop entering here, courtyard
after courtyard, corridor after corridor, shop and back-shop, do enter,
and you'll leap to the other side of the mirror of this country that people
don't dare name]

The last clause here intertextually evokes Lewis Carroll's *Through the
Looking-Glass, and What Alice Found There* (1871). The impression is
of Méa Shéarim as utopia, in both senses of the word – an 'ideal' place
for an ultra-Orthodox Jewish man (although not for an Ultra-Orthodox
woman, as Rachel's tragic position at the end of the novel confirms), but
also a no-place; an anachronistic, *shtetl*-like world in the middle of a
twentieth-first-century capital.

As for depiction of the Western Wall, like other texts discussed above,
La répudiée lingers poetically on its Jerusalem stone. The first mention
of it conveys Rachel's affection for her bedroom made of white stones
precisely because they remind her of the Wall (17). When she leaves Méa
Shéarim and walks to the Wall, her vision accentuates the majesty and
luminosity of its stones:

> Le mur resplendissait dans le soleil du matin. Ses pierres blanches
> s'élevaient, majestueuses, sur les siècles. Les pierres polies du sol brillaient,
> renvoyant l'éclat blanc du Mur. (58)

> [The wall gleamed in the morning sun. Its majestic white stones rose over
> the centuries. The polished ground stones sparkled, reflecting the white
> brilliance of the Wall]

When devastated by her husband Nathan's rejection due to her assumed
infertility, she poignantly seeks emotional sustenance from the Western
Wall (69–70). And when Nathan has decreed their separation, in her
misery she instinctively goes again to the Western Wall, with which she
has an affectively charged tactile relationship (81). Finally, in a state of
high emotion at the discovery that it is not she but her husband who is
infertile, she goes yet again to the Western Wall, performing the ritual
of slipping between its stones a piece of paper. But rather than the
traditional written message, hers is a visual message: a photograph of
the husband she has adored and who has definitively repudiated her (91)
– whence the novel's title.

Michaël Sebban's *La terre promise, pas encore* (2002) is less enclosed
in its spatial range than *La répudiée*, but it too presents Jerusalem as in
many ways both compelling and oppressive. For the male Eli the sources

of that oppression largely differ from the gendered ones of Rachel in *La répudiée*, who as an ultra-Orthodox woman is cloistered in the quarter of Méa Shéarim with only limited visits to the Western Wall. However, one source of oppression is common to both novels: the social and existential constraints imposed by the complete divorce between religious and secular Jews in Jerusalem (62). Yet this is not the only or indeed the most important source of oppression experienced by Eli in Jerusalem. More significant is the general ambiance of tension, due again to deep divisions, but this time of a political as well as a religious-versus-secular nature:

> Petit à petit, je sentais que quelque chose changeait en moi. Ça commençait à monter, doucement. Il ne se passait rien de particulier. Il ne se passe jamais rien à Jérusalem. Non. C'était beaucoup plus subtil. Une pesanteur sourde se mettait doucement en place. M'entourait, m'habitait. [...] Qui est-tu? Quel est ton camp? J'avais beau essayer de leur expliquer, de m'expliquer, que c'étaient des conneries toutes leurs histoires de paix ou de guerre, de pros et d'antis, de religieux et de laïques. Impossible de se dérober. Il fallait une réponse et j'étais sommé de la donner. Et tous les jours des pierres s'ajoutaient aux pierres. M'emmurant davantage. (80–81)

> [Gradually, I felt something changing in me. The feeling started to rise, slowly. Nothing in particular was happening. Nothing ever happens in Jerusalem. No. It was much more subtle. A dull heaviness was slowly settling in. Surrounding me, inhabiting me. [...] Who are you? Which camp do you belong to? I tried in vain to explain to them, to explain to myself, that all their fuss about peace or war, pros or antis, the religious and the secular, was bullshit. It was impossible to shy away. An answer was needed and I was ordered to give it. And every day stones were added to stones. Walling me in more]

Given the positive poetics of stone in other texts depicting Jerusalem, the metaphor in the last two sentences here is startling. Where in other texts the stones of Jerusalem have been aesthetically and spiritually pleasing, here they are cumulative elements in what becomes an imprisoning wall (with possible allusion to the Western Wall). The antagonistic binaries enforced upon Eli, the demand actively to take one side against another, be it in clashes between pro-peace and Greater Israel supporters or between religious and secular Israelis, end up figuratively suffocating and literally depressing him:

> Ça finissait par me coller au sol, par m'empêcher de respirer, de rire même. J'étais dans un étau. La tension de Jérusalem m'avait cloué au sol. Arrimé. Sans que j'y prenne garde. (81)

[It ended up flooring me, stopping me from breathing, even from laughing. I was in a stranglehold. Jerusalem's tension had nailed me to the ground. Fastened me. Without realizing it was happening]

The tension of Jerusalem is amplified in a passage ranging from the quotidian to the metaphysical and the cosmic:

> Tout le monde y va de son coup de pompe de tension. Du marchand de cacahuètes qui t'arnaque chaque fois sur la monnaie et qui t'engueule si tu viens réclamer. Jusqu'à la lumière du soleil qui t'aveugle. En passant par tous les types qui te bousculent dans la rue. Et la tension produit de la tension qui se rajoute à la tension qui forme de la tension qui produit de la tension qui se rajoute à la tension. Et ça fait de la tension au kilo, sédimentée au malaise métaphysique, formatée aux dimensions de la ville d'or et de lumière.
>
> Jérusalem: capitale mondiale de la tension. (83–84)

[Everyone pumps up the tension in their own way. From the peanut seller who always swindles you on your change and bawls you out if you come back to claim the rest. To the light of the sun that blinds you. In between, all the guys who jostle you in the street. And the tension produces tension which adds to the tension which generates tension which produces tension which adds to the tension. And that makes tension by the kilo, sedimented onto the metaphysical unrest, formatted to the dimensions of the city of gold and light.

Jerusalem: the world capital of tension]

This is not the experience of Eli alone. The hypertension of Jerusalem is confirmed by his friend Vladi:

> – Je ne quitte pas Jérusalem, on m'en chasse. La vie y est devenue impossible. Tu as dû le remarquer toi aussi. La tension devient chaque jour plus insupportable. (186)

[I'm not leaving Jerusalem, I'm being driven out. Life there has become impossible. You must have noticed it too. Every day the tension becomes more unbearable]

The last word here, 'insupportable', is semantically echoed in the last word of Eli's devastated realization:

> J'avais donc vécu en Israël pendant trois ans, quitté la France, pour en arriver à cette conclusion, cette terrible évidence: Jérusalem est une ville impossible. (188)

[So I'd lived in Israel for three years, left France just to come to this conclusion, this obvious dreadful fact: Jerusalem is an impossible city]

Nuancing this conclusion is a later affirmation, made partly in response to the intense difficulty that Vladi and others have in leaving Jerusalem behind after having invested such high hopes in it:

> Il faudrait toutes les connaître, ces vies qui n'ont d'autre but que Jérusalem, pour comprendre ce qu'il en coûte de quitter cet endroit. (193)

> [You would have to experience them all, all those lives which have no goal other than Jerusalem, to understand what it costs to leave this place]

Eli here conveys an ambiguous epiphany:

> J'ai compris ce matin-là, en rentrant chez moi et en regardant le soleil se lever, qu'on ne quittait jamais tout à fait Jérusalem. On lui est lié pour toujours. Même si c'est une ville impossible quand on y a vécu. Et même quand on n'y a pas vécu. On ne le sait pas encore, c'est tout. (193)

> [I realized that morning, on my way back home and as I watched the sun rise, that you never leave Jerusalem completely. You're bound to it for ever. Even if it's an impossible city when you've lived there. And even when you haven't lived there. You just don't know it yet, that's all]

The reason for this permanent bond is not fully elucidated, but seems to be a psychic impasse caused by the unattainability set against the unrelinquishability of the high hopes invested in the Promised Land's epicentre. What is clear is the irreversible change that Jerusalem effects in all who have lived there, along with the inability to find peace dwelling anywhere else:

> Je cherchais la Terre promise, j'avais trouvé une ville impossible. Trois ans à Jérusalem, et je ne pourrai plus jamais vivre comme avant. Parce que, s'il est impossible de vivre à Jérusalem, il n'est possible de vivre nulle part ailleurs ou n'importe où. C'est la même chose. Au deuil près. Le deuil. Parce qu'il n'y a pas de Terre promise, pas encore. (194)

> [I was looking for the Promised Land, I'd found an impossible city. Three years in Jerusalem, and my life would never be the same again. Because, if it's impossible to live in Jerusalem, it's not possible to live anywhere else. It's all the same. Apart from the mourning. Mourning. Because there is no Promised Land, not yet]

The religious note struck by Sebban also resonates in *Sur la frontière* (2002) by Michel Warschawski, who was born and raised in France but moved to Jerusalem for further Talmudic studies. His distinction between Jerusalem and Israel asserts the former's non-representativity of the latter:

Jérusalem, pas Israël. Car j'avais bien senti qu'en Israël il y avait le
centre israélien et la périphérie juive. Le centre, c'était Tel-Aviv: une ville
moderne, laïque, occidentale. [...] Jérusalem au contraire était une ville
juive, une excroissance de la diaspora. (27)

[Jerusalem, not Israel. For I'd certainly felt that in Israel there is the Israeli
centre and the Jewish periphery. The centre was Tel Aviv: a western,
secular, modern city. [...] Jerusalem on the contrary was a Jewish city, an
outgrowth of the diaspora]

The essential Jewishness ascribed to Jerusalem rather than Israel as a
whole inheres in the capital city's visible religiosity and, Warschawski
contends, its rejection of Zionist modernity (30). The seductiveness
of Jerusalem mediated in Sebban's *Le Cadenas du marché Yéhouda*
(2008) certainly does not derive from its religiosity. While Sebban again
emphasizes the city's quintessential tensions (10), he also expresses
something about that seductiveness which, while cognitively elusive, is
affectively and existentially vital:

je retrouve les sensations que Paris m'avait fait oublier. On ne quitte
Jérusalem que pour s'y retrouver [...] je sais que vivre loin de Jérusalem,
c'est vivre loin de la vérité. (23)

[I rediscover the sensations that Paris had made me forget. You only leave
Jerusalem to find yourself there again [...] I know that to live far away
from Jerusalem is to live far away from truth]

The ineffability of Jerusalem's magnetism is later voiced in terms of
radical alterity:

À peine revenu à Jérusalem, l'étrangeté de cette ville submergeait mon
insouciance tahitienne. Rien n'est comme ailleurs ici et il faut faire avec.
Accepter que cet endroit est soumis à des lois particulières, renoncer
à tout vouloir comprendre. Il faut parfois lâcher les armes, déserter le
champ de bataille. (54–55)

[Hardly had I returned to Jerusalem than the strangeness of this city
engulfed my Tahitian carefreeness. Nothing is as it is elsewhere and you
have to get on with it. To accept that this place is subject to specific laws,
to give up wanting to understand everything. Sometimes you have to lay
down arms, desert the battlefield]

Henri Raczymow's *Eretz* (2010) returns to the religiosity of Jerusalem
emphasized by Warschawski in *Sur la frontière*. Like the latter, Raczymow
contrasts the capital city with Tel Aviv: 'les religieux irrédentistes de

Jérusalem versus les athées pacifistes et favorables aux compromis de Tel-Aviv' (37) ['Jerusalem's religious advocates for the return of biblical territory versus the pacifist atheists of Tel Aviv who supported compromise']. Indeed it is because of its religiosity that Raczymow feels excluded from Jerusalem (55). However, like Sebban and others, he also apprehends in Jerusalem a radical alterity, and to this he adds a sense of its violence:

> Peut-être après tout tu aurais aimé cette étrangeté de Jérusalem, cette radicalité acre [*sic*] et âpre et violente, sans concession à la mode, à l'Occident, au bon goût, à l'élégance, à tout ce qui pourrait s'apparenter à du plaisir, à de la sensualité ... (80)

> [Perhaps you would after all have liked that strangeness of Jerusalem, that sharp, bitter and violent radicality, which makes no concession to fashion, to the West, to good taste, to elegance, to anything that might resemble pleasure, sensuality ...]

This statement is immediately followed by a literary tracking shot evoking iconic alterity, Méa Shéarim, and suggesting the contagion of its ethos and (counter)aesthetic:

> Nous traversons donc Méa Shéarim, le quartier fameux des *haredim*, construit sur le modèle d'un ancien *shtetl* de Pologne ou de Galicie. Mais c'est tout Jérusalem qui semble être devenu Méa Shéarim! Les *haredim* partout! Ils ont tout envahi. Jérusalem leur appartient. Pas un homme sans ses *tsitsit*. Pas une femme dont on puisse deviner les genoux ou les bras. Elles portent toutes ces vêtements archivieillots, des vêtements de pauvresses. (80–81)

> [So we're going through Méa Shéarim, the famous Haredi quarter, constructed on the model of a former Polish or Galician *shtetl*. But the whole of Jerusalem seems to have become Méa Shéarim! The Haredim are everywhere! They've invaded everything. Jerusalem belongs to them. There's not a single man without his *tzitzit*. Not a single woman whose knees or arms you can make out. The women all wear really old-fashioned clothes, paupers' clothes]

Like other writers examined above, Raczymow depicts Jerusalem as deeply mysterious, in fact so mysterious it is almost magical – but for him, menacingly so:

> Jérusalem continue de me faire peur. De m'intimider. De tenir ses distances. Non comme une femme trop belle pour moi, mais comme un espace sacré qui me serait (encore) interdit. Un peu comme le *Schloss* de Kafka pour son héros K. Ou bien cet espace relève pour moi de ce que les

ethnologues appellent le « mana », une puissance magique attachée à un être ou à un lieu ou à n'importe quoi de symbolique. (97)

[Jerusalem continues to frighten me. To intimidate me. To keep its distance. Not like a woman too beautiful for me, but like a sacred space that is (again) out of bounds to me. A bit like Kafka's *Schloss* for his hero K. Or maybe for me this space is to do with what ethnologists call 'mana', a magic power attached to a being or a space or anything symbolic]

That mystery and menace are counterbalanced by something also conveyed by other authors considered above: Jerusalem's seductiveness. But this too is destabilizing:

Retour à Tel-Aviv dans une grande tristesse. Il y a à Jérusalem quelque chose dans l'air qui nous rend comme ivres, quelque chose d'hystérique qui fouette l'âme. (105)

[Return to Tel Aviv in great sadness. There's something in the air in Jerusalem that seems to make us drunk, something hysterical that fires up the soul]

Despite his earlier protestations of exclusion from Jerusalem, Raczymow is drawn to and melancholic in separation from it (105). And yet the concluding pages of *Eretz* come full circle, returning to Raczymow's initial fear of Jerusalem (150) and to the various roots of that fear: 'Ces collines compliquées, ces tensions visibles, cette religiosité qui m'est vite insupportable ...' (150) ['Those intricate hills, those visible tensions, that religiosity that quickly becomes unbearable to me ...']. In the second clause here, Raczymow concurs with Sebban's dramatic depiction of Jerusalem in *La terre promise, pas encore.*

The paradoxes in these various literary snapshots of Jerusalem resist rational explanation. In a dialectical interplay, there is its mystery, seduction and even its intoxicating effects, set against the tension that pervades it (which may at least partially stem from its situation as a divided city – politically, religiously and even architecturally), the fear it inspires, and an extreme alterity that for the non-religious Jew is alienating. Marco Koskas's reflection in *Mon cœur de père* (2012) provides a fitting end note:

toute la mystique juive, et la raison d'être d'Israël, c'est que les Juifs sont en exil hors de Jérusalem. Nous ne sommes pas censés être nostalgiques de Tunis, mais de Jéru. (102)

[the whole of Jewish mysticism, and Israel's reason for being, is that Jews are in exile outside of Jerusalem. We're not supposed to be nostalgic for Tunis, but for Jeru]

For the secular Jew, analogy with missing limb syndrome might not be entirely inapt: amputated of religious faith in Jerusalem as the one and only proper dwelling place for Jews, s/he still feels something intensely alive that is materially absent. For many secular Jews, Jerusalem is therefore a site of passionate affective investment, but ultimately an aporetic ideal.

6.2. Israel as marked by madness

The previous section discussed literary portraits of Jerusalem, which is constructed as locus of madness in Michaël Sebban's *La terre promise, pas encore* (2002): '– Tu t'imagines le nombre de tapés qui débarquent dans cette ville. Tous les illuminés de la planète passent par ici' (106) ['Imagine the number of nutters who turn up in this city. Every crank on the planet passes through']. The present section will home in on this notion of madness but extend it from Jerusalem to Israel more generally. Psychoanalyst Daniel Sibony posits a Gordian knot, implying that Israelis' desire to be 'normal' is so obsessive that it is a form of madness in itself:

> Des Israéliens « fous » de normalité se dépriment de voir qu'il faut encore légitimer Israël; ils croient que le légitimer c'est le rendre encore plus normal; que la loi symbolique c'est celle de la norme. (187–88)

> [Israelis who are 'mad' in their obsession with being normal get depressed when they see it's still necessary to legitimize Israel; they believe that to legitimize it is to make it still more normal, that the symbolic law is the law of the norm]

Sibony views the putative normality of Israel as dyadic, and casts one of its two sides as bordering on psychopathology: 'La « normalité » d'Israël oscille entre un narcissisme candide, vaguement autiste, et une plate rationalité' (188) ['Israel's "normality" swings between a guileless, vaguely autistic narcissism, and a dull rationality']. For Sibony, the obsessive fantasy of normality derives at least partly from Israel's sense of existential threat, undergirded by a history of Jewish persecution and murder since time immemorial (200). Fear of annihilation produces certain paradoxes and dangers:

depuis le nazisme, il y a la peur que ça puisse revenir à tout moment [...]
En même temps, trouver que cette peur est abusive, c'est revendiquer
une normalité de façade; c'est risquer de *s'effacer soi-même* dans une
normalité forcée. (Sibony, 201)

[since Nazism, there's the fear it could return at any moment [...] At the
same time, to consider this fear excessive is to claim an outward show of
normality; it's to risk *erasing yourself* in a forced normality]

Indeed, for Sibony, 'Israël est malade de normalité, de rupture avec
son histoire, avec la transmission qui le fonde' (239) ['Israel is ill with
normality, with rupture from its history, with the transmission that is
its foundation']. Sibony explains this apparent oxymoron in terms of a
manically object- or results-oriented ethos in Israel (239).

In a less abstract idiom than Sibony's, Martine Gozlan also touches
on Israel's uneasy relationship with 'normality'. Referring to Avraham
Yehoshua, an Israeli writer viscerally attached to but fiercely critical of
his country, she remarks:

Il illuminait la problématique que vient de pulvériser Nadia dans
le soir vertigineux de Hébron: la capacité du peuple juif à vivre
« normalement ». (125)

[He illuminated the issues that Nadia had just demolished in the vertiginous
evening of Hebron: the Jewish people's ability to live 'normally']

Further, the sanity of two aspects of Israeli society is questioned:
Messianism – with, she argues, 'le délire messianique' (Gozlan, 124)
['Messianic delirium'] still palpable in Hebron – and the occupation
of the Territories in general: 'David Ben Gourion rêvait d'un pays
normal. Où est la normalité dans les territoires?' (Gozlan, 124) ['David
Ben Gurion dreamed of a normal country. Where is normality in the
Territories?']. In counterpoint, one inhabitant of these Territories whom
she cites dethrones the ideal of normality:

– Mais je ne veux pas que ce soit un pays normal. Je veux un pays juif, au
goût juif. Et Hébron est à nous, les juifs y ont toujours vécu! (Gozlan, 125)

['But I don't want this to be a normal country. I want a Jewish country, to
Jewish tastes. And Hebron is ours, Jews have always lived there!']

The political obverse of this stance is also conveyed in Gozlan's citation
of Yehoshua:

Et, naturellement, quand je disais, au lendemain de la guerre des Six

Jours, qu'il fallait rendre la terre pour avoir une paix, on me considérait comme un fou! La folie, en Israël, c'est d'être normal. (127)

[And, of course, when I said just after the Six-Day War that land would have to be given back to obtain peace, people thought I was mad! Madness in Israel is being normal]

Finally, from political conceptions of the normality/madness binary, Gozlan moves to a gendered perspective, diagnosing psychiatric disorders in significant proportions of ultra-Orthodox Jerusalemite men which are exposed in their vicious treatment (physical battery) of women:

Violence cachée. Pathologique. Car des pans entiers de la communauté ultra-orthodoxe sont saisis par une démence qui n'a plus rien à voir avec les comportements habituels des juifs religieux. Certains orthodoxes songent même à ouvrir un hôpital psychiatrique, où les médecins se soumettraient aux décrets des rabbins pour soigner névrosés, psycho-pathes et dépressifs. (195–96)

[Hidden violence. Pathological violence. For whole sections of the ultra-Orthodox community are gripped by a madness which no longer has anything to do with the habitual behaviour of religious Jews. Some Orthodox Jews are even thinking about opening up a psychiatric hospital, where doctors would submit to rabbis' decrees in order to treat neurotics, psychopaths and depressives]

Though more figuratively, Diana Pinto too observes psychiatric disorders, along with denial of the reality principle, within the human collectivity that is Israel – insisting, moreover, that this observation is made by many Israeli themselves:

Le super-Israël aux prouesses mondiales devient subitement Israël l'autiste atteint du syndrome d'Asperger, l'État bipolaire, schizophrénique, paranoïaque, psychotique et psychorigide: bref celui qui nie le principe de réalité. Ce sont là des métaphores fortes, très fortes, voire terrifiantes. Ce ne sont pas les miennes. Des Israéliens de tout bord politique, les plus orthodoxes et les plus laïcs, les plus jeunes et les plus vieux, venant des origines culturelles les plus diverses, les ont librement évoquées devant moi comme autant d'évidences et avec un ton qui n'avait rien à voir avec le si célèbre humour juif. (2012, 19)

[The super-Israel with global prowess suddenly becomes the autistic Israel suffering from Asperger's Syndrome, the psycho-rigid, psychotic, paranoid, schizophrenic, bipolar state: in short, a state which denies the reality principle. These are strong, very strong, indeed terrifying metaphors. They're not my own. Israelis of every political stripe, the most Orthodox and the most secular, the youngest and the oldest, from the most diverse of cultural backgrounds, have freely invoked them before me as just so many obvious facts and in a tone that had nothing to do with that famous Jewish humour]

Sibony's and Gozlan's nuanced approaches to the question of Israel's 'madness', whereby a normatively stigmatizing charge is sometimes mitigated by a sense that Israel's abnormal conduct is completely logical given Jews' abnormal history of persecution, is rather more bluntly reflected in the first of our primary texts. Joseph Kessel's *Terre d'amour et de feu* (1965) recurs to the very foundations of Zionism and its proleptic production of the Israeli state. Referring to the Zionist annual conference's refusal of the British offer in 1903 of a Jewish homeland in Uganda (see Chapter 1), and the delegates' resolve to hold out for nothing less than Palestine, he comments in lapidary terms that reprise the Shakespearean motif of the wise Fool:

> Cela semblait, cela était de la folie.
> Les événements donnèrent raison aux fous. (9)

> [It seemed – and it was – madness.
> Events were to prove the mad right]

A less bullish approach is taken by Esther Orner's *Fin et suite* (2001). There are hints of Pinto's charge (2012, 71) of Israeli schizophrenia, but Orner's lexis of division is non-pathologizing:

> Et si tu as dû quitter le pays, tu lui es restée attachée jusqu'à la fin de tes jours. Ne l'incriminant jamais de tes échecs. Ces échecs qui parfois nous dépassent font partie de nos pauvres vies. Tu as toujours su que nous étions un peuple divisé. (82)

> [And even though you had to leave the country, you remained attached to it to the end of your days. Never attacking it for its failures. Those failures that are sometimes beyond us are part of our poor lives. You always knew that we were a divided people]

And in *Une année si ordinaire* (2004), Orner evokes the gulf noted above between Israel's ideal of normality and its structural tendency to what other countries see as its abnormality:

> je me suis aussi souvenue que j'étais venue ici à l'âge de treize ans pour être ou devenir normale. Etre enfin comme tous les peuples! Quelle idée saugrenue. Weitzmann ne manque pas de souligner le talent que nous avons à nous retrouver dans des situations les plus anormales. (57)

[I also remembered that I'd come here at the age of thirteen in order to be or to become normal. Finally to be like all peoples! What a crazy idea. Weitzmann makes sure he highlights the gift we have for finding ourselves in the most abnormal of situations]

She semi-seriously admits that Israel is a country of overactive (cf. Sibony, 239) madmen, but implies that a grain of madness is necessary to bear the intense pressures of their situation:

> Oui, nous sommes un pays de fous, c'est comme les Galeries Lafayette disait une amie, à chaque instant il se passe quelque chose.
>   Sans un grain de folie, serions-nous capables de vivre une telle situation? Et ceux qui ne le peuvent s'en vont. (58)

[Yes, we're a country of madmen, it's like the Galeries Lafayette, a friend said to me: there's always something going on.
     Without a touch of madness, would we be able to survive such a situation? And those who can't, leave]

Thus Israel's madness is defiantly conceded but also explicated (and arguably neutralized) as a psychological safety valve for coping with unique circumstances. Zenatti's *Quand j'étais soldate* (2002) also takes this tack, but places more emphasis on the existential extremes of Israel's unique circumstances:

> Nous sommes un pays de fous situé entre les chansons, la mer et la guerre. Un pays où la mort est envisageable, dès dix-huit ans, mais cette éventualité ne rend personne plus intelligent. (46; cf. Sibony, 200)

[We're a country of madmen situated between songs, sea and war. A country where death is imaginable from the age of eighteen, but this prospect doesn't make anyone more intelligent]

However, the homodiegetic narrator of Zenatti's *Ultimatum (En retard pour la guerre)* (2006) strenuously opposes tolerance of a particular form of 'madness': that of panic-stricken paranoia prompted by the mnemonic regime of the Shoah. This novel restages a much more recent historical reality – Tel Aviv and Haifa being hit by Iraqi Scud missiles in 1991 – which ignited fear that Israel could be sucked into the Gulf War:

> Alors je refuse de suivre Tamar sur le chemin qui mène aux forêts de bouleaux de Pologne et d'Ukraine. Je vois la folie nous y guetter, incandescente encore du sang des morts, tapie sous les fougères. Si nous cédons à la terreur que nous inspirent les deux mots associés, Gil nous trouvera tout à l'heure en train de courir dans l'appartement, échevelées et moites, le regard fiévreux, ou bien nous balançant en psalmodiant les

mots terribles sur tous les tons, avec dans la voix tantôt un étonnement enfantin, tantôt les accents butés de celui qui dit non à la réalité, débordantes de détresse, miaulant comme des femmes blessées, voix démentes, voix chevrotantes de sorcières: Les chambres ... le gaz ... les chambres ... le gaz ... . Les chambres ... le ... (73)

[So I refuse to follow Tamar down the path that leads to the birch forests of Poland and Ukraine. I see madness lying in wait for us there, still glowing from the blood of the dead, lurking under the ferns. If we give way to the terror with which the two associated words fill us, Gil will soon find us running around in the apartment, frenzied and clammy, our gaze feverish, or rocking back and forth chanting terrible words in all sorts of tones, sometimes with a childlike astonishment in our voices, sometimes with the stubborn stresses of somebody denying reality, overflowing with distress, mewing like injured women, voices crazy, the quavering voices of witches: 'The chambers ... the gas ... the chambers ... the gas ... . The chambers ... the ...']

The narrator's friend, who has recently given birth, holds a contrary view, that to underplay the acute stress created by acute military threat to Israel is in itself a form of madness – an instance of what Sibony called 'Des Israéliens « fous » de normalité' (187):

– Je suis allée à la Goutte de Lait ce matin, je leur ai dit que j'avais du mal à l'allaiter, que je sentais bien qu'il restait sur sa faim. Il pleure tout le temps depuis que nous sommes rentrés de l'hôpital. Tu sais ce qu'ils m'ont demandé, ces demeurés? « Es-tu particulièrement stressée en ce moment? PARTICULIÈREMENT STRESSÉE! EN CE MOMENT! Mais non, bien sûr que non! Tout va pour le mieux dans le meilleur des mondes, n'est-ce pas? Ils sont dingues, dingues, dingues. C'est un pays de fous, je te dis, un pays de fous, fils de fous et descendants de fous. (Zenatti, 2006, 126)

[I went to the Drop of Milk this morning. I told them that I was having problems breastfeeding, that I felt he wasn't getting enough milk. He cries all the time since we got back from the hospital. Do you know what they asked me, those halfwits? 'Are you especially stressed at the moment?' ESPECIALLY STRESSED! AT THE MOMENT! No, of course not! Everything is for the best in the best of all possible worlds, isn't it? They're crazy, crazy, crazy. This is a country of madmen, I tell you, a country of madmen, sons of madmen and descendants of madmen]

And indeed, the narrator's earlier intransigence softens as she reads about the mental illnesses induced by this exceptional situation in which Israelis are, for their own safety, cloistered in hermetically sealed rooms.

She even comes to abandon her earlier moratorium on all mnemonic parallels with the Shoah:

> Cette situation d'enfermement conduit à une sensation d'étouffement qui elle-même favorise l'émergence de troubles psychiques ou psychotiques latents. L'exemple le plus évident étant bien sûr les rescapés de la Seconde Guerre mondiale, ou les enfants de rescapés, pour lesquels la chambre dont on ne peut sortir, associée à la menace du gaz, ravive un traumatisme douloureux. (141–42)

> [This situation of confinement leads to a sensation of suffocation which in itself contributes to the emergence of latent mental or psychotic disorders. The most obvious example of course being the survivors of the Second World War, or the children of survivors, for whom the room you can't get out of, associated with the threat of gas, revives a painful trauma]

Her first sentence in this extract is supported by a later empirical observation: 'Les hôpitaux psychiatriques sont surchargés depuis le début de la guerre. Impossible de trouver une place' (144–45) ['Psychiatric hospitals have been overcrowded since the start of the war. Impossible to get a place'].

This section has explored literary representations of madness/ unreason in Israel. The next section investigates a fundamental element of Israeli identity that exerts a magetism which also goes beyond normative conceptions of reason: the Hebrew language.

6.3. The force of the Hebrew language

Philosopher Elisabeth de Fontenay locates the reasons for that magnetism in Hebrew's status as the only form of continuity for a diasporized people before the creation of the state of Israel, and as a unifying factor for Israelis thereafter (199). The latter is also highlighted by Diana Pinto:

> Dernier point, qui est sans doute le tout premier élément de cette nouvelle unité: la langue. Il ne faut pas minimiser l'importance de l'hébreu, désormais parlé par tous. (2012, 16)

> [One last point, which is no doubt the very first element in this new unity: language. The importance of Hebrew, from now on spoken by everyone, should not be played down]

For Pinto, the unifying force of Hebrew resides not just in providing a common language for people of multiple linguistic origins, but also in attenuating the importance of political divisions between left and right: 'La séparation traditionnelle entre gauche et droite ne peut que se relativiser à l'aune de cette langue neuve mais si ancienne [...]' (2012, 16) ['the traditional separation between left and right can only be relativized in terms of this new but very ancient language'].

In the primary literature, the use of Hebrew is variously valorized and subjected to critical scrutiny. Joseph Kessel's *Terre d'amour et de feu* (1965) limits itself to valorization, highlighting the pride of the Yishuv community not just in learning Hebrew but also in the language's usurpation of (diasporic) mother tongues:

> La conversation se tenait en russe. Je remarquai que la jeune femme, bien qu'elle vînt de l'Ukraine, s'exprimait avec difficulté dans cette langue.
> – Je l'ai presque oubliée, dit-elle avec une sorte de fierté sombre. Nous ne parlons qu'hébreu. (50)

> [The conversation was conducted in Russian. I noticed that the young woman, although she came from Ukraine, found it hard to express herself in this language.
> 'I've almost forgotten it', she said with a sort of sombre pride. 'We only speak Hebrew']

Like de Fontenay and Pinto, Kessel emphasizes the unifying force of Hebrew, but in his case proleptically, from the perspective of the early Zionists:

> Et, en vérité, il semble qu'il y ait en Palestine non point un peuple d'Israël, mais dix. Cependant les chefs sionistes espèrent amalgamer ces éléments si divers. Ils ont foi pour cela dans le temps, dans les mariages de plus en plus mélangés [...] et surtout dans la puissance unificatrice de la langue. (79)

> [And, to tell the truth, it seems that in Palestine there is not one people of Israel, but ten. However, the Zionist leaders hope to amalgamate these elements that are so diverse. For that they have faith in time, in more and more mixed marriages [...] and above all in the unifying power of the language]

Kessel contends that a common language is *the* essential factor for a people's survival: 's'il ne possède pas de langue qui lui soit propre, c'est un peuple mort' (79) ['if it doesn't have its own language, it's a dead people']. Hebrew is metaphorized as a once dead body that has been restored to life, warmth and vitality by Zionism in Palestine (80). Such a restoration is deemed to be in the order of a miracle – a mystical phenomenon eluding rational explanation; and the word 'miracle' is also chosen later on to describe the process by which a language previously reserved for Talmudic and philological study has become the vernacular among Palestinian Jews (80). Interestingly, Kessel points to strong similarities between Hebrew and Arabic (both are of course Semitic languages) in their guttural syllables and in their common 'emphase naturelle de l'Orient' (81) ['natural oriental grandiloquence']. However, what some readers may view as suspect Orientalism is matched by political considerations. For instance, Kessel deploys a simile that presents the speaking of Hebrew as a symbol of Zionist ideals: 'L'hébreu est devenu comme le drapeau du sionisme' (81) ['It's as if Hebrew has become the flag of Zionism']. The patriotic imperative to speak Hebrew is also evinced in the following:

> Combien de fois, dans les rues de Tel-Aviv, ne me suis-je pas entendu crier:
> – *Rak Ivritt* (seulement l'hébreu).
> C'est un cri national, un cri de ralliement. Il exprime la volonté d'unir, de lier un peuple jusque-là dispersé, un patriotisme qui couvait depuis des siècles, et qui se réveille aujourd'hui avec la résolution de triompher. (81)

> [How many times, in the streets of Tel Aviv, have I not heard people crying:
> '*Rak Ivritt* (Hebrew only)'.
> It's a national cry, a rallying cry. It expresses the will to unite, to bind together a people that was previously dispersed, a patriotism that had lain dormant for centuries, and is now awakening determined to triumph]

In fact, such is the patriotic investment in Hebrew as a national language unifying Jews in their historic homeland of Palestine that Hebrew becomes a metonym for (the modern) Jew, as the following exchange succinctly illustrates:

> – Tu n'as pas honte, dit-il en yddisch, de cette cigarette, un samedi?
> – Le jeune homme ouvrit paresseusement les paupières, toisa le réprimandeur, et répondit en hébreu:
> – Juif, parle le juif. (82)

> ['Aren't you ashamed', he said in Yiddish, 'of that cigarette on a Saturday?'
> The young man lazily opened his eyelids, looked up and down the person who'd reprimanded him, and replied in Hebrew:
> 'Jewish, speak Jewish']

That insistence on speaking Hebrew alone despite the diverse linguistic origins of immigrants to Palestine and later to Israel recurs in Marc Hillel's *Tu vivras dans ton sang* (1971), as does Kessel's insistence on the oriental sounds of the language:

> Arrivé en 1945 en Palestine, Yasha connaissait également l'hébreu; heureusement, car les deux tiers de nos camarades, originaires du pays, n'utilisaient ou ne voulaient utiliser d'autre langue que celle-là. L'attitude intransigeante des sabras, en la matière, présentait pour nous, les nouveaux venus, un certain avantage; elle nous obligeait à nous familiariser rapidement avec cet idiome rugueux, aux consonances orientales très prononcées. (258)

> [When he arrived in Palestine in 1945, Yasha also knew Hebrew; fortunately, as two-thirds of our comrades, born in the country, used no other or wanted to use no other language. The *sabras*' uncompromising attitude on this subject was for us, the newcomers, something of an advantage; it forced us to familiarize ourselves quickly with that rugged language with its very distinct oriental sounds]

Hebrew figures in two modes in a later Hillel novel, *Les Oranges de Jaffa* (1981), set in 1964. One – which presents rather more cynically a point previously made by Kessel – is Hebrew as a tool of Zionist propaganda used to impose a unified national identity:

> Doron, pour annoncer son collègue plus précisément chargé de la propagande à bord, avait employé l'hébreu, langue sacrée pour les juifs de l'Exil mais qui cessait de l'être pour devenir nationale dans le pays. (109)

> [To announce the colleague of his who was more specifically responsible for propaganda on board, Doron had used Hebrew, a sacred language for Jews of the Exile but which was ceasing to be so and instead becoming a national language in the country]

Another, linked to the first, is Hebrew as an onomastic imperative: 'En Israël, on peut changer de nom comme on veut, à condition de prendre un nom hébreu bien entendu' (49) ['In Israel, you can change your name if you want, provided that you take a Hebrew name of course']. Similarly, Paula Jacques's autofictional novel *Un baiser froid comme la lune* (1983), set in the late 1950s, reflects the onomastic duty of Israeli citizens to choose a Hebrew name, and so obliterate their diasporic origins:

> L'usage exigeait que l'immigré adopte un prénom israélien, voire même un patronyme hébraïque, comme pour souligner que, perdant son pays natal, il consentait à perdre jusqu'au souvenir de sa perte. (217)

[Custom required that the immigrant adopt an Israeli first name, indeed even a Hebrew patronymic, as if to emphasize that, in losing his native country, he consented to lose even the memory of his loss]

In addition to the onomastic duty, Jacques's novel notes a duty previously witnessed by Kessel (82) – that of speaking only Hebrew, to the complete exclusion of any other language (in Jacques's case, within the *kibbutzim*):

Tamar Gadol, la *Madrikha*[4] chargée de l'éducation des adolescents, baptisa Mélissa du prénom d'Illana: « chêne » au féminin. Celle-ci ne s'y résigna pas davantage qu'à l'apprentissage de l'hébreu qu'elle put bientôt parler à peu près clairement. La seule langue autorisée au kibboutz s'imposait à sa compréhension, malgré elle. (217)

[Tamar Gadol, the *madrikha* responsible for the teenagers' education, gave Mélissa the new first name of Illana: the feminine form of 'oak'. Mélissa no more resigned herself to this than to learning Hebrew, which she could soon speak more or less clearly. The only language allowed in the *kibbutz* imposed itself on her understanding, against her wishes]

While Mélissa's change of name is imposed and resented, Jean-Luc Allouche's in his autobiographical *Les jours innocents* (1984) is self-initiated when he goes to Israel in the late 1960s. Pressure to renounce names containing any traces of Arabic or Berber is conveyed:

Souvent, ils changeaient de nom, renonçaient aux patronymes à consonance arabe ou berbère, dont ils portaient le stigmate, et adoptaient des noms bibliques ressuscités, grandiloquents et naïfs. (82)

[Often, they changed names, gave up Arabic- or Berber-sounding patronymics, whose scars they bore, and adopted revived biblical names that were grandiloquent and naïve]

The presence of a form of ethnic cleansing even within Hebrew names is implied:

il changea une lettre de son nom hébraïsé, dont la présence et, surtout, la prononciation, malaisée aux gorges « occidentales », révélaient l'Orient en lui. (83)

[he changed a letter of his Hebraized name, whose presence and, above all, pronunciation, difficult for 'western' throats, revealed the Orient within him]

But at that early point during his stay in Israel Allouche seems to have been oblivious to such discrimination against Arabic or Berber, dazzled

as he still was by the resurrection of an originally religious language and
by its new power beyond the domain of the sacred:

> Longtemps, il s'extasia, comme le plus candide des touristes, de la
> résurrection de la langue. Il s'émerveilla d'en lire les signes sur les
> enseignes ou sur les marchandises. Mieux que tout, elle donnait corps
> au miracle: elle pouvait donc tout exprimer, de la vie et des jours. Les
> mots sacrés s'animaient aux réalités les plus triviales et traduisaient la
> formidable vitalité qui secouait le pays. (84–85)

> [For a long time, like the most naïve of tourists, he went into raptures
> about the resurrection of the language. He marvelled at reading its
> signs on shop boards or on merchandise. Better than anything, it gave
> substance to the miracle: it could thus express everything in life and
> in everyday matters. The sacred words came to life in the most trivial
> of realities and conveyed the tremendous energy that was shaking the
> country]

It is noteworthy that Allouche, like Kessel (80), uses the word 'miracle'
to express incredulous wonder at a sacred language's ability to express
the everyday realities of secular life. Recurring to the ruling Ashkenazi
elite's rejection of exilic languages, and particularly Arabic, registered by
Allouche, we find this feature in Michel Warschawski's *Sur la frontière*
(2002) too. What is new is that Warschawski both equates the rejection
with class differentials and challenges the shibboleth of Hebrew as a
unifying factor in Israel's multicultural population:

> L'« autre Israël » [...] c'était la périphérie: les « villes de développement »
> du Néguev et de Galilée ou les villages agricoles, misérables moshavim
> du corridor de Jérusalem, où après quinze ans on ne parlait toujours pas
> hébreu. C'est là qu'était concentrée la majorité des immigrants venus des
> pays arabes, religieux pour la plupart ou pour le moins traditionalistes,
> très attachés à leur culture et à leurs rites, mais sommés de changer leur
> mode de vie et de pensée pour être dignes du nouvel État juif. (219–20)

> [The 'other Israel' [...] was the periphery: the 'development towns' of
> the Negev and Galilee or the agricultural villages, wretched *moshavim*[5]
> of the Jerusalem corridor, where after fifteen years people still didn't
> speak Hebrew. It was there that you found concentrated the majority
> of the immigrants from Arab countries, for the most part religious or
> at least traditionalist, very attached to their culture and to their rites,
> but commanded to change their way of life and thinking in order to be
> worthy of the new Jewish state]

Moving back three years, Esther Orner's *Autobiographie de Personne*

(1999) focuses not so much on the political as on the (inter)personal, affective and symbolic dimensions of Hebrew usage in Israel. The narrator comments that her daughter (a character based on Orner herself) and her son-in-law 'parlaient, plutôt ils criaient, dans la langue du pays. Comme si cette langue avait été créée pour ça' (70) ['spoke, or rather they shouted, in the language of the country. As if this language had been created for that purpose']. The second sentence implies a tendency to emotional excess in speakers of Hebrew. In what initially appears to be a contrast, the narrator also observes that the word 'patience' is used with uncommon frequency in Hebrew (88). But shortly afterwards the initial contrast is lessened by the observation that in Hebrew, the word for patience is derived from the word for suffering (88) – which brings us back full circle to the tendency of Hebrew-speakers to the emotional excesses of crying or shouting. A reflection in Karin Bernfeld's *Les Portes de l'espérance* (2003) reinforces Orner's sense that Hebrew promotes verbal expression of emotional excess, but Bernfeld goes a step further in implying its promotion of agressivity:

> J'ai l'impression de haïr l'hébreu. L'impression qu'on ne peut que brailler cette langue.
> Dans les rues, les voix qui s'emmêlent, violentes, les cris. Pourquoi pas parler sans gueuler?
> [...] La langue des engueulades, elle s'y prête si bien. (212)

> [I feel as if I hate Hebrew. I feel that you can only bawl in this language.
> In the streets, the violent voices that get mixed up, the shouts. Why not speak without yelling? [...] The language of slanging matches, it lends itself so well to them]

Bernfeld's other reflections on Hebrew belong more to the realm of the political, recalling Allouche's remarks on imposed distinctions between Arabic and Hebrew, but this time remarking on a particular and in itself stigmatizing use of Arabic permitted in Hebrew: 'en hébreu, on utilise surtout les mots arabes pour les insultes' (174) ['in Hebrew, people use Arab words above all for insults'].

Orner's *Une année si ordinaire* (2004) also analyses Hebrew through a political prism. One instance is light-hearted in tone – 'Guerre – *Milhama*. La racine de ce mot donne *Lehem*, du pain. Très marxiste l'hébreu!' (212) ['War – *milhama*. The root of this word gives *lehem*, bread. Very Marxist, Hebrew!'] – though the implicature that war is akin to daily bread casts Israel in a sombre light. Another is more serious in tone, implying a link between muteness and violence: 'J'y

pense, en hébreu, les mots violence (*alimouth*) et muet (*ilem*) ont la
même racine' (16) ['I think about it: in Hebrew, the words violence
(*alimouth*) and mute (*ilem*) have the same root']. Does this suggest
a political awareness built into Hebrew of the fact that muteness –
involuntary or imposed silence – is a form of symbolic violence? Some
readers may ignore this political potential and see Orner's observation
as reflecting a slightly Kabbalistic *poesis* of Hebrew. However, while
Orner certainly highlights the spiritual richness of Hebrew lexis, she
does so from the perspective of cultural politics, via competing linguistic
claims. Countering the charge made by translators that Hebrew is an
impoverished and inflexible tongue, she points out that new words are
being created daily in Hebrew, that the Hebrew speaker can innovate
without being accused of creating neologisms, and that if French has
a wide lexis of abstract and philosophical words, Hebrew can boast
greater breadth and nuance in its spiritual lexicon: 'Il ne me viendrait
pas à l'idée d'incriminer la langue française car un même mot l'âme en
désigne deux distincts en hébreu' (52) ['It wouldn't occur to me to call
the French language into question because the same word, *âme*, has two
distinct ones in Hebrew'].

Valérie Zenatti's one reference to Hebrew in *Une bouteille dans
la mer de Gaza* (2005) is placed firmly in the realm of the political:
that of the contemporary Israeli–Palestinian conflict. The Palestinian
protagonist Naïm's recollection of a key childhood memory points to
strong similarities between Hebrew and Arabic (cf. Kessel, 1965, 81),
and underscores the importance for peace of linguistic accommodation
with the Other:

> Quand Yasser Arafat est arrivé à Gaza, en 1994, mon père est entré
> dans ma chambre avec un livre à la main et m'a dit: « Naïm, à partir
> d'aujourd'hui, tu vas apprendre l'hébreu. Nous allons être en paix
> avec les Israéliens, c'est une bonne raison pour apprendre leur langue
> sérieusement. » C'est ainsi que tous les soirs, après mes devoirs, j'ai étudié
> le *Aleph Beth*, et toute votre langue, qui ressemble tant à la nôtre. (156)

> [When Yasser Arafat arrived in Gaza in 1994, my father came into my
> bedroom with a book in his hand and said to me 'Naïm, from today,
> you're going to learn Hebrew. We're going to be at peace with the Israelis,
> it's a good reason for learning their language seriously'. So it was that
> every evening, after homework, I studied the *Aleph Beth*, and your entire
> language, which is so like ours]

In *Cela ne sera pas un rêve* (2009), Line Meller-Saïd sustains this political focus but reverts to a period before the creation of the state of Israel when the Polish-Jewish protagonist Léa, dreaming of emigration to Palestine, is passionately inspired by learning Hebrew as a political as well as spiritual act:

> L'étude de cette langue devient sa priorité. Elle s'y adonne avec fougue. La figure du père de l'hébreu moderne la hante. LA RENAISSANCE D'ISRAËL ET DE SA LANGUE SUR LA TERRE DES PÈRES: en elle se martèle à son tour, aux limites du conscient, cette ritournelle structurante, obsédante, d'un rêve éveillé quasi prophétique d'Éliezer Ben Yehouda,[6] à la source de son autobiographie, *Le rêve traversé*. (15)

> [Studying this language becomes her priority. She devotes herself to it enthusiastically. The figure of the father of modern Hebrew haunts her. THE REBIRTH OF ISRAEL AND OF ITS LANGUAGE IN THE LAND OF THE FATHERS: within her, in its turn, on the margins of the conscious, is pounding away this obsessive, structuring ritornello of a quasi-prophetic waking dream of Eliezer Ben-Yehuda, at the root of his autobiography, *A Dream Come True*]

Hebrew becomes a vital form of spiritual and affective nourishment for Léa and for the other young people among whom she encourages its use (20). But emphasis is also placed on the political imperative of speaking Hebrew – to the detriment of Yiddish, which is downgraded to a language of exile and enslavement (20). That downgrading is also recorded in *Eretz* (2010), where Henri Raczymow recalls an elderly woman in Israel who spoke only in Hebrew telling him that as a child she was forbidden to use Yiddish, 'jargon des Juifs du ghetto qui courbaient l'échine comme chacun sait' (123) ['the jargon of ghetto Jews who, as everyone knows, were submissive']. Unlike Meller-Saïd, Raczymow questions this prohibition of Yiddish for the greater glory of Hebrew and reports the concrete defiance of the prohibition by a Yiddish speaker whose Zionist credentials are impeccable:

> Il s'agit d'une simple ponctuation au discours du président, mais pourquoi chante-t-elle en hébreu au cours d'une réunion de membres actifs d'une société dont la vocation est de défendre le yiddish et, pour ce faire, d'utiliser cette langue? On donne ensuite la parole au vieil homme en bout de table, qui nous dit, sans à-propos évident, avoir été jadis membre du Palmach (unité juive de combat avant la création de l'État). Il sort de son portefeuille sa carte du Palmach et se met à chanter, quant à lui, une chanson en yiddish. (123–24)

> [It's a mere punctuation in the president's speech, but why is she singing

in Hebrew in the middle of a meeting of active members of a society whose purpose is to defend Yiddish and, to achieve this, to use that language? Next up to speak is an old man at the end of the table, who tells us, without any obvious relevance, that in bygone days he had been a member of the Palmach (Jewish combat unit before the creation of the state). He takes out of his wallet his Palmach card and starts to sing, for his part, a song in Yiddish]

In *Mon cœur de père* (2012) Marco Koskas takes a different approach, by reaffirming the imperative of speaking Hebrew for anyone who wants to live in Israel but at the same time observing that even speaking it with a foreign – in this case French – accent can be frustrating (10), due to the alienation felt by the formally diasporic speaker from the 'authentically' Israeli collectivity. This is offset by his later-expressed approval for Israel's founding fathers' imposition of Hebrew as a federating language, without which linguistic incoherence ('la tour de Babel') would have prevailed (109). As Anne Rabinovitch's *Chacune blesse, la dernière tue* (2012) makes clear, *ulpan* – intensive instruction in Hebrew – is offered free by the Israeli state to all new immigrants (18). But the financial gratui-tousness of the instruction is anything but gratuitous in the other sense of the word: it is a deliberate state policy to integrate all new immigrants via a common language. Whilst such a policy is not unknown in other countries, Israel has certainly been a pioneer in devoting sizeable state funds to the promotion of a national language. This is precisely because it is not *just* a national language, but also a language of sacred Jewish texts wherein lie the origins of Jewish identity. Thus Hebrew is the tool with which Israel has sought, not always unproblematically, to unify the linguistically diverse Jews arriving in the country each year.

6.4. Frontier *topos*

If unity is the goal of Hebrew promotion policies in Israel, it is antinomic to the *topos* examined in this section. The frontier axiomatically denotes divisions, and it is to the various frontiers, be they literal or metaphorical, of Israel and its people that attention will now turn. In certain cases, these frontiers will shade into liminalities, where divisions are more muted and more fluid.

Idith Zertal argues that the absence of a recognized consensual frontier has served to stimulate what she calls the fantasy of Greater Israel, qui était mise en œuvre avec une inflexible fermeté dans les territoires, détourna le cours de l'histoire d'Israël et conduisit finalement à l'assassinat d'un Premier ministre. (257)

[which was implemented with rigid firmness in the Territories, diverted the course of Israel's history and finally led to the assassination of a prime minister]

Tracing the use of the term 'Grand Israël' ['Greater Israel'] back to the 1930s and to diverse Zionist plans for the division of Palestine, she notes that varying discourses within these debates drew on a lexicon and imaginary of the human body, with the threat that losing even a tiny part of the land would be tantamount to amputation (257–58). Martine Gozlan focuses on figurative rather than geographical frontiers: between Israelis and Palestinians, but also between Israelis of differing ideological hues. The first type of frontier features in the situation of Axelle, a settler in the Occupied Territories who lives physically very close to Arabs but has never visited an Arab town (90), and Gozlan muses, 'Quelle chose étrange, cet éloignement de ce qu'on côtoie et cette curiosité pour ceux dont on nie la réalité politique ...' (91) ['What a strange thing, that distance from what you rub shoulders with and that curiosity about those whose political reality you deny ...']. The incongruity lies not only in the physical proximity set against the actual separation of the two opposed communities, but in the fact that they resemble each other culturally – denoting at least a potential liminality rather than an insurmountable frontier:

Axelle est cachée jusqu'aux cheveux, au nom de la *tsniout*, la pudeur, concept ombrageux partagé avec l'autre, l'ennemi, le Palestinien d'en face. (104)

[Axelle is covered right up to her hair, in the name of *tsniout*, modesty, a prickly concept shared with the other, the enemy, the Palestinian on the other side]

The second metaphorical frontier, or rather plurality of frontiers, etched by Gozlan divides Israelis among themselves:

– Le plus grand désastre d'Israël, continue Carmela [...] c'est celui des relations entre Israéliens. Nous n'avons aucun contact les uns avec les autres. Religieux et non-religieux ne s'adressent pas la parole. Les Tel-Aviviens ne parlent pas aux colons, les gens de Jérusalem disent que Tel-Aviv n'est pas une ville pour les vrais juifs et pourtant ... (113)

['Israel's greatest disaster', continues Carmela [...] 'is relations between

Israelis. We have no contact with each other. The religious and the non-religious don't address a word to each other. People from Tel Aviv don't speak to the settlers, people from Jerusalem say that Tel Aviv isn't a city for real Jews and yet …']

One major frontier mentioned by Carmela, between religious and secular Israelis, is illustrated vividly by a recent scandal:

> En décembre 2011, Naama Margolese, huit ans, a été agressée et insultée par des haredim, des hommes en noir, qui ont craché sur sa tenue « immodeste ». L'affaire a déclenché un énorme scandale. Le 27 décembre, dix mille manifestants occupaient les rues de Beth Shemesh pour protester contre les fanatiques. Ils étaient soutenus par le Premier ministre Benyamin Netanyahou. (162)

> [In December 2011, Naama Margolese, aged eight, was attacked and insulted by Haredim, men in black, who spat on her 'immodest' attire. The affair triggered a huge scandal. On 27 December, 10,000 demonstrators occupied the streets of Beth Shemesh to protest against the fanatics. They were supported by the Prime Minister Benyamin Netanyahu]

This frontier is also observed by Pinto, who nuances it as a division between the growing number of religious Israelis and the secular Zionism of the state's founding fathers and their descendants (2012, 23–24). As with Russian nesting dolls, yet more frontiers within frontiers are revealed by Gozlan: those between religious Israelis – conservative Jews and ultra-Orthodox Jews – and between the sexes within ultra-Orthodox Israeli communities (162–63). Of the first, Gozlan observes:

> C'est qu'il existe une nuée de sectes au centre du monde religieux. Toutes se déchirent à belles dents. Au cœur de chaque Israël, comme d'habitude, d'autres Israëls se combattent. (166)

> [There's a horde of sects at the centre of the religious world. All of them savagely rip each other apart. At the heart of each Israel, as usual, other Israels are fighting]

This suggests a final, striking frontier, not between two or more human beings, but within each single Israeli, who internalizes but fails to integrate his or her opposites.

The first of the primary texts to portray frontiers is Joseph Kessel's *Terre d'amour et de feu* (1965). Kessel uses precisely the word 'frontière' to designate the gulf between the uncultivated parts of Palestine occupied by Arabs and those populated by Jews, the latter unambiguously presented as superior in their rich cultivation and harmony (17). Paula Jacques, in

Un baiser froid comme la lune (1983), makes ostensibly similar remarks on the boundary separating Arab and Jewish land (242), but differs from Kessel in two respects. She is writing about such land after the creation of the state of Israel; and unlike his, her words are certainly not a paean to cultivated Jewish land accompanied by denigration of unproductive Arab land. As seen in Chapter 1, Jacques in fact depicts Jewish land as being cultivated with ruthless, monetary calculation via the simile of Swiss finance, 'proliférait comme l'action suisse en bourse' (242) ['proliferating like Swiss shares on the stock market'], while Arab land is presented as being in harmony with a nature whose offerings should not be rushed (242).

The signal importance of the concept of the frontier is indicated in the very title of Michel Warschawski's *Sur la frontière* (2002), which in certain respects figures the type of frontier depicted by Kessel and Jacques but extends its cognitive range in several directions. Warschawski describes his text as:

> le récit d'une expérience, passionnante et passionnée, sur les frontières séparant États, communautés et réalités, qui font la trame de ce que l'on appelle le « problème palestinien ». (7)

> [the narrative of a gripping and passionate experience on the frontiers separating states, communities and realities, which form the fabric of what is called the 'Palestinian problem']

He also defines himself as 'un militant de la frontière' (7), and specifies two pages later that he has chosen to live and fight *on* the frontier, implying a wish to at best destroy, at worst erode the boundaries dividing Israelis and Palestinians. The following extract evokes that intense personal investment and its heavy personal cost – trial and imprisonment on suspicion of having aided terrorism:

> L'accusation de soutien au terrorisme ayant fait long feu, c'est autour de la frontière que se sont confrontées les parties, dans ce que le procureur général avait appelé le *no man's land* entre Israéliens et Palestiniens, mais aussi entre légalité et illégalité. Si c'est moi qui le premier avait utilisé ce terme, ce n'est que progressivement que j'ai saisi à quel point toute ma vie, personnelle et militante, a été le résultat du choix délibéré de vivre et de me battre sur la frontière. (9)

> [Since the accusation of support for terrorism didn't last long, it's around the frontier that the two parties confronted each other, in what the public prosecutor had called the no man's land between Israelis and Palestinians, but also between legality and illegality. Even if I were the

first to have used this term, it was only gradually that I grasped to what extent my whole life, on both the personal and the activist level, has been the result of a deliberate choice to live and fight on the frontier]

However, Warschawski does not neglect other boundaries dividing Israelis, one of which – the boundary between religious and secular Israelis – has been alluded to by Gozlan and Pinto above, and another of which, the boundary between Ashkenazi and Sephardi/Mizrahi Jews, has been examined in Chapter 3:

> Les trente-cinq dernières années de ma vie ont été, en fait, une longue marche sur la frontière, ou plutôt sur les différentes frontières où se côtoient l'État d'Israël et le monde arabo-musulman, Israéliens et Palestiniens, mais aussi Juifs et Israéliens, religieux et laïcs, Juifs d'Europe et Juifs d'Orient. (9–10)

> [The last thirty-five years of my life have, in fact, been a long march along the frontier, or rather on the different frontiers where there is a mixing of the state of Israel and the Arab-Muslim world, Israelis and Palestinians, but also Jews and Israelis, the religious and the secular, European Jews and oriental Jews]

Warschawski's is by far the most conscious and the most sustained exploration of the frontier *topos* in all the primary texts. Indeed, he argues for its centrality not just to his own life but to that of all Israeli citizens (the final two clauses below echoing Gozlan, 166):

> « La frontière est un concept central dans la vie de tout Israélien: elle est un élément formateur dans notre vie à tous, délimite nos horizons, sert de ligne de démarcation entre menace et sentiment de sécurité, entre ennemis et frères. Dans un pays qui est à la fois un ghetto et un bunker assiégé, la frontière est omniprésente, et à chaque pas nous nous y heurtons. Oui, la frontière est non seulement dans le cœur de chaque soldat, comme le dit la chanson, mais dans celui de chaque citoyen d'Israël, élément constitutif de son être. (17)

> [The frontier is a central concept in the life of all Israelis: it is a formative element in all our lives, defines the scope of our horizons, serves as a demarcation line between threat and a feeling of security, between enemies and brothers. In a country which is at the same time a ghetto and a besieged bunker, the frontier is everywhere, and with every step we take we bang into it. Yes, the frontier is not only in the heart of every soldier, as the song says, but in the heart of every citizen of Israel, a constitutive part of his or her being]

This declaration presents the frontier as an ideological meme in Israeli society. Sub-units within the overarching unit include the image that Israelis have of the Arab world on the other side of the frontier as constituting a minatory desert, paradoxically empty yet occupied (the word is not innocent) by a hostile population (29). Later on, the frontier is mediated as the antithesis of a bridge between the two peoples; referring to the frontier between internationally recognized Israel and the Occupied Territories, he observes that:

> Palestiniens et Israéliens traversaient quotidiennement la frontière, mais, alors que les premiers rencontraient Israël et le peuple israélien à chacun de leurs pas, les Israéliens, eux, ne voyaient personne. (179)

> [Palestinians and Israelis crossed the frontier on a daily basis, but, while the former met Israel and the Israeli people with every step they took, the Israelis, for their part, saw nobody]

The Israeli blindness to Palestinians denoted in the last clause is, it is implied, a willed one.

Certain permutations of the frontier *topos* in Warschawski's text challenge normative expectations of the political left, right and centre. One is the view of a liberal and pacifist journalist, Dankner, that while peace means an opening of frontiers, this opening must lead to Israel's definitive integration with the West and to turning its back on the Arab world (200). In contrast to this is the alignment of right-wing Israelis with an opening of frontiers that will also open up the possibility of reconciliation with the Arab world:

> *Pour M. Shemesh et, peut-être, pour une majorité d'Israéliens qu'on a l'habitude d'étiqueter à droite, la paix c'est aussi l'ouverture de la frontière, mais pas celle qui mène à Florence ou à Londres. La paix, c'est la possibilité de se réconcilier avec le monde arabe dont ils sont issus, de retrouver les liens avec cette culture et, surtout, de briser le mur qui les coupait de leur propre arabité, de leur identité meurtrie. (200)*

> [For Mr Shemesh and, perhaps, for a majority of Israelis who tend to be labelled 'right-wing', peace is also the opening of the frontier, but not the frontier leading to Florence or London. Peace is the possibility of reconciliation with the Arab world from which they came, of recovering links with this culture and, above all, of breaking the wall which cut them off from their own Arabness, from their wounded identity]

The last sentence here reiterates the notion of Semitic brotherhood between Arabs and Sephardic/Mizrahi Israelis treated briefly in Chapter

4, and of a possible Levantinization of Israel touched upon in Chapter
3. That these evolutions should be associated with right-wing Israelis
at first seems perverse, but it should be acknowledged that the majority
of religious, traditionalist and right-wing Israelis are of Sephardic or
Mizrahi origin. Perversity is a word used by Warschawski himself,
albeit for different reasons – to characterize the unilateral and imposed
separation of Israelis and Palestinians:

> Rares furent les Israéliens qui comprirent la perversité de cette séparation
> unilatérale et imposée. En juin 1995, je demandai à Naomi Hazan,
> députée du Meretz, ce qu'on pouvait faire contre le bouclage. Elle eut
> l'air surprise et me répondit: « Rien. Le bouclage, c'est le début de la
> séparation, un pas vers l'État palestinien. C'est ainsi que l'on habitue
> l'opinion publique aux futures frontières. » (209)

> [Very few Israelis understood the perversity of this unilateral and imposed
> separation. In June 1995, I asked Naomi Hazan, a Meretz member of
> parliament, what could be done against the cordoning off. She looked
> surprised and replied: 'Nothing. Cordoning off is the start of separation,
> a step towards the Palestinian state. This is how we get public opinion
> used to the future frontiers']

The response of Hazan, a member of parliament for Meretz (a left-wing
party aiming for peace between Israelis and Palestinians via a two-state
solution) could be seen as somewhat bleak. Her vision of this solution
as consisting purely in complete separation and new frontiers admits
no possibility of positive relations between Israelis and Palestinians:
on the contrary, it projects a future whereby each annihilates the other
symbolically.

Valérie Zenatti's narrative voice in *Quand j'étais soldate* (2002) is
that of a much younger, less politically mature Israeli, but it brings out
powerfully that same sense of absolute separation and alterity dividing
Israelis and Palestinians found in Warschawski's text (and also evinced
by Gozlan). On her first trip to the Occupied Territories, the 18-year-old
narrator is stunned by the utterly alien and desolate reality encountered
there (214). Whilst she has literally crossed a geographical frontier –
that separating Israel from the Occupied Territories – her overwhelming
sense of this frontier is not geographical but temporal and cultural:
'l'impression d'avoir traversé une frontière, mais pas une frontière
géographique. Où suis-je? Cent, deux cents ans en arrière?' (214) ['the
sense of having crossed a frontier, but not a geographical one. Where
am I? A hundred, two hundred years back in time?']. Although she could

be charged with condescendingly implying Palestinians' backwardness, a more charitable interpretation would stress her shock at their poverty. Also of significance is her new cognizance of the Palestinians' sadness and their hatred for the Israeli bus visitors amongst whom she numbers, viewed by them as their oppressors. Sadness is also felt by the 'enemy' side in the one, potent, reference made by Michaël Sebban's *Le Cadenas du marché Yéhouda* (2008) to frontiers:

> Le désordre des voitures et des charrettes des marchands ne concerne plus que les touristes escortés et les Arabes du coin. La vieille ville est devenue ce que ce pays est devenu, un entrelacement de frontières hermétiques. Et je ne suis pas le dernier à m'en plaindre même si je m'en désole. (57)

> [The chaos of the cars and the traders' carts now only concerns escorted tourists and local Arabs. The old town has become what the country has become, a network of hermetic frontiers. And I'm not the only one to complain about it even if it upsets me]

The potency of this sadness derives from its positing of the Old City of Jerusalem, famously divided, as synecdoche for the whole of Israel: an Israel riven by frontiers that hermetically seal off diverse communities from the Other, whether along ethnic, religious-versus-secular or political lines. That Israel emerges vividly in the next, short section, which homes in on perhaps the most pronounced of those political lines.

6.5. The frontier between Israelis living in internationally recognized Israel and those in the Occupied Territories

The desolation of Zenatti and Sebban resurfaces in Sebban's *La terre promise, pas encore* (2002). In addition, this semi-autobiographical novel emphasizes the cultural and cognitive frontiers sealing off hyper-modern, economically privileged young Israelis from the harsh reality of life in the Occupied Territories:

> *– Les filles, à Tel-Aviv, elles ont été voir* Pulp Fiction. *Le lendemain, elles se font fait piercer des oreilles aux orteils. Tu crois qu'ils s'imaginent qu'ici, à un quart d'heure, c'est les Territoires?* (43)

> [The girls in Tel Aviv went to see *Pulp Fiction*. The next day, they got piercings done from ear to toe. Do you imagine that those people give a thought to the fact that they're only fifteen minutes from the Territories?]

However, the response to this question intimates an inchoate but palpable sense that these young Israelis are not so blissfully ignorant as they might seem:

> – *Bien sûr qu'ils le savent, c'est pour ça qu'ils ont fait Tel-Aviv. Ils veulent faire comme si tout était normal, mais comme rien n'est normal, alors ils exagèrent. Ils veulent faire plus normal que normal.* (143)

> [Of course they know, that's why they went to Tel Aviv. They want to behave as if everything were normal, but as nothing is normal, well, they're pushing it. They want to behave more normal than normal]

The last two sentences reprise the *topos* examined above in section 6.2. of Israelis' preoccupation, not to say obsession, with normality, deriving from the actual abnormality of their situation. One facet to that abnormality is the obligation to do a month's reserve duty in the Occupied Territories each year, in addition to the three compulsory years of military service. This enforces a periodic crossing of and thus re-cognizance of the frontier between internationally recognized Israeli boundaries and the Occupied Territories. Later on in the novel, dialogue between unnamed interlocutors conveys a huge gap between the two demographics, the settlers being scorned as paranoid (121–22). Eli's Israeli friend Haïm confirms that gap, although this time stress is placed not on scorn, but rather on the indifference of geographically 'legitimate' Israelis towards the Territories and their inhabitants:

> Vus de Tel Aviv, les Territoires c'est loin. [...] C'est triste à dire, mais ici, dans l'ensemble, les gens se foutent des Territoires et de Jérusalem. (162–63)

> [Viewed from Tel Aviv, the Territories are far away. [...] It's sad to say, but here, on the whole, people don't give a damn about the Territories and Jerusalem]

That indifference is echoed by another friend, Vladi, who, in response to Eli's question about what to do with the Palestinians in order to secure Israelis' long-term future in Israel, responds bluntly '– Qu'on leur file un État, qu'on se tire des Territoires et qu'on soit enfin tranquilles' (183) ['Let's give them a state, let's pull out of the Territories and finally get some peace and quiet']. However, the qualifier he adds to this blunt comment, 'Si c'est possible', evinces pessimism about Israelis ever truly being able to make that break, due to the tenacity of the advocates of Greater Israel. This brings us back full circle to the abnormality of the Israelis' affective state. The last section of this chapter will briefly consider one avatar of that state, which is a deeply figurative form of the frontier motif.

6.6. Figurative frontier:
Israel's consumption and ejection of its people

In Esther Orner's *Autobiographie de Personne* (1999), the first-person narrator (based on Orner's mother) remarks, echoing Leviticus 18:25, that Israel is a land that vomits its inhabitants (96). This clearly exercises her, for two pages later she returns to and dwells upon it:

> Mais cette terre qui vomit ses habitants, ça me travaille. Où c'est écrit demandait maman pour une chose qui n'avait pas de sens. Mais là il paraît que c'est vraiment écrit. (98)

> [But this land that vomits out its inhabitants, it bothers me. Where's it written down demanded mum for something that made no sense. But in this case it seems it really is written down]

However, there is a counterpoint to this – 'C'est aussi une terre qui avale ses habitants' (98) ['It's also a land that swallows its inhabitants'] – which for its part alludes to Numbers 13:32. She qualifies this by adding:

> Ceux qui l'ont cherché. Après tout il faut faire attention où on pose ses pieds. Ça c'est sûr. Une terre qui a des pouvoirs. Des qualités. Une terre qui engloutit ou mange ses habitants, ça s'est vu. Mais une terre qui vomit c'est autre chose. (98–99)

> [They were asking for it. After all, you have to be careful where you venture. That's for certain. It's a land that has powers. Qualities. A land that swallows or eats its inhabitants, that's not unknown. But a land that vomits is something else]

Orner's fourth and fifth sentences mediate Israel as powerful and endowed with other positive features, but her last sentence represents Israel as a country of conundrum. No elucidation is offered either for its vomiting out of its people or for its devouring of them. The frontier between the two violent actions, between Israeli citizens' interiority and exteriority to their own country, constitutes a compelling enigma.

6.7. Endnote

To a greater or lesser extent, enigma colours many of the elements examined in this chapter. Treatment of Jerusalem, found in 11 of the primary texts, emphasizes the following: the city's inexplicably hypnotic lure, which is often crystallized in the image of the Western Wall (four of the primary texts); the city's aesthetically and spiritually charged stone (also in four primary texts); its ineffable secrets, including the antinomy between its seductiveness (five) and oppressive tensions (three); and, condensing many of these elements, the otherworldly, almost oneiric quarter of Méa Shéarim (four). Six of the primary texts suggest that Israel is marked by madness, but they do so parallactically, such that (like the image of Jerusalem) the concept emerges in contrasting forms, some of the texts relativizing the whole construct of madness – implying that what appears highly irrational from outside Israel conforms to a logic of its own within the unique circumstances of Israeli lives. The Hebrew language features in no fewer than 13 of the primary texts, where both its spiritual value and its state manipulation for political reasons emerge. Finally, the trope of the frontier, interpreted pluralistically, is present in seven of the primary texts, which collectively foreground the multiple divisions, contradictions and paradoxes by which Israeli society is riven.

Ultimately, the metaphysics and *poesis* of Israel emerging in this chapter are beyond rational analysis. They are shot through with conflict (a salient theme of this book, dominating in three different avatars three of its chapters) between the emotional and the spiritual on the one hand, and the conceptual and the political on the other. The only clear implicature is what subtends this conflict: the immense pull of its constituent parts. Within them, Israel appears to encapsulate two of the three qualities of the (early) Kantian sublime. In *Observations on the Feeling of the Beautiful and Sublime* (1764), Kant maintained that the sublime came in three forms: the noble, the splendid and the terrifying. Israel cannot be described as noble – no more than any other nation state in the world, for all are ruled by self-interest. But in its mediation by the primary texts at least, Israel does reveal glittering shards of both the (aesthetically and spiritually) splendid and the (politically) terrifying.

Notes

1 See http://www.levitt.com/slideshow/so1p05.

2 Nicault is the author of *Une histoire de Jérusalem: 1850–1967* (Paris: CNRS Éditions, 2008).

3 On 'the female experience of Jewish space governed by male law', see Nolden (199–200).

4 A *madrikha* is a community leader or guide.

5 A *moshav* (plural, *moshavim*) is an agricultural co-operative settlement.

6 Ben-Yehuda was the key figure in the revival of Hebrew in modern times.

CHAPTER SEVEN

Supplement

The final paragraph of the Introduction refers to both consensus and dissensus in Francophone Jewish writers' affective and cognitive responses to Israel. In this book, treatment of those responses has been guided by, though not limited to, Martha Nussbaum's conception of emotions as 'appraisals or value judgments, which ascribe to things and persons outside the person's own control great importance for that person's own flourishing' (4). A good number of the responses have manifested not just unreflecting emotion but also 'appraisals or value judgments'. Most have revealed the ascription of 'great importance' to Israel for the flourishing of Jewish characters in the case of novels, and for the authors themselves in the case of autobiographical/autofictional texts.

This final chapter – as its title indicates, a supplement, rather than a conclusion, to its predecessors – returns to these processes of consensus and dissensus. It throws them into sharper relief by presenting the varied answers given by writers I interviewed (or, in three cases, to whom I sent questionnaires) in 2011, all of whom are treated in this book, to questions that have informed elements of the entire study. A British Academy grant allowed me to interview 13 authors and receive question-naires responses from three others. This represents just under half the authors treated (27) in the present study; but a sample of 48.15% forms a reasonable set of empirical data. The diversity of answers given to the eight interview questions[1] posed systematically to all 13 authors was marked, indicating in its turn the diversity of these authors' affective investments in and cognitive framings of Israel. Nonetheless, a number of recurring points did emerge, and this is where the notion of antiphony appears apt for it denotes a phenomenon of responsive singing or chanting not dissimilar to the common refrains found in these points.

I will begin with the cognitively weighted points, giving a brief digest before considering in more detail the affective points, which – to sustain the musical metaphor – showed rather more counterpoints. The cognitively weighted points included the following: that the 'special', indeed unique, relationship between France and Israel originated historically in France's being the first country in the world to emancipate Jews (in the wake of the French Revolution), but also, more sinisterly, in France's collaborationist Vichy regime, one of the main accomplices to the Nazi Judaeocide; that the relationship improved dramatically between 1945 and 1950, then developed in the 1950s and 1960s into a more pragmatic exchange, in which France was the chief vendor of arms to Israel, thereby increasing the latter's military strength; and that this relationship degenerated again after the Six-Day War in 1967. All of the writers questioned concurred in seeing that degeneration as stemming from France's wish to keep on good terms with Arab countries, and thus continue to influence and benefit commercially from its trade links with them. Many of these Arab countries were ex-French colonies representing ongoing commercial interests for France, compared to which her commercial interests in the single and tiny country of Israel were negligible. Another recurring point was that the large Francophone community in Israel is generally well integrated, but that, conversely, Israelis tend to perceive France as an increasingly dangerous bastion of antisemitism. Linked to this was a generally strong affirmation of Zionism, and the impression that French anti-Zionism can easily become a smokescreen for antisemitism. On the other hand, few of the authors interviewed supported the declaration by the CRIF (Conseil représentatif des institutions juives de France [Representative Council of French-Jewish Institutions]) of unfailing solidarity with Israel, where 'unfailing' connoted 'uncritical'. Almost all recognized that Palestinians had rights that were currently being denied, and almost all endorsed a two-state solution. Possible points of synergy between France, Israel and Europe were seen as being less political than artistic, particularly literary and cinematic.

Given limitations of space and, more importantly, the central hermeneutic of this book, namely the role of affect in the rapport Francophone Jewish writers have with Israel, the second and final part of this chapter will concentrate on the first of the eight questions asked of each writer: 'Que représente Israël pour vous, sur le plan affectif?' ['What does Israel represent for you, emotionally?']. Answers to that question often revealed an incapacity for scotomization (in psychoanalytic theory, scotomization is the mind's ability to erase a traumatic or overwhelming experience) *vis-à-vis* the two thousand-year-old history of Jewish persecution and, in the twentieth century, mass extermination. Unsurprisingly, this ascotomization is most apparent in the responses of Ashkenazi Jews born before, during or very shortly after the Second World War. The oldest of the authors interviewed, Esther Orner (1937–), replied thus:

> Israël disons pour moi, c'est le pays rêvé. Ça commence assez tôt. Après la guerre. J'ai été cachée pendant la guerre, mes parents ont été déportés, mon père n'est pas revenu, ma mère est revenue, elle n'a pas beaucoup parlé etc. [...] C'était une maison triste bien sûr, la majorité de cette famille avait été déportée et c'était les restes, ce qu'on appelle en hébreu 'sheérith Israël', ce sont les 'restes d'Israël'. Dans notre optimisme, nous disons qu'il peut y avoir toutes les catastrophes mais qu'il restera toujours un reste d'Israël. Et donc les restes de cette famille, c'était une maison triste et ce qui m'a sortie de là, ce sont les mouvements de jeunesse sionistes, d'une part et je les ai tous fréquentés. [...] Israël était présente. Pour moi, c'était quelque chose qui m'interpellait.

> [Let's say that for me, Israel is the dream country. It began quite early on. After the war. I was hidden during the war; my parents were deported. My father didn't return; my mother did. She didn't speak much etc. [...]. Of course it was a sad house, most of this family had been deported and it was the remnants, what in Hebrew is called *shearith Israel*, these are the 'remnants of Israel'. In our optimism, we say that there can be all sorts of catastrophes but there will always remain a remnant of Israel. And so the remainder of this family was a sad house and what got me out of it were the Zionist youth movements, on the one hand, and I got involved in all of them. [...] Israel was present. For me, it was something that called out to me]

Here Orner exploits the dual meaning of the word 'Israël': the Jewish people, and the state created in 1948. Affectively, what is striking in her response is the status of the country as a dream, an ideal that provided a bulwark against despair provoked by the European Judaeocide. The metaphysics of absence and presence inform her reply: while most of her family were absent in death, Israel, in both senses of the word, was physically, reassuringly present, even if only in the unintended remnants ('restes') of the Judaeocide. Another striking affect in Orner's words is produced by interpellation, a sense of Israel having figuratively hailed her childhood and adolescent self. Interpellation influences subjectivation; and this notion of Orner's subjectivity having been at least partly forged by Israel is reinforced in her later comment 'Israël c'était presque une deuxième nature, c'était pas mythifié' ['Israel was almost a second nature, it wasn't mythified'].

Ascotomization is also apparent in Myriam Anissimov's (1943–) response to the same question:

> C'est vraiment peut-être un des centres de mon existence, parce que je viens d'une famille dont tous les membres ont été exterminés pendant la Seconde Guerre mondiale.

> [It's really perhaps one of the central points of my existence, because I come from a family all of whose members were exterminated during the Second World War]

But, as with Orner, Israel had provided, if not a compensation for that decimated family, at least a positive pole in her imaginary. For Anissimov,

> [Israël] représente dans mon imaginaire à peu près la même chose que l'insurrection du ghetto de Varsovie. Le refus de se laisser exterminer, même quand la situation est désespérée.

> [Israel represents in my imagination more or less the same thing as the Warsaw Ghetto Uprising. The refusal to let yourself be exterminated, even when the situation is desperate]

In addition to representing courageous revolt, the antithesis of the stereotype of Jews submitting like sheep to slaughter, Israel is also a site of intense emotional investment for Anissimov, to the point where she uses as dramatic a term as 'passion':

> Ma relation à Israël est aussi passionnelle et émotionnelle que ma relation à la langue yiddish [...] quand j'entends parler yiddish, je le ressens avec tout mon corps, toute mon âme qui est alors mobilisée. J'ai aussi cette relation émotionnelle avec Israël. C'est l'âme du peuple juif. J'en fais partie.

> [My relationship with Israel is as passionate and emotional as my relationship with the Yiddish language [...] when I hear Yiddish being spoken, I feel it with my whole body, my whole soul, which is then mobilized by it. I also have this emotional relationship with Israel. It's the soul of the Jewish people. I'm part of it]

As with Yiddish, so with Israel Anissimov has a relationship that plainly incorporates the bodily dimension of affect established in the Introduction. It is, she stresses, a relationship of deep attachment: 'Israël constitue pour moi un attachement de nature profonde' ['For me, Israel constitutes an attachment of a profound nature']. The lexicon of depth and attachment, foregrounded in the Introduction too via reference to theoretical/philosophical texts by Bruno Chaouat and Elisabeth de Fontenay, is also deployed by Henri Raczymow (1948–) – 'Israël est une terre spéciale à mes yeux. J'y suis profondément attaché' ['In my eyes Israel is a special land. I'm profoundly attached to it'] – and by Yaël Hassan (1952–) – 'mon attachement envers Israël est immense et l'a toujours été, que je sois là-bas ou ici, cet attachement reste de même nature, il reste intense' ['my attachment to Israel is huge and always has been; whether I'm there or here, that attachment remains the same, it remains intense']. Returning to Anissimov, it is clear that (and again as for Orner) Israel partly represents an *ersatz* family:

> Chaque jour, je lis les informations sur la situation en Israël pour voir si « nous sommes » encore là. C'est une relation familiale […] Israël est une partie de ma famille, une partie de mon être. […] D'une certaine manière, ma famille c'est Israël.

> [Every day, I read the news about the situation in Israel to see if 'we' are still there. It's a family relationship […] Israel is a part of my family, a part of my being. […] In a sense, Israel is my family]

The same affectively invested seme of Israel as family is mobilized by Karin Bernfeld (1976–), a much younger writer than Orner, Anissimov and Raczymow:

> c'est ma famille, c'est le lieu où j'allais quand j'étais petite pour pouvoir rencontrer mes grands-parents, mes cousins, mes tantes. Donc forcément, il y a un lien affectif très fort.

> [it's my family, it's the place I used to go when I was a child to meet my grandparents, my cousins, my aunts. So, inevitably, there's a very strong emotional link]

The daily anxiety about Israel's safety, indeed its very existence, expressed by Anissimov was also voiced in my interview with Jean-Luc Allouche (1949–), although two distinctions need to be made here. First, he is a Sephardic Jew of Algerian origin whose family had been spared the Shoah in Europe, and second, he was referring specifically to the crisis of the Six-Day War in 1967 and 'la montée de la tension, l'angoisse que beaucoup de gens ont eue pendant les mois d'attente' ['the rising tension, the anxiety that many people felt during the months of waiting']. His own anxiety was so great that, though a good student, he failed his *baccalauréat*, having been glued to his transistor radio for news on the day of the first exam. A year later, he moved to Israel as a student and fell in love; not with a human being, but with the state-imposed language of Israel: 'je tombe amoureux d'un substitut, c'est la langue hébraïque' ['I fell in love with a substitute, the Hebrew language'].

In sharp contrast to Allouche's love for the Hebrew language – a language that could be viewed as a metonym of Israel, such is its centrality to Israel's identity (see Chapter 6) – what Paula Jacques (1949–) initially felt was animosity. This was, admittedly, due to very different circumstances, for her childhood/early teenaged stay in one of its *kibbutzim* was forced upon her (her family having been expelled qua Jews from her native Egypt, her father being dead and her mother unable to look after her):

> il fallait absolument couper les racines et, moi, j'étais une petite bourgeoise et qui rêvait, je sais pas moi, de la France [...] contrainte d'apprendre cette langue que je n'avais pas l'intention d'apprendre puisque ma mère par ailleurs m'écrivait que le mois prochain elle me ferait venir à Paris.

> [it was absolutely essential to cut yourself off from your roots and I, I was a bourgeois little girl who dreamed, I don't know, of France [...] forced to learn this language that I had no intention of learning since my mother also used to write to me saying that the next month she'd have me brought to Paris]

In addition to resentment at this linguistic imposition, which aimed to sever her diasporic roots (see Chapter 6), she found the entire system of raising children in the *kibbutz* 'très dure' ['very hard'], feeling 'emprisonnée' ['imprisoned'] in the institution. But later in life, and despite her sympathy for the plight of the Palestinians, her hostile feelings for Israel as a whole transmuted into something like an attachment, as for Anissimov, Hassan and Raczymow above. Unusually among the authors interviewed, Jacques explicitly presents this attachment as potentially going beyond the cognitive and the rational:

> J'ai senti qu'il y avait des liens, des liens qui peut-être dépassaient l'intelligence et le raisonnement qu'étaient la marche de ces gens-là vers ce pays et qu'ils y avaient droit dans une certaine mesure, non pas à cause de la Bible, non pas à cause des prédictions mais parce que c'est un peuple en détresse et qui avait trouvé une terre.

> [I felt that there were links, links that perhaps exceeded the intelligence and reasoning represented by the march of those people towards this country, and that in a sense they were entitled to it, not because of the

Bible, not because of predictions but because they were a people in distress who had found a land]

At the time of our interview (2011), Jacques's relationship with Israel was emotionally mixed: she could not repress a shudder at her earliest memories of it, and yet was also moved, enthused and stunned by its human heterogeneity and vibrancy. In spite of her opposition to its government's policies on the Palestinian question, she had finally found in Israel 'un plaisir extraordinaire' ['an extraordinary pleasure'], a love for 'la façon des Israéliens de vivre [...] dans un mode frénétique de liberté de parole' ['the way Israelis live [...] with a wild freedom of speech'] and love too for both its energy and its admixture of eastern and western cultures. Love is also a word used by Marco Koskas (1951–), who ascribes it to all Jews *vis-à-vis* Israel: 'peu ou prou, tous les juifs aiment Israël. Bien sûr, c'est un amour plus ou moins critique mais c'est de l'amour quand même' ['all Jews love Israel, more or less. Of course, it's a love that can be critical to different degrees but it's still love'], and by Hassan (1952–), who recalls her love for Israel without any of Koskas's qualification: 'j'ai posé les pieds dans ce pays, je l'ai aimé immédiatement et intensément' ['I set foot in this country and I loved it immediately and intensely'].

Alongside the love for Israel professed by these writers there is often ambivalence. This is the predominant emotion evinced by Michel Warschawski (1949–), but in stronger terms than Jacques and Koskas. While Israel is the only country where Warschawski feels at home, it also constitutes for him 'un régime politique que j'abhorre, colonial et militariste, contre lequel je lutte sans concession' ['a political regime that I loathe, colonialist and militaristic, which I fight uncompromisingly']. For Ami Bouganim (1951–), too, Israel is a home from which he has no intention of moving – such is its intellectual, religious and emotional grip on him – but of which his cognitive assessment is pessimistic. That pessimism is born of what he views as its Messianic miscalculations:

> Aujourd'hui, Israël représente pour moi une aventure messianiste qui est en train de tourner mal. [...] Ce n'est pas pour cela que je vais prendre mes cliques et mes claques et que je vais partir – ce serait trop tard. Je ne ressens pas moins, intellectuellement, religieusement et émotionnellement.

> [These days, Israel represents for me a Messianic adventure which is going wrong [...] Nevertheless, I'm not going to pack my bags and leave – it would be too late. My feelings are no less intense, emotionally, religiously and intellectually]

Bouganim also sees negative emotions circulating in Israel that go beyond his own: 'Aujourd'hui, on peut déceler nombre de symptômes de crispation, de désarroi et de désertion' ['These days, you can detect many symptoms of tension, distress and defection']. These he explains in terms of Messianism, propaganda and the pain that any territorial concessions to the Palestinians would bring:

> nous sommes dans une logique messianiste qui considérerait toute concession comme une terrible régression. Ce serait douloureux, voire insoutenable. On est pris dans un engrenage où l'endoctrinement se mêle à la peur, à l'espoir et à la vanité.
>
> [we're caught in a Messianic logic which would view any concession as a terrible regression. It would be painful, indeed intolerable. We're caught up in a system where indoctrination mingles with fear, hope and futility]

Ambivalence further threads its way through the remarks of Hassan, whose immediate and intense love for Israel was tempered upon arrival in the country by cognition of her Otherness:

> mon idée était que je rentrais à la maison, je rentrais chez moi. Et très vite, je me suis aperçue que ce n'était pas le cas, parce qu'en Israël aussi j'étais une étrangère finalement. Parce que d'abord, quand je suis arrivée, je ne parlais pas l'hébreu, parce que quand je l'ai parlé, j'avais un accent français, parce que j'avais ma culture quand même, ma culture française.
>
> [I had the notion was that I was going back to my house, I was going home. And very quickly, I realized that this wasn't the case, because in Israel too I was, ultimately, a foreigner. Because firstly, when I arrived, I didn't speak Hebrew; because, when I did speak it, I had a French accent; because I had my own culture after all, my French culture]

Yet she was able to adapt relatively quickly, helped by an openness to cultural diversity and by awareness of its ubiquity (see Chapter 3) in Israel:

> Je m'étais dit, voilà, il ne faut pas gommer tout ça, mais réapprendre d'autres choses. Et donc, très vite, je me suis dit que même en Israël, j'aurai ma part d'étrangeté [...] Autant l'étrangeté en France était gênante, autant elle ne l'était pas en Israël. [...] je me sentais bien dans ce fourmillement d'origines différentes.
>
> [I told myself, right, you mustn't erase all of that, but relearn other things. And so, very quickly, I told myself that even in Israel, there'd be part of me that was foreign. [...] While foreignness in France made me

feel uncomfortable, in Israel it didn't at all. [...] I felt good in this mass
of different origins]

Of a younger generation, Eliette Abécassis (1969–) nonetheless
experienced a similar bipolarity between her Frenchness and her
aspiration to settle in Israel:

> je suis très enthousiaste à l'idée de ce peuple, du retour vers la terre. Et
> c'est assez paradoxal parce qu'en même temps, je suis très française,
> j'écris en français. À chaque fois que je vais en Israël, je me sens encore
> plus française, et en même temps, en vivant ici, je sens que j'aimerais vivre
> là-bas. Donc voilà, ça représente comme un ailleurs familier.

> [I'm very enthusiastic about the idea of this people, of return to the land.
> And it's quite paradoxical because at the same time, I'm very French, I
> write in French. Every time I go to Israel, I feel even more French, and at
> the same time, living here, I feel that I'd live to live there. So there you are,
> it represents something like an elsewhere that is familiar]

Abécassis's last sentence above (where 'ailleurs' refers to Israel) echoes
certain of Anissimov's musings:

> Ma culture est française. Néanmoins, mes émotions n'y sont pas toujours
> toutes liées. J'éprouve des sentiments complexes vis-à-vis de la France.
> Je sais que j'appartiens à sa culture, que j'ai été formée dans ses écoles et
> qu'une majeure partie de ma vie est liée à la France, mais une partie de
> mon esprit est ailleurs.

> [My culture is French. Nonetheless, my emotions aren't always linked
> to it. I have complex feelings about France. I know that I belong to its
> culture, that I've been educated in its schools and that a major part of my
> life is linked to France, but a part of my mind is elsewhere]

Penultimately, it is the positive that predominates in Abécassis's vision
of Israel, which for her, as for Bouganim and Warschawski, represents
a home (although in their case it is a literal as opposed to her symbolic
home), a nodal point of belonging: 'C'est-à-dire comme une sorte de vraie
maison, une protection, un endroit, le lieu auquel j'appartiens profondément' ['That's to say like a sort of real home, a form of protection,
a place, the place to which I belong deeply']; but her final clause
shows once more the leaking in of ambivalence, for this is a home 'que
peut-être je ne rejoindrai jamais' ['that maybe I'll never get to']. Finally,
the second youngest of the authors interviewed, Chantal Osterreicher
(1974–), also spontaneously engaged the lexicon of ambivalence, all

the while stressing her highly charged attraction to Israel. When at the age of 17 Osterreicher arrived in a *kibbutz* in the Negev desert, she was 'vraiment bouleversée' ['really overwhelmed']; she states that 'Affectivement, j'avais été vraiment touchée et je n'avais qu'une idée en tête, c'était revenir' ['Emotionally, I'd been really touched and I only had one idea in my head: to go back there']. Such was the affective pull that she later emigrated from France to Israel:

> Israël [...] avait déjà une place particulière à mon cœur à l'époque, maintenant encore plus puisque je me suis mariée en Israël, mes enfants sont nés en Israël. Bon, après il peut y avoir des sentiments plus ambivalents par rapport à Israël puisque j'y vis maintenant depuis huit ans, je n'ai plus disons la naïveté du premier jour en arrivant en Israël.

> [Israel [...] already had a special place in my heart at the time, now even more so since I got married in Israel, my children were born in Israel. Well, afterwards there can be more ambivalent feelings about Israel since I've been living there for eight years now. Let's say that I'm not so naive as the first day I arrived in Israel]

But elective affinities with Israel in this younger French-Jewish *émigrée* to the country finally trump ambivalence: 'si je m'imaginais vivre quelque part, ailleurs, je ne pourrais pas m'empêcher de regarder tous les jours ce qui se passe en Israël' ['if I imagined living somewhere else, I wouldn't be able to stop myself looking every day at what was happening in Israel']. Despite the ambivalences expressed by many of these writers, Israel is often evaluated by them in eudaimonistic terms.

This book has sought both to respect an *epoché* on the highly polemical status of Israel in global politics, and to parse the divergences but also the many convergences in Francophone Jewish writers' affective and conceptual relationships with the country, which are undergirded by the 'special relationship' between France and Israel that was documented in the Introduction. This final chapter's analysis of the interviews with a selection of those writers serves as a form of *mise en abyme* for such relationships. The very coexistence of polyphony and antiphony precludes the drawing of any unitary conclusion. For Israel resists attempts to pin it down, and seems like no other nation in the passions it incites. Perhaps the only viable conclusion to this book is that Israel's 'identity' is a *hapax legomenon* within the text of human culture.

Notes

1 The eight questions were as follows (for a selection of replies to them, see Cairns, 2015):

1. Que représente Israël pour vous, sur le plan affectif et/ou spirituel? [What does Israel represent for you, emotionally and/or spiritually?]

2. Avez-vous déjà vécu, ou passé une importante période de temps, en Israël? Si c'est le cas, quelles ont été vos impressions du pays et de sa communauté francophone? Y avez-vous fait l'expérience de préjugés contre les Juifs de la diaspora? [Have you ever lived, or spent a significant period of time, in Israel? If so, what were your impressions of the country and of its French-speaking community? Did you experience prejudices against diasporic Jews there?]

3. Croyez-vous qu'il existe (ou bien qu'il existait par le passé) entre la France et Israël une relation privilégiée? Si oui, comment expliquer cette relation privilégiée, et en quoi consiste-t-elle? [Do you think there is (or was in the past) a privileged relationship between France and Israel? If so, how do you explain this privileged relationship, and in what does it consist?]

4. Que pensez-vous de l'affirmation de la part du CRIF (Conseil représentatif des institutions juives de France) d'une solidarité indéfectible avec Israël, et de son soutien pour une résolution pacifique du conflit au Moyen Orient? [What do you think of the assertion of the CRIF (Representative Council of French Jewish Institutions) of an unfailing solidarity with Israel, and of its support for a peaceful resolution to the Middle Eastern conflict?]

5. Êtes-vous sioniste ou antisioniste? Quelles sont les raisons de votre positionnement sur cette question aujourd'hui extrêmement délicate? [Are you Zionist or anti-Zionist? What are the reasons for your position on this currently very delicate question?]

6. Quels sont vos propres attitudes et sentiments à l'égard de la politique israélienne? A titre d'exemple, comment avez-vous réagi à la condamnation faite par la France d'Israël dans l'affaire de la flotille à destination de Gaza? [What are your own attitudes and feelings about Israeli politics? For example, how did you react to France's condemnation of Israel in the Gaza-bound flotilla affair?]

7. Que pensez-vous de l'hypothèse très répandue selon laquelle la montée des agressions antisémites en France depuis le début de la Deuxième Intifada s'explique en grande partie par le fait que le conflit israélo-palestinien se rejoue plutôt que se résout dans la banlieue, où vivent de nombreux jeunes Arabes « radicalisés » et violemment antisionistes? [What do you think of the very widespread hypothesis that the rise in antisemitic attacks in France since the start of the Second Intifada is largely due to the fact that the Israeli–Palestinian conflict is acted out rather than worked through in

the *banlieue*, where many young 'radicalized' and fiercely antisemitic Arabs live?]

8. D'une perspective juive, quels sont selon vous les liens, les « points chauds », et les points de synergie entre la France, Israël, et l'Europe? [From a Jewish perspective, what do you think are the links, the 'flashpoints' and the points of synergy between France, Israel and Europe?]

Bibliography

Primary Texts

Abécassis, Eliette, *L'Or et la cendre* (Paris: Ramsay, 1997)

——, *La répudiée* (Paris: Albin Michel, 2000)

——, *Sépharade* (Paris: Albin Michel, 2009)

Allouche, Jean-Luc, *Les jours innocents* (Paris: Lieu commun, 1984)

Anissimov, Myriam, *La Soie et les cendres* (Paris: Payot, 1989)

Azoulai, Nathalie, *Les Manifestations* (Paris: Éditions du Seuil, 2005)

Bernfeld, Karin, *Les Portes de l'espérance* (Paris: Flammarion, 2003)

Bouganim, Ami, *L'arbre à vœux* (Waterloo: Avant-propos, 2010)

——, *Entre vents et marées* (Paris: Éditions Stavit, 1998)

——, *Le cri de l'arbre* (Tel Aviv: Stavit, 1983)

Boukhobza, Chochana, *Sous les étoiles* (Paris: Seuil, 2002)

——, *Le Troisième Jour* (Paris: Denoël, 2010)

——, *Un été à Jérusalem* (Paris: Balland, 1986)

Cohen, Marcel, *Miroirs* (Paris: Gallimard, 1980)

Finaly, Patricia, *Le gai ghetto* (Paris: Gallimard, 1970)

Francos, Ania, *Les Palestiniens* (Paris: Julliard, 1970; first published 1968)

——, *Sauve-toi, Lola!* (Paris: Barrault, 1983)

Frydman, Sarah, *La Marche des vivants* (Paris: Albin Michel, 1997)

Hassan, Yaël, *Souviens-toi Leah!* (Paris: Eden, 2004)

Hillel, Marc, *Les Oranges de Jaffa* (Paris: Garnier frères, 1981)

——, *Tu vivras dans ton sang* (Paris: Garnier frères, 1971)

Jacques, Paula, *Gilda Stambouli souffre et se plaint* (Paris: Mercure de France, 2002)

——, *Un baiser froid comme la lune* (Paris: Mercure de France, 1983)

Kessel, Joseph, *Terre d'amour et de feu* (Paris: Plon, 1965)

Koskas, Marco, *Destino* (Paris: Grasset, 1981)

——, *Mon cœur de père* (Paris: Fayard, 2012)

Meller-Saïd, Line, *Cela ne sera pas un rêve* (Paris: Éditions Jean-Paul Bayol, 2009)

Moses, Emmanuel, *Papernik* (Paris: Bernard Grasset, 1992)

Orner, Esther, *Autobiographie de Personne* (Geneva: Éditions Métropolis, 1999)

——, *Fin et suite* (Geneva: Éditions Métropolis, 2001)

——, *Une année si ordinaire* (Geneva: Éditions Métropolis, 2004)

Osterreicher, Chantal, *L'Insouciance d'Adèle* (Paris: Dorval Éditions, 2006)

Peskine, Brigitte, *Buena Familia* (Paris: Nil, 2000)

Rabinovitch, Anne, *Chacune blesse, la dernière tue* (Paris: Alma, 2012)

——, *Les étangs de ville d'Avray* (Paris: Actes Sud, 1987)

Raczymow, Henri, *Eretz* (Paris: Gallimard, 2010)

Rosenthal, Olivia, *Les Fantaisies spéculatives de J. H. le sémite* (Paris: Editions verticales/Le Seuil, 2005)

Sebban, Michaël, *Le Cadenas du marché Yéhouda* (Paris: Hachette Littératures, 2008)

——, *Lehaïm. À toutes les vies* (Paris: Hachettes Littératures, 2004)

——, *La terre promise, pas encore* (Paris: Ramsay, 2002)

Warschawski, Michel, *Sur la frontière* (Paris: Stock, 2002)

Zenatti, Valerie, *Quand j'étais soldate* (Paris: L'École des loisirs, 2002)

——, *Ultimatum (en retard pour la guerre)* (Paris: Éditions de l'Olivier, 2006)

——, *Une bouteille dans la mer de Gaza* (Paris: L'École des loisirs, 2005)

Secondary Texts

Anderson, Benedict, *Imagined Communities: Reflections on the Origin and Spread of Nationalism* (New York: Verso, 1991)

Arendt, Hannah, 'La tradition cachée', in *La Tradition cachée. Le Juif comme paria* (Paris: Christian Bourgois, 1993), 178–82

Auron, Yair, *Israeli Identities: Jews and Arabs Facing the Self and the Other* (Oxford/New York: Berghahn Books, 2012)

Badiou, Alain and Finkielkraut, Alain, *L'Explication. Conversation avec Aude Lancelin* (Paris: Nouvelles Éditions Lignes, 2010)

Balibar, Etienne, Brauman, Rony, Butler, Judith et al., *Antisémitisme, l'intolérable chantage: Israël, une affaire française* (Paris: La Découverte, 2003)

Barnavi, Élie and Rosenzweig, Luc, *La France et Israël: une affaire passionnelle* (Paris: Perrin, 2002)

Benbassa, Esther, *Être juif après Gaza* (Paris: CNRS Éditions, 2009)

Ben-Rafael, Eliezer and Ben-Rafael, Miriam, *Sociologie et sociolinguistique des francophonies israéliennes* (Frankfurt am Main: Peter Lang, 2013)

Blanc, Aurélia, 'Communauté, mon amour?', *Respect* (October–December 2012a), 52–53

——, 'L'inquiétude des Juifs de France', *Respect* (October–December 2012b), 62–63

Boniface, Pascal, *Est-il permis de critiquer Israël?* (Paris: Éditions Robert Laffont, 2003)

Boyarin, Daniel, *Unheroic Conduct: The Rise of Heterosexuality and the Invention of the Jewish Man* (Berkeley: University of California Press, 1997)

Braudel, Fernand, *Memory and the Mediterranean* (New York: Alfred Knopf, 2001)

Brauman, Rony and Finkielkraut, Alain, *La discorde: Israël-Palestine, les Juifs, la France. Conversations avec Élisabeth Lévy* (Paris: Mille et une nuits, 2006)

Brubaker, Rogers and Cooper, Frederick, 'Beyond "Identity"', *Theory and Society*, 29.1 (February 2000), 1–47

Burg, Avraham, *Vaincre Hitler: pour un judaïsme plus humaniste et universaliste*, trans. Orit Rosen and Rita Sabah (Paris: Fayard, 2008)

Butler, Judith, *Parting Ways: Jewishness and the Critique of Zionism* (New York/ Chichester: Columbia University Press, 2012)

Cairns, Lucille, 'Israël, entre rêve et réalité', *Continuum: Revue des Écrivains Israéliens de Langue Française*, nos. 11/12 (2014–2015), 167–207

——, 'Jewish Children's Homes in Post-Holocaust France: Personal *Témoignages*', in Seán Hand and Steven T. Katz (eds), *Post-Holocaust France and the Jews, 1945–1955* (New York: New York University Press, 2015), 139–55

——, *Post-War Jewish Women's Writing in French* (Oxford: Legenda, 2011)

——, 'Righteous Realism versus Postmodern Play: The Israeli-Palestinian Conflict in Female-Authored French Fiction', *Modern and Contemporary France*, 22.1 (Spring 2014), 71–84

Chaouat, Bruno, 'Nouvelles questions juives après le 11 septembre', *Controverses* (June 2007), 156–74

——, 'L'affect sioniste', *Revue Cités*, 47–48 (August 2011), 189–204

Charbit, Denis, *Les Intellectuels français et Israël* (Paris: Éditions de l'éclat, 2009)

Cohen, Charles, 'Israël-Palestine: une passion française', *Respect* (October– December 2012), 64–66

Dayan-Rosenman, Anny, 'The Israeli-Palestinian Conflict in France: A Conflict in Search of Novelistic Representations', in Nathalie Debrauwere-Miller (ed.), *Israeli–Palestinian Conflict in the Francophone World* (New York/London: Routledge, 2010), 81–92

Debray, Régis, *À un ami israélien. Avec une réponse d'Élie Barnavi* (Paris: Flammarion, 2010)

Derrida, Jacques and Roudinesco, Élisabeth, *De quoi demain: dialogue* (Paris: Fayard: Galilée, 2001)

Eytan, Freddy, *Sarkozy, le monde juif et Israël: mariage d'amour ou de raison?* (Paris: Alphée-J. P. Bertrand, 2009)

Fontenay, Elisabeth de, *Actes de naissance. Entretiens avec Stéphane Bou* (Paris: Le Seuil, 2011)

Frenk, Levana, 'Le procès Eichmann et nous', *Continuum*, 8 (2011), 30–31

Gabizon, Cécilia, *OPA sur les Juifs de France: enquête sur un exode programmé* (Paris: Grasset, 2006)

Gelblum, Arieh, 'Chodesh Yamim Hiyiti Oleh Chadash' [For a Month I was a New Immigrant], series in *Ha'aretz*, 22 April 1949

Giroud, Françoise, 'Cette Shoah qui ne passe pas', *Le Monde*, 12 June 2002, <http://archives.desinfos.com/giroud20612.html>

Gozlan, Martine, *Israël contre Israël. L'autre menace* (Paris: Archipel, 2012)

Groenendyk, Eric, 'Current Emotion Research in Political Science: How Emotions

Help Democracy Overcome Its Collective Action Problem', *Emotion Review*, 3.4 (October 2011), 455–63

Halperin, Eran, Canetti-Nisim, Daphna and Hirsch-Hoefler, Sivan, 'The Central Role of Group-based Hatred as an Emotional Antecedent of Political Intolerance: Evidence from Israel', *Political Psychology*, 301 (2009), 93–123

Harding, Jennifer and Pribram, E. Deirdre (eds), *Emotions: A Cultural Studies Reader* (London and New York: Routledge, 2009)

Harris, Rachel S., 'Israel: Finding the Levant within the Mediterranean, *The Levantine Review*, 1.1 (Spring 2012), 106–17

Hazan, Eric, *Un État commun entre le Jourdain et la mer* (Paris: La Fabrique, 2012)

Hecker, Marc, *La défense des intérêts de l'État d'Israël en France* (Paris: Harmattan, 2005)

——, *Intifada française? De l'importation du conflit israélo-palestinien* (Paris: Éditions Ellipses, 2012)

Herschthal, Eric, 'Israel's Black Panthers Remembered', *The Jewish Week*, 29 June 2010, <http://www.thejewishweek.com/arts/film/israel%27s_black_panthers_remembered>

Hochberg, Gil Z., *In Spite of Partition: Jews, Arabs, and the Limits of Separatist Imagination* (Princeton/Oxford: Princeton University Press, 2007)

Hoffenberg, Valérie, 'Nos différences', *L'Arche*, 638 (August 2012), 66

Hogan, Patrick Colm, 'Fictions and Feelings: On the Place of Literature in the Study of Emotion', *Emotion Review*, 2.2 (April 2010), 184–95

Kant, Immanuel, *Observations on the Feeling of the Beautiful and Sublime* (1764)

Karsh, Efraim, *Fabricating Israeli History: The 'New Historians'* (London/Portland: Frank Cass, 2000)

Khazzoom, Aziza, 'The Great Chain of Orientalism: Jewish Identity, Stigma Management and Ethnic Exclusion in Israel', *American Sociology Review*, 68 (August 2003), 481–510

Londres, Albert, *Le Juif errant est arrivé* (Paris: Arléa, 2010) (first published by Albin Michel in 1930)

Marcus, Paul, *Soixante ans d'amour contrariées: les relations franco-israéliennes de 1948 à aujourd'hui* (Paris: Cherche Midi, 2008)

Marty, Éric, 'L'angélisme des belles âmes', *Le Monde*, 11 October 2000

——, *Bref séjour à Jérusalem* (Paris: Gallimard, 2003)

Massumi, Brian, *Parables for the Virtual: Movement, Affect, Sensation* (Durham/London: Duke University Press, 2002)

Memmi, Albert, *Juifs et Arabes* (Paris: Gallimard, 1974)

Nicault, Catherine, *Une histoire de Jérusalem: 1850–1967* (Paris: CNRS Éditions, 2008)

Nietzsche, Friedrich, *The Birth of Tragedy*, trans. W. Kaufmann (New York: Vintage Books, 1967)

——, 'The Will to Power', in Oscar Levy (ed.), *The Complete Works of Friedrich Nietzsche*, 15 (Edinburgh and London: T. N. Foulis, 1910)

——, *Thus Spoke Zarathustra: A Book for Everyone and No One*, trans. R. J. Hollingdale (Harmondsworth: Penguin Books, 1969)

Nolden, Thomas, *In Lieu of Memory: Contemporary Jewish Writing in France* (New York: Syracuse University Press, 2006)

Nordau, Max, 'Muskeljudentum' (based on 'Jüdische Turnzeitung' of June 1900), *Zionistische Schriften* (Cologne/Leipzig: Jüdischer Verlag, 1909)

Nussbaum, Martha C., *Upheavals of Thought: The Intelligence of Emotions* (Cambridge: Cambridge University Press, 2001)

Ohana, David, 'Zarathustra in Jerusalem: Nietzsche and the "New Hebrews"', in Wistrich, Robert and Ohana, David (eds), *The Shaping of Israeli Identity: Myth, Memory and Trauma* (London: Frank Cass, 1995), 38–60

Orès, Sandra, 'Ceux qui tentent un nouveau destin', *L'Arche* (July–September 2014), 24–27

Ortony, Andrew, Clore, Gerald L. and Collins, Allan, *The Cognitive Structure of Emotions* (New York: Cambridge University Press, 1988)

Penslar, Derek J., 'Zionism, Colonialism and Postcolonialism', *Journal of Israeli History: Politics, Society, Culture*, 20.2–3 (2001), 84–98

Pinto, Diana, *Israël a déménagé* (Paris: Stock, 2012)

——, '« *Plus jamais ça* ». Europe, Israël: les malentendus', *Le Débat*, 161 (2010), 144–57

Primor, Avi, *Le Triangle des passions: Paris, Berlin, Jérusalem* (Paris: Bayard, 2000)

Rachlevsky, Seffi, *Messiah's Donkey* (Tel Aviv: Yediot Aharonoth Publishers, 1998)

Rafowicz, Olivier, 'Il nous manque', *L'Arche* (December 2013), 104–05

Roei, Noa, *Shifting Sights: Civilian Militarism in Israeli Art and Visual Culture* (unpublished doctoral thesis, University of Amsterdam, 2012)

Rosman, Miriam, *La France et Israël 1947–1970. De la création de l'État d'Israël au départ des Vedettes de Cherbourg* (Paris: Honoré Champion, 2009)

Rothberg, Michael, *Multidirectional Memory: Remembering the Holocaust in the Age of Decolonization* (Stanford: Stanford University Press, 2009)

Salomon, Jacques (propos recueillis par), 'Catherine Nicault: « La solution n'est pas à portée de main, ni à portée de ma génération »', *L'Arche* (January–March 2013), 58–59

Segev, Tom, *Le Septième Million* (Paris: Liana Levi, 2003)

Serero, Lisa, 'L'aliya: un aboutissement?', *Respect* (October–December 2012), 43–44

Shohat, Ella, 'Sephardim in Israel: Zionism from the Standpoint of Its Jewish Victims', in McClintock, Anne, Mufti, Aamir and Shohat, Ella (eds), *Dangerous Liaisons: Gender, Nation and Postcolonial Perspectives* (Minneapolis: University of Minnesota Press, 1997), 39–68

Sibony, Daniel, *Proche-Orient, psychanalyse d'un conflit* (Paris: Seuil, 2003)

Sieffert, Denis, *Israël-Palestine, une passion française: la France dans le miroir du conflit israélo-palestinien* (Paris: La Découverte, 2004)

Smith, Anthony D., *Myths and Memories of the Nation* (Oxford: Oxford University Press, 1999)

Starr, Deborah A. and Somekh, Sasson (eds), *Mongrels or Marvels: The Levantine Writings of Jacqueline Shohet Kahanoff* (Stanford, California: Stanford University Press, 2011)

Taguieff, Pierre-André, *La nouvelle judéophobie* (Paris: Mille et une nuits, 2002)

Waintrater, Meïr, 'You, Zionist! Uses and Misuses of the Z-Word in Current Political Discourse', <http://www.chgs.umn.edu/news/>

Weitz, Yechiam, 'Political Dimensions of Holocaust Memory in Israel During the 1950s', in Wistrich, Robert and Ohana, David (eds), *The Shaping of Israeli Identity: Myth, Memory and Trauma* (London: Frank Cass, 1995), 129–45

Wetherell, Margaret, *Affect and Emotion: A New Social Science Understanding* (Los Angeles/London: Sage, 2012)

Wistrich, Robert S., *From Ambivalence to Betrayal: The Left, the Jews, and Israel* (University of Nebraska Press, 2012)

Wistrich, Robert and Ohana, David (eds), *The Shaping of Israeli Identity: Myth, Memory and Trauma* (London: Frank Cass, 1995)

Yakira, Elhanan, *Post-sionisme, post-Shoah. Trois essais sur une négation, une délégitimation et une diabolisation d'Israël* (Paris: Presses universitaires de France, 2010)

Zertal, Idith, *La Nation et la mort: la Shoah dans le discours et la politique d'Israël*, trans. Marc Saint-Upéry (Paris: Éditions la Découverte, 2004)

Zipperstein, Steven J., 'Menachem Begin: A Life', *Fathom*, 4 (Autumn 2013), 73–75

Index